Investigating Discourse and Texts

Linguistic Insights

Studies in Language and Communication

Edited by Maurizio Gotti,
Emeritus Professor,
University of Bergamo (Italy).

Volume 306

Stefania Maci / Giovanni Garofalo (eds.)

Investigating Discourse and Texts

Corpus-Assisted Analytical Perspectives

PETER LANG
Lausanne - Berlin - Bruxelles - Chennai - New York - Oxford

Bibliographic information published by die Deutsche Nationalbibliothek
Die Deutsche Nationalbibliothek lists this publication in the Deutsche Nationalbibliografie; detailed bibliographic data is available on the Internet at ‹http://dnb.d-nb.de›.

Library of Congress Cataloging-in-Publication Data
A CIP catalog record for this book has been applied for at the Library of Congress.

The volume was produced with the financial support of the Department of Languages, Literatures, and Foreign Cultures at the University of Bergamo, within the framework of the 'Department of Excellence' project.

ISSN 1424-8689
ISBN 978-3-0343-4753-2 (Print)
E-ISBN 978-3-0343-4800-3 (E-PDF)
E-ISBN 978-3-0343-4801-0 (E-PUB)
DOI 10.3726/b21393

Published by Peter Lang Group AG, Lausanne, Switzerland

info@peterlang.com
http://www.peterlang.com/

Contents

Part I: CADS as a methodological approach

Part II: Case studies

GIOVANNI GAROFALO / STEFANIA M. MACI[1]

Investigating discourse and texts through Corpus-Assisted Discourse Studies (CADS)

1. Corpus-Assisted Discourse Studies: A methodological synergy to analyse discourse and text-building strategies

In recent decades, qualitative discourse analysis has generated a substantial amount of valuable research that has contributed to our comprehension of linguistic patterns beyond individual sentences (Jaworski and Coupland 2014). This research has also shed light on how language, power and social dynamics mutually interplay through an intricate network of established social practices perpetuated by the verbal conduct of speakers. In particular, the seminal works by Fairclough (1992, 1995, 2003), van Dijk (1993, 1998) and Wodak and Meyer (2001)—to name but a few—demonstrated how discourse puts ideology and power into action and, specifically, how communication is involved in forming and upholding unequal power dynamics, disadvantage, and discrimination (Gillings et al. 2023: 5). This consolidated line of research, known as *Critical Discourse Studies* / *Critical Discourse Analysis* (CDS / CDA), openly declared its politically-committed goals, as its main purpose was not merely investigating social injustices but also redressing them, through an eclectic methodological framework that drew from various disciplines adjacent to linguistics (e.g., sociology, anthropology or social sciences). At the heart of this speculation was the Foucaultian notion of *discourse*, conceived as a system of statements, practices,

1 The individual contributions of the two authors to this chapter are as follows: Giovanni Garofalo drafted Section 1 and its corresponding references, while Stefania M. Maci wrote Section 2.

and ideas that shape and produce knowledge within a specific historical and social context (Foucault 1969). Discourses are not just about language, but they encompass a broader network of power, knowledge, and social structures. Moreover, discourses are never neutral, seeing as how they convey power and contribute to the construction of reality and the shaping of social norms and identities. For this reason, discourses are closely knit to mechanisms of social control and exert influence over how people think, behave, and understand the world around them.

As rightly observed by Gillings, Mautner and Baker (2023: 6), CDS / CDA usually relies on meticulous perusal and interpretative analysis of individual texts. However, this approach encounters a challenge, as in-depth reading and detailed description are feasible primarily with a limited corpus, such as a few newspaper articles or a small number of transcripts of oral texts. Consequently, the real issue at the heart of CDS / CDA is the representativeness of the texts upon which qualitative speculation is carried out. Indeed, one might wonder to what extent the analyst gives in to the temptation of selecting specific textual instances precisely because they contain those ideological/sociological features that they aim to highlight. It was precisely to address these inherent limitations of CDS / CDA that Corpus Linguistics (CL) came onto the scene of discourse studies, around the 1990s of last century (Leech and Fallon 1992; Caldas-Coulthard 1993; Stubbs and Gerbig 1993; Krishnamurthy 1995; Stubbs 1997). Being essentially empirical and based on machine-readable, authentic and representative corpora, CL allows for automatic processing of a huge quantity of texts which can be enriched with various metadata, thus avoiding the risk of 'cherry picking' involved in the intuition-based approach of qualitative discourse analyses (Gillings et al. 2023: 36).

Among the earliest and most significant attempts to bring together CL and CDA, a special mention should be given to Paul Baker's volume, *Using Corpora in Discourse Analysis* (2006), a reference book which paved the way for further research conducted primarily within the framework of the Lancaster University and focused on the ways sociopolitical domination is reproduced in discourse (Baker et al. 2008). It should be noted, however, that the label *CADS (Corpus-Assisted Discourse Studies*) was mostly used in the body of research that emerged in Italy through the initiatives of individual scholars (Partington et al. 2004;

Morley and Bayley 2009; Partington et al. 2013) who focused on socio-political discourse analysis, which included unveiling significant ideological metaphors, discourse prosody and other recurring patterns in the language of political figures and institutions. As a result of the synergy between CL and CDA, CADS 'explore discourse (i.e., language as a social practice) through examining corpora', which 'allows one to survey a corpus in its entirety rather than focusing only on certain texts' (Gillings et al. 2023: 1). In addition, CADS are notably insightful as they are informed by a variety of theoretical perspectives, inherent to the methodologies underpinning them. While discussing the relevance and interdependence of the two fundamental components of CADS, Baker et al. (2008: 274) raise a series of interrelated issues and make the following key observations:

> [i]n the combination of methods normally used by CDA and CL, [. . .] neither CDA nor CL need be subservient to the other (as the word 'assisted' in CADS implies), [since] each contributes equally and distinctly to a methodological synergy. More precisely, we address the following interrelated questions.
> 1. What are the respective merits and limitations of methods of analysis traditionally used by CL and CDA when the focus is on issues that CDA traditionally examines?
> 2. What should be the nature of such a methodological synergy?
> 3. How can the combination in research projects, and their potential theoretical and methodological cross-pollination, benefit CDA and CL?
> 4. How helpful and /or justified is the distinction between what have traditionally been termed quantitative and qualitative approaches in linguistics?

As a summary of the responses to the aforementioned questions, it suffices to recall that the synergy between CL and CDA involves their combined application to gain deeper insights into language, power dynamics, and social structures. This synergy emerges when researchers combine the strengths of both approaches. On the one hand, CL offers quantitative tools for systematically analyzing extensive language datasets, revealing non-obvious patterns and frequencies in language use, thus reducing the potential bias of the analyst. On the other, CDA focuses on the qualitative interpretation of texts, disclosing ideological subtleties / power dynamics and contextualizing recurring linguistic features within social, political, and cultural settings. By so doing, 'discourse studies (DS) can be enriched and made more rigorous by computer assistance' (Gillings et al. 2023: 45), while the combination of quantitative and qualitative methodologies enhances the investigation of discourse, enabling scholars to understand how language both mirrors and shapes social reality, ideologies, and power dynamics.

Through the CADS methodology, it becomes possible to address questions such as (Gillings et al. 2023: 1): how does language portray a specific social group? Which linguistic decisions align with certain ideological stances? Do discursive portrayals evolve over time? What significance do specific linguistic selections hold in institutional discourses? The common thread among all CADS studies is their focus on a specific social issue (e.g., inequality, poverty, racism, gender-related prejudice, violence or discrimination, etc.), transcending mere linguistic concerns. Alternatively, research may arise from a broader curiosity about the connections between a given social practice and its associated linguistic preferences. In brief, CADS effectively aid in dissecting the intricacies of discourse, making it appealing not only to linguists but also to researchers exploring the interplay between discourse and society across disciplines such as sociology, psychology, law, management, and beyond. Actually, a characteristic feature of CADS is their frequent reliance on methodological triangulation, i.e., resorting to an eclectic mix of techniques and methodological approaches to analyse a given social phenomenon. In this regard, Baker and Egbert (2016: 3) argue that

> methodological triangulation facilitates validity checks of hypotheses, anchors findings in more robust interpretations and explanations, and allows the researcher to respond flexibility to unforeseen problems and aspects of the research. Such triangulation can involve using multiple methods, analysts, datasets, and it has been used for decades by social scientists as a means of explaining behavior by studying it from two or more perspectives (Webb et al. 1996; Glaser and Strauss 1967; Newby 1977; Layder 1993; Cohen and Manion 2000).

In addition to serving as an effective methodology to examine social phenomena according to quantifiable linguistic evidence, CADS can provide a crucial contribution to the study of textuality / text production norms in both specialized and non-specialized contexts. In fact, the synergy between CL and discourse studies at large allows researchers to analyse the data through a functionalist lens and delve, by way of example, into multiple aspects of the text-building process (Douglas et al.

1998; Gries 2009a, 2009b; Kabanoff 1997; Lindquist, 2009; O'Keeffe and McCarthy 2022; Popping 2000) such as:

1. *Pattern recognition:* CADS enable the identification of recurring linguistic patterns within a corpus of texts, unveiling how texts are structured and organized.
2. *Genre analysis:* By studying various genres within a corpus, CADS reveal how text organization varies across different communicative contexts and genres.
3. *Cohesion and coherence:* Through CADS, researchers can examine lexico-grammatical devices that contribute to the coherence and cohesion of texts, enhancing our understanding of their organization.
4. *Functional analysis:* CADS facilitate the examination of linguistic choices that fulfill specific textual functions, elucidating how texts are organised to convey meaning effectively.
5. *Thematic exploration:* Researchers can employ CADS to uncover prevalent themes and topics across texts, shedding light on how texts are structured around particular key concepts.
6. *Discourse markers and structure:* CADS allow for the analysis of discourse markers and their role in signaling transitions and overall discourse structure, both in specialised and in general language.
7. *Comparative study:* Through CADS, text organization and lexico-grammatical features can be compared across different contexts, time periods, or genres, revealing variations and trends.

A mere glance at the index of this volume is enough to realize the multiplicity of research areas falling under the scope of CADS. Some chapters in the first part of the book appear more directly related to the first part of the acronym, Corpus Linguistics (CL), e.g., the preliminary reflections on the linguist's complex role in Sentiment Analysis or in performing grammatical tagging, an operation that adds value to corpora and makes them suitable for multiple research purposes. Both chapters fall within the gambit of functional text analysis, which correlates recurring structures with specific discourse functions. Conversely, the chapters dealing with the conventional traits of specialized phraseology (e.g., the lexical bundles employed in tourism communication in hotel webpages in German) or with the analysis of particular constructions at the interface of syntax and phraseology (e.g., the study of the WAY-construction in English and Spanish, of 'why-fragments' in contemporary English, or of 'if clauses' in American English) could be categorised under the broader umbrella of 'recurrent pattern recognition' or 'genre analysis'. On the other hand, the majority of studies in the second part of the volume are oriented towards the second component of the CADS acronym ([Critical] Discourse Studies) and examine the social practices deployed in specific discourses, e.g., electoral debates, TV series, social media like Twitter, or medical communication.

Last but not least, it is worth mentioning the potential limitations of CADS, thoroughly reviewed by Taylor and Marchi (2018). It must be emphasized that CADS are effective when this methodology is aligned with both the available data and the research questions. Its applicability varies and it may deemed essential for some projects, useful but non-essential or not worth it for others. Indeed, methodological competence involves knowing when and how to bring CADS to bear or whether to use it at all. While CADS' potential is now beyond question, their primary shortcomings can be outlined as follows (Gillings et al. 2023: 45–46):

1. CADS are unavoidably biased towards *lexis*, requiring identifiable words for analysis. This methodology is less suitable when the research question pertain to general discourse phenomena lacking clear 'lexical hooks' and unfolding over lengthy stretches of discourse, like argumentative strategies or extended metaphors.
2. They focus on *words*, limiting understanding of meaning in longer texts or dynamic social interactions.
3. CADS do not readily lend themselves to *identifying absent phenomena / language patterns*, as they primarily look for present elements. Comparisons between corpora can be helpful (Duguid and Partington 2018: 56), but interpretation remains the researcher's responsibility.
4. CADS lean toward *textual data*, omitting non-verbal context like images, sounds or gestures. In this regard, advances

in multimodal analysis are emerging, for example, Bednarek and Caple (2014: 151) proposed a new method called Corpus-Assisted Multimodal Discourse Analysis (CAMDA), combining corpus-based analysis with detailed scrutiny of other semiotic resources (also see Bednarek and Caple, 2017; Caple, 2018; Caple et al. 2020).

5. The metadata usually available in large corpora may *lack contextual factors*, hindering accurate analysis of age, gender, ethnicity, etc. The availability of a wider range of metadata in corpora annotation may result in broader research possibilities.
6. CADS *cannot eliminate bias entirely*, as key research design decisions remain subjective, e.g., decisions involving how to construct a corpus, which annotation scheme and software is considered more suitable for the analysis, the order of analytical steps, the frequency or statistical saliency thresholds, etc. (see Baker 2015: 286).

In the light of the above, one might even question whether the term 'limitations' fully applies. In fact, CADS should be assessed based on its intended purpose: if a method seems limiting, it might not be flawed but mismatched with research goals. Aligning the method with the research questions and to the data available undoubtedly enhances its potential.

2. Volume structure

The volume is divided into two parts. While the first part, CADS as a methodological approach, focuses on the corpus linguistic methodological approach to discourse analysis, the second part offers case studies.

The first part begins with Antonio Moreno-Ortiz's chapter 'The linguist's role in sentiment analysis: from knowledge provider to data annotator'. Here the author gives an overview of linguistic studies, corpus linguistics and computational linguistics used by researchers to present practical use cases, methods, systems, problems, advantages and disadvantages of different approaches, including sentiment analysis, lexicon-based and machine learning-based approaches, and transformer-based models, which represent the state of the art in natural language processing.

The investigation by Mª Paula Santalla del Río, Eva Mª Domínguez Nova and F.co Mario Barcala Rodríguez, 'Hypervalues in tagsets and its impact in the automatic morphosyntactic annotation of Spanish' aims to improve the quality of corpora enriched with morphosyntactic annotation to enable more searchable and better-secured corpora for discourse and translation studies. More specifically, the study evaluates the impact of values, called hypervalues, representing more than one unitary value for a grammatical category (whose relevance in a real text must be identified by context) in tagsets on annotation by applying it to a Spanish written corpus. Using the XIADA tagger, a statistical tagger based on second-degree Markovian models, three tagsets were developed corresponding to the three types of hypervalue treatment considered: Tagset with lexically assigned hypervalues that are neither manually nor automatically disambiguated, Tagset without hypervalues, and Tagset with hypervalues and their breakdowns. To evaluate the performance of the XIADA tagger, each elaborated tagset was run on a Spanish press corpus of about 52,000 words, after training the tagger with a corpus of 15,000 words. The evaluation is quantitative, with the first type showing better performance in automatic tagging. Qualitative insights into the errors due to the type of tag set used are also given.

Maricel Esteban-Follonosa's study, 'Methodological proposal for the selection and prioritisation of lexical bundles in professional discourse', discusses the methodology used in a corpus study of lexical bundles of online advertising texts of German accommodation websites. The main aims are to produce an inventory of lexical bundles characteristic of this discourse, to contribute to improving the writing of similar texts by non-native speakers, and to contribute to the development of a multilingual dictionary specialised in tourism discourse. For the study, the *Korpus der deutschsprachigen Hotelswebseiten* (KoDeHo) was compiled (2.4 million tokens) and divided into three diatopic subcorpora. In the study, the index of mixed values (such as frequency, mutual information index and simple mathematical index as proposed by the Sketch Engine platform) is proposed as a methodological tool for ordering lexical bundles, as it is of pedagogical, lexicographic and traductological interest.

The study by Luisa González-Romero, 'Between the construction and the phraseological unit. The *way*-construction in English and Spanish' presents an interesting analysis of the WAY /CAMINO construction in English and Spanish respectively. In English, the WAY construction has gained attention in recent literature because it is considered a conventional pairing of form and function in constructionist models: the syntactic pattern [SUBJi [V [POSSi way] OBL]] conveys the implication that the subject referent moves along the path denoted by the prepositional phrase, there seems to be agreement on the non-existence of this construction in Spanish, since Spanish is a verb-framed language that encodes the path of motion and the motion itself in the verb, while manner is expressed independently as an adverbial or gerundive element. This paper explores the possibility that there is a sentence type in Spanish that is syntactically and semantically equivalent to the English WAY construction. The analysis shows that the WAY construction exists in Spanish, although it is much less productive than in English and has the same features as its English counterpart. This finding indicates the existence of a continuum between the grammatical construction with free slots in which verbs from different semantic classes can alternately express either physical or abstract motion, and the phraseological unit that conveys a metaphorical meaning derived from the fixed combination of the verbs *make* and *find*, *encontrar* and *hacer*, and the nouns *way/camino* in their figurative use.

The study by Yolanda Fernández-Pena and Javier Pérez Guerra, 'Why *why* fragments? A corpus-based constructionist analysis of their form and meaning', analyzes fragments in contemporary English, which are independent linguistic expressions that can function as full sentence constituents. Fragments may convey an 'orthodox' interrogative interpretation of a complete *why*-clause, a potentially added 'modal' meaning, or the added 'presupposition of uniqueness'. The analysis examines *why*-fragments evidenced in representative samples from the spoken and written components of the British National Corpus 1994. The *why*-fragments are examined by considering variables such as categorial design, lexical, categorial and case mismatches between antecedents and remnants, and interpretation. The null hypothesis is the lack of a relationship between the enriched interpretation of *why*-fragments and their linguistic characterisation. To confirm or reject the null hypothesis, the data are modelled around independent linguistic predictors and the response variable 'literal' vs. 'enriched interpretation'. The binomial fixed-effects regression model revealed significant trends: *why* plus 'pronominal/adverbial' constructions tend to convey the canonical meaning of the corresponding complete sentences, while the '*why* + bare infinitive' construction favours an enriched interpretation.

The second part of the volume presents readers with interesting case studies of corpus approaches to discourse analysis, beginning with the chapter by Rosalía Rodríguez-Vázquez and Claudia de la Iglesia Sanjuán, 'The intonation of directive (in)subordinate *if*-clauses in American English: a corpus study', which also examines fragments. Fragments are characterised as structurally non-canonical but semantically felicitous constituents that are fully intelligible in the context in which they are uttered. Although fragments in written English have received some attention from a syntactic and communicative perspective, the description and classification of fragments in spoken English is comparatively sparse. This chapter aims to fill the existing research gaps by analysing, describing and classifying the intonational contours of a particular group of fragments, namely directive insubordinate *if*-clauses that occur without a main clause or are syntactically independent of it. Given that the intonation of directive rebellious *if*-clauses in British English (BE) shows a falling contour, the study aims to examine whether this is also true in the case of spoken American English (AmE). The results of the analysis of subordinating and subordinating *if*-clauses in the Santa Barbara Corpus of Spoken American English show that the former exhibit a falling contour in all positions within the utterance, i.e. initial, medial and final, irrespective of their subtype, while the latter exhibit (a) a falling contour when final and (b) a rising contour in some cases when in initial and medial positions. Moreover, these observations prove that recalcitrant *if*-clauses show a comparatively high degree of intonational 'fixation', which supports their syntactic and semantic marking as fragments.

The investigation carried out by Encarnación Almazán Ruiz and Aroa Orrequia Barea, 'A critical discourse analysis of 2020 US presidential debates', focuses on presidential debates as key elements of democracy, and aims to analyse the 2020 US presidential debates (28,499 tokens; 4,915 types) between Joe Biden and Donald Trump using a Corpus-assisted Discourse Studies (CADS) and Sentiment Analysis approach. The study shows that the overall polarity of Trump's speeches is negative, while that of Biden's speeches is neutral. Since the semantic orientation of the text is determined by the polarity of the words it contains, the study shows that Trump uses more negative and polarising words than Biden. Such a choice of words has an impact on the electorate, as it can evoke rejection towards certain social groups and even provoke social divisions.

The analysis of Carmen Gregori-Signes, 'Who's friends with the victim? A corpus-based stylistic approach to the analysis of the TV Series *The Killing*', deals with TV crime fiction. Although television crime fiction is one of the most widely used genres today, many of its features have not yet been sufficiently researched. Most research on fictional dramas has focused on the perpetrator, the detective or even the plot, often relegating the murder victim to the background in literature. This article argues that the functional role of the victim in the development of the narrative plot is worthy of further investigation. Using a corpus-based stylistic methodology, the frequency and distribution of terms for victim by the different characters in the first two seasons of the TV cult series *The Killing* was examined. The results showed that the choice of victim names functions as a key element that gives continuity to the main plot and helps the viewer to determine the status and importance of the characters in the fictional world.

The main topic of the contribution by Ignacio M. Palacios-Martínez and Paloma Núñez-Pertejo, 'The role of age in English Twitter discourse', is Twitter discourse and the influence of the age of the participants on the language used in the social network. To analyse the language, a contrastive analysis is conducted using two datasets: a set of posts from three British rappers and songwriters in their mid-twenties and a set from three well-known London singers in their 1950s and 1960s.The results first show features common to both groups of speakers that differ little or not at all, such as intensifiers, clipped words, abbreviations, emojis, multimodal communication and the use of spellings that reflect spoken language. It also identifies features that are present in both groups but are significantly different from each other. The results show that age, which plays an important role in traditional forms of expression, also has an impact on new digital genres such as Twitter.

Also Gema Alcaraz-Mármol and Jorge Soto-Almela focus on Twitter in their chapter 'A contrastive corpus-assisted study of the portrayal of Afghan women in the Twitter discourse during the 2021 Taliban takeover'. In this research, Twitter was used as a source to create a corpus of tweets about the withdrawal of international troops from Afghanistan and the announcement of a transitional Taliban government. This had consequences for the population, especially for women who sought help from the international community. The study analysed tweets in Spanish posted in Spain and in English posted in the US that contained the hashtags and keywords *Afganistán/Afghanistan*. Over 5,000 tweets in Spanish and over 16,000 tweets in English were collected, with the lemmas *mujer* and *woman* in the top 10 in each language. The semantic preference of the lemmas *mujer* and *woman* was also investigated based on their collocates. The results indicate that the lemma *mujer* appears in more tweets than the lemma *woman*, suggesting that US tweets mention the topic of women in relation to the conflict in Afghanistan to a lesser extent. The semantic preference of the lemmas *mujer* and *woman* for words of victimisation and feminism varies proportionally from country to country.

The final chapter by Stefania M. Maci, Cherubino Di Lorenzo and Catello Vollono, '*All together now*: disentangling Beatles' song titles in medical research articles' seeks to understand the reasons for the use of Beatles' song titles in the titles of medical research articles (RAs). To this end, 546 article titles were collected and linguistically analysed over a period of 57 years (1965–2022). The titles were then classified according to three different perspectives: (1) level of informativeness; (2) information packaging and meaning; (3) degree of accessibility and referential transparency. The results show that Beatles' quotations have gradually expanded over the years, with a preference for compound and nominal titles. In terms of the way in which information is packaged, titles are primarily *focus* ones and constructed with no specialized language. Results suggest that by quoting a Beatles song title, the author of the publication is clearly exploiting an attention-seeking device with startling effect. Such an approach does not seem to be dependent on a specific time, academic journal, medical field, or Beatles song. They can therefore be defined as *attractors*.

References

Baker, Paul / Egbert, Jesse (eds.) 2016. *Triangulating Methodological Approaches in Corpus-Linguistic Research*. New York / London: Routledge.

Baker, Paul / Gabrielatos, Costas / KhosraviNik, Majid / Krzyżanowski, Michał / McEnery, Tony / Wodak, Ruth. 2008. A Useful Methodological Synergy? Combining Critical Discourse Analysis and Corpus Linguistics to Examine Discourses of Refugees and Asylum Seekers in the UK press. *Discourse & Society* 19/3, 273–306.

Baker, Paul. 2006. *Using Corpora in Discourse Analysis*. Bloomsbury.

Baker, Paul. 2015. Does Britain Need Any more Foreign Doctors? Inter-Analyst Consistency and Corpus-Assisted (Critical) Discourse Analysis. In N. Groom / M. Charles / S. John (eds.), *Corpora, Grammar and Discourse: In Honour of Susan Hunston*. Amsterdam: John Benjamins, 283–300.

Bednarek, Monika / Caple, Helen. 2014. Why Do News Values Matter? Towards a New Methodological Framework for Analysing News Discourse in Critical Discourse Analysis and Beyond. *Discourse and Society* 25/2, 135–58.

Bednarek, Monika / Caple, Helen. 2017. *The Discourse of News Values: How News Organizations Create Newsworthiness*. New York: Oxford University Press.

Biber, Douglas / Conrad, Susan / Reppen, Randi. 1998. *Corpus Linguistics: Investigating Language Structure and Use*. Cambridge: Cambridge University Press.

Caldas-Coulthard, Carmen R. 1993. From Discourse Analysis to Critical Discourse Analysis: The Differential Re-presentation of Women and Men Speaking in Written News. In J. M. Sinclair / M. Hoey / G. Fox (eds.), *Techniques of Description: Spoken and Written Discourse*. London: Routledge, 196–208.

Caple, Helen. 2018. Analysing the Multimodal Text. In C. Taylor / A. Marchi (eds.), *Corpus Approaches to Discourse: A Critical Review*. London: Routledge, 85–109.

Caple, Helen / Huan, Changpeng / Bednarek, Monika. 2020. *Multimodal News Analysis Across Cultures*. Cambridge: Cambridge University Press.

Cohen, Louis / Manion, Lawrence. 2000. *Research Methods in Education*. London: Routledge.

Duguid, Alison / Partington, Alan. 2018. Absence: You Don't Know What You're Missing. Or Do You? In C. Taylor / A. Marchi (eds.), *Corpus Approaches to Discourse: A Critical Review*. London: Routledge, 38–59.

Fairclough, Norman. 1992. *Discourse and Social Change*. Cambridge: Polity Press.

Fairclough, Norman. 1995. *Critical Discourse Analysis. The Critical Study of Language*. London / New York: Longman.

Fairclough, Norman. 2003. *Analysing Discourse. Textual Analysis for Social Research*. London / New York: Routledge.

Foucault, Michel. 1969. *L'archéologie du savoir*. Paris: Gallimard.

Gillings, Mathew / Mautner, Gerlinde / Baker, Paul. 2023. *Corpus-Assisted Discourse Studies*. Cambridge: Cambridge University Press.

Glaser, Barney G. / Strauss, Anselm L. 1967. *The Discovery of Grounded Theory: Strategies for Qualitative Research*. Chicago: Aldine.

Gries, Stefan Th. 2009a. *Quantitative Corpus Linguistics with R: A Practical Introduction*. New York: Routledge.

Gries, Stefan Th. 2009b. What Is Corpus Linguistics? *Language and Linguistics Compass* 3, 1–17.

Jaworski, Adam / Coupland, Nikolas (eds.) 2014. *The Discourse Reader*. London: Routledge.

Kabanoff, Boris. 1997. Computers Can Read as Well as Count: Computer-Aided Text Analysis. *Organizational Research. Journal of Organizational Behavior* 18/S1, 507–511.

Krishnamurthy, Ramesh. 1995. *Ethnic, Racial and Tribal. The Language of Racism?* London: Routledge.

Layder, Derek. 1993. *New Strategies in Social Research*. Cambridge: Polity Press.

Leech, Geoffrey / Fallon, Roger. 1992. Computer Corpora: What Do They Tell Us about Culture? *ICAME Journal* 16, 29–50.

Lindquist, Hans. 2009. *Corpus Linguistics and the Description of English*. Edinburgh: Edinburgh University Press.

Morley, John / Bayley, Paul (eds.) 2009. *Corpus-Assisted Discourse Studies on the Iraq Conflict. Wording the War*. London: Routledge.

Newby, Howard. 1977. In the Field: Reflections on the Study of Suffolk Farm Workers. In C. Bell / N. Newby (eds.), *Doing Sociological Research*. London: Allen and Unwin, 108–209.

O'Keeffe, Anne / McCarthy, Michael. 2022. *The Routledge Handbook of Corpus Linguistics*. 2nd ed. London: Routledge.

Partington, Alan / Duguid, Alison / Taylor, Charlotte. 2013. *Patterns and Meanings in Discourse. Theory and Practice in Corpus-Assisted Discourse Studies (CADS)*. Amsterdam / Philadelphia: Jon Benjamins.

Partington, Alan / Morley, John / Haarman, Louann (eds.) 2004. *Corpora and Discourse*. Bern: Peter Lang.

Popping, Roel. 2000. *Computer-Assisted Text Analysis*. London: Sage.

Stubbs, Michael. 1997. Whorf's children: Critical comments on critical discourse analysis (CDA). In A. Ryan / A. Wray (eds.), Evolving Models of Language. Clevedon: Multilingual Matters, 100–116.

Stubbs, Michael. 2001. *Words and Phrases: Corpus Studies of Lexical Semantics*. London: Blackwell.

Stubbs, Michael / Gerbig, Andrea. 1993. Human and Inhuman Geography: On the Computer-Assisted Analysis of Long Texts. In M. Hoey (ed.), *Data, Description, Discourse: Papers on the English Language in Honour of JohnMcH Sinclair on His Sixtieth Birthday*. London: Harper Collins, 64–85.

Taylor, Charlotte / Marchi, Anna (eds.) 2018. *Corpus Approaches to Discourse: A Critical Review*. London: Routledge.

van Dijk, Teun A. 1993. Principles of Critical Discourse Analysis. *Discourse & Society* 4/2, 249–83.

van Dijk, Teun A. 1998. *Ideology. A Multidisciplinary Approach*. London: Sage.

Webb, Eugene J. / Campbell, Donald T. / Schwartz, Richard D. / Sechrest, Lee. 1966. *Unobstrusive Measures*. Chicago: Rand McNally.

Wodak, Ruth / Meyer, Michael (eds.) 2001. *Methods of Critical Discourse Studies*. London: Sage.

Part I
CADS as a methodological approach

ANTONIO MORENO-ORTIZ

The linguist's role in sentiment analysis: From knowledge provider to data annotator

1. Introduction

In this day and age, Internet users take for granted the ability to create online content easily. In fact, most may not even be aware that they are actually generating such content when they update their Facebook status, create an Instagram story, or post a product review on Amazon; but companies and organizations were quite aware of this soon after the technologies that make this possible were introduced in the early 2000's. Apart from the obvious business opportunities that these new functionalities enabled, the user-generated data was seen by many as an endless source of valuable information to exploit. Data mining, a term that had been in use by the database community since the 1990's, took on a whole new dimension. Since the World Wide Web is mostly (80–90 %) made up of unstructured data,[1] especially text, the term *text mining* was coined to refer specifically to the act of distilling knowledge from this particular type of data. The connection with linguistically-motivated inquiry was obvious to the early proponents of the field. In fact, Hearst (1999: 4) states:

> If we extrapolate from data mining (as practiced) on numerical data to data mining from text collections, we discover that there already exists a field engaged in text data mining: corpus-based computational linguistics! Empirical computational linguistics computes statistics over large text collections in order to discover useful patterns. These patterns are used to inform algorithms for various subproblems

1 https://techjury.net/blog/big-data-statistics/.

> within natural language processing, such as part-of-speech tagging, word sense disambiguation, and bilingual dictionary creation.

The last sentence is particularly relevant to this article, because it defines very well the role corpus linguists were fulfilling at the time: that of knowledge providers, which they extracted from corpora using quantitative and qualitative methods and materialised as insights that could then be used to model a language. However, the availability of these massive amounts of user-generated content (UGC) has fuelled a critical shift during these years: research on linguistic data is not the exclusive concern of (corpus/computational) linguistics anymore, as companies and organisations worldwide regard UGC as a rich pool of information from which valuable —in economic terms—knowledge can be obtained. As a result, Natural Language Processing (NLP) has evolved from a mere set of techniques that provide ad-hoc solutions to low-level language processing problems (e.g., tokenization, part-of-speech tagging, syntactic parsing) to a fully-fledged field of study that effectively tackles complex linguistic challenges such as sentiment analysis, text summarisation, human-like dialogue systems, and other natural language tasks that require sophisticated solutions.

Big data, the overused term that is meant to refer to the processing of very large collections of data, usually of diverse nature (both structured and unstructured) and provenance, requires not just accessibility to the dataset itself, but also the availability of highly sophisticated software that can effectively extract useful information/knowledge, on the one hand, and powerful hardware on which to run these algorithms on the data, on the other. In present-day NLP praxis, this materialises as machine/deep learning algorithms and specialised hardware, such as graphics or tensor processing units (GPUs and TPUs), which can run said Artificial Intelligence algorithms.

The combination of all these circumstances—commercial interest and therefore large-scale investment, data availability, and technical capabilities—has produced a new generation of extremely powerful language processing applications, such as voice assistants, chatbots, or high-quality machine translation, as well as a slew of tools and methodologies that are not only valuable to businesses, but also, I believe, to the language researcher. Among these applications, Sentiment Analysis (SA) or opinion mining has become one of the most salient subfields of NLP in the last two decades. In this chapter I set out to describe the evolution of the methods employed to tackle this task, which attempts to automatically classify an opinionated text according to the polarity it conveys.

From a linguistic perspective, evaluative language has traditionally been the concern of discourse analysis, where researchers have focused on the subtle ways in which opinion is expressed, with few—but noteworthy—attempts to provide systematic and computationally-tractable methodologies, although research has been limited to very specific genres. In traditional, rule-based approaches to computational linguistics this valuable knowledge has been useful to implement practical systems to process language. This body of research, however, seems now to be decoupled from NLP, both in terms of methods and textual genres, as current state-of-the-art NLP techniques are based on training predictive models from large amounts of raw text, without resorting to manually encoding the kind of specialised knowledge that is derived from traditional linguistic studies.

Thus, in this article I address the following questions: (1) how are probabilistic models replacing humans as knowledge providers? (2) Is there still a role to be fulfilled by language researchers in the development of present-day NLP systems? (3) Can language researchers actually benefit from these intelligent systems? This pursuit entails an understanding of both perspectives in terms of objectives and methods, as well as an illustration of how some synergy between them might be put into actual practice.

2. Evaluation in linguistics

> Linguists have underestimated the extent to which grammatical and discourse structures serve affective ends. (Ochs and Schieffelin 1989: 7).

Although a dictionary definition of the word may give us a good indication of what is meant by *evaluation*, it is necessary to define it from the point of view of linguistics. Thompson and Hunston (2000: 5) define evaluation as follows:

> Evaluation is the broad cover term for the expression of the speaker or writer's attitude or stance towards, viewpoint on, or feelings about the entities or propositions that he or she is talking about. That attitude may relate to certainty or obligation or desirability or any of a number of other sets of values.

From a sentiment analysis perspective, this definition aligns perfectly with its goals, which essentially come down to discovering linguistic productions that express attitude, stance, viewpoint, or feelings towards the entities being discussed. Evaluation has also been defined as a 'departure from the norm'. This is the case in those authors that have focused on texts which are not evaluative in nature, or at least should not be classed as such in principle. Thus, Labov (1972) lists a number of lexical and grammatical devices, such as intensifiers, comparative structures, and correlatives, that depart from the 'basic narrative syntax', which, in turn, is characterised by certain other linguistic devices, such as past tenses and adverbials of instrument, place, and time. Under this view, evaluation is seen as the exception rather than the norm.[2]

In stark contrast, some linguists, such as Émile Benveniste, have positioned subjectivity as central to language itself:

> Language is marked so deeply by the expression of subjectivity that one might ask if it could still function and be called language if it were constructed otherwise (Benveniste 1971: 225).

If evaluation is so important, then we should expect to find a multitude of works devoted to studying its means of expression. Nevertheless, as Hunston (1989) states in her seminal work, evaluation, or subjectivity, and the mechanisms that speakers use to express it, have received little attention from linguists. The reason she mentions is that evaluation has no agreed-upon definition and the role it plays in discourse is not clear. Finegan (1995) provides other reasons why evaluation itself has received little attention:

---

2 Labov, however, is one of the first authors to emphasize the importance and relevance of evaluation in language in general and personal narratives in particular. In his ethnographical analysis of "fight narratives" in black English vernacular, he describes the evaluation part of the narrative as "the point" of the narrative (Labov 1972: 366).

> The discourse sense of subjectivity is not now paramount in linguistic analysis, and has never been, in part because structural and formal linguistics more typically focus on language as the expression of objective propositions, on occasion displaying a curious indisposition even to recognize the self in discourse (2).

There are, nevertheless, a good number of authors that have paid attention to the phenomenon of evaluation in a systematic way. Labov and Waletzky (1967) distinguish two functions of narratives: referential and evaluative. Unlike most discourse-oriented studies, they take the clause as the basic unit of analysis and, in fact, formally define a narrative as a sequence of clauses that meet certain conditions (Labov and Waletzky 1967: 27–28). They go on to establish five main components: orientation, complication, evaluation, resolution, and coda. Because of their clause-based approach, an analysis of a narrative should then map each clause in the text to one of these functions. Similarly, Winters (1982) in his *Contextual Grammar of English* takes the dichotomy situation vs. evaluation—in other words, what we *know* vs. what we *think*—to study clause relations.

Thompson and Hunston (2000: 21) summarise the work carried out in this direction, i.e., identifying the linguistic features that signal evaluation, and point out three categories:

1. Comparators: comparative adjectives and adverbs, adverbs of degree, comparator adverbs, and expressions of negativity (morphological, such as affixes; grammatical, such as *not*, *never*, *hardly*; and lexical, such as *fail*, or *lack*).
2. Markers of subjectivity: modals, non-identifying adjectives, report and attribution structures, marked clause structures (such as clauses beginning with *it* and *there*) and pseudo-clefts.
3. Markers of value: lexical items of varied nature and indications of the presence of goals and (non-)achievement.

As we will see in Section 3.1 below, language elements described here form the basis of the contextual valence shifter systems that have been proposed and implemented within lexicon-based approaches to sentiment analysis, as they materialise as formal markers that not only signal the presence of evaluation or subjectivity, but may also shift the orientation of sentiment words.

The work of Ken Hyland regarding evaluation in academic texts is also of extreme relevance in this context. Although Hunston (1989, 1993) needs to be recognized for her ground-breaking work on the role of evaluation in scientific texts, Hyland takes this idea even further, and does not hesitate to place academic texts in a category he calls *review genres*: '(...) what academics mainly do is evaluate. Their research and publishing is a continual round of comparing methods, assessing sources, weighing up outcomes, contrasting claims and considering data'. (Hyland and Diani, 2009: 1). Like Hunston, Hyland claims that academic texts are far from being the objective, faceless kind of discourse that they have typically taken to be, as evaluation is an inherent aspect of human nature. Ultimately, this idea is rooted in the social constructivist position, which questions the notion of an objective reality and argues that 'everything we see and believe is actually filtered through our theories and our language, sustained by everyday social processes or research and communication' (Hyland 2009: 12).

The corpus linguistics developments on the notion of semantic prosody (or preference) are also quite relevant in this context. As stated by Stewart (2013), the concept (and term) of semantic prosody is attributed to Sinclair (1991) and, although its definition seems to be rather elusive, it refers to the observation that certain words that do not, per se, convey a particular semantic orientation somehow determine the presence of lexical items that do have one. For example, the phrasal verb 'set in' determines subjects that 'refer to unpleasant states of affairs', such as *rot, decay, malaise, despair, ill-will, decadence*, etc. (Sinclair 1991: 74–75). Other examples given by authors in this tradition are *utterly*, *bent on*, and *symptomatic* (Louw 1993), *commit*, *somewhat*, and *prevail* (Bublitz 1996), the verb *peddle* (Partington 1998), or the phrasal verb *break out* (Stewart 2013).

Semantic prosody/preference may be understood as a more general phenomenon that does not exclusively determine the presence of sentiment words. Instead, it may also determine other semantic categories, but what is of relevance to sentiment analysis is this particular type, what Bednarek (2008) calls 'POS/NEG collocations', as sentiment dictionaries are meant to contain all lexical items that signal a certain orientation. In this regard, if a word (e.g., the verb *commit*) is known to convey, albeit indirectly, a particular sentiment, then it should be included in the sentiment dictionary. This would allow certain unmarked collocations, e.g., 'commit deeds', to be classified as negative. The undesired side effect is that many of the lexical items said to convey semantic prosody of the type POS/NEG collocation display polysemy. For example, *commit* also has the, rather positive, sense of 'devote oneself to' (a laudable undertaking). In Section 3.2 below, I describe how, for practical applications, probabilistic methods can be useful in these situations.

This section would not be complete without making special mention of the work on appraisal carried out by scholars within the Systemic Functional Linguistics (SFL) framework of M.A.K. Halliday and his colleagues. In SFL, the related concepts of evaluation, affect, subjectivity, attitude, opinion, etc., fall under the umbrella term *appraisal*, and the linguistic framework crystalises in what is known as Appraisal Theory (Martin and White 2005). Within the broader SFL framework, appraisal is one of the three major components that construe interpersonal meaning—the other two being *negotiation* and *involvement*. Like the other two components, appraisal realises its discourse semantics function by lexicogrammatical (evaluative lexis, modality, negation, intensification, etc.) and phonological (loudness, pitch, phonasthesia) means. The appraisal event itself, known as the evaluation, is said to be achieved as the instantiation of three major aspects: (i) *attitude*, which refers to the core emotion (positive or negative) that is expressed towards the appraised entity, and encompasses three semantic regions: the emotional region (affect), the ethical region (judgement), and the aesthetic region (appreciation); (ii) *engagement*, which attempts to qualify the heteroglossy of an appraisal statement, that is, the speaker's position with regard to it: whether they disclaim it, proclaim it, entertain it, or attribute it to others. Finally, (iii) *graduation* accounts for the more direct intensification and downtoning linguistic mechanisms that further modulate the expression of appraisal.

The several examples and case studies carried out by Appraisal Theory proponents (Martin and Rose 2003; Martin and White 2005) illustrate that this framework is quite capable of describing and explaining in detail the expression of evaluative language. However, few attempts have been made to implement it in actual sentiment analysis systems, as most applications of the theory take the form of case studies or proof-of-concept, and even in these scenarios researchers have reported some serious limitations, such as the difficulty of identifying appraisal groups and attitude categories (Soo-Guan Khoo et al. 2012).

In addition, the framework does little in terms of providing useful data in order to achieve the main objective of sentiment analysis: automatically identify polarity expressions and the entities they refer to.

3. Sentiment analysis in practice

The main goal of sentiment analysis is to identify 'people's opinions, sentiments, evaluations, appraisals, attitudes, and emotions towards entities such as products, services, organizations, individuals, issues, events, topics, and their attributes' (Liu 2011: 459). The actual tasks tackled by Sentiment Analysis are polarity detection and emotion recognition, performed by the use of a classification task (Cambria et al. 2017). Text classification is in fact one of the most basic NLP tasks, whereby a document is classified as belonging to one of two or more classes. This is accomplished by using a *classifier*, i.e., a predictive model that reads the input text and outputs a certain class, sometimes with a confidence score (i.e., how confident the classifier is that the document belongs in that class). Figure 1 is a simple representation of this process.

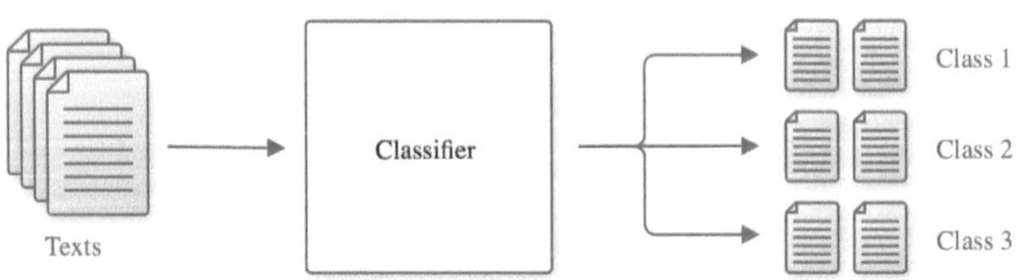

Figure 1: A text classification task.

Text classification is applied to a multitude of tasks and tools, such as spam filters, topic identification, and, of course, sentiment classification. For example, in Figure 1, Class 1 could be *positive*, Class 2 *negative*, and Class 3 *neutral*.

Classification techniques, like other processes that attempt to emulate intelligent behaviour, can be implemented in many ways. The traditional approach is a series of IF-THEN statements (or *production rules*), which together form a rule-based system. Rule-based systems have been employed since the beginning in computing, as they form the basis of most programming languages. They are sometimes referred to as 'the simplest form of artificial intelligence' (Grosan and Abraham, 2011: 149). A rule-based system contains a set of production rules, a set of facts, and an interpreter that controls the application of the rules given the facts. Thus, these systems require expert knowledge of the domain at hand, as well as engineering skills to encode this knowledge as a set of facts and rules.

In sentiment analysis, the facts would specify which words and expressions are positive and negative, and the rules would define how the proportion of positive versus negative words is to be measured to come up with a global sentiment score for the document. Context can also be accounted for by a set of such rules (e.g. 'IF a negation particle precedes a sentiment adjective, THEN its polarity is inverted'). Lexicon-based sentiment analysis systems are, for the most part, rule-based systems, where the required static facts (e.g., sentiment lexicon) and procedural knowledge (e.g., context rules) have been obtained from certain knowledge sources—corpora, dictionaries, computational lexicons, etc.—and encoded by a knowledge engineer.

As opposed to this type of deterministic systems, machine learning uses probabilistic (or stochastic) methods to mimic intelligent behaviour. Instead of relying on expertly-encoded, distilled knowledge, the learning algorithms are able to obtain that knowledge themselves from large amounts of data, in this case text. Generally speaking, corpus-based (i.e., machine learning) approaches are predominant both in industry and research, since they have been shown to excel in classification tasks.

Current state-of-the-art in sentiment classification is offered by machine-learning approaches in the form of neural networks that use Transformers, i.e., deep learning models that aim to solve certain text-related tasks (bi-directional attention, word and sentence prediction, sequence-to-sequence tasks) while handling long-range dependencies with ease. Language models based on the Transformers architecture include two of the most successful ones to date: Google's BERT (Devlin et al. 2019) and OpenAI's GPT (Brown et al. 2020). Both have been shown to improve on previous top benchmark scores across numerous NLP tasks, both in natural language understanding and generation, including sentiment analysis (Wolf et al. 2020).

Before we go into detail as to how each of these approaches actually achieves its goals, it seems quite apparent that rule-based methods call for already available linguistic knowledge: lexical (what specific words and multi-word expressions denote or connote semantic orientations), morphosyntactic and structural—what inflectional, phrase-level and sentence-level mechanisms may modify those words—, and pragmatic and discourse-level (how the wider context determines the analysis in terms of genre or social constraints). All of these have been the concern of linguistic studies and the results obtained have the potential to be encoded and formalised as facts and rules.

3.1. Deterministic methods

Lexicon-based methods of performing sentiment analysis are said to be deterministic because they use deterministic data, i.e., a set of words that make up a lexicon where sentiment information about those words is stored and, sometimes, a set of rules that can contextualise the semantic orientation of those words in actual usage. Examples of such sentiment dictionaries include The Harvard General Inquirer (Stone and Hunt 1963), MPQA (Wilson et al. 2005), Bing Liu's Opinion Lexicon (Hu and Liu 2004), SentiWordNet (Baccianella et al. 2010), SO-CAL (Taboada et al. 2011), EmoLex (Mohammad and Turney 2010), VADER (Hutto and Gilbert 2014), Lingmotif-Lex (Moreno-Ortiz and Pérez-Hernández 2018), and SenticNet (Cambria et al. 2020). These resources generally consist of word lists with varying degrees of information, from simple polarity to emotion classification.

However, the semantics (including polarity) of individual words and phrases may be altered by the context in which they appear, sometimes to the point that they actually mean exactly the opposite of what they initially denote, which is especially true of sentiment words. For example, the positive word 'happy' will invert its polarity simply by a preceding negative adverb, such as 'not' or 'never'. A good lexicon-based sentiment analysis system, therefore, needs to account for such contextual shifters, which is not an easy task. For instance, we can implement a rule that inverts the sentiment of 'happy' when it is preceded by 'never' within a span of 3 words, which would correctly classify as negative expressions such as 'I was never really happy there', but would incorrectly classify cases like 'I've never been so happy before'. Various systems of contextual shifters have been developed within the field of sentiment analysis (e.g., Kennedy and Inkpen 2006; Moreno-Ortiz and Pérez-Hernández 2018; Polanyi and Zaenen 2006; Taboada et al. 2011). Nonetheless, the level of difficulty that sentence-level context handling poses pales in comparison to higher-order linguistic levels of analysis; discourse-related phenomena, such as the metaphorical usage of words, irony, sarcasm, understatements, or humblebragging—all of which are pervasive in social media, one of the major genres that sentiment analysis has been applied to—constitute a serious problem for which no practical solutions are offered at present.

These knowledge sources are also deterministic because they have been compiled and curated by humans and therefore are known to be true, or at least supposed to be true; this means that the performance of these systems is entirely a function of the data they are based on. Their underlying model is also deterministic: if more positive words than negative words are found in a text, then the text is predicted to be positive. When analysis errors occur, they are attributed to bad or incomplete data: a certain sentiment word is missing, a valence shifter was wrongly applied, pragmatic features have not been accounted for, some additional world or common-sense knowledge is required. The underlying assumption is that it is possible to collect all of the necessary facts and rules necessary for the model to perform optimally. This does not only apply to a lexicon-based sentiment analysis system, but to each and every formal grammar and computational implementation of linguistic theories. Nevertheless, the facts and rules of language have repeatedly been shown to be much too elusive and organic to be restrained by the deterministic straightjacket. Otherwise, after seven decades of implementations of linguistic theories, at least one would have emerged as a viable framework to develop real-world language applications, which is, arguably, not the case.

1 I hated the da vinci code ... .

2 Well, I am not going to lie, The Da Vinci Code SUCKED!

3 And better...- We all know Da Vinci code is bogus and inaccurate.

4 The Da Vinci Code sucked like a Hoover.

5 we saw the da vinci code, which kinda sucked in an okay way.

6 Da Vinci Code sucked, but talking through it definitely did not suck.

7 She was just absolutely adorable in Amélie, one of my favorite films, and while The Da Vinci Code pretty much suc ked, she looked good in it.

8 god, i just thought i hated the da vinci code, now i see how very wrong i was ... .

Figure 2: Lingmotif's text representation of 8 movie reviews. Darker background colour is red (i.e., negative) in the original.

To understand the problems that we attempt to tackle, Figure 2 shows the text representation, as rendered by Lingmotif 2 (Moreno-Ortiz 2017, 2021), of 8 tweets with opinions from the UMICH SI650 dataset of movie reviews.[3]

Strictly speaking, examples 1 to 7 convey a negative opinion on the movie itself, and text 8 expresses a positive opinion. Examples 1 through 4 are rather straightforward: negative items are found in all of them, and therefore the global polarity for each tweet is correctly calculated (as represented by the red background colour). Examples 5 and 6 both contain one negative and one positive item. In such cases Lingmotif uses a simple strategy based on the end-focus principle, assigning more weight to those elements that are located at the end, which is why both tweets are classified as positive; but this is obviously not always correct. Example 7 illustrates a common problem in SA tasks: the opinion holder evaluates entities other than the one they are supposedly judging; in this case the user positively evaluates an actress and the role she played in a different movie, for which a positive opinion is voiced, whilst the opinion of the actual movie is negative. Finally, example 8 poses a more complex type of difficulty: the adversative structure 'thought [NEG] . . . now i see . . . wrong' inverts the polarity of the verb 'hate' and determines the global polarity of the opinion (which Lingmotif wrongly classifies as negative).

3 These text representations are generated from the individual tokens after being processed by Lingmotif; therefore, the original spellings have been normalised. The original dataset is available at https://www.kaggle.com/c/si650winter11.

I have deliberately chosen one-sentence documents (tweets) to illustrate how difficulties are present even when discourse structure is extremely simple, but its relevance and impact on global sentiment identification increases proportionally with text length. For example, in user reviews it is common to discuss the pros and cons of a product or service, sometimes including comparisons with competing products.

A consumer review example may be useful to understand the pervasiveness of the described issues. Figure 3 shows the text representation produced by Lingmotif 2.0 of a consumer product review (of a phone case) taken from Amazon.

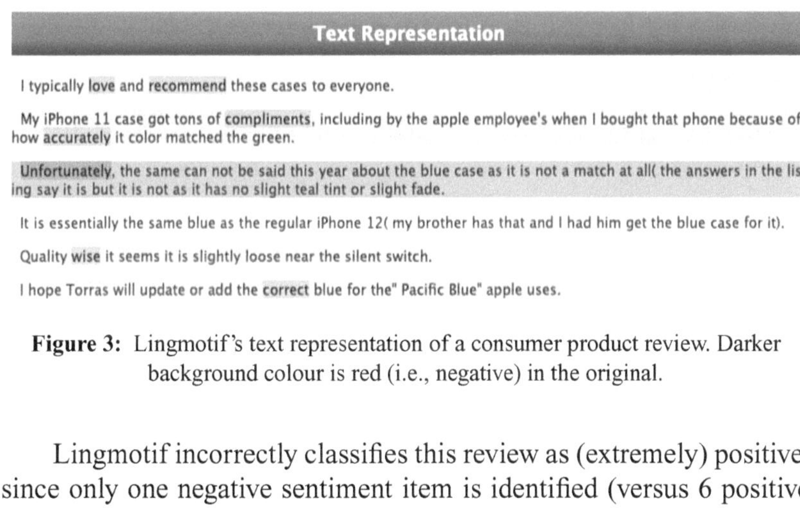
Text Representation

I typically love and recommend these cases to everyone.

My iPhone 11 case got tons of compliments, including by the apple employee's when I bought that phone because of how accurately it color matched the green.

Unfortunately, the same can not be said this year about the blue case as it is not a match at all(the answers in the list ing say it is but it is not as it has no slight teal tint or slight fade.

It is essentially the same blue as the regular iPhone 12(my brother has that and I had him get the blue case for it).

Quality wise it seems it is slightly loose near the silent switch.

I hope Torras will update or add the correct blue for the" Pacific Blue" apple uses.

Figure 3: Lingmotif's text representation of a consumer product review. Darker background colour is red (i.e., negative) in the original.

Lingmotif incorrectly classifies this review as (extremely) positive, since only one negative sentiment item is identified (versus 6 positive ones). This is due to three main reasons:

1. All comments in the first two sentences concern the reviewer's previous experience with other models of the same brand, not the one under consideration.
2. There are two lexical issues: one derived from the incorrect spelling of 'quality wise' (missing hyphen) and the other from the fact that the adjective 'loose' has a negative connotation in this particular domain.
3. Lingmotif's current set of context rules is unable to manage long-distance dependencies, therefore missing the fact that the verb 'hope' in the last sentence implies that the positive idea in 'update or add the correct...' is an unfulfilled wish on the part of the reviewer.

Lingmotif can make use of ad hoc, domain-specific lexicon plugins, which provide a means to adapt to different genres and text types where certain lexical items have a certain semantic orientation ('loose' is negative in this example but it may be neutral or even positive applied to other products or services). However, it is clear at this point that pursuing the strictly lexical path (with minimal context handling) by developing domain-specific plugins may be worth the effort in certain scenarios and can overcome some limitations, but it is questionable whether this path is optimal in terms of efficiency and efficacy.

3.2. Probabilistic methods

Machine learning (ML) algorithms have been in use since the 1960's, but during the last two decades we have witnessed their widespread use in real-world applications in many different fields of research and development.

In regular programming, we tell the computer exactly what steps to take to solve a problem, which works very well in many scenarios such as solving an equation; however, there are other tasks that do not lend themselves to this approach: how can we break down the process of identifying a particular object in a picture or, more specifically, the text understanding process into minute, step-by-step detail? The analysis process that I described in the previous section, used by lexicon-based SA tools such as Lingmotif, is nothing but an extreme procedural simplification of a much more complex cognitive process that our brains are somehow able to deal with effortlessly.

Machine learning attempts to teach computers to solve these complex problems by feeding learning algorithms examples of the problem and letting them figure out how to do it by themselves. Although 'classical' ML algorithms (Naïve Bayes, decision trees, Support Vector Machines, etc.) have been (and still are) successfully used to solve practical NLP problems, including sentiment analysis, it is Deep Learning and neural networks that have revolutionised the field. Currently, state-of-the-art performance in all language-related tasks is offered by the Transformer architecture (Vaswani et al. 2017), and therefore it has rapidly become the dominant architecture in NLP (Wolf et al. 2020). It draws on the concept and practice of 'pretraining', i.e., creating a language model from a very large corpus in an unsupervised manner which can later be repurposed for different specific applications by 'finetuning' it on smaller, labelled (i.e., annotated) corpora.

Table 1 shows the classification results of the movie tweets discussed in the previous section (Figure 2) using an implementation of the Transformer architecture. For the experiments in this section I used the default sentiment analysis pipeline offered by the HuggingFace Transformers library (Wolf et al. 2020) with two different models. Model 1 is the BERT-based 'DistilBERT base uncased finetuned SST-2' model,[4] which produces a binary classification (positive/negative) and is finetuned on the Stanford Sentiment Treebank (SST-2) dataset; it achieves an accuracy of 91.3 %. Model 2 is Cardiff NLP's roBERTa-based 'twitter-roberta-base-sentiment' model,[5] which considers 3 classes (positive/neutral/negative). It is trained on 58 million tweets and finetuned on the TweetEval (Barbieri et al. 2020) benchmark. This means that Model 1 is best suited to classify product reviews, whereas Model 2 was specifically developed to tackle tweets.

Table 1: Classification of movie reviews using a Transformer-based classifier.

Text	**Model 1**		**Model 2**	
	Class	**Score**	**Class**	**Score**
1. 'I hated The Da Vinci Code'	NEG	0.9993	NEG	0.9118
2. 'Well, I'm not gonna lie, The Da Vinci Code SUCKED!'	NEG	0.9953	NEG	0.9011
3. 'And better. . .-We all know Da Vinci code is bogus and inaccurate.'	NEG	0.9995	NEG	0.8076
4. 'The Da Vinci Code sucked like a Hoover.'	NEG	0.9997	NEG	0.9129
5. 'we saw the da vinci code, which kinda sucked in an okay way.'	NEG	0.9852	NEG	0.9050
6. 'Da Vinci code sucked, but talking through it definitely did not suck.'	NEG	0.8380	NEG	0.5593
7. 'She was just absolutely adorable in Amélie, one of my favorite films, and while The Da Vinci Code pretty much sucked, she looked good in it.'	POS	0.9998	POS	0.9252
8. 'god, i just thought i hated the da vinci code, now i see how very wrong i was. . .'	NEG	0.9997	NEG	0.9440

4 https://huggingface.co/distilbert-base-uncased-finetuned-sst-2-english.

5 https://huggingface.co/cardiffnlp/twitter-roberta-base-sentiment.

In terms of classification, results are better for both models than those achieved by Lingmotif, as 6 of the 8 texts are classified correctly. Also, the only one that is classified as positive is rather doubtful, as many human readers would probably classify it as positive too. In almost all cases the confidence score is very high, including the two classification errors (texts 7 and 8). Interestingly, both models show the lowest score for one of the doubtful cases (text 6).

Let us now see how these probabilistic models deal with the longer consumer review in the previous section (Figure 3), which is reproduced here together with the raw output of the two classifiers:

> "I typically love and recommend these cases to everyone. My iPhone 11 case got tons of compliments, including by the apple employee's when I bought that phone because of how accurately it color-matched the green. Unfortunately the same cannot be said about the blue case as it is not a match at all (the answers in the listing say it is but it is not as it has no slight teal tint or slight fade). It is essentially the same blue as the regular iPhone 12 (my brother has that and I had him get the blue case for it). Quality wise it seems it is slightly loose near the silent switch. I hope Torras will update or add the correct blue for the 'Pacific Blue' apple uses."
>
> **Model 1: [{'label': 'NEGATIVE', 'score': 0.9782788157463074}]**
>
> **Model 2: [{'label': 'positive', 'score': 0.9140385389328003}]**

Here model 1 correctly predicts the text to negatively evaluate the product, with a very high confidence score, too. However, model 2 classifies the text as positive, which is most probably due to the fact that this model has been trained on Twitter data and thus is ill-equipped to cope with consumer reviews. Unfortunately, we have no way to know what words or n-grams led to these results; perhaps the model was able to pick up on cues such as the fact that most positive words are in sentences where the past tense is used, maybe it took the word 'loose' as negative, or perhaps that the review ends with the expression of a hope for improvement. There is just no way to ask the model how it reached that decision; this is because of the well-known 'explainability' issue (or lack thereof) of machine learning and modern Artificial Intelligence in general. Indeed, these algorithms excel at discovering correlation in massive datasets, but offer little to nothing in the way of causation. Ultimately, the researcher is left to come up with likely interpretations of the results, as I have done in the examples above. Important steps are being taken towards an explainable AI (Barredo Arrieta et al. 2020), but current technology cannot offer 'explanations' of its own predictions; they simply act as black boxes that take an input and produce an output based on their probabilistic model.

These informal experiments are not meant to be proof of the superiority of one approach over the other. Rather, the aim is simply to illustrate the following observations:

- Rule-based, linguistically-motivated language processing is hard to develop and delivers subpar performance. Nonetheless, their results are transparent and fully interpretable, which is useful to the language researcher. The development process also appeals to—and calls for—language experts, which act as knowledge providers and knowledge engineers.
- Probabilistic models are the current state-of-the-art not only in sentiment analysis but across all other language-related practical tasks (summarisation, language understanding and generation, question answering, machine translation, etc.). Model development involves very little knowledge about how language works, as this is something that the algorithms discover by themselves, but highly specialised technical knowledge and hardware is required. Their usefulness to the language researcher is limited, as they cannot offer insights into the language they analyse. They are useful to evaluate other systems, since they are currently the benchmark.

Thus, neural networks are somehow capable of extracting the relevant features about language from language data and condensing them into an abstract (and opaque) model that can then be used to perform complex tasks that mimic human abilities rather successfully.

We are now in a position to address the question that gives title to this article: given the current state of affairs, what is the role of the linguist?

4. Discourse annotation for language model finetuning and linguistic inquiry

In this section I present a proposal for finetuning pre-trained language models to incorporate discourse information, in an attempt to solve some of the challenges that were highlighted in Section 3.1 and which impact both lexicon-based and machine learning sentiment analysers. This approach embodies one of the objectives of the DisParSA project,[6] currently under development.

Annotated corpora are essential to machine learning, as they provide the necessary labelled data required to train models in a supervised manner, including the finetuning of pretrained models. At the same time, the annotated corpus is a rich source of information that can provide interesting and useful insights as to how language is used.

The annotation schema for sentiment analysis we have implemented for the project is multi-layered, as we encode the following categories of information:

- Lexical polarity: where we annotate lexical units with positive or negative semantic orientation.
- Aspect: for aspect-based sentiment analysis, where we identify the relevant features, characteristics or components of the target entity being evaluated, together with the polarity expressed toward each aspect.
- Named entities: only those relevant to the evaluation act (opinion holder, evaluated entity, reader, etc.).
- Discourse units describing the communicative functions present in the text.

Currently, our main research focus is the discourse annotation layer. All other data categories have been implemented in our Lingmotif software in previous research efforts, but it is the first time that we attempt to introduce a discourse component.

---

6 Discourse Parsing for Sentiment Analysis (DisParSA). Project funded by the Spanish Ministry of Science and Innovation [grant number PID2020-115310RB-I00].

Discourse annotation can take many shapes and focus on different aspects, as discourse is a polyhedral, multi-faceted phenomenon. Rhetorical Structure Theory (RST) is a compositional model of discourse structure developed by Mann and Thompson (1988) and subsequently implemented as an automatic parser by Marcu (1997, 1999) and others. Following a descriptive approach, it aims to identify the structure of a text by segmenting it into 'elementary discourse units' (EDUs) which are related to each other and reflect the overall organisation and coherence of a text by postulating a hierarchical structure based on the idea that every part of a text has a function.

RST has been shown to be useful in lexicon-based sentiment analysis by many researchers. Voll and Taboada (2007) and Taboada et al. (2008) opened the path to employ discourse information as part of the equation to calculate global document polarity in general, and using RST in particular, to discover the relevant EDU and give more importance to the sentiment items found in those segments. This has been the main strategy followed by other authors: Chenlo et al. (2014) used RST for ranking global sentiment in blog posts and also applied it at the sentence level on news and product reviews text, while Bhatia et al. (2015) employed RST representations to improve the calculation of document classification by reweighting sentiment items in discourse units according to their status and relations.

One particular attempt to use RST is of special interest to us: Schouten and Franciscar (2016) found that although their approach produced high-quality linguistic information, it did not perform as well as machine learning-based approaches. The relevance of this work to ours lies in the fact that they applied RST to aspect-based sentiment analysis (our ultimate goal). Furthermore, their results underwent a strict performance evaluation process, since it was carried out in the controlled environment imposed by an organised shared task (SemEval). Thus, this work is a particularly reliable source in terms of performance.

An alternative which we believe to be more suitable to our ends is that of discourse units, as posited by Biber et al. (2007). This notion agrees with the basic RST assumption that every part of the text has a function, but it does not attempt to assign such functions down to the clause level, nor to connect all of them by means of labelled relationships, which are a means to achieve discourse parsing. Although several discourse parsers have been developed based on RST, reliability is generally low, as multiple parsers recurrently output different parses of the same text. They also rely on syntax parsers, which are not very reliable themselves when it comes to social media text (our main focus), since defining features of the genre, such as bad or missing punctuation marks, pose a serious problem.

Biber et al. (2007)'s notion of discourse units focuses on the functions that segments of a text have within that text, rather than on the relationships that the units hold among themselves. The discourse structure of a text is thus derived from the sequence of those functional discourse units[7] in that text. An analysis of discourse organisation under this emerging framework consists of seven steps, which can be applied using a top-down or bottom-up approach. The former proceeds as follows (Biber et al. 2007: 13):

1. Determine the analytical framework (i.e., the set of possible classes of FDUs).
2. Segmentation of the text into discourse units.
3. Classification by application of the categories in 1.
4. Linguistic analysis of each unit.
5. Linguistic description of discourse categories.
6. Derive text structure from the sequence of FDUs.
7. Describe patterns of discourse organisation across a corpus.

This approach has recently been applied to spoken language discourse annotation by Egbert et al. (2021), who developed a methodological framework for segmenting conversations into functional units and annotating their function. In their analysis of conversations, they identify a number of functions that are recurrently carried out by discourse units and assign them certain labels, such as sharing feelings and opinions ('fel'), engaging in conflict ('con'), joking around ('jok'), figuring

7 The term "functional discourse unit", which we will refer to as "FDU", is actually not used by the authors. Nevertheless, in my view, it is an appropriate term because it reflects well what its identification is based on (its function) and distinguishes from other types of discourse units based on semantic relations or other features. The term FDU is, however, used by Egbert et al. (2021).

things out ('fto'), etc. The authors consider it a coding framework that 'opens up an entirely new sub-field of descriptive corpus linguistics' (Egbert et al. 2021: 733).

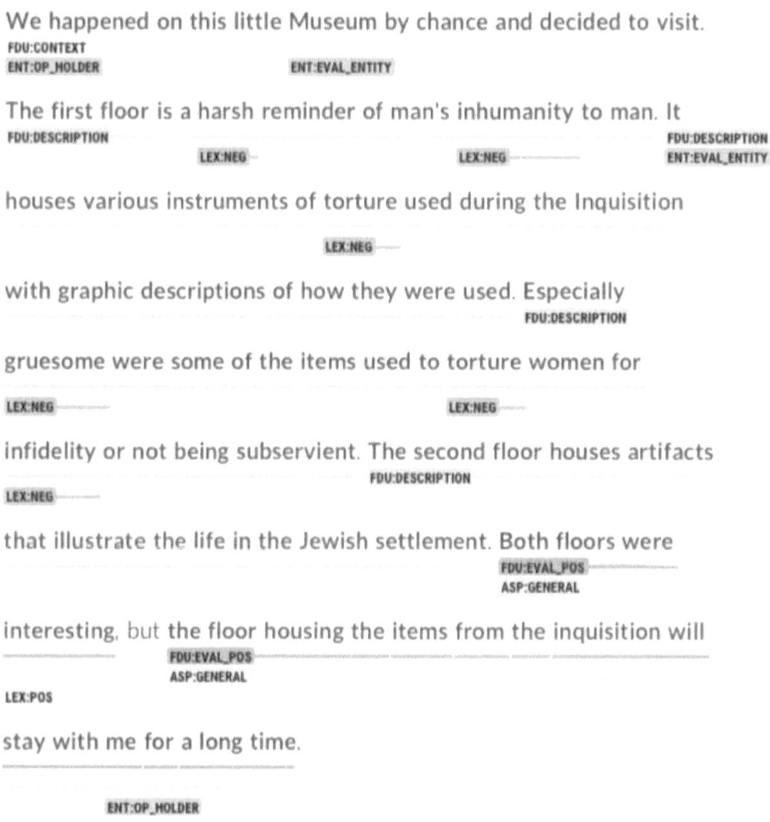

Figure 4: Annotated consumer review following the DisParSA framework.

The coding framework that we have designed for our project, although developed separately and simultaneously, is very close to this one, as both are inspired by the same ideas and concepts. Of course, we focus on opinion texts rather than conversations, as our interest lies there. Currently we have developed the analytical framework for consumer reviews of the hospitality industry, a genre that we are very familiar with from previous work (Moreno-Ortiz et al. 2019). As an annotation tool we employ Prodigy (Montani et al. 2022), a commercial, server-based corpus annotation tool especially designed for machine learning purposes. Prodigy does not support multi-layer annotations, so we annotate the different layers using encoded labels whose first three characters designate each of the four layers: FDU, LEX(icon), ENT(tity), and ASP(ect). Figure 4 shows an example of annotation.

This is an interesting example because it illustrates several important aspects. This review of a museum consists of six FDUs. The first one is of type 'context'; it is followed by four FDUs of type 'description', where objective information is provided, and concludes with two evaluative units where the actual opinion is given. In all this text only one sentiment word is mentioned that actually contributes to the overall positive evaluation of the museum ('interesting'). All other polarity words (6) are negative, but they are irrelevant to the evaluation itself as they are simply describing the content of the museum. This information is key to correctly assigning the overall polarity of the evaluation expressed in the text, but it is only available if we have access to a discourse component that is able to identify functions.

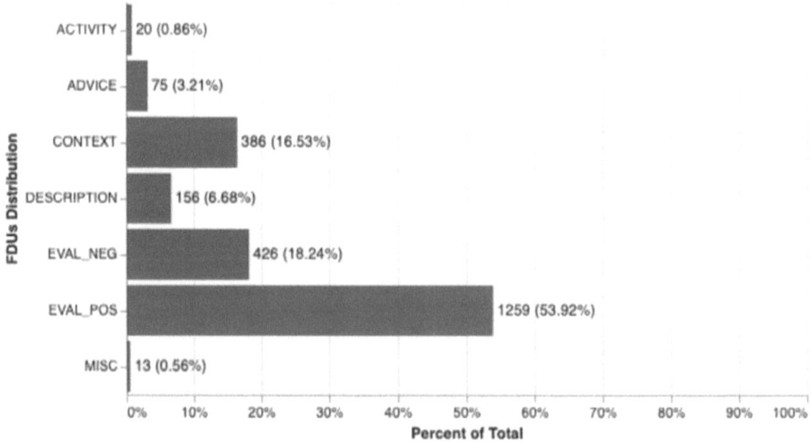

Figure 5: FDUs distribution example.

Our intention is to annotate a sizable corpus that is sufficient to fulfil two objectives: (1) provide information on how evaluation is actually expressed, and (2) use the data to finetune a pre-trained Transformer model so that it can recognise these segments automatically. We access the annotated data contained in the different layers using a custom script that reads the annotations and generates a number of useful reports and statistics, including visualisations. Figures 5 and 6 provide examples of such visualisations for a set of 190 reviews of hotels.

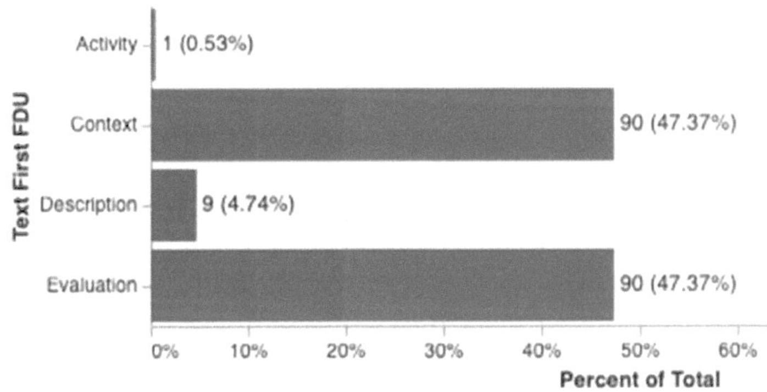

Figure 6: Text first FDU.

The script currently generates 12 such visualisations in the form of bar graphs and heat maps, along with the basic descriptive statistics, all integrated in an HTML document. It also generates a report listing each of the annotated FDUs, with links to the FDUs they subsume. From the examples here it is easy to see how 'context' is the most frequent FDU after 'eval' (Figure 5), a fact that needs to be taken into account when assigning the overall polarity to a text, or that it is just as likely for a review to start with context as it is that the global evaluation is provided at the very beginning (Figure 6).

It is still soon to offer conclusive results in terms of discourse analysis, as the annotation process has only recently started, but we are confident that we have created a viable framework, based on actual data, to study evaluative language and analyse how speakers structure and organise the information when we communicate our opinion about a certain item or topic.

5. Conclusions

We are now in a position to answer the three questions that were posed in the introduction. Computational Linguistics and Natural Language Processing methods are evolving at warp speed, as a new generation of Artificial Intelligence technology finds effective applications in so many areas of human life, especially language. To answer the first question—'how are probabilistic models replacing humans as knowledge providers?'—when it comes to actual natural language tasks, probabilistic models of language offer state-of-the-art performance, but are of little use to the language researcher, as they are unable to provide useful insights into the data. Conversely, deterministic approaches to language processing based on the collection of facts and rules are able to provide valuable cues as to how evaluative language is used and the effect it produces in linguistic productions, but offer poorer performance in terms of the main task at hand (sentiment classification); they are also harder to develop if a reasonable degree of quality is desired.

From a NLP perspective, linguistic studies have traditionally provided input as a source of specialized, detailed knowledge about language, which engineers have attempted to turn into a collection of facts and rules to create applications. This role seems to be less relevant now, as learning algorithms are capable of deriving this knowledge from raw text using intelligent algorithms. Therefore, the answer to the second question—'is there still a role to be fulfilled by language researchers?'—is yes, but the profile is shifting towards that of *data provider*. The insights derived from linguistic studies are of course still useful and necessary but, for the current generation of language technology, annotated corpora are more valuable than distilled knowledge. In this respect, it is also important to stress that generating high-quality annotated corpora, with the required level of granularity, undoubtedly requires considerable linguistic knowledge and expertise on the part of the coder. Therefore it is an activity particularly well-suited to the language expert.

Finally, to the question 'can language researchers actually benefit from these intelligent systems?', the answer is a resounding yes. Firstly, because these language models, being based on actual data, serve as benchmarks to evaluate and contrast hypotheses and rule-based applications. Secondly, because the current architectures require high-quality language data in the form of annotated corpora created by language specialists, and, as we have shown, these resources not only are useful for this paractical application, but are also a powerful tool for linguistic inquiry.

References

Baccianella, Stefano / Esuli, Andrea / Sebastiani, Fabrizio. 2010. SentiWordNet 3.0: An Enhanced Lexical Resource for Sentiment Analysis and Opinion Mining. In *Proceedings of the International Conference on Language Resources and Evaluation*. Valletta, Malta, 2200–2204.

Barbieri, Francesco / Camacho-Collados, Jose / Espinosa Anke, Luis / Neves, Leonardo. 2020. TweetEval: Unified Benchmark and Comparative Evaluation for Tweet Classification. In *Findings of the Association for Computational Linguistics: EMNLP 2020*. Online: Association for Computational Linguistics, 1644–1650.

Barredo Arrieta, Alejandro / Díaz-Rodríguez, Natalia / Del Ser, Javier / Bennetot, Adrien / Tabik, Siham / Barbado, Alberto / Garcia, Salvador. 2020. Explainable Artificial Intelligence (XAI): Concepts, Taxonomies, Opportunities and Challenges toward Responsible AI. *Information Fusion* 58/June, 82–115.

Bednarek, Monika. 2008. Semantic Preference and Semantic Prosody Re-Examined. *Corpus Linguistics and Linguistic Theory* 4/2, 119–139.

Benveniste, Emile. 1971. *Problems in General Linguistics*. Coral Gables, FL.: University of Miami Press.

Bhatia, Parminder / Ji, Yangfeng / Eisenstein, Jacob. 2015. Better Document-Level Sentiment Analysis from RST Discourse Parsing. In *Proceedings of the 2015 Conference on Empirical Methods in Natural Language Processing*. Lisbon, Portugal: Association for Computational Linguistics, 2212–2218.

Biber, Douglas / Connor, Ulla / Upton, Thomas A. 2007. *Discourse on the Move: Using Corpus Analysis to Describe Discourse Structure*. Amsterdam; Philadelphia: John Benjamins.

Brown, Tom / Mann, Benjamin / Ryder, Nick / Subbiah, Melanie / Kaplan, Jared / Dhariwal, Prafulla / Neelakantan Arvind. 2020. Language Models Are Few-Shot Learners. In Larochelle, H. / Ranzato, M. / Hadsell, R. / Balcan, M.F. / Lin H. (eds.), *Advances in Neural Information Processing Systems*, Vol. 33. Curran Associates, Inc, 1877–1901.

Bublitz, W. 1996. Semantic Prosody and Cohesive Company: Somewhat Predictable. *Leuvense Bijdragen: Tijdschrift Voor Germaanse Filologie* 8(5/1–2), 1–32.

Cambria, Erik / Dipankar, Das / Bandyopadhyay, Sivaji / Feraco, Antonio. 2017. *A Practical Guide to Sentiment Analysis*. 1st ed. Socio-Affective Computing 5. Springer International Publishing.

Cambria, Erik / Li, Yang / Xing, Frank Z. / Poria, Soujanya / Kwok, Kenneth. 2020. SenticNet 6: Ensemble Application of Symbolic and Subsymbolic AI for Sentiment Analysis. In *Proceedings of the 29th ACM International Conference on Information & Knowledge Management*. CIKM '20. New York, NY, USA: Association for Computing Machinery, 105–114.

Chenlo, José M. /Hogenboom, Alexander / Losada, David E. 2014. Rhetorical Structure Theory for Polarity Estimation: An Experimental Study. *Data & Knowledge Engineering* 94, 135–147.

Devlin, Jacob / Chang, Ming-Wei / Kenton Lee / Toutanova, Kristina. 2019. BERT: Pre-Training of Deep Bidirectional Transformers for Language Understanding. In *Proceedings of the 2019 Conference of the North American Chapter of the Association for Computational Linguistics: Human Language Technologies, Volume 1 (Long and Short Papers)*. Minneapolis, Minnesota: Association for Computational Linguistics, 4171–4186.

Egbert, Jesse / Wizner, Stacey / Keller, Daniel / Biber, Douglas / McEnery, Tony / Baker, Paul. 2021. Identifying and Describing Functional Discourse Units in the BNC Spoken 2014. *Text & Talk* 41/5–6, 715–737.

Grosan, Crina / Abraham, Ajith. 2011. *Intelligent Systems*. Vol. 17. Intelligent Systems Reference Library. Berlin, Heidelberg: Springer Berlin Heidelberg.

Hearst, Marti A. 1999. Untangling Text Data Mining. In *Proceedings of the 37th Annual Meeting of the Association for Computational Linguistics on Computational Linguistics*. ACL '99. USA: Association for Computational Linguistics, 3–10.

Hu, Minqing / Liu, Bing. 2004. Mining and Summarizing Customer Reviews. In *Proceedings of the Tenth ACM SIGKDD International Conference on Knowledge Discovery and Data Mining*. Seattle, WA, USA: ACM, 168–177.

Hunston, Susan. 1989. *Evaluation in Experimental Research Articles*. Birmingham, UK: University of Birmingham.

Hunston, Susan 1993. Evaluation and Ideology in Scientific Writing. In Ghadessy, M. (ed.), *Register Analysis: Theory and Practice*, Pinter, 57–74.

Hutto, C. J. / Gilbert, Eric. 2014. VADER: A Parsimonious Rule-Based Model for Sentiment Analysis of Social Media Text. In *Proceedings of the International AAAI Conference on Web and Social Media*, 216–225.

Hyland, K. (2009). *Academic Discourse: English in a Global Context*. London, UK: Continuum.

Hyland, K. / Diani, G. (2009). Introduction: Academic Evaluation and Review Genres. In Hyland, K. / Diani, G. (eds.), *Academic Evaluation: Review Genres in University Settings*. London, UK: Palgrave Macmillan, 1–14.

Kennedy, Alistair / Inkpen, Diana. 2006. Sentiment Classification of Movie Reviews Using Contextual Valence Shifters. *Computational Intelligence* 22/2, 110–125.

Labov, William. 1972. *Language in the Inner City: Studies in the Black English Vernacular*. Conduct and Communication. University of Pennsylvania Press.

Labov, William / Waletzky, Joshua. 1967. Narrative Analysis: Versions of Personal Expeerience. In Helm, J. (ed.), *Essays on the Verbal and Visual Arts: Proceedings of the 1966 Annual Spring Meeting of the American Ethnological Society*. Proceedings of the Annual Spring Meeting of the American Ethnological Society. American Ethnological Society.

Liu, Bing. 2011. *Web Data Mining*. Berlin, Heidelberg: Springer.

Louw, Bill. 1993. Irony in the Text or Insincerity in the Writer? The Diagnostic Poten- Tial of Semantic Prosodies. In Baker, Mona / Francis, Gill / Tognini-Bonelli, Elena (eds.), *Text and Technology: In Honour of John Sinclair*. Amsterdam: John Benjamins, 157–175.

Mann, William C. / Thompson, Sandra A. 1988. Rhetorical Structure Theory: Toward a Functional Theory of Text Organization. *Text – Interdisciplinary Journal for the Study of Discourse* 8/3, 243–281.

Marcu, Daniel. 1997. The Rhetorical Parsing of Unrestricted Natural Language Texts. In *35th Annual Meeting of the Association for Computational Linguistics and 8th Conference of the European Chapter of the Association for Computational Linguistics*. Madrid, Spain: Association for Computational Linguistics, 96–103.

Marcu, Daniel. 1999. Discourse Trees Are Good Indicators of Importance in Texts. In Mani, Inderjeet / Maybury, Mark (eds.), *Advances in Automatic Text Summarization*. The MIT Press.

Martin, James R. / Rose, David. 2003. *Working with Discourse: Meaning Beyond the Clause*. Bloomsbury Academic.

Martin, James R. / White, Peter R. R. 2005. *The Language of Evaluation: Appraisal in English*. Basingstoke: Palgrave Macmillan.

Mohammad, Saif M. / Turney, Peter D. 2010. Emotions Evoked by Common Words and Phrases: Using Mechanical Turk to Create an Emotion Lexicon. In *Proceedings of the NAACL HLT 2010 Workshop on Computational Approaches to Analysis and Generation of Emotion in Text*. Association for Computational Linguistics, 26–34.

Montani, Ines / Honnibal / Van Landeghem, Sofie / Boyd, Adriane / Peters, Henning / Samsonov, Maxim / Geovedi, Jim. 2022. Prodigy v1.11.8. Explosion.

Moreno-Ortiz, Antonio. 2017. Lingmotif: Sentiment Analysis for the Digital Humanities. In *Proceedings of the 15th Conference of the European Chapter of the Association for Computational Linguistics*. Valencia, Spain: Association for Computational Linguistics, 73–76.

Moreno-Ortiz, Antonio. 2021. *Lingmotif 2*. Málaga, Spain: Universidad de Málaga.

Moreno-Ortiz, Antonio / Pérez-Hernández, Chantal. 2018. Lingmotif-Lex: A Wide-Coverage, State-of-the-Art Lexicon for Sentiment

Analysis. In *Proceedings of the Eleventh International Conference on Language Resources and Evaluation (LREC 2018)*. Miyazaki, Japan: European Language Resources Association (ELRA), 2653–2659.

Moreno-Ortiz, Antonio / Salles-Bernal, Soluna / Orrequia-Barea, Aroa. 2019. Design and Validation of Annotation Schemas for Aspect-Based Sentiment Analysis in the Tourism Sector. *Information Technology & Tourism* 21/4, 535–557.

Ochs, Elinor / Schieffelin, Bambi. 1989. Language Has a Heart. *Text – Interdisciplinary Journal for the Study of Discourse* 9/1, 7–26.

Partington, Alan. 1998. *Patterns and Meanings: Using Corpora for English Language Research and Teaching*. Amsterdam: John Bejamins.

Polanyi, Livia / Zaenen, Annie. 2006. Contextual Valence Shifters. In *Computing Attitude and Affect in Text: Theory and Applications*. Dordrecht, The Netherlands: Springer, 1–10.

Schouten, Kim / Frasincar, Flavius. 2016. COMMIT at SemEval-2016 Task 5: Sentiment Analysis with Rhetorical Structure Theory. In *Proceedings of SemEval-2016*. San Diego, California: Association for Computational Linguistics, 356–360.

Sinclair, John M. 1991. *Corpus, Concordance, Collocation*. Oxford University Press.

Soo-Guan Khoo, Christopher / Nourbakhsh, Armineh / Na, Jin-Cheon. 2012. Sentiment Analysis of Online News Text: A Case Study of Appraisal Theory. *Online Information Review* 36/6, 858–878.

Stewart, Dominic. 2013. *Semantic Prosody: A Critical Evaluation*.

Stone, Philip J. / Hunt, Earl B. 1963. A Computer Approach to Content Analysis: Studies Using the General Inquirer System. In *Proceedings of the May 21–23, 1963, Spring Joint Computer Conference*. ACM, 241–256.

Taboada, Maite. 2016. Sentiment Analysis: An Overview from Linguistics. *Annual Review of Linguistics* 2, 325–347.

Taboada, Maite / Brooks, Julian / Tofiloski, Milan / Voll, Kimberly / Stede, Manfred. 2011. Lexicon-Based Methods for Sentiment Analysis. *Computational Linguistics* 37/2, 267–307.

Taboada, Maite / Voll, Kimberly / Brooke, Julian. 2008. Extracting Sentiment as a Function of Discourse Structure and Topicality. In

Technical Report TR 2008–20. Simon Fraser University, School of Computing Science.

Thompson, Geoffrey / Hunston, Susan. 2000. Evaluation: An Introduction. In Susan Hunston / Geoff Thompson (eds.), *Evaluation in Text. Authorial Stance and the Construction of Discourse*. Oxford: Oxford University Press, 1–27.

Vaswani, Ashish / Shazeer, Noam / Parmar, Niki / Uszkoreit, Jakob / Jones, Llion / Gomez, Aidan N. / Kaiser, Łukasz / Polosukhin, Illia. 2017. Attention Is All You Need. In *Proceedings of the 31st International Conference on Neural Information Processing Systems*. NIPS17. Long Beach, California, USA: Curran Associates Inc., 6000–6010.

Voll, Kimberly / Taboada, Maite. 2007. Not All Words Are Created Equal: Extracting Semantic Orientation as a Function of Adjective Relevance. In Mehmet A. Orgun / John Thornton (eds.), *AI 2007: Advances in Artificial Intelligence*. Lecture Notes in Computer Science. Berlin, Heidelberg: Springer, 337–46.

Wilson, Theresa / Wiebe, Janyce / Hoffmann, Paul. 2005. Recognizing Contextual Polarity in Phrase-Level Sentiment Analysis. In *Proceedings of the Conference on Human Language Technology and Empirical Methods in Natural Language Processing*. HLT '05. Stroudsburg, PA, USA: Association for Computational Linguistics, 347–354.

Wolf, Thomas / Debut, Lysandre / Sanh, Victor / Chaumond, Julien / Delangue, Clement / Moi, Anthony / Cistac, Pierric 2020. Transformers: State-of-the-Art Natural Language Processing. In *Proceedings of the 2020 Conference on Empirical Methods in Natural Language Processing: System Demonstrations*. Online: Association for Computational Linguistics, 38–45.

MARÍA PAULA SANTALLA DEL RÍO / EVA MARÍA DOMÍNGUEZ NOYA / FRANCISCO MARIO BARCALA RODRÍGUEZ

Hypervalues in tagsets and their impact on the automatic morphosyntactic annotation of Spanish

1. Introduction

In this study we describe an experiment which sought to improve the quality of corpora enriched with morphosyntactic annotation. By increasing the quality of morphosyntactic annotation, corpora with greater guarantees of robustness can be made available to discourse scholars and translators. With this in mind, the impact on annotation of including hypervalues in tagging systems was evaluated here. Specifically, we applied three tagsets to a corpus of written Spanish, the only difference between these being in the way that hypervalues were handled in the tagsets.

The performance of automatic part-of-speech annotation depends on a large number of factors, ranging from the language and the kind and genre of the texts to be tagged, to the tagger itself and the size of both the training corpus and the tagset used in tagging. All of these factors have been analysed widely. In Spanish, for example, the impact of the tagger used is analysed in Pla, Molina and Prieto 2001 and in Parra and Martínez 2015; meanwhile, Aliwy, Radie and Hamed 2015 consider the impact of language and tagsets in the tagging task. However, to the best of our knowledge no previous research in any language has focused on the impact of the specific aspect of the tagset that we will address here, that is, how it deals with hypervalues where these can be introduced.

The concept of hypervalue as we use it in this study has not, as far as we know, been used previously in morphosyntactic annotation, and hence does not appear as such in the glossaries of terms of recent Corpus Linguistics manuals, for example in Rojo 2021. In the field of corpus morphosyntactic annotation, the closest concept is that of the *portmanteau* tag (Burnard 2007[1]; Baker 2006: 131; Smith 1997; Leech et al., 1994), first used in the annotation of the BNC. Yet this concept, as we will explain in Section 2.1, differs in significant ways from that of hypervalue. This, as we will discuss in Section 2.1, is a complex value which, for a part of speech like gender, number or tense, covers (in a system of morphosyntactic tags) more than one possible simple value for that part of speech, and does so simultaneously; for example, feminine and masculine for gender, singular and plural for number or present and past for tense.

In what follows, Section 2 establishes the concept of hypervalue in the context of morphosyntactic annotation, as well as the different ways of dealing with hypervalues within annotation. Section 3 goes on to describe how we sought to determine the impact that each of these ways of dealing with hypervalues has on the results of annotation; the resources used for the evaluation are described (the corpus, the tagsets, the lexicons and the tagger), as well as the design of these (three different evaluations, each of which uses the whole corpus, differently divided in each case into training and test corpora). Section 4 presents the results of the evaluations, both quantitatively and, more briefly, qualitatively. Finally, Section 5 offers some conclusions.

2. Morphosyntactic annotation

The morphosyntactic annotation of a corpus consists of adding to each element an indication of the word class or part of speech to which it belongs, as well as an indication of the grammatical values shown by

---

1 Burnard prefers the term *ambiguity tag.*

the grammatical categories that affect each word class (gender, number, tense, mood, etc.). Likewise, each item is normally assigned a lemma, that is, the canonical representation of the inflection related to the word class of the item and to the grammatical categories that affect that class. Thus, for example, in the ESLORA corpus (*vid.* Section 3.4), wherever the item *voy* appears, it is assigned the label VIP1S, indicating that it is a **v**erb form, in **i**ndicative mood, in **p**resent tense, **1**st person **si**ngular, and has the lemma *ir*.

The components of any annotation system comprise, on the one hand, the tag system itself (the set of representations of the type VIP1S, that is, the *tagset*, together with the description of its content, the *tag definitions*, verb, indicative, present, 1st person, singular), and on the other hand, the description of how the labels in question are applied to the corpus, the *guidelines*, these being especially useful in circumstances where it may not be clear which label to assign.

It is of course the case that different tag systems will differ in the number of tags they contain. Such differences in the overall size of tagsets can be due to *granularity*, that is, the depth and detail of the information contained in the tags themselves. Some systems aim at greater detail than others. For example, a tagset might or might not differentiate between subtypes of verbs: Gerund periphrastic auxiliary (G), Infinitive periphrastic auxiliary (I), Main verb (M), Passive auxiliary (P), Compound tense auxiliary (X). Spanish verbs, excluding differences relating to conjugational and morphological regularity, have around 56 different word forms, which thus require 56 different tags, leading to 56 * 5 tags if the subtypes of verbs noted above are also distinguished (VGIP1S, VIIP1S, VMIP1S, VPIP1S, VXIP1S instead of just VIP1S). Likewise, the distinction of degree and diminutive, augmentative, etc. forms in adjectives can also multiply the number of tags required, hence the need to distinguish, for example, Augmentative (A), Comparative of superiority (#), Diminutive (D), Positive (+) and Superlative ($) (AAMS, A#MS, ADMS, A+MS, A$MS, instead of just AMS, for adjective, masculine, singular).

2.1. Hypervalues

A further issue that conditions the size of a tagset, although one which has not received much attention to date, is the treatment of hypervalues, that is, how to annotate the grammatical values of words which, at least when isolated, can represent more than one inflectional value for a given part of speech.

To take an example, adjectives like *elegante* can modify masculine or feminine nouns (or their equivalents) or neuter pronouns. Tagsets can account for this in three ways:

- Model 1: a single tag is always assigned to *elegante* and encompasses all three values, masculine, feminine and neuter: AIS (adjective, masculine/feminine/neuter, singular). Thus, only one tag, in which the letter I stands for a hypervalue for the grammatical category of gender, is required to tag *elegante* in any context.
- Model 2: as many tags are used as there are possible gender values for *elegante*, each one assigned according to the context of the item without limiting its scope in any way: AMS (adjective, masculine, singular), AFS (adjective, feminine, singular), ANS (adjective, neuter, singular). Thus, three tags, in which no hypervalues are found for the grammatical category of gender, are used to tag *elegante* according to the context in which it appears.
- Model 3: as many tags are used as there are possible gender values and subsets of gender values, each one assigned to the item according to a limited context (for example, text between strong punctuation marks [colon, semicolon, period, and question or exclamation marks]): AMS (adjective, masculine, singular), AES (adjective, masculine/feminine, singular), AFS (adjective, feminine, singular), ANS (adjective, neuter, singular), AAS (adjective, masculine/neuter, singular), AIS (adjective, masculine/feminine/neuter, singular). Hence there are six tags; in three of these E, A and I stand for hypervalues for the grammatical category of gender, and in the other three no hypervalues are found. All of them are required to tag *elegante* according to the context in which it appears.

In the tagset the number of tags per word class, then, increases from Model 2 to Model 1, and then to Model 3 (although see Section 3.2 on possible exceptions to this tendency). Meanwhile, the number of tags that each word can have out of context grows progressively from Model 1 to Model 2 to Model 3, with no exceptions in this case. In Table 1, below, we illustrate all these points with the tagset that we use in our evaluation. The number of tags necessary in each model to tag the adjective word class in Spanish is shown, distinguishing only gender and number; also shown is how many of these tags must be used to tag the adjective *elegante*[2] in real contexts:

Table 1: Tags needed for the adjective word class/*elegante* in each model.

	Model 1	**Model 2**	**Model 3**
tags for the adjective word class	9	5	12
tags for the item *elegante*	1	3	6

Model 1 requires more tags for a word class with all its inflectional patterns than Model 2, whereas Model 2 needs more labels to tag a word in all its possible contexts than Model 1. Model 3 combines both these circumstances to some extent. All this is the case because contextual disambiguation is not offered by the first model (hence, for items in which it is grammatically necessary, it requires hypervalues and only hypervalues); the second model always disambiguates (and thus does not require hypervalues); and the third model does so where this is possible (and hence requires hypervalues and disaggregated values).

Having introduced the concept of hypervalue, we will conclude this section by exploring its relation to its possible precedent *portmanteau* or *ambiguity* tag. Ambiguity tags are described in Burnard 2007 as follows:

2 The specific tags can be seen in Appendix 1.

> These tags indicate that the automatic tagger was unable to determine, with sufficient confidence, which was the correct category, and so left two possibilities for users to disambiguate themselves, if they should wish to do so. For example, in the case of VVD-VVN, the first (more likely) tag, say for a word such as *wanted*, is VVD: past tense of lexical verb; and the second (less likely) tag is VVN: past participle of lexical verb.

Although the concepts of ambiguity tags and hypervalues are both used to represent more than one morphosyntactic categorization, there are notable differences between them. First, the former can concern word class identification, while hypervalues are restricted to grammatical categories. Also, even when ambiguity tags involve grammatical categories exclusively, they are still multiple tags, not a single tag. These two differences, however, are themselves due to a third, principal difference, which has to do with how they are handled during the process of annotation. Ambiguity tags only exist after the process has been carried out and they are not part of the tagset handled by the tagger, whereas hypervalues form part of the tags included in the tagset handled by the tagger during the tagging process. This also means that ambiguity tags are neither present in the training corpora used by probalistic taggers, nor do they compete with other tags in the tagging process. Completely the reverse situation pertains for tags including hypervalues.

3. The evaluation

To evaluate the effect that each of the models distinguished in terms of the use of hypervalues has on morphosyntactic annotation, we used a series of resources (a corpus, three annotation systems or tagsets, three lexicons or dictionaries, and a tagger). These resources are described in the following four subsections, followed in Section 3.5 by an explanation of how they were used in our evaluation.

3.1. The corpus

Table 2, below, describes the corpus used in the evaluation. It comprises press texts extracted[3] from three newspapers (*El Correo Gallego*, *El Mundo* and *El País*) and classified into sections. Unbracketed numbers here refer to orthographic words (word forms between spaces or punctuation marks) plus punctuation marks; bracketed numbers refer to words only.

Table 2: The corpus for evaluation.

	El Correo Gallego	El Mundo	El País	Total
Culture		4,463 (3,796)	3,351 (2,865)	7,814 (6,661)
Sport	5,755 (4,813)	4,461 (4,076)	3,789 (3,242)	14,205 (12,131)
Economy		1,162 (1,008)	1,795 (1,577)	2,957 (2,585)
Galicia	1,100 (970)			1,100 (970)
International			11,631 (10,143)	11,631 (10,143)
Local	5,349 (4,577)			5,349 (4,577)
National	340 (303)		6,382 (5,609)	6,722 (5,912)
Opinion	3,502 (3,049)		765 (668)	4,267 (3,717)
Society	616 (554)		2,547 (2,259)	3,163 (2,813)
Total	16,662 (14,266)	10,086 (8,880)	30,260 (26,363)	57,208 (49,509)

3 Dates: El Correo Gallego (1999-11-24, 1999-12-01, 1999-12-05, 2000-01-05, 2000-01-07, 2000-01-23, 2000-01-28, 2000-01-30, 2000-03-08, 2000-03-26, 2000-05-05, 2000-05-28, 2000-07-16, 2000-07-23, 2000-07-30, 2000-10-11), El Mundo (2002-01-02), El País (2002-01-02, 2002-01-23, 2002-01-26).

To carry out the evaluation, the complete corpus was disambiguated manually in three different versions: each of these uses one of the annotation models described above. Both the raw corpus and these disambiguated versions can be downloaded at the web pages that describe the tagsets that encode each of the models, cited below (see Section 3.2, note 4).

3.2. The tagsets

The following table sets out the number of tags in each model, both in total and by word class; it also shows, for each class, the number of symbols needed to cover the simple values, and where appropriate the hypervalues, identified for each of the grammatical categories that affect them. This gives us an idea of the degree of granularity aimed at. The adverb, conjunction, interjection and preposition word classes, which in the three models give rise to a single tag each (W, C, I, P), without any specification of grammatical category, are not included in the table (although the totals do include them)[4].

---

4 The tagsets for each of the models including hypervalues, and for the volume of information indicated in the table, can be consulted at the following web pages (the design of the annotation follows the recommendations proposed by the EAGLES Group, Leech and Wilson 1996):

• Model 1, https://gramatica.usc.es/~mpsr/XIADA-es/FVII-XIADA-es-Manual-de-anotacion-v4.1-modelo-CAES.html.

• Model 2, https://gramatica.usc.es/~mpsr/XIADA-es/FVII-XIADA-es-Manual-de-anotacion-v4.1-modelo-FVII.html.

• Model 3, https://gramatica.usc.es/~mpsr/XIADA-es/FVII-XIADA-es-Manual-de-anotacion-v4.1.html.

Table 3: The size of the *tagsets*.

			Simple values/hypervalues in each category						
Word class	**Mod.**	**N.º of tags**	**Case**	**Gen.**	**Mood**	**Num.**	**Pers.**	**Word subclass**	**Tense**
Adj.	1	9		5		3			
	2	5		3		2			
	3	12		6		3			
Det.	1	93		6		3	5	15	
	2	91		3		2	6	15	
	3	136		6		3	7	15	
Pron.	1	114	7	6		3	7	14	
	2	136	7	3		2	6	14	
	3	198	7	6		3	7	14	
Noun	1	9		3		3		2	
	2	4		2		2		2	
	3	9		3		3		2	
Verb	1	64		3	8	2	5		7
	2	67		3	6	2	3		7
	3	78		4	8	2	5		7
Total	1	293							
	2	307							
	3	437							

As we noted in Section 2.1, when hypervalues are taken into account the number of tags per word class increases from Model 2, to Model 1 and then to Model 3. As we can see in Table 3 for pronouns and verbs, there are exceptions to this tendency. These exceptions, which most frequently have to do with closed-class words, occur in the following context: when, as well as the inflectional model presenting a hypervalue, there are no other inflectional models of the word class in question that, for some of its word items, present the simple values that underlie the hypervalue under consideration. For example, the possessive determiner *su* has the hypervalue 7 (third person singular and plural) for the category person in Model 1, and since there are no other inflectional models of the possessive determiner in the third person that discriminate the values of the third person singular and plural, there is only one label available in Model 1 (the one that includes the hypervalue); however, two are needed in Model 2, one for the third person singular and another for the third person plural. When this happens, contrary to what we saw in Section 2.1 for adjectives, the total number of tags per word class and in the tagset might, as in our case, be slightly higher in Model 2 than in Model 1.

In addition, three further observations must be made on Table 3, relating to the category of case, the total number of tags, and the issue of proper nouns. Regarding the category of case, due to the difficulties in disambiguation that this entails, it is always treated in the three models according to the characteristics of Model 1. Hence, in all three models we have the same number of symbols, which is thus the total number of hypervalues and simple values possible for case. These simple values and hypervalues are then lexically assigned to the specific word forms of the personal pronouns, each of which, then, always exhibits the same symbol for case in the disambiguated corpus.

Turning to the total number of tags in the tagsets, and also in the disambiguated corpora, this includes 10 more, corresponding to punctuation marks, numbers, dates, times, abbreviations, words in other languages, non-classifiable elements, and orality markers (Model 3 was used in the tagging of an oral corpus, see Section 3.4).

Finally, with respect to proper nouns, seven tags are also added. These are treated in the same way in all the models. Thus, annotation involves selecting a tag (all simple values and hypervalues included for gender and number), taking context into account. In Model 3, nine labels should theoretically be necessary to cover proper nouns, as follows: NPEL, NPEP, NPES, ~~NPFL~~, NPFP, NPFS, ~~NPML~~, NPMP, NPMS, but in fact the number is seven, since two of these (indicated with strikethrough) are morphologically impossible. Translated into what the specification of gender and number allows in their cases (E and L, being hypervalues, are not possible symbols in Model 2), the same possibilities, assigned in the same way, are functional in the other models (where E and L are not possible symbols, they simply disappear): thus, in Model 1, the tags for proper nouns are exactly the same as in Model 3; in Model 2: NP, NPP, NPS, NPF, NPFP, NPFS, NPM,

NPMP, NPMS. Whereas in Models 1 and 3 NPEL, NPEP and NPES are assigned during the annotation, in Model 2 NP, NPP and NPS are assigned.

3.3. The lexicons

It is also interesting to observe the size of the dictionaries (computational lexicons) arising from each of the models 1, 2 and 3 (also available at the web pages cited in note 4). Table 4 shows these data. Obviously, it is expected that the greater the number of entries per lemma in the lexicon[5], the greater the complexity of the disambiguation, which is the fundamental operation of annotation.

Table 4: The size of the lexicons.

		Entries			**Entries per lemma**		
Word class	**Lemas**	**1**	**2**	**3**	**1**	**2**	**3**
Adjetives	22,089	75,857	111,086	152,933	3.43	5.03	6.92
Determiners	274	682	843	1,001	2.49	3.08	3.65
Pronouns	268	676	949	1,130	2.52	3.54	4.22
Common nouns	58,274	128,319	134,233	140,311	2.20	2.30	2.41
Verbs	5,555	355,293	415,899	476,900	63.96	74.87	85.85
Adv., prep., conj., int.[6]	4,563	4,588	4,588	4,588	1.01	1.01	1.01
Total	91,023	565,415	667,598	776,863	6.21	7.33	8.53

5 Appendix 2 clarifies, on the basis of the structure of the lexicon itself, exactly what the concepts of lemma and entry consist of.

6 The difference between the number of lemmas/entries in adverbs, prepositions, conjunctions, and interjections may be surprising, and arises due to the presence in the lexicon of a number of graduated adverbs (*brillantísimamente*, *un poquito*, etc., which constitute the same lemmas as *brillantemente* and *un poco*, respectively).

As we noted in Section 2.1, the number of entries per lemma, that is, tags per items of open-class words, increases from Model 1 to Model 2 to Model 3.

3.4. The tool: The XIADA tagger

The experiment was carried out using the XIADA tool (http://corpus.cirp.gal/xiada/). This statistical tagger, developed jointly by the *Centro Ramón Piñeiro para a Investigación en Humanidades* (CIRP) and the COLE group of the Universities of A Coruña and Vigo to automatically tag the *Corpus de Referencia do Galego Actual* (CORGA) (http://corpus.cirp.gal/corga), is based on secondary-order Hidden Markov models, i.e., statistical models in which the calculations relating to the morphosyntactic labels of a word depend on the previous two (Brants 2000). The tagger was intended to contribute to the design and development of resources for the incorporation of Galician into Information and Communication Technologies and, at the same time, to make it possible to obtain data for the study of lexical, grammatical, discursive aspects, etc. of that language.

The Etiquetador/Lematizador do Galego Actual (XIADA) contains—among other modules—ones for sentence segmentation, tokenization, morphosyntactic annotation, and lemmatization. It also has linguistic restriction rules (Barcala et al. 2007) and pruning rules (Domínguez 2016) that serve to increase significantly its success rate. Specifically, in relation to its coverage, precision and robustness in analysis, data provided by Domínguez, Barcala and Molinero 2009 confirm that it has a success rate in line with state of the art tools in the field (96 %) (García and Gamallo 2010; Pla et al. 2001; Parra and Martínez 2015). The tagger code was released in 2019, along with the resources that it uses (https://github.com/crpih/xiada).

Although other taggers for Spanish (TreeTagger, Schmid 1994; TreeTagger-IULA, Martínez et al. 2010; FreeLing, Padró 2012; IXA, Agerri et al. 2014) were available, in order to use one of them we would have needed to adapt it to work with our resources (the tagsets, the lexicons and the training corpora). We thus considered that it was more practical and productive, in terms of our knowledge of the tool and future control of the whole process of annotation, to use the XIADA tagger, initially developed in the research group for Galician, but which at that moment had already been adapted and applied to the tagging of (spoken) Spanish within the framework of the ESLORA project (Barcala et al. 2018; Vázquez Rozas et al. 2020). It was, then, on the basis of our prior involvement in the ESLORA project that XIADA was chosen for the evaluation described in the present study, using the resources described in the previous sections: a corpus to carry out the disambiguation (an unannotated part of the corpus described in Section 3.1), a training corpus from which to derive its Markovian model (a different part of the same corpus, now annotated, described in Section 3.1,), a tagset (Section 3.2), and a lexicon (Section 3.3).

3.5. The design of the evaluation

Three evaluations were carried out, in each of which 60 % of the corpus was used as a training corpus and the rest as the test. In the extraction we made sure that there would always be texts from all the differentiated sections, both in the training and test corpora, the proportions here being broadly in relation to the corpus as a whole. Table 5 shows the sizes of the training and test corpora used in each of the evaluations. Size here refers to tagged units[7] (whether orthographic words, multiword units, disaggregated contractions, or punctuation marks):

Table 5: Size of training and test corpora for evaluations A, B and C.

		Evaluation A		**Evaluation B**		**Evaluation C**	
	Corpus	**Training**	**Test**	**Training**	**Test**	**Training**	**Test**
Culture	7,266	4,369	2,897	4,613	2,653	4,595	2,671
Sport	13,400	8,143	5,257	7,926	5,474	7,319	6,081
Economy	2,839	1,582	1,257	1,819	1,020	1,806	1,033
Galicia	987	625	362	623	364	625	362
International	11,131	6,553	4,578	6,090	5,041	7,139	3,992
Local	4,982	2,757	2,225	2,978	2,004	2,905	2,077

Continued

7 The concept of a tagged unit is clarified in Appendix 3.

Table 5: *Continued*

		Evaluation A		Evaluation B		Evaluation C	
National	6,393	3,774	2,619	3,766	2,627	3,714	2,679
Opinion	4,164	2,560	1,604	2,631	1,533	2,550	1,614
Society	2,969	1,910	1,059	1,861	1,108	1,861	1,108
Total	54,131	32,273	21,858	32,307	21,824	32,514	21,617

3.5.1. Ambiguity in real texts

As we have already done for the number of entries per lemma in the lexicon, which illustrates the degree of ambiguity that each model imposes on the lexicon, it is also interesting to observe the degree of effective ambiguity that each model imposes on the tagged corpus prior to disambiguation, that is, the number of tags that each unit of the corpus is assigned from the lexicon: the tagger has to operate on these using its Markov model. This number is shown for each evaluation in Table 6, Table 7 and Table 8:

Table 6: Ambiguity in real texts generated by the three models. Evaluation A.

Evaluation A		**N.º of tags before disambiguation (b)**			**N.º of tags per tagged unit (b/a)**		
Word class	**N.º of tagged units (a)**	**Model 1**	**Model 2**	**Model 3**	**Model 1**	**Model 2**	**Model 3**
Adj.	1,153	2,174	3,589	5,784	1.89	3.11	5.02
Det.	3,626	5,479	7,357	9,564	1.51	2.03	2.64
Pron.	1,030	4,474	9,233	14,341	4.34	8.96	13.92
Noun	5,116	13,776	14,010	14,336	2.69	2.74	2.80
Verb	2,776	5,358	7,822	10,390	1.93	2.82	3.74
Adv.-Conj.-Intj.-Prep.	5,196	6,546	6,550	6,546	1.26	1.26	1.26
Other	2,961	8,976	8,977	8,975	3.03	3.03	3.03
Total	21,858	46,783	57,538	69,936	2.14	2.63	3.20

Table 7: Ambiguity in real texts generated by the three models. Evaluation B.

Evaluation B		**N.º of tags before disambiguation (b)**			**N.º of tags per tagged unit (b/a)**		
Word class	**N.º of tagged units (a)**	**Model 1**	**Model 2**	**Model 3**	**Model 1**	**Model 2**	**Model 3**
Adj.	1,158	2,103	3,546	5,679	1.82	3.06	4.90
Det.	3,556	5,334	6,977	8,965	1.50	1.96	2.52
Pron.	1,047	4,432	9,025	14,492	4.23	8.62	13.84
Noun	5,122	13,625	13,879	14,170	2.66	2.71	2.77
Verb	2,778	4,996	7,337	9,751	1.80	2.64	3.51
Adv.-Conj.-Intj.-Prep.	5,296	6,679	6,681	6,677	1.26	1.26	1.26
Other	2,867	7,940	7,941	7,942	2.77	2.77	2.77
Total	21,824	45,109	55,386	67,676	2.07	2.54	3.10

Table 8: Ambiguity in real texts generated by the three models. Evaluation C.

Evaluation C		**N.º of tags before disambiguation (b)**			**N.º of tags per tagged unit (b/a)**		
Word class	**N.º of tagged units (a)**	**Model 1**	**Model 2**	**Model 3**	**Model 1**	**Model 2**	**Model 3**
Adj.	1,180	2,327	3,698	5,998	1.97	3.13	5.08
Det.	3,630	5,526	7,363	9,488	1.52	2.03	2.61
Pron.	1,025	4,635	9,309	14,782	4.52	9.08	14.42
Noun	5,195	14,995	15,190	15,599	2.89	2.92	3.00
Verb	2,561	5,696	7,960	10,439	2.22	3.11	4.08
Adv.-Conj.-Intj.-Prep.	5,103	6,514	6,508	6,506	1.28	1.28	1.27
Other	2,923	7,932	7,932	7,934	2.71	2.71	2.71
Total	21,617	47,625	57,960	70,746	2.20	2.68	3.27

As was also expected, the ambiguity generated in real texts increases progressively from Model 1 to Model 2 to Model 3.

4. Results

Table 9, below, presents the results of the tests carried out for each evaluation (A, B and C) and for each model (1, 2 and 3), as well as the averages of the three evaluations for each of the models. We have evaluated the full coincidence in the test corpora of the **word form TAB tag (TAB lemma)**, and for the **word form TAB first character of tag (rest of tag TAB lemma)**. That is, the correct identification of both class and inflectional category values, on the one hand, and only word class, on the other.

Table 9: Results of the evaluation.

Model	Eval. /Average (of Eval. A, B, C) Model	Tagged units	Wrong tag	%	Wrong word class	%
1	A	21,858	729	3.34	491	2.25
1	B	21,824	728	3.34	537	2.46
1	C	21,617	773	3.58	516	2.39
1	Average 1	21,766.33	743.33	3.42	514.67	2.36
2	A	21,858	940	4.3	474	2.17
2	B	21,824	931	4.27	491	2.25
2	C	21,617	935	4.33	495	2.29
2	Average 2	21,766.33	935.33	4.30	486.67	2.24
3	A	21,858	1,116	5.11	474	2.17
3	B	21,824	1,085	4.97	501	2.3
3	C	21,617	1,099	4.08	507	2.35
3	Average 3	21,766.33	1,100.00	5.05	494.00	2.27

From the former perspective (full tags), the most efficient model is 1, followed by 2, then 3. But the same does not occur from the latter perspective (word class), where the most efficient model is 2, closely followed by 3, then 1.

4.1. *Brief qualitative remarks*

Table 10 shows the tagging errors (the second tag has been assigned where the first one should have been assigned) that are repeated more than 50 times across the total number of evaluations.

Table 10: Quantitative analysis.

Model 1			Model 2			Model 3		
Rank	**Freq.**	**Error**	**Rank**	**Freq.**	**Error**	**Rank**	**Freq.**	**Error**
163	57	AAS/ NCMS	194	53	C/ PLMS	265	51	PLFS/ C
164	72	AIS/ AES	195	66	NCMS/AMS	266	66	NCMS/ AMS
165	80	NCMS/ Cifra	196	67	PLMS/ C	267	71	PLMS/ C
166	100	C/ PLIL	197	74	AMS/ NCMS	268	73	AMS/ NCMS
167	100	PLIL/ C	198	80	NCMS/ Cifra	269	80	NCMS/ Cifra
168	125	NPEL/ NPMS	199	132	NP/ NPMS	270	131	NPEL/ NPMS
169	156	AES/ AIS						

As expected, the greater the number of tags, the greater the variety of tagging errors (Model 1: 169, Model 2: 199, Model 3: 270). Consistency between the three models is also observed with respect to errors involving proper nouns, which are treated in the same way in all three models (errors involving NP labels). There is also a considerable number of errors involving conjunctions (C) and relative pronouns (PL) in all three models, as well as errors involving adjectives (A) and common nouns (NC) in the three models, with a greater incidence in 2 and 3. Finally, the extraordinary occurrence of errors involving adjectives with fully open gender (I, masculine/feminine/neutral) and restricted to two values (E, masculine/feminine) in Model 1 stands out. This is, nevertheless, an error that does not fit in this model, where an adjective, if associated with tag AIS, cannot be associated with tag AES, and vice versa. This is an important observation because it can be solved methodologically and will eliminate a significant number of errors (228) in Model 1, which will further improve its efficiency for full tag evaluation.

5. Conclusions

In line with an increase in the number of tags due to increased granularity, the increase in the number of tags relating to the treatment of hypervalues has the effect of increasing the error rate of the automatic annotation process (the error rate increases through Model 1, Model 2 and Model 3). This is because as the number of tags increases the greater is the ambiguity, in both the lexicon and, more notably, in the real texts. However, such an effect is not maintained if we look exclusively at the number of errors in the word class assignment (the rate of erroneously assigned word classes increases from Model 2 to Model 3 to Model 1). That said, it is worth noting that the assignment of hypervalues in Model 3, which has been tested against itself, could also be tested with Model 2 as a reference. This would allow us to evaluate errors and uncertainties (a hypervalue is assigned that covers the simple value which should have been assigned) in a different way. This in turn would avoid considering some of the current errors in Model 3 as such, hence improving its results, in that some cases would become uncertainties instead of errors. On the other hand, the choice of either of these approaches in the design of an annotation system must also take into account user satisfaction. This itself must also be evaluated, because although it is true that Model 1 is less frequently wrong, it is also the case that it forces the user to discriminate values when this becomes necessary. Models 2 and 3, on the other hand, are more frequently wrong, yet provide the user with the discriminated values, completely so in the case of 2, and in 3 where this is possible in certain circumstances. Finally, it would also be interesting to compare the stability in the degree of errors found in our present evaluation (using newspaper texts) to similar evaluations using other text types and language registers.

Appendix 1

The group of tags necessary in each model to cover the adjective part of speech, with their description and examples. Those that should be associated with the item *elegante* have been highlighted: in Model 1, a single tag that is applied to the item in the corpus in any circumstance (for this reason, in this model the examples do not appear contextualized), and several tags in Models 2 and 3, each of which is applied to the item *elegante* in the corpus in relation to the context (hence the examples here are contextualized). The complete tag systems can be seen at the urls indicated in note 4.

Model 1

AAS, Adj. Masc./Neut. Sing., relativo
AEP, Adj. Fem./Masc. Plur., insoportables
AES, Adj. Fem./Masc. Sing., gran
AFP, Adj. Fem. Plur., guapas
AFS, Adj. Fem. Sing., guapa
AIL, Adj. Fem./Masc./Neut. Plur./Sing., papanatas
AIS, Adj. Fem./Masc./Neut. Sing., interesante
AMP, Adj. Masc. Plur., guapos
AMS, Adj. Masc. Sing., san, don

Model 2

AFP, Adj. Fem. Plur., guapas; Son unas mujeres inteligentes; Son las alarmas antincendios.
AFS, Adj. Fem. Sing., guapa; Es una mujer inteligente; Es una alarma antincendios.
AMP, Adj. Masc. Plur., guapos; Son unos hombres inteligentes; Son los mecanismos antincendios.
AMS, Adj. Masc. Sing., Es un hombre guapo/inteligente; Es el mecanismo antincendios.
ANS, Adj. Neut. Sing., Eso es lo más bueno/interesante/papanatas que he oído nunca.

Model 3

AAS, Adj. Masc./Neut. Sing., Es relativo; Todo me parece muy elegante/papanatas.
AEL, Adj. Fem./Masc. Plur./Sing., Hacer de guardaespaldas papanatas es su especialidad.
AEP, Adj. Fem./Masc. Plur., Hay bastantes guardaespaldas más bien insoportables/soplagaitas.
AES, Adj. Fem./Masc. Sing., Bastante guardaespaldas insoportable/papanatas hay ya en el mundo.
AFL, Adj. Fem. Plur./Sing., Ya está bien de crisis aguafiestas, por favor.
AFP, Adj. Fem. Plur., guapas; Son unas mujeres inteligentes; Son las alarmas antincendios.
AFS, Adj. Fem. Sing., guapa; Es una mujer inteligente; Es una alarma antincendios.
AIS, Adj. Fem./Masc./Neut. Sing., Es interesante/burdeos.
AML, Adj. Masc. Plur./Sing., No más análisis antidoping, por favor.
AMP, Adj. Masc. Plur., guapos; Son unos hombres inteligentes; Son los mecanismos antincendios.
AMS, Adj. Masc. Sing., Es un hombre guapo/inteligente; Es el mecanismo antincendios.
ANS, Adj. Neut. Sing., Eso es lo más bueno/interesante/papanatas que he oído nunca.

Appendix 2

Lexicons consist of series of associations `word form TAB tag TAB lemma`. The number of associations of this class, that is, the number of lines in the lexicon, reflects the number of entries. The concept of lemma reduces this count to the count of different associations regarding only the first character of the label (which refers to the word class) and the lemma. For the word form *elegante* in Model 3, the entries in the lexicon are as follows (in this series there are two lemmas, the different associations that arise from the count of what is highlighted in bold in the entries).

elegante	**A**AS	**elegante**
elegante	**A**ES	**elegante**
elegante	**A**FS	**elegante**
elegante	**A**IS	**elegante**
elegante	**A**MS	**elegante**
elegante	**A**NS	**elegante**
elegante	**N**CES	**elegante**
elegante	**N**CFS	**elegante**
elegante	**N**CMS	**elegante**

Appendix 3

Each of the non-blank lines of the disambiguated corpus, from which we extract a minimal sample here, is a tagged unit. Clearly, this does not necessarily coincide with an orthographic form such as those described in Section 3.1. *Unas cuantas*, for example, contains two orthographic forms, but a single tagged unit.

```
no      W       no

sería   VIC3S   ser
```

```
elegante        ANS     elegante
,       Q       ,
tras    X       tras
unas cuantas    DNFP    unos cuantos
historias       NCFP    historia
,       Q       ,
dejar   VNP     dejar
sin     X       sin
reflejar        VNP     reflejar
la      DAFS    el
jornada NCFS    jornada
final   AFS     final
.       Q       .
la      DAFS    el
crónica NCFS    crónica
de      X       de
sociedad        NCFS    sociedad
.       Q       .
```

References

Agerri, Rodrigo / Bermúdez, Josu / Rigau, German. 2014. IXA Pipeline: Efficient and Ready to Use Multilingual NLP tools. In Calzolari, Nicoletta / Choukri, Khalid / Declerck, Thierry / Loftsson, Hrafn / Maegaard, Bente / Mariani, Joseph / Moreno, Asuncion, Odijk, Jan / Piperidis, Stelios (eds.), *Proceedings of the Ninth International Conference on Language Resources and Evaluation*. Reykjavik: ELRA, 3823–3828.

Aliwy, Ahmed Hussein / Radie, Rosual Ali / Hamed, Hiba Sarteel. 2015. HMM Based POS Tagging System for 8 Different Languages and Several Tagsets. Engineering and Technology Journal 33/2B, 326–337

Baker, Paul 2006. *A Glossary of Corpus Linguistics*. Edinburgh: Edinburgh University Press.

Barcala, Francisco M. / Domínguez, Eva M. / Fernández, Alba / Rivas, Raquel / Santalla, María Paula / Vázquez, Victoria / Villapol, Rebeca. 2018. El corpus ESLORA de español oral. Diseño, desarrollo y explotación. *CHIMERA. Romance Corpora and Linguistic Studies* 5/2, 217–237.

Barcala, Francisco M. / Molinero, Miguel Á. / Domínguez, Eva M. 2007. XML Rules for Enclitic Segmentation. In Moreno-Díaz, Roberto et al. (eds.), *Computer Aided Systems Theory*, 4739, *Lecture Notes in Computer Science*. Berlin-Heidelberg-New York: Springer-Verlag, 273–281.

Brants, Thorsten. 2000. TnT—A Statistical Part-of-Speech Tagger. In *Proceedings of the Sixth Applied Natural Language Processing Conference*. Seattle-Washington: Association for Computational Linguistics, 224–231.

Burnard, Lou. (ed.) 2007. *Reference Guide for the British National Corpus (XML Edition)*. http://www.natcorp.ox.ac.uk/docs/URG/

Domínguez, Eva M. 2016. O etiquetador probabilístico de XIADA e o seu teito de acerto: a elaboración de regras lingüísticas. In González, Manuel (ed.), *Lingua, pobo e terra. Estudos en homenaxe a Xesús Ferro Ruibal*. Santiago de Compostela: Xunta de Galicia—Centro Ramón Piñeiro para a investigación en humanidades, 213–232.

Domínguez, Eva M. / Barcala, Francisco M. / Molinero Miguel Á. 2009. Avaliación dun etiquetador automático estatístico para o galego actual: Xiada. *Cadernos de Lingua* 30–31, 151–193.

García, Marcos / Gamallo, Pablo. 2010. Análise morfossintáctica para Português Europeu e Galego: Problemas, Soluçoes e Avaliaçao. *Linguamática* 2–2, 59–67.

Leech, Geoffrey / Garside, Roger / Bryant, Michael. 1994. CLAWS4: The Tagging of the British National Corpus. In *Proceedings of the 15th International Conference on Computational Linguistics (COLING 94-Kyoto, Japan)*, 622–628.

Leech, Geoffrey / Wilson, Andrew. 1996. *Recommendations for the Morphosyntactic Annotation of Corpora*. Technical Report. Advisory Group of Language Engineering Standard (EAGLES).

Martínez, Héctor / Vivaldi, Jorge / Villegas, Marta. 2010. Text Handling as a Web Service for the IULA Processing Pipeline. In *Web Services and Processing Pipelines in HLT: Tool Evaluation, LR Production and Validation*. Paris: ELRA, 22–29.

Padró, Lluís. 2012. Analizadores Multilingües en FreeLing. *Linguamática* 3/2, 13–20.

Parra, Carla / Martínez, Héctor. 2015. Choosing a Spanish Part-of-Speech Tagger for a Lexically Sensitive Task. *Procesamiento del Lenguaje Natural* 54, 29–36.

Pla, Ferrán / Molina, Antonio / Prieto, Natividad. 2001. Evaluación de un etiquetador morfosintáctico basado en bigramas especializados para el castellano. *Procesamiento del lenguaje natural* 27, 215–222.

Rojo, Guillermo. 2021. *Introducción a la lingüística de corpus*. Londres: Routledge.

Schmid, Helmut. 1994. Probabilistic Part-of-Speech Tagging Using Decision Trees. In *Proceedings of International Conference on New Methods in Language Processing (Manchester, UK)*, 44–49.

Smith, Nicholas. 1997. Improving a Tagger. In Garside, Roger / Leech, Geoffrey / McEnery, Anthony (eds.), *Corpus Annotation: Linguistic Information from Computer Text Corpora*. London: Longman, 137–150.

Vázquez, Victoria / Barcala, Francisco M. / Domínguez, Eva M. / Fernández, Alba / Rojo, Guillermo / Santalla, María Paula. 2020. Codificación y anotación del habla en un contexto bilingüe: el corpus ESLORA de español de Galicia. In Gallego, Ángel J. et al. (eds.), *Dialectología digital del español, Anexo 80 de Verba,* 189–224.

MARICEL ESTEBAN-FONOLLOSA

A proposal for the selection and prioritization of lexical bundles in specialised discourse[1]

> *Whatever the extraction method, there are so many constructions that there is ever a need for prioritization and organization.*
>
> (Simpson-Vlach y Ellis, 2010: 30)

1. Introduction

This chapter discusses the methodology used in a corpus-driven study of lexical bundles as found in online promotional texts, more specifically, German accommodation websites. A *mixed value* index is proposed as a means ordering these bundles, which are of practical interest in terms of their potential application in pedagogical and lexicographical fields.

In Section 2, below, we give an introduction to formulaic language and previous research on lexical bundles, followed by a description of the methodology adopted for the present study (Section 3), the main goals of which are:

1 The current research was carried out within the framework of the research project FFI2019-108783RB-100: "Construction Grammar and Phraseology German and Spanish Constructional Idioms through Corpora". This project, funded by the Spanish Ministry of Science and Innovation, is developed by the research group FRASESPAL under the direction of Carmen Mellado Blanco.

(i) to generate an inventory of the lexical bundles characteristic of this particular text type, towards their application in the teaching of German as a Foreign Language with a specific focus on the field of tourism; (ii) to provide tools aimed at fostering improvements in the writing of similar texts by non-native professionals; and (iii) to contribute to the development of a specialised multilingual dictionary of tourism (Esteban-Fonollosa, 2021).

We then describe the *Korpus der deutschsprachigen Hotelswebseiten* (KoDeHo), which is compiled according to the criteria of balance and representativeness (Biber, 1993; Lemnitzer and Zinsmeister, 2006; McEnery and Wilson, 2012). It is a monolingual corpus, extends to 2.4 million tokens, and is subdivided into three dialectal sub-corpora. After this description, we briefly explain how the lexical bundles were extracted, which reliability thresholds were established (Fuster-Márquez, 2014; Steyer, 2013), and which filtering and classification criteria were used.

Following this we discuss the mixed value index, the main focus of the current research. This index is proposed as a quantitative sorting criterion, one which combines the values typically included in quantitative studies of this type, such as frequency, the Mutual Information Index, and the simple maths index, this latter tool included in the Sketch Engine (2013) platform. In the discussion of the results we argue that the use of the mixed value index is an effective statistical technique for assessing the relevance of lexical bundles in an analysis of specialised discourse. The findings of the study are of potential interest in a variety of areas, most notably language teaching, lexicography and traductology.

2. Formulaic language and lexical bundles

The formulaic nature of language has to do with the fact that languages operate on the basis of a confluence of the usual, the conventionalised, the exemplary and the variable, all at different linguistic levels. Formulaic language is related to Eugenio Coseriu's concept of repeated discourse. As Ruiz (1997: 25) points out, as early as 1964 Coseriu, 'in a work referring to the lexicon, used the term repeated discourse, which includes the units of phraseology, in opposition to the free discourse technique'[2]. Furthermore, Zuluaga (1980) considers the repetition of phraseological units to be a constitutional factor in language, leading to the establishment of the expression in a certain form, and excluding other forms which, according to the prevailing system, would also be possible[3] (Corpas 1996).

Early interest in this area focused on the syntagmatic relations of words, as Firth (1969) set out in 1951, based on the concept of collocation, this, of course, predating the technological developments that corpus linguistics would subsequently introduce. It was found that describing the meaning of a word involves a consideration of 'the company words keep'. In this Firthian sense, Sinclair's (1991) approach is based on the notion of the ambivalent nature of linguistic communication: both written and spoken forms are the result of a relationship between linguistic freedom in the process of choice (*open choice principle*) and the conventional use of many semi-prefabricated features which are used as single units. Sinclair calls this second aspect of communication the *idiom principle*, and in this he refers not only to idioms or sequences that are completely fixed and non-compositional in the sense of traditional or 'taxonomic' phraseology (Groom 2017), but also, and indeed above all, to phraseological elements in which parts can be analysed and remain variable. Whereas research with a restricted or partial corpus of texts is unlikely to provide all the answers here, there is enough evidence to claim that one language looks like another in this sense when viewed as a whole (cf. Filatkina 2018). That is, corpus linguistics can provide evidence of this 'idiom principle' which, until recently, linguists could not obtain with absolute accuracy, and which to a great extent could only be derived through his or her intuition, ability, and professional experience (Sinclair 1991).

---

2 "[...]dentro de un trabajo referido al léxico, acuña el término discurso repetido, que recoge las unidades de la fraseología, como opuesto a la técnica libre del discurso." (Ruiz 1997: 25) (my own translation).

3 "[...] conduce a la fijación de la expresión en una forma determinada, quedando excluidas por la norma lingüística social otras formas que, según el sistema, también serían posibles." (Corpas 1996: 21) (my own translation).

Research into formulaic language developed principally from the 1970s onwards. As Wood (2002) notes, British lexicography played a fundamental role here, based on the observation of language performance in large corpora of language in use, where it was possible to identify the tendency of words to co-occur or appear together. Formulaic language itself embraces to a very broad set of units, and these are of relevance in language acquisition (Pawley and Syder 1983; Wray and Perkins 2000), pragmatics (Coulmas 1981; Nattinger and DeCarrico 1992), discourse (Altenberg 1998) and the cognitive processing of language (Wray 2008). As a concept, formulaic language involves sets of formulaic sequences, and differs from phraseology in that the latter concerns just one specific type of formulaic language (Wood 2015). Wray and Perkins (2000) define formulaic sequences as pluriverbal units of language, either continuous or discontinuous, which appear to be prefabricated in the sense that they are stored and retrieved from memory as a whole. On the same lines, Wood (2015) observes that there is broad agreement that formulaic language is a pluriverbal phenomenon, with units carrying a single meaning or function and being of a prefabricated nature.

In terms of research methodologies, a distinction is made between *top-down* approaches, which classify formulaic language by means of semantic or syntactic criteria, and *bottom-up* or distributional methods, in which corpus analysis and frequency thresholds are used to identify sequences, sometimes classifying these according to discursive functions; this second approach is fundamentally inductive in nature (Wood 2015). According to Steyer (2013), corpus linguistics has become a hyperonym, one which brings together different methods and approaches that have in common the analysis and evaluation of mass data. Technical advances in corpus linguistics since the 1990s have made it possible to observe the formulaic nature of languages in ever-greater detail.

Research on lexical bundles goes back to the early work of Altenberg (1993), who proposed a methodology for identifying recurrent sequences as defined by their frequency, and with grammatical and functional analysis used to categorise these (Hyland 2012). In a broad sense, such sequences contribute to the meaning and coherence of a text in a specific context. Biber et al. (1999) define lexical bundles as recurrent lexical sequences of three or more words, regardless of their idiomaticity and structure, which appear as such in normal discourse. They are, then, extended collocations that occur together statistically more frequently than by chance. They can be searched for and identified using automated corpus analysis in which frequency and distribution criteria are established, given that the same bundles will tend to appear in different documents. Frequency data on lexical bundles has the advantage that patterns of use can be identified which might otherwise go unnoticed by researchers, but which do indeed need to be explained (Biber et al. 2004). Frequency is only one indicator of whether a sequence of several words is prefabricated; sequences with idiomatic meanings are often rare, but are clearly prefabricated (Biber et al. 2004).

The methodology followed for the identification of bundles involves finding sequences which, whilst not necessarily idiomatic in nature and usually not consisting of grammatically complete units (Biber 2005), as *in the case of*, do function as basic discourse-building units (Biber et al. 2004: 372). Most lexical bundles consist of incomplete sequences that link two structural units. Thus they are formulaic sequences in that they are fixed in the discourse, although not strictly in the sense of Wray (2002), who argues that to be considered thus they must also be stored in the mental lexicon as units (Hyland 2012: 150).

An additional issue to be taken into account is length. In English, three-word lexical bundles tend not to be especially interesting, while five-word bundles are comparatively rare and often involve smaller, internal bundles. For these reasons, four-word bundles are perhaps the most researched in the literature, at least in the context of English, not least because they present a wide diversity of structures and functions. An approach based on the frequency of occurrence of words allows us to consider sequences that are not intuitively recognisable as such. Thus, Biber et al. (2004) claim that linguists have often not addressed the presence of high frequency multiword sequences in texts because their focus has tended to be on grammatical phrases and clauses, without taking into account the possibility of lexical units that cross grammatical structures. Biber and colleagues have shown how lexical bundles do have identifiable discourse functions, and as such are part of the communicative range of speakers, even if they do not correspond to the structures traditionally recognised in linguistic research, where they have often been seen as marginal, or indeed ignored, despite such a decision being subjective rather than reflecting linguistic realities (Hyland 2012).

Biber et al. (1999) define lexical bundles as continuous sequences of words that allow us to differentiate registers. Since that pioneering work, numerous studies, especially in the field of language teaching (Simpson-Vlach and Ellis 2010; Salazar 2011), as well as in academic discourse and more specific domains such as hotel websites (Fuster-Márquez 2014), have highlighted the role of lexical bundles in determining the idiosyncrasy of text types.

3. Methodological approach

The methodology used in the present study is inductive and corpus-driven, and as such combines quantitative and qualitative analysis. Tognini-Bonelli (2001) notes that corpus linguistics has traditionally distinguished between two approaches to analysis, *corpus-based* and *corpus-driven*. The first, also referred to as *introspective*, uses a corpus to identify examples of a phenomenon previously observed or intuited, while the second approach studies language based on the phenomena drawn directly from a corpus. Fuster-Márquez (2020) observes that for the analysis of lexical bundles, this second, inductive approach is fundamental.

For the present study we adopt a largely inductive approach which focuses on the extraction and classification of lexical bundles characteristic of hotel websites, this as a prior step to the detailed analysis of these bundles. However, bearing in mind the possibility of variation in our data, we have also taken a deductive approach in exploring these (inductively extracted) bundles. The advantages of such a combination of introspective and empirical-deductive methods has been discussed elsewhere (Steyer 2013; Bubenhofer 2009).

Our aim is to provide an analysed list of word combinations that are characteristic of hotel website texts in German, and which are of potential interest in teaching German. To this end we have used the methodology originally proposed by Biber et al. (1999) to establish contrasts between different registers or discursive genres in English; it is an approach which both Fuster-Márquez (2014) and Fuster-Márquez and Pennock (2015) have used in the study of phraseological aspects of the language of British hotel websites. The methodology identifies lexical bundles, these defined as recurrent, fixed sequences of words that present specific structures and perform specific functions in texts of the same discourse type. As such, the bundles constitute a good starting point for exploring phraseological differences between registers, genres, and disciplines (Römer 2009).

In terms of pedagogy, lexical bundles from a specific discourse are of particular interest, in that the most frequent and most useful vocabulary in a language is usually favoured in foreign language teaching (cf. Salazar 2011), both in general and specialised domains. Our current approach, then, is a means of identifying high-frequency fixed sequences in German language use, which can serve as a reference point in the development of teaching materials, both in the general field of tourism and more specifically in the hospitality sector. If we can establish the most characteristic lexical bundles in this specific context, we can go on to teach students how to adapt their language use to the target audience here, that is, potential customers.

3.1. Corpus description

For this study we have compiled a corpus of urban hotel websites from Germany, Austria, and Switzerland, which we have called *Korpus der Deutschsprachigen Hotelwebseiten*—KoDeHo (Corpus of German-speaking hotel websites). In order to enhance the representativeness of the corpus, the following criteria were taken into account in the selection of texts: geographical location, classification of hotels, location within the city, and whether or not a hotel was part of a hotel network.

KoDeHo comprises 982 texts from 982 accommodation websites, with a total of 2,334,787 tokens and 288,094 types. It is structured in three sub-corpora, reflecting the three geographical regions of the German-speaking countries included: Germany, Austria, and Switzerland. Table 1 sets out the distribution of the texts by country, indicating the number of tokens and types, as well as the cities from which the samples were taken.

The number of hotels selected by geographical location and cities is unequal, due to differences in the density of population and hotels in each case. This was an intentional. It serves to enrich the corpus, in the sense that the population density and tourist interest of the locations have, in our opinion, an influence on the importance of the promotional discourse of the texts themselves.

Table 1: Distribution of hotels, types, tokens, and cities by country.

Country	Texts	Types	Tokens	Cities numb.	Cities
Germany	655	172,983	1,427,280	22	Augsburg, Berlin, Dresden, Düsseldorf, Erfurt, Frankfurt, Freiburg, Hamburg, Hannover, Heidelberg, Koblenz, Köln, Leipzig, Mainz, München, Münster, Nürnberg, Osnabrück, Potsdam, Regensburg, Rostock, Stuttgart
Austria	243	78,239	694,833	9	Bregenz, Eisenstadt, Graz, Innsbruck, Klagenfurt, Linz, Salzburg, Sankt Pölten, Wien
Switzerland	84	36,872	212,674	7	Basel, Bern, Chur, Luzern, Schaffhausen, St. Gallen, Zürich
Total	**982**	**288,094**	**2,334,787**	**38**	

Figure 1 shows the distribution by country of the percentage of cities, texts, number of types and total number of tokens in each of the countries considered. In all columns, the highest percentage is always Germany, followed by Austria and Switzerland, in that we have taken into account population size. Of particular note, while the texts collected from Switzerland represent 8 % of the whole, in terms of types they represent almost 15 %. This is due to the more extensive texts and more extensive websites found in Switzerland. Similarly, in the case of Austria, whereas the percentage representation in cities, texts and types is around 25 % of the total, the percentage of tokens it is around 30 %. Meanwhile, the percentage of texts collected in Germany is around 70 %, but the number of tokens and types drops to 59 %.

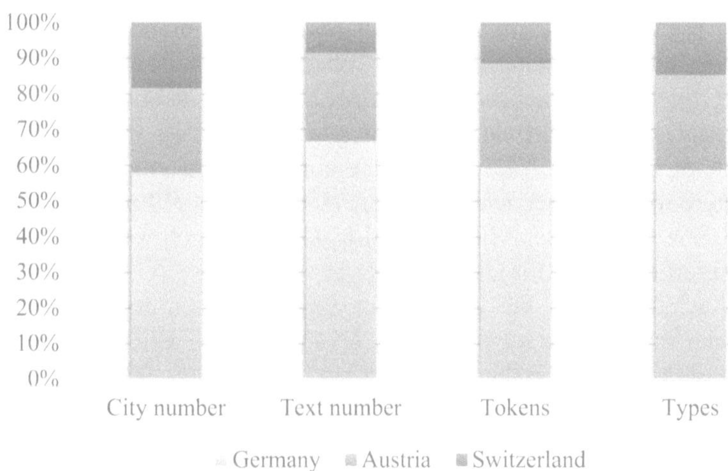

Figure 1. Percentage of cities, number of texts, number of tokens, and number of types per country

The varying lengths of the texts collected are directly related to the similarly differing lengths of the website texts from which they are drawn. Promotional texts in the form of downloadable documents have not been included; these typically contain more detailed information about menus, characteristics of rooms, organisation of events and other services offered by a hotel, etc. Furthermore, FAQ sections, reservation forms and information request forms have been excluded, as have texts setting out terms and conditions, contracts or company policies, and the processing of user data (*Impresion*, *Datenschutz*, etc.), in that these belong to the legal-commercial domain.

3.2. Extraction of n-grams

In this preliminary step, we used the N-grams tool of the Sketch Engine platform to automatically extract n-grams of three to five words from KoDeHo. This was done independently, i.e., separately, according to their length, in a frequency-based ordering of the n-grams. The reason for doing so, rather than using a single extraction procedure, was to avoid any possible bias due to the length variable, in that there is a correlation between the length of the n-gram and its frequency: the shorter the n-gram, the more frequent it will be. In the search, the parameters of the default search were maintained: case-sensitive, with punctuation marks, hyphens and numbers not considered as tokens. Contractions, whether of a preposition and determiner (*vom*, *zum*) or of a verb and pronoun, plus compounds with an internal hyphen (*U-Bahn*, *Kabel-TV*), were considered as single tokens, a procedure that has been adopted in previous studies of English (Biber et al. 1999: 990; Fuster-Márquez 2014: 90) and which we consider to be justified here also for German.

In what follows the criteria for filtering the n-grams will be described, this towards identifying the lexical bundles which are characteristic of these texts, in the sense of Biber et al.'s (1999: 992) definition of register.

3.3 N-gram filtering and obtaining a list of lexical bundles

After obtaining the lists of three-, four- and five-word n-grams independently, we filtered the data using two sets of criteria: quantitative and qualitative or formal ones. The quantitative criteria involve establishing a threshold or minimum frequency level, on the one hand, and a minimum number of documents in which the sequences to be studied appear, on the other. The qualitative criteria concern the non-inclusion of certain words, such as abbreviations and proper nouns. In addition, we established a further set of criteria which allow us to order the lexical bundles according to variables which are based on previous research into lexical bundles in specialised discourse.

3.3.1. Quantitative criteria for semi-automatic n-gram filtering

One of the criteria, of procedural nature, is to consider a recurrent sequence of words as a lexical bundle, to ensure a minimum occurrence, at a pre-established threshold, in a particular corpus. This minimum number of occurrences is known as the frequency threshold. Biber et al. (1999) studied four-word lexical bundles in conversation and academic prose, and establish frequency thresholds of ten occurrences per million. By contrast, Biber et al. (2004) considered lexical bundles for analysis when they reach a frequency threshold of 40 occurrences per million and in a minimum of 20 documents, in a study to determine those lexical bundles that define a discourse, genre, or register. Since five- and six-word sequences are less frequent, Biber et al. (1999) consider lower frequency thresholds here. Fuster-Márquez (2014: 92) establishes a relatively high or restrictive threshold of 29 occurrences per million words and an occurrence in at least 16 different documents for an investigation of four-word lexical bundles in hotel websites in English, in light of the fact that the language exhibited by hotel websites tends to be more repetitive than other text types.

Using thresholds of occurrence in a minimum number of documents allows us to exclude those n-grams that have a high frequency but are found mainly in one text or a small number of texts from the same source. Considering the thresholds of previous studies, and looking specifically at the data in our corpus, we established a relatively low initial threshold, in that we wanted to avoid the possibility of sequences from certain frames not being detected, since variations of certain frames may not be excessively frequent. For the same reason, we filtered the data manually to exclude sequences above the established thresholds but which were detected in hotels of the same network, since these might have skewed the results. This step was carried out after observing the most immediate cotext of these n-grams using the concordance tool in the AntConc programme (Anthony 2020).

In order to obtain a list of the lexical bundles from our corpus, the thresholds established were 48 occurrences per million in twelve different documents for three-word n-grams, a minimum of 20 occurrences in twelve different documents for four-word n-grams, and 14 occurrences in ten different documents for five-word n-grams. In KoDeHo, this entailed trigrams with 48 occurrences or more, four-word n-grams with 20 occurrences, and five-word n-grams with 14 occurrences.

After semi-automatic filtering following these thresholds of frequency and number of documents, and manual filtering using the formal criteria (described in the following section), we obtained a total of 174 three-word lexical bundles, 228 four-word bundles, and 70 five-word ones. Thus, a total of 472 lexical bundles, which is a manageable dataset for the analysis and classification aimed at in the study.

3.3.2. Qualitative criteria for semi-automatic filtering of n-grams

Given our dataset of three-, four- and five-word bundles, these filtered semi-automatically using frequency and distributional criteria, we determined additional criteria of a more subjective nature in order to filter the lists, this towards identifying bundles which were of potential interest for language-teaching purposes.

Salazar (2011: 48), in a pedagogical study of lexical bundles in academic medical texts, establishes a number of qualitative filtering criteria which can be considered as subjective. We agree with her claim that such criteria are part of a methodological rather than a theoretical decision, yet they are necessary in order to obtain a list of lexical bundles which, for our purposes, define the selected texts and are relevant for the teaching of German for specific purposes.

The following filtering criteria for exclusion, then, were considered:

- Abbreviations: frequently-occurring word sequences in apposition or which involve overlapping: *Di Mi Do Fr*, *m zu Fuß*, *m vom Hotel entfernt*, *x Übernachtung inkl. Frühstück*.
- Proper nouns: the most frequently-used proper nouns in these texts are the names of hotels, cities or places of interest: *Hotel Altstadt Vienna*, *in Frankfurt am Main*. However, these are largely excluded in advance due to their low frequency or because they are often found in only a few documents.
- Ending with a determiner: such sequences usually overlap with other (larger or smaller) ones: *mit Blick auf den*, *in der Nähe des*, *bieten wir Ihnen ein*, *guten Start in den*, *im Zentrum der*, *ein individuelles Angebot für Ihre*. The presence of the determiner does not provide any additional information that would motivate

their inclusion as such, although it may be important information for further analysis, like the fact that some sequences alternate a genitive or prepositional complement introduced by *von*. Indeed, in Biber et al. (1999) and subsequent studies by the same group, lexical bundles which end in a determiner, such as *the nature of the*, are indeed considered. However, German is a more flexible language in this sense, and unlike in English the determiner changes form according to gender and number, so that the data on frequency would be partial or lower. In Salazar's (2011: 50) research on English, sequences of this type are also excluded in compiling a list of lexical bundles in the academic medical discourse, again with pedagogical aims.

- Fragments of other bundles: these sequences sometimes include a coordinating conjunction and sometimes fragments of other, longer lexical bundles: *freuen uns auf Ihre, und um das Hotel, Sie an der Rezeption, mit viel Liebe zum, oder rufen Sie uns an, ganze Familie und der ideale*.
- Overlaps: Biber et al. (1999) note the existence of bundles that can be extended into larger sequences, and this is the case with overlaps of two bundles of different sizes in KoDeHo. So, for sequences in which there is an overlap, in almost all cases we have excluded the less frequent bundle, e.g.: *eine große Auswahl* is included, whereas *eine große Auswahl an* is excluded; *rund um die* is excluded, but *rund um die Uhr* or *rund um das Hotel* is included. However, those lexical bundles of different lengths that overlap and do not have the same frequency have been included, as they might indicate variation in a bundle.
- Series of function words: we excluded these lexical bundles because of their low transparency and sometimes because they are fragments of other bundles. Their appearance in the initial data is because they consist of words which are very frequent in the corpus and whose nature is purely grammatical: *Sie sich von uns, Sie sich auf ein, Sie links in die, wir für Sie ein, Sie uns einfach*.
- Numbers: in the extraction of the n-grams, numbers and symbols were not considered, so numerals are also been excluded, although we understand that quantification and numerals are

certainly important in the discourse of hotel websites. However, they would typically constitute framing elements, with a variant element of quantification, such as: *oder zwei Einzelbetten, Doppelbett oder zwei, für zwei Personen.*

- Noise: sequences that, due to layout issues, appear with incomplete words or that involve elements of web navigation, such as: *mit der U, s Hotel in, auf der B.*

In the case of lexical bundles that include grammatical mistakes, such as **mit den öffentlichen Verkehrsmittel*, **in der Nähe des Hotel*, these are included in the listings in uncorrected form, since our aim is to reflect language in use. We consider these as purely typographical errors.

Hence, our methodology involves quantitative, computer-assisted extraction criteria and qualitative, formal criteria, all of these latter driven at least in part by subjective choices by the researchers. There is, then, the potential for a bias in the results, yet such subjectivity is an inherent element of this kind of research. As Salazar (2011: 67) points out, intuitive decisions are nothing new in studies of this type; indeed, he cites previous phraseological studies in which human judgement was used as a methodological support for corpus-based approaches (Altenberg and Eeg-Olofsson, 1990; De Cock et al. 1998), this mainly to determine which items should be prioritised and to remove results that were 'uninteresting from a phraseological point of view' (Altenberg and Eeg-Olofsson, 1990: 7). According to Salazar, a selectional procedure based on intuition is especially necessary in studies which aim to identify lexical bundles for teaching. It is therefore a decision that is partly subjective and methodological, rather than theoretical.

4. Methodological proposal for selecting and prioritizing lexical bundles

Once the lexical bundles from the KoDeHo corpus had been filtered, we carried out a number of calculations that allowed us to organise the list according to the relevance and typicality of the items. This was, then, a multidimensional ordering, and to establish such an order of significance the calculations used three different indexes. The first was the norm index, which relates the value of the frequency and the number of documents in which the lexical bundle appears. The second was the *Mutual Information Index* (MII), which calculates the mutual attraction of the words that form part of each n-gram in terms of their occurrence together in the same corpus by chance. The third and final index was the so-called simple maths value provided by Sketch Engine, which relates the normalised frequencies of an n-gram in a study corpus to a reference corpus, in this case KoDeHo and *German Web 2013* (deTenTen13), from which we used the subcorpus *Domain of states with official language German* (Sketch Engine 2013). The following sections describe the calculation of these indexes in more detail.

4.1. Norm index between frequency and number of documents in which a lexical bundle occurs

The most usual way to establish the order of importance of the n-grams is to use the frequency of occurrence of those in the documents considered. Such an approach, however, ignores the fact that the n-grams are distributed differently across the corpus texts. One interesting approach is to consider the importance of n-grams appearing frequently in a sufficiently significant number of texts, an approach seen in other research (Biber et al. 1999; Fuster-Márquez 2014; Fuster-Márquez and Pennock 2015; Römer 2010). In this way, sequences with the same author or that occur in just a few texts are discarded. One way to simultaneously consider the frequency of occurrence of n-grams and the number of documents in which they appear is to consider n-grams as characterised by a vector:

$$V = (F, N)$$

where F is the frequency of occurrence and N the number of documents in which the n-gram occurs. Because F and N in general attain different values within different ranges, and also as a means of considering the frequency and number of documents in the same way, it is better to use the relative values of F and N defined thus:

$$f = \frac{F}{\max(F_i)}$$

$$n = \frac{N}{\max(N_i)}$$

This results in the vector of the type:

$$v = (f, n)$$

The order is determined by applying the Euclidean norm of each vector as the ordering value, which is defined as:

$$\|v\| = \left(f^2 + n^2\right)^{\frac{1}{2}}$$

The higher the ||v|| the more important the n-gram. When comparing the results of this index with those of the absolute frequency of occurrence of each n-gram in the corpus, we observed that the ordering of the n-grams underwent little variation. We therefore decided to use the frequency index for further selection and to exclude the norm index, in that it added complexity but no specific advantage. Having excluded from the filtering process those n-grams that were concentrated in a small number of texts, or which pertained to a specific hotel, hotel chain or hotel group, information on the number of documents in which they appeared was only moderately relevant.

4.2. Mutual Information Index

Alternatively, n-grams can be ordered using the Mutual Information Index (MII). Some research on lexical bundles in specialised discourse has used this index as a filtering criterion (Salazar 2011). Specifically, the Pointwise Mutual Information (PMI) allows us to measure the statistical association between two variables and is defined as follows:

$$PMI = log_2 \frac{p(x,y)}{p(x)p(y)}$$

PMI compares the probability of observing *x* and *y* together (the joint probability) with the probabilities of observing *x* and *y* independently, where *x* and *y* are words that are part of a collocation. If there is a genuine association between *x* and *y*, then the probability P(*x*, *y*) will be far greater than the probability p(*x*) p(*y*), and consequently PMI(*x*, *y*) ≫0. If there is no interesting relation between *x* and *y*, then p(*x*, *y*)≈p(*x*) p(*y*), and hence PMI(*x*, *y*)≈0. If *x* and *y* are in complementary distribution, then p(*x*, *y*) will be much smaller than p(*x*) p(*y*), forcing PMI(*x*, *y*) ≪0 (Church and Hanks 1990).

The PMI compares the probability of observing *x* and *y* together (the joint probability) with the probability of observing *x* and *y* independently, where *x* and *y* are words that are part of a collocation. If there is a genuine association between *x* and *y*, then the probability of them being together, P(*x*, *y*), will be far greater than the probability p(*x*) p(*y*), and consequently PMI(*x*, *y*) ≫0. If there is no interesting relation between *x* and *y*, then p(*x*, *y*)≈p(*x*) p(*y*), and hence PMI(*x*, *y*)≈0. If *x* and *y* are in complementary distribution, then p(*x*, *y*) will be much smaller than p(*x*) p(*y*), forcing PMI(*x*, *y*) ≪0 (Church and Hanks 1990).

The PMI is mathematically defined to compare only two variables, but there are two ways to extend this definition to more variables (Van de Cruys 2011) based on the interaction of information and total correlation, which is necessary in the case of the current research into lexical bundles, which range from three to five words.

The interaction of information or co-information is based on the notion of conditional mutual information. This is the mutual information of two random variables conditioned on a third. The information on specific interaction can be defined as:

$$SI_1 = log_2 \frac{p(x,y)p(y,z)p(x,z)}{p(x)p(y)p(z)p(x,y,z)}$$

Total correlation or multiple information quantifies the amount of information that is shared between different random variables, and thus expresses how a particular group of random variables is related. In analogy to the definition of mutual point information, the correlation can be defined for specific instances of M random variables as:

$$SI_2(x_1, x_2, \ldots, x_M) = log_2 \frac{p(x_1, x_2, \ldots, x_M)}{\prod_{i=1}^{M} p(x_i)}$$

In the case of three random variables (M=3) it is expressed as:

$$SI_2 = log_2 \frac{p(x_1, x_2, x_3)}{p(x_1)\,p(x_2)\,p(x_3)}$$

The second method (SI2), which generally yields better results than the first, is a direct extension of the PMI; it is easier to calculate and has been used in linguistics for collocation extraction (Villada 2005).

We used this index for the subsequent ordering of lexical bundles for two reasons: it takes into account the tendency of words to appear together, and also offers a somewhat different ordering than the one derived from frequency and the index which is called *simple maths* on the Sketch Engine platform, which was used to compare our corpus and the general German reference corpus, as explained in the following section.

4.3. *Keyness scoring factor in Sketch Engine which compares a specific corpus and a reference corpus*

In order to reveal how special a n-gram is in a specific corpus compared to a reference corpus, the frequency of occurrence of the n-gram in the two corpora are compared. We did this out using the Sketch Engine platform. By means of the K n-grams option in the N-grams tool (see Kilgarriff 2009) the programme calculates a score for each n-gram, defined as:

$$Score = \frac{frel_{espec} + n}{frel_{ref} + n}$$

Table 2 explains the meaning of the elements of the *simple maths* index:

Table 2: Meaning of elements of the formula of the *simple maths* index.

Score	The keyness scoring factor
$frel_{espec}$	The relative frequency per million in the specific corpus
$frel_{ref}$	Relative frequency per million in the reference corpus
n	A smoothing factor which takes the default value of 1

This score is basically the quotient of the relative frequencies per million of both corpora with a smoothing factor. The higher the score of a n-gram, the more typical it is of the specific corpus.

The score here, together with the absolute frequency index of our corpus and the PMI, was used to order the lexical bundles under investigation in terms of their pedagogical interest. The way in which these three factors were used is described in the following section.

4.4. Mixed value: Ordering on the basis of three indexes

As noted above, it is possible to order the n-grams according to their significance arising from the application of the defined parameters. Because each index highlights one type of lexical bundle as the most relevant, we considered combining these indexes in order to avoid the bias involved in calculating them with only part of the variables. On these lines, Simpson-Vlach and Ellis (2010) use frequency and MI as the criteria to obtain a list of lexical bundles with pedagogical applications, aiming thus to obtain a more reliable metric, one that avoids excluding less frequent but nevertheless relevant bundles. In this case, the authors used experts to consider these values, something that we do not see as appropriate in the present study, due to its highly subjective nature.

The previous section described a method for comparing the specific corpus to a reference corpus. As a result, a prioritisation of the n-grams using these three criteria is obtained. The following formula was applied to order the lexical bundles on the basis of the indexes, considering the criteria described above. A vector represented by its order was associated with each n-gram by applying the criteria of absolute frequency, pointwise mutual information and score in the comparison of the study and reference corpora, in order to extract key n-grams:

$$vmix=(Ord_F, Ord_{MP}, Ord_{SCORE})$$

Table 3 explains the meaning of the elements of the mixed value index formula:

Table 3: Meaning of elements of the mixed value index formula.

Vmix	The vector that considers the three orderings of the n-gram
Ord_F	The ordinal of the n-gram ordered by frequency
Ord_{MI}	The ordinal of the n-gram ordered by Pointwise Mutual Information
Ord_{SCORE}	The ordinal of the n-gram ordered by score in the corpus comparison

The Euclidean norm of the vector was used as the ordering criterion:

$$\|vmix\| = \left(Ord_F{}^2 + Ord_{MI}{}^2 + Ord_{score}{}^2\right)^{1/2}$$

Hence we obtain a value that considers all three orders, and thus the variables involved in the investigation of lexical bundles. Table 4 shows the top fifteen bundles according to this calculation. We observe that the mixed value returns as more prototypical some sequences that offer greater fixedness and lower frequency, which we identify as closer to the lexical pole than to the grammatical one.

Table 4: Top fifteen lexical bundles according to each ordering.

	Frequency ordering	**MI ordering**	***simple maths* ordering**	***Mixed value index* ordering**
1	*nichts mehr im Wege*	*in der Altstadt von*	*handelt es sich um*	*viel Liebe zum Detail*
2	*WLAN im ganzen Haus*	*in der Nähe von*	*bei uns können Sie*	*zu einem unvergesslichen Erlebnis*
3	*mit einer großen Auswahl*	*erreichen Sie das Hotel*	*herzlich Willkommen im Hotel*	*Doppelbett oder zwei Einzelbetten*
4	*lassen Sie sich verzaubern*	*in der Zeit von*	*weitere Informationen erhalten Sie*	*Leistungen und praktische Informationen*
5	*in der Innenstadt von*	*in der Innenstadt von*	*auf der Suche nach*	*wie zu Hause fühlen*
6	*seien Sie unser Gast*	*Sie und Ihre Gäste*	*wir freuen uns darauf*	*Start in den Tag*
7	*von seiner schönsten Seite*	*buchen Sie Ihr Hotel*	*auf der linken Straßenseite*	*mit Rat und Tat*
8	*jedes Zimmer verfügt über*	*bei uns im Hotel*	*in den letzten Jahren*	*Anreise mit dem Flugzeug*
9	*auch innerhalb der Familie*	*Informationen finden Sie in*	*mitten in der Stadt*	*der ideale Ausgangspunkt für*
10	*wenige Gehminuten vom Hotel*	*pro Nacht und Zimmer*	*direkt vor dem Hotel*	*lässt keine Wünsche offen*
11	*wir würden uns freuen*	*bei uns können Sie*	*der perfekte Ort für*	*nach Wahl des Küchenchefs*
12	*in nur wenigen Gehminuten*	*buchen Sie Ihr Zimmer*	*mit den öffentlichen Verkehrsmittel*	*rufen Sie uns an*
13	*Ihre Nutzung der Website*	*mit Dusche und Badewanne*	*ganz nach Ihren Wünschen*	*Wir freuen uns auf*
14	*eine Auszeit vom Alltag*	*verwöhnen wir Sie mit*	*nur wenige Gehminuten entfernt*	*gerne beraten wir Sie*
15	*immer für Sie da*	*Aufenthalt in unserem Hotel*	*die Seele baumeln lassen*	*alle Zimmer verfügen über*

5. Conclusions

This study of lexical bundles has allowed us to identify elements of formulaic language commonly used in German hotel websites in what is considered to be native-speaker usage. This is a pioneering study in German, given the current lack of work on phraseological units of this kind in the specialised discourse of tourism.

The corpus methodology used here has been shown to be fundamental in this type of analysis of German, bearing in mind the importance of obtaining conclusions based on large language samples capable of revealing linguistic routines used in such texts.

The filtering process used has drawn on previous studies, but with certain methodological refinements. We used both frequency thresholds and also the criterion that bundles should appear in texts from various sources, so as to avoid the excessive influence on the results of combinations used by a single writer or in a single source, such as texts pertaining to a specific hotel chain; that is, sequences considered to be excessively idiosyncratic were excluded.

The index of mixed value used to order bundles according to their relevance as characteristic elements of the texts studied is innovative in terms of its quantitative dimension. This index allows us to consider three other indexes used in previous research on lexical bundles in specific kinds of discourse that also have a pedagogical, lexicographical and translation-based aims.

The combination of these different indexes (the mutual information index, the frequency index, and the simple maths index), which provided us with varying results, has allowed us to avoid the bias inherent in focusing on just one variable, and to consider all the quantitative variables deemed to be important in determining the specificity of our present corpus.

References

Altenberg, Bengt. 1993. Recurrent Verb-Complement Constructions in the London-Lund Corpus. In J. Aarts / P. Haan / N. Oostdijk (eds.), *English Language Corpora: Design, Analysis and Exploitation. Papers from the Thirteenth International Conference on English Language Research on Computerized Corpora.* Amsterdam: Rodopi, 227–245.

Altenberg, Bengt. 1998. On the Phraseology of Spoken English: The Evidence of Recurrent Word-Combinations. In A. P. Cowie (ed.), *Phraseology: Theory, Analysis, and Applications.* Oxford: Oxford University Press, 101–122.

Altenberg, Bengt / Eeg-Olofsson, Mats. 1990. Phraseology in Spoken English. In J. Aarts / W. Meijs (eds.), *Theory and Practice in Corpus Linguistics*. Amsterdam: Rodopi, 1–26.

Anthony, Laurence 2020. *AntConc (Version 3.5.9)* [Computer Software]. Tokyo, Japan: Waseda University. https://www.laurenceanthony.net/software.

Biber, Douglas. 1993. Representativeness in Corpus Design. *Literary and Linguistic Computing* 8/4, 243–257. DOI: 10.1093/llc/8.4.243.

Biber, Douglas. 2005. Paquetes léxicos en textos de estudio universitario: Variación entre disciplinas académicas. *Revista Signos* 38/57, 19–29. [online]. http://www.redalyc.org/articulo.oa?id=157013764002.

Biber, Douglas / Conrad, Susan / Cortes, Viviana. 2004. If You Look at . . .: Lexical Bundles in University Teaching and Textbooks. *Applied Linguistics* 25/3, 371–405.

Biber, Douglas / Johansson, Stig / Leech, Geoffrey / Conrad, Susan / Finegan, Edward. 1999. *Longman Grammar of Spoken and Written English.* Harlow: Pearson.

Bubenhofer, Noah. 2009. *Sprachgebrauchsmuster: Korpuslinguistik als Methode der Diskurs- und Kulturanalyse*. Berlin: de Gruyter.

Church, Kenneth Ward / Hanks, Patrick. 1990. Word Association Norms, Mutual Information, and Lexicography. In *27th Annual Meeting of the Association for Computational Linguistics*, *Association for Computational Linguistics.* Vancouver: British Columbia, 76–83.

Corpas, Gloria. 1996. *Manual de fraseología española*. Madrid: Gredos.

Coulmas, Florian. 1981. *Routine im Gespräch. Zur pragmatischen Fundierung der Idiomatik.* Wiesbaden: Athenaion.

De Cock, Sylvie / Granger, Sylviane / Leech, Geoffrey / McEnery, Tony. 1998. An Automated Approach to the Phrasicon of EFL Learners. In S. Granger (ed.), *Learner English on Computer*. London-New York: Addison Wesley Longman, 67–79.

Esteban-Fonollosa, Maricel. 2021. *Lenguaje formulaico del alemán en páginas web hoteleras de los países de lengua alemana: un estudio basado en paquetes léxicos*, Thesis. Valencia: Universitat de València.

Filatkina, Natalia. 2018. *Historische formelhafte Sprache. Theoretische Grundlagen und methodische Herausforderungen.* Berlin: De Gruyter.

Firth, John Rupert. 1969. *Papers in Linguistics: 1934–1951*, 1st, 4th reprint. London, Oxford: University Press.

Fuster-Márquez, Miguel. 2014. Lexical Bundles and Phrase Frames in the Language of Hotel Websites. *English Text Construction* 7/1, 84–121. https://doi.org/10.1075/etc.7.1.04fus

Fuster-Márquez, Miguel / Fernández-Domínguez, Jesús. 2020. Overused Bundles in the Written Academic English of Spanish EFL Students Corpus Analysis in Academic Discourse. In M. L. Carrió-Pastor (ed.), *Academic Discourse and Learner Corpora*, Vol. 1, 282–299.

Fuster-Márquez, Miguel / Pennock-Speck, Barry. 2015. Target Frames in British Hotel Websites. *International Journal of English Studies*. Murcia: Servicio de publicaciones Universidad de Murcia 15/1, 51–69. https://doi.org/10.6018/ijes/2015/1/213231.

Groom, Nicholas. 2017. *Phraseology: A Critical Reassessment [PowerPoint]*. Invited talk, Idiomaticity Workshop. University of Oslo, Norway. https://www.hf.uio.no/ilos/english/research/projects/idiomaticity/events/groom_oslo_20170902.pdf.

Hyland, Ken. 2012. Bundles in Academic Discourse. *Annual Review of Applied Linguistics* 32. Cambridge: Cambridge University Press, 150–169.

Kilgarriff, Adam 2009. Simple maths for keywords. In M. Mahlberg / V. González Díaz / C. Smith (eds.), *Proceedings of the Corpus Linguistics Conference 2009* (CL2009), 171. https://ucrel.lancs.ac.uk/publications/CL2009/

Lemnitzer, Lothar / Zinsmeister, Heike. 2006. *Korpuslinguistik: eine Einführung*. Tübingen: Narr.

McEnery, Tony / Andrew, Wilson. 2012. *Corpus Linguistics: Method, Theory and Practice.* Cambridge: Cambridge University Press.

Nattinger, James R. / DeCarrico, Jeanette S. 1992. *Lexical Phrases and Language Teaching*. Oxford, England: Oxford University Press.

Pawley, Andrew / Syder, Frances Hodgetts. 1983. Two Puzzles for Linguistic Theory: Nativelike Selection and Nativelike Fluency. In J. C. Richards / R. W. Schmidt (eds.), *Language and Communication*. London: Longman, 191–225.

Römer, Ute. 2009. The Inseparability of Lexis and Grammar: Corpus Linguistic Perspectives. *Annual Review of Cognitive Linguistics*, 7, 141–163.

Römer, Ute. 2010. Establishing the phraseological profile of a text type: The construction of meaning in academic book rewiews. *English Text Construction* 3/1, 95–119.

Ruiz, Leonor. 1997. Aspectos de fraseología teórica española. *Cuadernos de filología: Anejo 24*. València: Universitat de València.

Salazar, Danica J. L. 2011. *Lexical Bundles in Scientific English: A Corpus-Based Study of Native and Non-Native Writing*, Thesis. Barcelona: Universitat de Barcelona.

Simpson-Vlach, Rita / Ellis, Nick C. 2010. An Academic Formulas List: New Methods in Phraseology Research. *Applied Linguistics* 31, 487–512. doi: 10.1093/applin/amp058.

Sinclair, John M. 1991. *Corpus, Concordance, Collocation. Describing English Language*. Oxford: Oxford University Press.

Sketch-Engine. German Web 2013 (deTenTen13) [online]. https://www.sketchengine.eu/.

Steyer, Kathrin. 2013. *Usuelle Wortverbindungen: zentrale Muster des Sprachgebrauchs aus korpusanalytischer Sicht*. Tübingen: Narr.

Tognini-Bonelli, Elena. 2001. *Corpus Linguistics at Work*. Amsterdam: John Benjamins.

Van de Cruys, Tim. 2011. *Two Multivariate Generalizations of Pointwise Mutual Information*. Cambridge: RCEAL, University of Cambridge.

Villada Moirón, Begoña. 2005. *Data-Driven Identification of Fixed Expressions and Their Modifiability*, Thesis. The Netherlands: University of Groningen.

Wood, David. 2002. Formulaic Language in Acquisition and Production: Implications for Teaching. *TESL Canada Journal*, 1–15.

Wood, David. 2015. *Fundamentals of Formulaic Language: An Introduction*. London: Bloomsbury Academic.

Wray, Alison. 2002. *Formulaic Language and the Lexicon.* Cambridge: Cambridge University Press.

Wray, Alison. 2008. *Formulaic Language: Pushing the Boundaries.* Oxford: Oxford University Press.

Wray, Alison / Perkins, Michael. 2000. The Functions of Formulaic Language: An Integrated Model. *Language & Communication* 20/1, 1–28.

Zuluaga, Alberto. 1980. *Introducción al estudio de las expresiones fijas.* Frankfurt a. M./Bern: Peter Lang.

LUISA GONZÁLEZ-ROMERO

Between the construction and the phraseological unit: The *way*-construction in English and Spanish[1]

1. Introduction

The so-called *way*-construction in English has been the focus of research of many recent studies because, among other things, it constitutes a clear example of the concept of 'grammatical construction', that is, a conventional pairing of form and function. In Goldberg's (1995) influential analysis of this sentence type, the syntactic pattern [$SUBJ_i$ [V [$POSS_i$ *way*] OBL]], as illustrated in (1) and (2), is argued to convey the implication of the subject referent moving along the path, real or abstract, denoted by the prepositional phrase despite the fact that the meanings of the individual words do not, or may not, express motion:

(1) The firefighters pushed their way into the building.
(2) Her boyfriend cried his way to forgiveness. (Szczesniak 2013: 181–2)

In contrast to English, this pattern is said to be non-existent in Spanish (Pedersen 2013; Mateu 2000), as we can see from the ungrammaticality of (3b) and (4b):

(3a) Peter fought his way out of the restaurant.
(3b) *Pedro peleó su camino fuera del restaurant. (Pedersen 2013: 242)
(4a) Adele moaned her way out of the stage.
(4b) *Adele gimió su camino fuera del escenario. (Mateu 2000: 17)

1 The research reported in this chapter was conducted within the framework of Project UPO-1254742, funded by the European Regional Development Fund (80%) and the Regional Government of Andalusia (FEDER Andalucía 2014-2020).

This lack has been argued to be related to the fact that Spanish is, following Talmy's (1985, 2000) typology of motion events, a verb-framed language (Mateu 2000, 2005). According to Talmy, languages which belong to this typological pattern encode the path of motion and the motion itself in the verb, whereas manner (or cause), if present in the sentence, is expressed independently as an adverbial or gerundive element, as in (5). In satellite-framed languages such as English, the verb conflates the information about motion and manner (or cause), and the path is expressed by satellites, that is, verb particles such as *out*, usually combined with a preposition, as in (6):

(5) La botella entró a la cueva flotando. (Talmy 1985: 69)
(6) I run out of the house. (Talmy 1985: 103)

This typological distinction may explain why the syntactic patterns instantiated by the sentences in (7b) and (8b), provided by the Glosbe Dictionary, where motion is expressed by the verbal elements *escabullirse* and *abrirse paso*, and the information about manner is conveyed by the adverbials *con una broma* and *combatiendo*, are probably the most frequent and natural ways to translate into Spanish the English examples in (7a) and (8a):

(7a) Graham tried to joke his way out.
(7b) Graham intentó escabullirse con una broma.
(8a) He fought his way across two continents, facing and overcoming dangers you could not possibly imagine.
(8b) Se abrió paso, combatiendo, a través de dos continentes, enfrentándose y escapando a peligros que no podríais concebir.

The *way*-construction is rather productive in Present Day English and the semantic range of verbs that can be found in it has increased over time and is still doing so (see Perek 2018). Among the verbs most strongly linked to the construction are *make* and *find* as they are two of the most common predicates in every period since the first occurrences of the pattern.[2] As regards Spanish and despite the above observations about

2 In the corpus analysis of the *way*-construction in different varieties of English carried out by Brunner and Hoffman (2020), *make* and *find* amount for almost 50 % of the tokens. The same number is provided by McColm (2019), not only for English, but also for German and Dutch, which also exhibit a parallel *way*-construction.

its typological nature and the assumed absence of *way*-constructions, this syntactic pattern has been very recently attested, although marginally, in this language (see González Romero 2022).

Drawing on these recent findings and on the basis of a contrastive analysis of two corpora of real tokens of the sequence [SUBJ$_i$ [V [POSS$_i$ *way/camino*] (OBL)]] with the verbs *make* and *find* and *hacer* and *encontrar*, the first aim of this study is to provide further evidence that a sentence type syntactically and semantically equivalent to the English *way*-construction also occurs in Spanish. The comparison of the corpora will identify similarities, general trends of usage and potential mismatches between the two languages and will, additionally, provide a detailed description of the *way*-construction with the verbs *make* and *find*, which, despite having a central role in English, has received little attention in the literature in favour of other occurrences of the construction with more unusual and semantically richer verbs. Secondly, this work seeks to show that, together with the expression of physical and abstract movement typically associated with the *way*-construction, the sequence analysed may behave in both languages as a phraseological unit with the meaning 'advance in life or become successful in a profession', which suggests the existence of a continuum between the syntactic and the lexical sides of language.

The paper is structured as follows. Section 2 provides methodological details about the corpora chosen for the compilation of the data sets as well as the selection criteria applied. Section 3 gives a brief account of the main features of the English *way*-construction according to some relevant earlier works. Section 4 presents the main findings of the contrastive analysis of the English and Spanish *way*-constructions attested in the corpora. The semantic characterization of the construction is completed in Section 5, where its frequent reading of difficult movement is examined in both languages. Section 6 deals with the comparison of the phraseological units in English and Spanish. In Section 7, a unified treatment of the *way*-construction and the phraseological unit in terms of the syntax-lexicon continuum is put forward. Finally, Section 8 summarizes the main conclusions drawn from the study.

2. Corpora and selection criteria

The data used in this study comes from two comparable and giga-token corpora: The English data has been extracted from the *NOW Corpus* (News on the Web) (Davies 2016), whereas the Spanish material has been retrieved from *Corpus del Español: NOW* (News on the Web) (Davies 2018). Both corpora contain billions of words from web-based newspapers and magazines from English and Spanish speaking countries. The English corpus is composed of data from 2010 to the present time and is constantly growing. The Spanish corpus consists of material from 2012–2019. Since the *way*-construction with *make* and *find* is extremely frequent, the search was limited to British English in a time spam of one year, 2019, in order to have a sample bigger enough to reach reliable conclusions but not much bigger than the Spanish one, where the construction is not easy to attest. For this reason, the full corpus was used when collecting the Spanish tokens although the search was geographically restricted to Spanish spoken in Spain.

The initial search for the corpora involved retrieving all the tokens of the pattern [SUBJ [V [POSS *way/camino*]]]. Due to the extremely high number of examples returned by the English corpus, the search was limited to third person singular subjects (POSS = *his, her, its*) and to present, past and bare verbal forms (V = *make(s), made, find(s), found*). In Spanish no restrictions were applied. The tokens obtained were then examined manually and the analysis revealed that the sequence instantiates two different patterns: the first one illustrates the *way*-construction as defined above, whereas the second corresponds to a phraseological unit with a metaphorical meaning. Occurrences were classified as *way*-constructions when they met the following criteria, adopted from the ones proposed by Mondorf (2011: 402) and Perek (2018: 71):

a. the possessive element is co-referential with the subject,
b. the sentence entails motion, either physical or abstract,
c. if the nouns *way* and *camino* are followed by a prepositional (or adverb) phrase, it must describe the path or goal of motion.[3]

3 As will be explained in more detail in Section 3, most accounts of the English *way*-construction, including those in Mondorf (2011) and Perek (2018), hold the

Tokens of the syntactic pattern under analysis were grouped as phraseological units when:

a. the possessive element is co-referential with the subject,
b. the sentence does not entail actual motion,
c. the nouns *way* and *camino* are used in a metaphorical sense,
d. if the nouns *way* and *camino* are followed by a prepositional (or adverb) phrase, it simply provides locative information.

Table 1 shows the distribution of tokens attested in the English and Spanish corpora:

Table 1: Distribution of *way*-constructions and phraseological units in the corpus.

SYNTACTIC PATTERN	**Tokens retrieved**	***Way*-Constr.**	**Phrase. unit**
[SUBJ$_i$ [MAKE [POSS$_i$ *way* (OBL)]]]	1390	1191	25
[SUBJ$_i$ [FIND [POSS$_i$ *way* (OBL)]]]	446	392	23
[SUBJ$_i$ [HACER [POSS$_i$ *camino*] (OBL)]]	224	55	149
[SUBJ$_i$ [ENCONTRAR [POSS$_i$ *camino*] (OBL)]]	432	85	300

Although this work is not devised as a quantitative research study in the strictest sense, the unbalanced number of constructions identified in each corpus, together with the fact the data in the English NOW corpus for the year 2019 is around two billion words and the full Spanish NOW corpus contains about 7.6 billion words, gives an indication of the high productivity of the *way*-construction in (British) English as compared with the Spanish variety analysed, where it is very uncommon but, undoubtedly, possible. On the contrary, the phraseological unit, although attested in both languages, is much more productive in Spanish than in English, where it is extremely rare.

view that directional phrases are compulsory in the construction. However, due to the fact that the idea of movement can be conveyed without such an element, it has been regarded as an optional constituent when collecting the data for this study.

3. Brief overview of the *way*-construction

The well-known definition of 'construction' provided by Goldberg (2006: 5), states that 'Any linguistic pattern is recognized as a construction as long as some aspect of its form or function is nor strictly predicted from its components parts or from other constructions recognized to exist'. Several reasons have been given to justify treating the *way*-construction as such in this constructionist sense. From a syntactic point of view, it is often noted that in many cases the argument structure of the verb is not properly projected since neither the postverbal NP nor the directional PP is licensed by the verb. As Jackendoff (1990: 211) originally observed, verbs attested in this pattern cannot occur with both an NP and a PP complement, as shown in (9). In addition, the construction is possible with verbs that do not normally admit a direct object, such as *talk* in (10) (Perek 2018: 67):

(9) *Bill belched (a belch) out of the restaurant.
(10) We talked our way into the VIP area.

The peculiar nature of the *way*-construction is further highlighted by the opposite phenomenon: the following examples from Jackendoff (1990: 212) show that potential transitive verbs, such as *eat*, cannot take canonical direct objects in the construction:

(11a) We ate our way across the U.S.
(11b) *We ate our hot dogs our way across the U.S.

These unusual features of the *way*-construction lead Jackendoff (1990: 218) to describe it as 'a fairly outrageous example of mismatch between syntactic and conceptual structure'.

Along with the structural features just described, the semantic properties of the *way*-construction make it also possible to classify it as a construction. The meaning of these sentences is not compositional and cannot be predicted from the meaning of the verb which, in many cases, do not even express motion. Neither can the idea of movement be entailed by the noun *way* alone because, as Goldberg (1995: 199–200) points out, its mere presence in the sentence does not guarantee the expression of a motion event. In contrast with (12a), the example in

(12b), where the noun *way* is not co-referential with the subject, does not entail motion:

(12a) *Frank found his way to New York, but he hasn't gone yet.
(12b) Frank found a way to New York, but he hasn't gone yet.

Having excluded the verb and the noun *way* as the source of the idea of motion conveyed by the sentence, it could be argued that this notion arises from the presence of the directional PP. This element is usually considered a main component of the *way*-construction and is sometimes even regarded as compulsory for the pattern to be considered as such (see Marantz 1992; Takao 2000 or Fanego 2018, among others). However, this element is not necessary if the distance implied in the sentence can 'be expressed by the sequence of the verb and one's way alone' (Kuno et al. 2004: 80):

(13) But it quickly hushes up as another group gropes its way, begging for assistance.

The idea of movement expressed by these sentences cannot be thus predicted from the semantic composition of their particular lexical pieces but seems to be linked, as suggested by Perek (2018: 68), to the whole syntactic pattern, being therefore necessary to posit 'an independent pairing of form with meaning', i.e., a grammatical construction. Traugott and Trousdale (2013: 79) adopt Jackendoff's (2002) characterization of the constructional meaning associated to the *way*-construction and summarize its syntactic and semantic properties in the following template:

[SUB$_i$ [V POSS$_i$ *way*] (DIR)] ↔ [SEM'$_i$ traverse the path PP while/by doing V']

Building on previous accounts of the construction in Levin and Rapoport (1988) and Jackendoff (1990), Goldberg (1995) distinguishes two interpretations for the *way*-construction: means and manner. In the means interpretation, the most basic and frequent one, the verb lexicalizes the means by which the motion occurs and implies that 'the subject moves despite some external difficulty, or in some indirect way: the path is not already established, but must in some sense be created by the mover' (Goldberg 1995: 204). In the manner interpretation, the subevents referred to are simply simultaneous and the verb only expresses co-occurring manner (Goldberg 1995: 209). In this reading, much less common and not accepted by all speakers, there is no implication that a path must be created and, therefore, the subject's movement is not depicted as difficult or laborious. The paraphrases in (14) and (15) show this contrast:

(14a) He dug his way out of prison. (Goldberg 1995: 199)
(14b) He got out of prison by digging (a tunnel)
(15a) Sam moaned his way down the road. (Jackendoff 1990:211)
(15b) Sam went down the road while moaning.

Later works split Goldberg's original means interpretation into two different types. Both Israel (1996) and Perek (2018) posit a first category, labelled *means thread* by the former and *path-creation sense* by the latter, which implies the creation of a literal or figurative path, as in (16). In the second sense, termed *manner* by both authors, the verb conveys information about the way in which motion takes place, such as rate, path shape or manner itself, as in (17). To these two central schema, both authors add a third one, the *incidental activity* or *action* sense, exemplified in (18), which corresponds to Goldberg's manner interpretation and is regarded as a more recent innovation, dating back to the first decades of the 19th century:

(16) The steamers were using dynamite in an attempt to blast their way through the ice. (Perek 2018: 81)
(17) The wounded soldiers limped their way across the field. (Israel 1996: 218)
(18) Alfred Scanlon (. . .) coughed his way into the bedroom. (Perek 2018: 87)

According to Perek's (2018) diachronic study, the path-creation sense is the most common in all the periods he analyses (from 1830 to 2010) and, although the number of new verb types attested in the three schemas has increased along the years, the incidental-activity sense is still, as Goldberg (1995: 202) had already noted, still marginal and infrequent.

Together with the implication of difficult motion or overcoming of barriers pointed out by Goldberg, two additional sematic restrictions on the means interpretation are highlighted by the author. The first one is that the movement must be self-propelled (except for *work* and *find*), whereas the second states that motion must be directed; it cannot be aimless (Goldberg 1995: 212–4):

(19) *The butter melted its way out of the turkey.
(20) *She wandered her way over the field.

Both constraints have been claimed to be easily violated as many corpus examples clearly show that both non self-propelled, (21), and aimless movements, (22), are possible:

(21) The clothes were squeezing their way through the wringer. (Luzondo 2013: 353)
(22) James Bond womanising his way across the world (Hilpert 2014: 38)

Another remarkable feature displayed by English *way*-constructions is their ability to express actual, concrete movement in physical space as well as abstract motion, where the goal in not a real location:

(23) He made his way back to the Jeep.
(24) . . . you can research your way into Shakespeare's truth. (Mondorf 2011: 411)

For Perek (2018: 91–2), the abstract meanings conveyed by the *way*-construction arose as metaphorical extensions of concrete uses of certain common verbs frequently attested in the earlier stages of the construction, for example, *fight, struggle, find* or *make* in (23), and the later inclusion of new items which allow this kind of abstract use, such as *chat, joke, talk, buy*, or *research* in (24).

To my knowledge, it has not been until quite recently that a sentence type equivalent to the English *way*-construction in many formal and functional aspects has been argued to exist in Spanish. The results of the corpus analysis carried out in González Romero (2022) show that, although the construction is quite restricted in terms of its frequency and the range of verbs that occurs in it, both the path creation and the manner interpretations in the sense of Perek (2018) are attested. The first reading, as shown in (25)–(27), clusters around well delimited semantic classes: together with the basic verbs *hacer* and *encontrar*, the construction occurs with verbs of creation, such as *realizar* o *crear*, verbs of road buildind, for example, *trazar, forjar or allanar*, and verbs of fighting, such as *forzar*, *luchar* or *pelear* (González Romero 2022: 113–120):

(25) Los peces han evolucionado con una anatomía específica para permitirles hacer su camino a través del agua.
(26) Cada uno de los candidatos de este año trazó su camino a la estatuilla a golpe de papeles dramáticos.
(27) Los manifestantes (. . .) trataban de forzar su camino a la embajada de los Estados Unidos en Manila.

The manner interpretation is more exceptional than the path-creation sense and may occur with basic verbs of movement, such as *andar* in (28), or verbs of manner of motion, such as *serpentear* in (29) (González Romero 2022: 120–122):

(28) . . . parece que la película de Sonic empieza a andar su camino hasta nuestras salas de cine.

(29) Mientras serpentea su camino a través de las calles de la ciudad, usted será recibido por brillantes pegatinas rojas y verdes del movimiento anti-desalojo.

Finally, the rare incidental activity sense is not attested in González Romero's (2022) corpus.

4. English and Spanish *way*-constructions: A contrastive analysis

According to Goldberg (1995: 206), the verb *make* has a privileged status in the *way*-construction since it was the first one to appear in it and nowadays it is still the most frequently used. Semantically, it is strongly linked to the original meaning of the construction, the creation of a literal or metaphorical path. As regards *find*, even though it is not as productive as *make* in the corpus analysed, it also occurs very frequently in the *way*-construction.[4] Israel (1996: 221) observes that this verb, together with others like *keep, hold, take* or *snatch,* originally coded the idea of acquisition or maintenance of possession of path, a usage very common in early stages of the construction but which nowadays only *find* and a few other verbs still represent.

A quick look at the distribution of the corpora shows that *make* is, as expected in English, much more frequent than *find*, while in Spanish the tokens with *encontrar* outnumber those with *hacer*. A deeper analysis of

4 In Goldberg's (1995) corpus, the verb *make* amounts to 20 % of the tokens. Brunner and Hoffmann (2020: 17) reports that *find* makes up for 13.1 % of all the verbs in their sample; it is, however, outnumbered by *make,* which accounts for 34.8 % of the total number of instances.

the data indicates, in line with the most basic meaning of the construction, that *make* and *find* show a strong preference for the expression of physical movement, where both the path and the goal are concrete, with both human, occasionally animal, and inanimate subjects:

(30) Jen turned off the lamp and made her way downstairs into the living room, where the phone was already singing. (19-12-19, churchtimes.co.uk)
(31) The Night King (. . .) was finished when her Valyrian steel dagger found its way into his stomach. (19-04-29, Evening Standard)[5]

Similarly, the corpus of Spanish *way*-constructions shows a preference for the expression of literal movement with both human and inanimate subjects:

(32) Todo esto aporta indicios de que un grupo de H. Erectus pudo haber hecho su camino hacia el sudeste asiático continental, (. . .). (14-10-23, el Economista.es)
(33) Esta energía extra finalmente encontrará su camino de regreso a la atmósfera y aumentará las temperaturas en la Tierra. (12-01-30, europapress.es)

In a much lesser proportion, some tokens in the English corpus describe the figurative movement of both human and inanimate subjects through an abstract path, as in (34), or towards an abstract goal, as in (35):

(34) (. . .) she looks for love and makes her way through some awkward and painful dates. (19-05-29, plymouthherlad.co.uk)
(35) But even if liquidity is not the problem, money still does not find its way to the real economy. (19-12-23, eurogamer.net)

In the Spanish corpus the expression of abstract motion is also slightly less frequent, but equally possible with both human and inanimate subjects:

(36) Después de su infancia turbulenta, Lila es una persona que lucha para encontrar su camino hacia una vida corriente de casada. (15-05-20, El País)
(37) Este país más pronto que tarde, hará su camino hacia la libertad como estado. (15-06-20, Diario Vasco)

The high productivity and semantic richness of the English *way*-construction allows it to express a wide range of motion events. On the

5 Due to space limitations, some examples from the corpora have been shortened in order to remove information which is not relevant to properly understand the sentence exemplified.

contrary, the Spanish *way*-construction, probably due to his low productivity, is much more limited in this regard. It is worth remarking, nonetheless, that the construction is found in both languages in certain common contexts. One of them involves the description of physical motion related to natural events such as the movement of planets and stars, weather phenomena, and environmental issues, as in (38) and (39):

(38) An estimated eight million tonnes of plastic waste finds its way into the world's oceans every year. (19-04-03, BBC News)

(39) (. . .) los contaminantes orgánicos persistentes y otros productos manufacturados eventualmente encuentran su camino en la cadena alimentaria. (17-03-05, Lainformación.com)

When the reference is to abstract motion, English and Spanish share again similar contexts referring to video games and technological developments:

(40) The technology is still evolving but already it has found its way into households through the video game market (. . .). (19-10-17, chroniclelive.co.uk)

(41) (. . .) los científicos desarrollaron un sensor diminuto basado en un catéter que podría proporcionar una visión en tiempo real desde el interior de los vasos sanguíneos. Y ahora, el nuevo enfoque está encontrando su camino a las clínicas como parte de los procedimientos del mundo real. (16-09-29, ComputerHoy)

The functional similarity between English and Spanish *way*-constructions is not limited to these common contexts but, as pointed out above, to the fact that they are mostly used to express physical movement in both languages. They differ, however, in that this contrast is much sharper in English, which clearly favours the expression of physical movement, whereas the two types of motion are quite balanced in Spanish. A further distinction applies to the subject: while in English human subjects significantly outnumber inanimate subjects, in Spanish this second kind is slightly preferred.

5. On the difficulty reading of the *way*-construction

As mentioned in Section 3, the implication of external difficulties or obstacles to be tackled is central to the characterization of the English *way*-construction in Goldberg's influential analyses and is widely accepted in later accounts of this phenomenon (Israel 1996; Traugott and Trousdale 2013; Hilpert 2014; Perek 2018, among others). However, some other corpus-based works claim that, although this difficulty reading is strongly linked to the *way*-construction in the path-creation and manner interpretations, there are instances where no sense of difficult movement is found:

(42) (. . .) and she was transferred from the country theatres to London, where she laughed and danced her way into popularity. (Szczesniak 2013: 165)

In light of the absence of any sense of difficulty and effortfulness, Kuno et al. (2004: 85) propose that this implication is not an inherent meaning of the construction but can be instead be derived from the fact that it conveys the idea that the distance traversed is of a nontrivial or uncommon nature and that the movement is performed in an unusual manner. For Szczesniak (2013: 167), this reading, although not always available, is common enough to be taken as a prototypical meaning component of the construction but is not a necessary condition for the construction to be acceptable.

On the basis of the data analysed, the notion of difficult or hard movement associated with the *way*-construction should not be regarded, as far as the tokens with *make* and *find* are concerned, as a uniform and rigid meaning, but rather as a gradient where different nuances can be observed. In line with Goldberg's observations, many tokens in the corpus display a strong sense of difficulty which is explicitly highlighted by some element in the sentence, as in (43) and (44), where motion is hindered by physical or abstract barriers:

(43) (. . .) she often has to avoid up to half a dozen chuggers as she makes her way through the city centre (. . .). (19-09-20, derbytelegraph.co.uk)

(44) Concerns over a 'no-deal Brexit' are causing companies to tighten their belts until the UK finds its way out of the Brexit impasse. (19-05-24, Imperial College London)

Some other times the action itself is perceived as naturally implying a high degree of difficulty and significant obstacles, such as climbing a building in (45) or trafficking in illegal drugs in (46):

(45) But many do not know the story behind how he makes his way up to the top of one of the city's tallest buildings. (19-12-07, hulldailymail.co.uk)

(46) Most of this cocaine finds its way out through ports, where it is easier for gangs to bribe local officials. (19-12-21, dalymail.co.uk)

In some other instances, the meaning of difficulty becomes weaker and must be inferred from the neighbouring context or the speakers' knowledge of the world. In (47) and (48), for example, the subjects are likely to be surrounded by people who must be somehow dodged for them to reach their goal; in (49) the reference to the long time necessary for the technology to be available gives a glimpse of the high level of difficulty involved:

(47) President Trump has entered the House of Representatives. He is shaking hands with congressmen as he makes his way towards the podium. (19-02-05, Express.co.uk)

(48) To capture each picture, she will find her way to a quiet area with no one around (. . .). (19-01-15, Mirror.co.uk)

(49) But it would take almost two full centuries for the technology to make its way to wrists. Patek Philippe first made a commercial perpetual calendar wristwatch in 1925. (19-05-05, British GQ)

More than tough movement or barriers to overcome, the movement is sometimes perceived as gradual (Kuno et al. 2004: 84), indirect (Goldberg 1995: 204) or winding (Israel 1996: 220). In (50), the slow but continuous movement of the water can be perceived as gradual and winding, whereas the process of verification of news before been published in (51) may be seen as indirect motion undergone by an abstract entity:

(50) The sitting water will eventually find its way past seals and begin rusting the steel bearing shells. (19-10-12, road.cc)

(51) Our team of reporters had checked the validity of the story before it made its way onto our website and into print. (19-12-18, yorkshireeveningpost.co.uk)

Finally, as already noted in previous works, many examples apparently do not seem to convey any sense of difficulty. Particularly remarkable is the lack of this reading in many tokens with the verb *make* which describe the physical movement of human subjects. The following sentences, for example, only focus on the idea of the subject referent moving in a particular direction or to a particular place, information which is provided by the postverbal prepositional phrase. These tokens, nonetheless, are closely related to the core meaning of the *way*-construction in that the movement of an entity from one point to another always implies the creation of a figurative self-developed path resulting from the actor's own motion (Luzondo 2013: 358):

(52) She gracefully made her way down the stairs as she showed off her chic outfit. (19-04-16, Daily Mail)

(53) Following lunch, the President made his way from Buckingham Palace to Westminster Abbey and smiled for the camera while walking into the iconic building. (19-06-03, HELLO!)

In Luzondo's view, the existence of instances which do not convey the implication of difficult movement hindered by obstacles follows from the fact that 'the semantics of the *way*-construction can encode both the creation of a path due to the existence of obstacles, i.e. the *prototypical* sense of the configuration, and the creation of a path even though no barriers is present' (Luzondo 2013: 358).

Apart from the semantic elasticity of the *way*-construction itself pointed out by Luzondo (2013), among others, the wide range of meanings displayed by *make* and *find* in the construction may be argued to be the result of their high polysemy and semantic abstractness, which, as Perek (2018: 81) notes, make them not add much meaning to the sentence apart from the idea of motion conveyed by the *way*-construction itself, together with the information added by the context. Contextual clues are vital in this regard because, as seen in the examples above, they provide the sentence with its actual meaning.

The difficulty reading that so frequently arises in the English *way*-construction is also the preferred semantics of the Spanish pattern, where it is sometimes openly stated in the sentence. The manner adverbials *superando obstáculos* y *trabajosamente* in the following examples clearly suggest that the movement depicted is by no means easy:

(54) Cada equipo sale de un punto y siguiendo siempre una línea recta, harán su camino superando obstáculos hasta llegar a la meta. (18-03-12, Cadena SER)

(55) Admiro la elegancia de su método de cálculo, debe ser agradable pasear a través de estos campos a lomos del caballo de las matemáticas reales, mientras nosotros tenemos que hacer nuestro camino trabajosamente a pie. (12-09-17, 20minutos.es)

It is also frequent for this reading to be inferred from the surrounding context or our world knowledge. In (56), the textual reference to a faraway part of the planet implies a remarkable degree of difficulty, whereas in (57) the idea of travelling across the desert easily suggests a challenging and hard activity:

(56) En su artículo (. . .), el equipo describe sus investigaciones y ofrece una posible explicación de cómo estas sustancias químicas encontraron su camino a una parte tan remota del planeta. (15-02-27, Te Interesa)

(57) Mientras hacía su camino por el desierto, Heidin encontró una caravana de mercaderes y mulas y le compró tres caballos, monturas, maíz, harina, té, utensilios y botas. (13-02-03 lagranepoca)

The implication of indirect, gradual or sinuous movement found in English is also attested in Spanish. Notice in this regard the similarity between the following instances and the English sentences in (50) and (51), respectively, above:

(58) 'Con los años, las goteras ya han hecho su camino a través de las columnas del templo', apostillaba el cura. (16-08-22, Deia)

(59) El boca a boca viaja mucho más rápido que un libro, y de alguna manera siempre encuentra su camino hasta la producción, impresión y publicación. (13-04-25, traveler.es)

Sometimes, however, the construction does not seem to convey any implication beyond that of the movement of the subject along a path that must be created but sometimes may be also pre-established, as in (60):

(60) Más de la mitad de los turistas en Alaska (. . .) llegaron a través de una de las muchas compañías de cruceros. El resto, aproximadamente un tercio, volando, o hacen su camino desde los estados del sur en vehículos o por vía férrea. (13-07-19, lagranepoca)

6. The phraseological units with *way* and *camino*: A contrastive analysis

Together with the *way*-constructions examined in previous sections, the corpora analysed also contain instances of the sequence [SUBJ$_i$ [V [POSS$_i$ *way/camino*]]] which can be argued to illustrate the use of a phraseological unit (henceforth PU) where the nouns *way* and *camino* are understood in a metaphorical way:

(61) From relatively humble beginnings he made his way in a time when everything was very class-based. (19-03-17, The Sunday Post)

(62) 'William and Kate have a map in front of them. They're headed for monarchy', Burrell said, adding that the Queen and Charles have left Harry to find his way. (19-11-12, uk.news.yahoo.com)

(63) No importa si nadie te apoya o el qué dirán, tienes que hacer tu camino y luchar a muerte por conseguir lo que quieres. (13-05-09, El Mundo.es)

(64) Desgraciadamente, no todos los genios encuentran su camino, cada año unos cuantos se van por el desagüe. (15-01-15, eldiario.es)

Within the wide and sometimes confusing terminology in the field of phraseology, the term 'phraseological unit' will be used here in a broad sense to refer to '(...) a stable, cohesive combination of words with a fully or partially figurative meaning' (Naciscione 2010: 32). PUs do not have a compositional meaning and, therefore, speakers have to store them in their mental lexicon (Hoffmann 2017: 288).[6]

In the tokens attested in the corpora, the nouns *way* and *camino* do not refer to the actual path or route leading from one place to another but, as defined in English and Spanish, to 'a metaphorical path taken by a person through life or in pursuit of a particular goal, desire, etc.' (OED) and 'el rumbo de las personas, los negocios y las cosas' (Caballero y Rubio 1900: 214). Contrary to *way*-constructions, these occurrences do not express physical or abstract motion but describe the process of advancing in life or becoming successful in a job, activity, or profession. Thus, the sequence *make one's way* is defined in the OED as 'To advance or improve oneself in terms of wealth, rank, social status, etc.; to become prosperous or successful by one's own efforts; to get on in the world'. As regards Spanish, although the patterns *hacer/encontrar POSS camino* are not, to the best of my knowledge, listed in any dictionary, the synonymous PU *hacerse camino*, where the possessive element is replaced by a reflexive, does appear in the *Diccionario de la lengua española* (DLE) and some phraseological Spanish dictionaries such as Seco's (2004) and is defined as 'Alcanzar fama y provecho en la profesión u oficio que se

6 Gries (2008: 6) points out, however, that in some studies semantic non-compositionality is not a compulsory feature of phraseologisms.

ejerce' (Real Academia Española).[7] These units are very likely related to the conceptual metaphor LIFE IS A JOURNEY (Lakoff 1993) or LA VIDA ES UN CAMINO, which, as Mellado Blanco (2020: 52) points out, permeates Spanish phraseology.

The unbalanced number of English and Spanish *way*-constructions in the corpora mentioned in previous sections is reversed when it comes to the PU, which is highly productive in Spanish but is minimally represented in the English sample, where only a handful of examples have been attested (see Table 1 above). Again, this disproportion does not prevent us from obtaining relevant results. Whereas in the *way*-construction, the directional prepositional phrase is a substantial constituent of the pattern almost always necessary for the expression of movement, the PU does not need to include any compulsory prepositional component, as (61)-(64) above show. Besides, when it appears, this element does not have a directional but a locative meaning. The presence of such prepositional phrase is highly common in English, where the verbs *make* and *find* frequently collocate with the phrases *in the world* and *in life:*

(65) The teenager describes himself as a young freelance journalist trying to make his way in the world (. . .). (NOW, politico.eu)

(66) But it seems that he could not find his way in life again after leaving the Army. (19-09-06, hulldailymail.co.uk)

More often than not, the Spanish PU does not take any locative element, but when it does, the phrase mostly refers to the professional field where the subject develops their careers:

(67) Bautista se define como una persona discreta y trabajadora que hace su camino en el deporte de la raqueta. (16-10-15, MARCA.com)

(68) El ex boxeador Mike Tyson parece haber encontrado su camino en el mundo del entretenimiento. (13-05-13, Mujerhoy.com)

The dual meaning of the nouns *way* and *camino,* which denote a physical or abstract route travelled by the subject in the *way*-construction but a metaphorical path taken in the course of one's life in the PU, along

7 A similar pattern in Spanish is *abrirse camino*, which displays a very close meaning according to the DLE: 'Hallar, sugerir o allanar el medio de vencer una dificultad o mejorar de fortuna'.

with the oblique component, directional in the former but locative in the latter, seems to set the two sequences under analysis apart. However, the link between the *way*-construction and the PU may be argued to be the implication of difficult movement or overcoming of barriers. This notion, so recurring in the *way*-construction, also appears to be an integral semantic component of the PU because the idea of finding one's place in life or achieving success naturally implies undergoing a challenging and laborious process where obstacles and barriers of various types must be removed:

(69) (...) he did his best to overcome those obstacles and make his way in the world. (19-11-11, oxfordmail.co.uk)
(70) Tilley spent time on the dole as he studied, worked unpaid jobs and tried to find his way in the world when he was 24. (19-12-10, dailymail.co.uk)
(71) Eran niños durante la Guerra Civil, lo que adelantó su uso de razón en la más terrible de las adversidades: la muerte, el hambre, la destrucción, la incertidumbre... A partir de ahí, hicieron su camino conquista a conquista (...). (17-05-04, Heraldo.es)
(72) Me ha costado encontrar mi camino en la fotografía porque al principio vas dando tumbos pero luego poco a poco te metes en una vía única. (12-18-29, La Vanguardia)

Despite the considerable attention that the English *way*-construction has received over the last decades and the numerous corpus studies devoted to this topic, the existence of the PU just described has gone largely unnoticed. To my knowledge, only Traugott and Trousdale (2013: 85) mention what they call a 'sub-formula' of the *way*-construction with the verb *make* which 'involves adverse contexts in which the protagonist has encountered some difficulty and is understood to make the best way to wherever they are going'. The construction may contain an optional locative phrase which in the example provided by the authors is one of the most commonly attested in the present corpus:

(73) I will answer for it the book shall make its way in the world, much better than its master has done before it.

Furthemore, Traugott and Trousdale (2013: 88, fn 16) briefly refer to the fact that some tokens with the verb *find* retrieved from the *Corpus of Contemporary American English* (COCA) (Davies 2008-) are used in a figurative way with the sense 'managed to succeed', the same reading displayed by the tokens cited above.

7. Making our way into the lexicon-syntax continuum

One of the basic tenets upon which constructionist approaches to language are built is the hypothesis, widely known as the lexicon-syntax continuum, that linguistic knowledge is organised in terms of constructions which vary according to their complexity and abstraction, ranging from morphemes to abstract syntactic frames (see Goldberg 2006 and 2013; Hoffmann 2017; Croft and Cruse 2004, among many others). This continuum, as Begnini et al. (2015: 279) emphasize, 'allows the phraseologisms to be described more uniformly within the linguistic system, without relegating them to the lexicon'.

Given the lexicon-syntax continuum, the distinction between argument structure constructions and PUs is expected to get blurred in certain uses. Both Jackendoff (1997) and Goldberg (2013) note that there exist fixed expressions or semi-idiosyncratic examples with a specialised meaning, such as *wend one's way, worm ones's way* or *sleep ones's way*, derived from the *way*-construction. The same phenomenon also occurs, according to Goldberg, with the ditransitive, caused-motion and resultative constructions in English. In her view, the existence of such uses calls for a uniform analysis of constructions and idioms. In the same vein, Begnini et al. (2015: 280) observes that the ditransitive construction in Italian can also have a fixed phraseological instantiation which conveys the same meaning of transfer as the schematic construction in sentences such as *Anna ha dato a Giovanni del filo da torcere* ('Anna gave John a hard time').

Returning to the present analysis, the fact that the structural sequence [SUBJ$_i$ [V [POSS$_i$ *way/camino*]]] can instantiate in English and Spanish both the *way*-construction and the PU may also be argued to point to the existence of a continuum between the grammatical construction, a productive pattern that contains lexically open slots in which verbs from different semantic classes and directional phrases of various kinds may alternate in order to express motion through a literal or abstract path, and the PU, which conveys a metaphorical meaning that results from the lexically fixed and stable combination of the verbs *make, find, hacer* and *encontrar* and the nouns *way* and *camino* in their figurative use. Drawing on Jackendoff's and Benigni et al.'s accounts of the interface between syntax and the lexicon, the PUs analysed in the present work could be taken to be 'specialized fixed expression built out of the construction' (Jackendoff 1997: 173), or 'idiomatic instantiations of the schematic construction' (Begnini et al. 2015: 281). On the basis of the data analysed, the *way*-construction and the PU do not only share the same syntactic form but also a common semantic basis in both languages: the pervasive sense of difficulty and effort in the (actual or metaphorical) movement.

8. Concluding remarks

The corpus-based analysis presented in this work has provided us, despite the small size of the Spanish corpus, with valuable information that points out the occurrence of the construction in this language and shows the existence of significant semantic properties and recurring patterns of usage quite similar to those observed in the English corpus. As regards English, the data examined has unveiled the semantic richness of the *way*-construction with the verbs *make* and *find* and its versatile nature and ability to appear in many different contexts. The same applies to the PU, which exhibits in both languages common semantic properties, but differs as regards its productivity and the nature of the oblique constituent.

On the basis of the commonalities observed, a continuum between the schematic *way*-construction and the lexically fixed PU has been suggested, a proposal which tries to find its way into the on-going line of research which seeks to explore the connections between Construction Grammar and phraseology in order to analyse linguistic phenomena of different levels of complexity and abstraction under the same theoretical framework.

References

Benigni, Valentina / Ramusino, Paola C. / Mollica, Fabio / Schafroth, Elmar. 2015. How to Apply CxG to Phraseology: A Multilin-Gual Research Project. *Journal of Social Sciences*, 11/3, 275–288.

Brunner, Thomas / Hofmann, Thomas. 2020. The *Way*-Construction in World Englishes. *English World-Wide*, 41/1, 1–32.

Caballero y Rubio, R. 1900. *Diccionario de modismos (frases y metáforas)*. Madrid: Librería de Antonino Romero. Retrieved from https://www.bvfe.es/es/directorio-bibliografico-diccionarios-vocabularios-glosarios-tratados-y-obras-lexicografia/15179-diccionario-de-modismos-frases-y-metaforas.html

Croft, William / Cruse, David A. 2004. *Cognitive Linguistics.* Cambridge: Cambridge University Press.

Davies, Mark. 2008. *The Corpus of Contemporary American English* (COCA). Retrieved from https://www.english-corpora.org/coca/.

Davies, M. 2016. *NOW Corpus* (News on the WEB). Retrieved from https://www.english-corpora.org/now/

Davies, M. 2018. *Corpus del Español. NOW Corpus* (News on the Web). Retrieved from https://www.corpusdelespanol.org/now/

Fanego, Teresa. 2018. A Construction of Independent Means: The History of the *Way* Construction Revisited. *English Language and Linguistics*, 23/3, 671–699.

Glosbe Dictionary English-Spanish. Retrieved from https://en.glosbe.com/es/en

Goldberg, Adele E. 1995. *Constructions: A Construction Grammar Approach to Argument Structure*. Chicago: University of Chicago Press.

Goldberg, Adele E. 2006. *Constructions at Work. The Nature of Generalization in Language.* New York: Oxford UniversityPress.

Goldberg, Adele E. 2013. Argument Structure Constructions versus Lexical Rules or Derivational Verb Templates. *Mind & Language*, 28/4, 435–465.

González Romero, Luisa. 2022. Sobre la expresión del movimiento en el español actual: la construcción de CAMINO. In Cuartero Otal, Juan et al. (eds.), *La interfaz léxico-gramática. Contrastes entre el español y las lenguas germánicas.* Berlin: Peter Lang, 101–135.

Gries, Stefan Th. 2008. Phraseology and Linguistic Theory: A Brief Survey. In Granger, Silviane / Meunier. Fanny (eds.), *Phraseology: An Interdisciplinary Perspective.* Amsterdam/Philadelphia: John Benjamins, 3–25.

Hilpert. Martin. 2014. *Construction Grammar and Its Application to English.* Edimburgh: University Press.

Hoffmann, Thomas. 2017. The Renaissance of Constructions: From Constructions to Construction Grammars. In Dancygier, Barbara (ed.), *The Cambridge Handbook of Cognitive Linguistics.* Cambridge: Cambridge University Press, 284–309

Israel, Michael. 1996. The *Way* Constructions Grow. In Goldberg, Adele (ed.), *Conceptual Structure, Discourse and Language.* Stanford: CSLI, 217–230

Jackendoff, Ray. 1990. *Semantic Structures.* Cambridge, Mass.: MIT Press.

Jackendoff, Ray. 1997. *The Architecture of the Language Faculty.* Cambridge, MA: MIT Press.

Jackendoff, Ray. 2002. *Foundations of Language: Brain, Meaning, Grammar, Evolution.* Oxford: Oxford University Press.

Kuno, Susumu / Takami, Ken-ichi / Courtenay, Karen / Decker, Nan. 2004. The Way Construction and Unergativity. In Kuno, Susumu / Takami, Ken-ichi (eds.), *Functional Constraints in Grammar: On the Unergative-Unaccusative Distinction.* Amsterdam/Philadelfia: John Benjamins, 67–104.

Lakoff, George. 1993. *The Contemporary Theory of Metaphor.* In Ortony, Andrerw (ed.), *Metaphor and Thought*, 2nd ed. Cambridge: University Press, 202–251.

Levin, Beth / Rapoport, Tova. 1988. Lexical Subordination. *CLS* 24/1, 275–289.

Luzondo Oyón, Alba. 2013. Revisiting Goldberg's Semantic Constraints on the 'way' Construction. *RESLA* 26, 349–364.

Marantz, Alec. 1992. The *Way*-Construction and the Semantics of Direct arguments in English: A Reply to Jackendoff. *Syntax and Se-mantics*, 26, 179–188.

Mateu, Jaume. 2000. Paths and Telicity in Idiomatic Constructions: A Lexical-Syntactic Approach to the Way Construction. *Paper presented at 2000 ESSLLI Workshop on Paths and Telicity in Event Structure*, Universidad de Birmingham.

Mateu, Jaume. 2005. Arguing Our Way to the "Direct Object Restriction" on English Resultatives. *The Journal of Comparative Germanic Linguistics* 8, 55–82

McColm, Dan. 2019. *A Cross-Linguistic Investigation of the Way-Construction in English, Dutch, and German.* Unpublished doctoral dissertation, University of Edinburgh.

Mellado Blanco, Carmen. 2020. Simbología religiosa y metáforas del CAMINO en la Biblia. In Dal Maso, Elena (ed.), *De aquí a Lima. Estudios fraseológicos del español de España e Hispa-noamérica.* Venezia: Edizioni Ca'Foscari, 45–64.

Mondorf, Britta. 2011. Variation and Change in English Resultative Constructions. *Language Variation and Change* 22, 397–421.

Naciscione, Anita. 2010. *Stylistic Use of Phraseological Units in Discourse.* Amsterdam/ Philadelphia: John Benjamins.

Oxford English Dictionary Online (OED). Oxford University Press. Retrieved from https://www.oed.com/

Pedersen, Johan. 2013. The Way-Construction and Cross-Linguistic Variation in Syntax. Implications for Typological Theory. In Paradis, Carita / Hudson, Jean / Magnusson, Ulf (eds.), *The Construal of Spatial Meaning: Windows into Conceptual Space.* Oxford: University Press, 236–262.

Perek, Florent. 2018. Recent Change in the Productivity and Schematicity of the *Way*-Construction: A Distributional Semantic Analysis. *Corpus Linguistics and Linguistic Theory* 14, 65–97.

Real Academia Española. *Diccionario de la lengua española* (DLE). Retrieved from https://www.rae.es

Seco, Manuel / Andrés, Olimpia / Ramos, Gabino. 2004. *Diccionario Fraseológico documentado del español actual.* Madrid: Aguilar.

Szczesniak. Konrad. 2013. You Can't Cry Your Way to Candy: Motion Events and Paths in the x's Way Construction. *Cognitive Linguistics*, 24/1, 159–194.

Takao, Takayuki. 2000. Aspectual Nature of the Path Expression in the Way-Construction. *The Toyo Review,* 32, 11–23.

Talmy, Leonard. 1985. Lexicalization Patterns: Semantic Structure in Lexical Form. In Shoepen, Timothy (ed.), *Language Typology and Linguistic Description*, Vol 3. Cambridge: University Press, 57–149.

Talmy, Leonard. 2000. *Toward a Cognitive Semantics: Typology and Process in Concepts Structuring*. Cambridge, MA: MIT Press.

Traugott, Elizabeth C. / Trousdale, Graeme. 2013. *Constructionalization and Constructional Changes*. Oxford: University Press. Online corpora and dictionaries

YOLANDA FERNÁNDEZ-PENA / JAVIER PÉREZ-GUERRA

Why *why*-fragments? A corpus-based constructionist analysis of their form and meaning

1. Introduction[1]

This chapter presents a corpus-based analysis of *why*-fragments in contemporary English. Fragments are independent linguistic expressions that, though they lack an orthodox clausal design, have 'the potential to function as a [complete] clause constituent' (Bowie and Aarts 2016: 261). The concept of 'fragment' is defined as any functionally stand-alone and syntactically and prosodically independent constituent which is formally reduced but nonetheless semantically, discursively and pragmatically equivalent to the corresponding complete clause in propositional meaning, force and communicative function (Fernández-Pena 2021). This is the case of the fragmentary utterances[2] in (1)–(5), extracted from the British component of the *International Corpus of English* (ICE-GB; Nelson et al. 2002):

1. But now it was filthy; it smelled of dead things and dripped with slime. *That a star, the brightest star in the heavens, should come to this.* (~'How amazing it is that a star...') [ICE-GB: W2F-020 #110:1]
2. P.S. *Good luck to Simon for his exams!* (~'I wish good luck to Simon...') [ICE-GB: W1B-004 #111:3]

1 We are grateful to the Spanish State Research Agency and the European Regional Development Fund (grant no. PID2020-117541GB-I00), and the Regional Government of Galicia (grant no. ED431C 2021/52).

2 Relevant fragments are italicised throughout the paper.

3. There lies the problem. *Not much to entertain you with on the Nrth Line tonight* (~'There is not much to entertain you with...') [ICE-GB: W1B-010 #087:2]
4. B: They would have said 'she is little and small <,> and arrogant'
   A: *Why arrogant* (~'Why would they have said you are arrogant?') [ICE-GB: S1B-046 #106:1:A]
5. A: Emma do you want to second that
   H: Yeah *why not* (~'Why would I not want to second that?') [ICE-GB: S1B-079 #080:1:H]

The interpretation of a fragment is often identical to that of the corresponding complete clause, as in (2) and (3). In other cases, however, the meaning of the fragment can be somewhat different, conveying an additional nuance that is distinct from the 'orthodox' or 'canonical' meaning of its non-fragmentary counterpart. This leads to a peculiar form-meaning constructional pairing (Goldberg 2019: 73), as exemplified in (6), where the fragment in italics implies surprise or counter-expectation:

6. A: I hear that John may wear a tuxedo to the ball...
   B: *Him wear a tuxedo?!* (Akamajian 1984: 3)

In the case of the *why*-fragments illustrated in (5) above and (7) below, the *wh*-proform *why* is followed by the so-called 'remnant', which may be a nominal, adjectival, adverbial, prepositional or clausal constituent or a bare infinitival predicate:

7. a. Why *why*-fragments?
   b. Why so specific?
   c. Why now?
   d. Why in this paper?
   e. Why this type of fragment exists?
   f. Why deal with *why*-fragments?

Like other fragmentary constructions, *why*-fragments may convey the 'orthodox' or 'canonical' interrogative interpretation of a complete *why*-clause, but also an 'enriched' interpretation: either (i) a potential 'modal' meaning similar to the one of the corresponding complete clause with the modal auxiliaries *should* or *would* (Johnson 1975: 487;

Weir 2017: 406; Zaitsu 2018, 2020) or (ii) an added 'presupposition of uniqueness' (Weir 2014), as exemplified in (8) and (9), respectively:

8. Why deal with *why*-fragments? (~'Why should we deal with *why*-fragments?')
9. Why *why*-fragments? (~'Why *why*-fragments and not any other type of fragment?')

The enriched meaning expressed by the *why*-fragments in (8) and (9) cannot be derived from their component parts or from the canonical complete *why*-clause, showing that speakers and hearers conventionalise not only the specific design of the fragment as a unique construction but also its so-called 'conversational postulate' (Gordon and Lakoff 1971). *Why*-fragments may therefore be said to constitute a special pairing of form and meaning, i.e. a 'construction' (Goldberg 2006: 5) (see Section 2).

This chapter presents an analysis of the *why*-fragments attested in representative samples retrieved from the spoken components of the two editions of the *British National Corpus*: BNC1994 (BNC Consortium 2007) and Spoken BNC2014 (Love et al. 2017). The aim of the study is two-fold: firstly, to determine whether the enriched interpretation of *why*-fragments can be claimed to be motivated by linguistic factors; and, secondly, to explore the evolution of that conventionalised meaning in recent diachrony. A multivariate analysis of potential linguistic proxies for the enriched (versus canonical) interpretation of *why*-fragments was carried out, taking into account both formal (i.e. syntactic design of the construction: *why* + type of remnant; mismatches of category and case between antecedents and remnants; island violations between remnants and antecedent sites) and semantic/pragmatic (i.e. canonical versus enriched interpretation) variables. The null hypothesis H_0 is the lack of connection between the enriched interpretation of *why*-fragments and their linguistic characterisation. To either confirm or reject this hypothesis, the data were modelled around the independent linguistic predictors outlined above and the response variable 'canonical versus 'enriched interpretation'.

The chapter is organised as follows. Section 2 presents a constructionist account of fragments, while Section 3 focuses on the form and meaning of *why*-fragments, and offers a review of previous literature on the topic. Section 4 explains the aims and methodology of the study (Section 4.1), the variables analysed (Section 4.2), the statistical analysis (Section 4.3) and the results obtained (Section 4.4), and Section 5 proposes some conclusions and avenues for future research.

2. A constructionist account of fragments

The usage-based perspective adopted for this constructionist account assumes, among other principles: (i) that speakers are 'at once impressively creative and impressively repetitive' as far as their linguistic productions are concerned (Goldberg 2013: 26), and (ii) that these processes of creativity and repetition go beyond the level of individual lexical items and affect entire constructions (see Van de Velde et al. 2015). If constructions are 'part of a lexicon-syntax continuum' (Hoffman and Trousdale 2013: 1), there can be no radical division between (word-level) lexicon and (construction-level) syntax, as claimed, for example, by generative language models.

The analysis proposed here adopts the definition of 'construction' offered by so-called Cognitive Construction Grammar. The concept of construction has undergone substantial modification since Goldberg (1995) defined it in her seminal monograph on the subject. According to Goldberg (2006: 5),

> Any linguistic pattern is recognized as a construction as long as some aspect of its form or function is not strictly predictable from its component parts or from other constructions recognizable to exist. In addition, patterns are stored as constructions even if they are fully predictable as long as they occur with sufficient frequency.

The main condition for a linguistic expression to be regarded as a construction in Cognitive Construction Grammar is, therefore, at least partial or even slight non-predictability (see Hilpert 2019: 13). Subsidiarily, if the expression is semantically and structurally transparent (i.e. if it evinces no degree of non-predictability), it can also qualify as a construction provided it is sufficiently frequent in language.[3] The criterion of non-predictability is borrowed from other usage-based approaches, according to which expressions may develop 'special pragmatic implications that can lead to special meaning', when these implications are not derived from the sequences' forms and/or interpretations (Bybee 2013: 5). Goldberg (2019: 73) reformulates the conventional learned pairing of form and function, and provides a more psychological definition of construction:

> Learners create lossy [not fully specified] memory traces of formal patterns and their associated messages-in-context within their hyper-dimensional conceptual space. [. . .] New memory traces are related to previously existing memory traces, creating emergent clusters that relate formal properties with relevant aspects of the message-in-context.

In addition to non-predictability and sufficient frequency, the notion of construction adopted in this study also takes into account the following features:

- Efficiency. 'Fewer and shorter constructions are easier to learn and produce than more or longer constructions' (Goldberg 2019: 8). This study analyses the *why*-fragment, a construction type that, unlike its associated *why*-sentence construction, lacks the functional structure of a complete clause (i.e. verbal group, grammatical subject, etc.). The classification of *why*-fragments as constructions is in keeping with the efficiency principle of ease of processing in relation to reduced sequences defended by Cognitive Construction Grammar.
- Complexity. The (not always predictable) learned pairing of form and function in constructions is observed at varying levels, ranging from words (e.g. lexical alternation within a given argument-structure realisation, as in *give* versus *lend* in ditransitive constructions) to word-order issues (e.g. in transitive verb-particle constructions; see Cappelle 2006). As regards formal complexity, constructions may be either atomic (i.e. lexically

3 Over time, the defining criterion of high frequency, as established in Goldberg (1995), has become less restrictive (see Goldberg 2019: 54).

specified), as in single words and fixed phrases such as *Goodbye*, or fully/partially schematic (e.g. *call* NP_{agent} *a liar*, ditransitive Subj V Obj_1 Obj_2) (see Smirnova and Sommerer 2020: 5). This study presents an analysis of the semi-specified schematic *why*-fragment construction, which comprises the atomic governing item *why* and a schematic remnant realised by a range of constituent types.

- Productivity. As observed in Smirnova and Sommerer (2020: 9), productivity in Construction Grammar is conceptualised in terms of the range of lexical items that may enter a construction and the construction's extensibility to host new items. The productivity of the *why*-fragment construction is corroborated not only by the wide range of categories that may occupy its remnant slot but also by the taxonomy of these remnant categories, which has increased in recent years.
- Entrenchment. This notion corresponds to the degree of 'usualisation' or 'institutionalisation' (Brinton and Traugott 2005) of a construction by the community. To quote Goldberg (2019: 73),

> Constructions are accessed in a content-addressable way during both comprehension and production, which encourages entrenched formulations to be reused. [. . .] Novel expressions are licensed by existing constructions to the extent that the existing combination of constructions covers the hyper-dimensional space required to include the novel expression.

A feature that is common to all linguistic approaches is the recognition of alternation. While alternations between and among constructions is not a pivotal aspect of Cognitive Construction Grammar, Goldberg (2019: 6) acknowledges the activation of and, more importantly in the context of this study, 'competition' between multiple constructions when speakers produce utterances. What is more, the existence of alternatives is claimed to increase the constructions' productivity and frequency. To quote Goldberg (2019: 73) again, '[a] construction is strengthened, becoming more accessible, when new representations overlap with existing representations. The range of a construction is broadened when witnessed instances are more variable'.

Using Perek's (2021) terminology, this study analyses the high-level, alternation-based constructeme *why*-construction and the collostructional pair *why*-fragment/*why*-sentence (on the characterisation of sentences as constructions, see Hilpert 2019: 130). Since they belong to the same network and are linked to a single constructeme, allostructions cannot be completely different from a constructionist perspective. De Vaere et al. (2020: 99) concludes vaguely that allostructions should be 'sufficiently, though not completely, equivalent'. Also, as acknowledged by Cappelle (2006), allostructions do not necessarily occur in complementary distribution. In fact, 'they may substitute for one another without bringing about a change in (truth-conditional) meaning', as occurs in the case of the *why*-allostructional pair (Cappelle 2006: 19).

Perek (2021: 601) points out that opting for one construction over another may depend not only on its central formal and semantic characteristics but also on processing factors (e.g. relative constituent lengths and complexity) or more discursive properties (e.g. given versus new informative loads). Constructional competition may therefore be analysed by weighing the contribution of linguistic predictors to a multi-variable scenario against the different constructions involved. Perek (2021: 601) claims that 'subjects rely on alternation-based generalizations more often than purely constructional ones in their sorting behavior'. This study identifies the linguistic factors that explain the competition or variation between orthodox *why*-sequences, whose interpretation corresponds to that of a complete *why*-sentence construction, and more conventionalised *why*-fragments, which convey enriched meanings.

3. On *why*-fragments: Form and function

Wh-constructions (defined here as conventionalised, non-compositional pairings of form and meaning showing some level of entrenchment) have already received a considerable amount of attention from linguists. Põldvere and Paradis (2019, 2020) examines so-called 'reactive *what-x*' constructions, as in *what and then a little robot brings it to you?*, which, unlike their corresponding sentential versions, convey a reaction and a request at the same time, and whose main constituents, the *wh*-proforms and the phrasal/clausal complements, are linked in a different way from traditional clausal syntactic relations. Kim and Davies (2019) analyses *what-with* absolute constructions, such as *What with him being a physician[, he's more pragmatic]*, whose non-compositional meaning involves a negative implication from the point of view of the speaker as well as their default interpretation as reason adjuncts. Neither of these readings is conveyed by either the corresponding complete clause (*Since he was a physician…*) or the prototypical absolute construction (*He being a physician…*). Michaelis and Feng's (2015) study focuses on the English Split Interrogative, as in *What are you, a senior?*, and the idiosyncratic properties that suggest that 'it is more than the sum of its parts; that is, it is not simply an *wh*-interrogative combined with a suggested response in the form of a tag' (p. 15). The so-called WHX construction (e.g. *what the hell…?*) is the focus of an article by Hugou (2017), which highlights both the intensity reading conventionalised by such expressions and the semantic bleaching undergone by the set of the nominals present in the construction. Fernández et al. (2007) analyses stand-alone *wh* non-sententials, such as *[Only wanted a couple weeks.] What?*, particularly in relation to their reprise reading, a value not attested in the corresponding reconstructed complete sentences. Massive pied-piping utterances (*[The doctor told me to eat.] Eat what?*), which have modal semantics, are the focus of Weir (2017). Finally, *wh*-exclamatives have been the subject of studies by Siemund (2015, 2017) and Heine et al. (2020): Siemund (2015, 2017) analyses the default exclamative and evaluative sentence functions fulfilled by *what-a/how*-constructions, while Heine et al. (2020) focuses on their surprise, factive, affective and quantificational interpretations.

Our study looks at *why*-fragments, whose characterisation as constructions derives from their idiosyncratic interpretation, their formal properties and the fact that they are not infrequent in English (to quote Zaitsu 2018: 1, they are 'incredibly frequent in production').

Formally, a *why*-fragment, also known as *why*-stripping (Kim and Abeillé 2019: 367), consists of a *wh*-proform and an overt non-*wh* remnant. The following categories may occur as focal remnants of *why*-fragments (see Section 4.2.2): nominal, adjectival, adverbial and prepositional phrases, Small Clauses and non-finite clauses (specifically, bare infinitival clauses; these are also referred to as 'matrix infinitival *why*-questions' in Bhatt 1998, 'tenseless clauses' in Collins 1991, and 'bare infinitive constructions' in Duffley and Enns 1996 and Huddleston and Pullum 2002: 835, 874).

The constructionist analysis of *why*-fragments is warranted by their conventionalised syntactic characteristics and special interpretation, which transform the *why*-fragment into a non-compositional form-meaning pairing. As regards form, *why*-fragments cannot be reconstructed as instances of ellipsis or sluicing for the following reasons (unless otherwise indicated, examples are taken from Kim and Abeillé 2019). Firstly, only *why* is attested in *why*-stripping, whereas *wh*-proforms other than *why* are possible in sluicing, as shown in (10):

10. John ate something, but I don't know *what* (~~John ate~~).

Secondly, *why*-fragments are mostly restricted to main clauses, while sluicing occurs in matrix and embedded clauses (see (10) above). Only *why*-fragments with adverbial remnants may be found in embedded contexts, as in (11):

11. It doesn't really matter anymore. You'll see *why shortly*.

Thirdly, *why*-fragments tolerate violations of connected prepositions, as in (12), case (13), and category (14)–(15):[4]

12. Robin's body had been found at the golf course just a half mile from her home under some leaves. *Why on the golf course?* [COCA 2005 SPOK]
13. They say that Saddam$_{\text{nominative}}$ is a dictator, but *why him*$_{\text{accussative}}$? [COCA 2003 SPOK]
14. What are these white men [so angry]$_{\text{Adjective Phrase}}$ about? [. . .] *Why [the anger]*$_{\text{Noun Phrase}}$*?* [COCA 2010 SPOK]
15. There is [safety issues]$_{\text{Noun Phrase}}$ as well. *Why that*$_{\text{pronoun}}$*?* [COCA 2004 SPOK]

4 Antecedents of the remnant are underlined throughout.

Fourthly, the remnant may not select the lexical item in the preceding clause but a synonym, as shown in (16), or even a discourse-new expression, in (17):

16. We've got to get over to your apartment fast. *Why the hurry?* [COCA 2008 FIC]
17. And as I understand it, Nicole, that's what drew you into the movement when you were 9 years old. *Why at that age?* [COCA 1999 SPOK]

Finally, the remnant in the *why*-fragment may correlate with an item attested in a complex syntactic environment in the antecedent clause or 'island' (e.g. coordinating construction (18), or modifier/complement of a noun phrase (19)). This would lead to ungrammaticality if the *why*-fragment were an instance of ellipsis, since extraction from an elliptical context would result in a movement violation:

18. Well, I think what's happening is both risky and immoral. *Why immoral?* [COCA 2009 SPOK] (Coordinate Structure Constraint)
19. A pack of lean dogs, all different colors, loped across the street far ahead of her. *Why dogs?* [COCA 1992 FIC] (Complex NP Constraint)

As far as meaning is concerned, although the interpretation of *why*-fragments can be equivalent to that of complete *why*-sentences (see, for example, Zaitsu 2018: 2, 2020), the fragments may also convey enriched meanings of uniqueness, as in (20) (see Nakao et al. 2012; Weir 2014: Yoshida et al. 2014, 2015), and of deontic modality, as in (21) (Gordon and Lakoff 1971: 481; Johnson 1975: 487; Huddleston and Pullum 2002: 835, 874; Zaitsu 2018: 1–3), which are not naturally conveyed by the corresponding complete *why*-sentences.

20. A: John danced with Mary.
    B: *Why with Mary?* (~'Why with Mary, and not with anybody else?') (Yoshida et al. 2015: 327)

21. Why take your dog on a walk in the rain? (~'Why should you take your dog on a walk in the rain?') (Zaitsu 2018: 3)

4. A corpus-based analysis of *why*-fragments

4.1. Aims and methodology

The aim of this study is to explore the diachronic evolution of the constructionalisation of *why*-fragments as special form-meaning pairings, where the formally reduced *why*-question conveys a meaning different from that of the complete *why*-clause: either a modal meaning, very similar to that of *should* or *would* (Johnson 1975: 487; Zaitsu 2018: 1), or a nuance of uniqueness or exclusiveness (Weir 2014). The methodology used was a multivariate analysis of potential linguistic proxies for the enriched (versus canonical) interpretation of the *why*-fragments.

The research questions proposed by the study are as follows:

1. Is the enriched interpretation of *why*-fragments motivated by linguistic factors?
2. Is that enriched interpretation favoured over time in recent diachrony?

To answer these questions, data were extracted from the spoken components of the two editions of the *British National Corpus*: BNC1994 (BNC Consortium 2007) and Spoken BNC2014 (Love et al. 2017).[5] It should be noted, however, that these two corpora are not fully comparable. The spoken component of BNC1994 contains transcriptions of both 'formal encounters from particular institutional settings', known as the 'context-governed part', and spontaneous conversations, known as the 'demographically-sampled part' (henceforth, BNC1994 DS) (Love et al. 2017: 321). It is only the latter, the 'conversational part' (Leech

5 The written components of the two editions of the BNC were also surveyed using CQPweb (https://cqpweb.lancs.ac.uk) for BNC1994 and #LancsBox X (Brezina and Platt 2022) for Written BNC2014 (Brezina et al. 2021). The data from Written BNC2014 had to be discarded, however, because #LancsBox X, currently the only platform where Written BNC2014 is available, (i) does not support punctuation searching and (ii) provides a contextual size (10 words before and after KWIC) that is too limited to carry out a qualitative analysis of the meaning of *why*-fragments.

et al. 2001: 2), that is comparable to Spoken BNC2014, where only recorded conversations in informal contexts are represented (see Love et al. 2017: 324–325). This is not the only point of difference, however. The two corpora also differ in size: whereas Spoken BNC2014 contains 11,422,617 words and 1,197,091 utterances (BNC2014 User Manual 2018: 17), BNC1994 DS contains only 4,233,962 words and 610,557 so-called 's-units' (i.e. elements 'more or less equivalent to sentences'; Burnard 2007).[6]

To retrieve the data, the study used the CQPweb interface[7] and four queries summarised by the following pattern:

why + (+) (+) (+) \?

The queries look for *why* followed by a minimum of one word and a maximum of four words before a question mark.[8] Instances containing five or more words between *why* and the question mark were not included because preliminary analyses confirmed that the occurrence of *why*-fragments with five words is anecdotal (Pérez-Guerra and Fernández-Pena 2022). Additionally, since '[t]he only feature of written punctuation retained in the Spoken BNC2014 transcription scheme is the question mark, which was to mark questions' (BNC2014 User Manual 2018: 37), only interrogative fragments were retrieved.

A total of 1,034 hits were extracted from BNC1994 DS and 2,676 from Spoken BNC2014. These data were manually pruned to exclude irrelevant instances (in italics below), such as canonical non-fragmentary main sentences (22), fragments with a *wh*-remnant (23) (see Kim and Abeillé 2019), and fragments which actually constituted two (potentially) different questions (24) or turns by different speakers (25):

6 Information retrieved from http://www.natcorp.ox.ac.uk/docs/URG/BNCdes.html#BNCcompo.

7 Access to the CQPweb interface: https://cqpweb.lancs.ac.uk.

8 The backslash (\) in the query is used to 'escape' the metacharacter (i.e. the use of the question mark as a wildcard) and, therefore, to match the literal character (see https://cqpweb.lancs.ac.uk/doc/cqpweb-simple-syntax-help.pdf).

22. what the hell? *Why won't you reply?* That's obviously her coming and trying isn't it (.) like trying to make amends [Spoken BNC2014: SK3B 1765]
23. A: well why didn't we go in for it?
    B: *why what?*
    A: why didn't we do a sheep? [Spoken BNC2014 ST64 54]
24. A: I won't [work] on New Year's Eve [. . .]
    B: *why you talking that off?*
    A: no [Spoken BNC2014: SNK6 174]
25. A: well *why*
    B: *all these then* [Spoken BNC2014: S6BS 2209–2210]

Cases where *why* occurs alone (26) or is followed by *not* on its own (27) and/or interpersonal or textual (non-ideational) material (28)–(31) were also discarded because they do not allow for constructional variation (see Alves-Castro 2020):

26. A: I can't print anything for you.
    B: *Why?*
    A: *Why?* Because the machine's been down since last Thursday. [BNC1994 DS: KPP 1256]
27. A: you can't have any more either
    B: *why not?*
    A: cos you've all had three sausages [Spoken BNC2014: S47C 329]
28. A: Put your foot back in there.
    B: *Why mum?* why doesn't, mum my foot on here. [BNC1994 DS KC5 629]
29. A: Ah, that's really funny! Erm could be nice about it.
    B: No!
    C: *Why not indeed?* [BNC1994 DS KCW 2871]
30. A: and then I was like you really can't have all three bottles of dad's red wine (.) so we erm
    B: *why the fuck not?*
    A: I felt bad [Spoken BNC2014: S37K 508]
31. I think it was Hasselblad supplied the cameras (.) so *why on earth?* [Spoken BNC2014: SVBJ 515]

Finally, non-fragmentary subordinate sentences (32), repetition of the same fragment by the same speaker (33), and unfinished (34) or unclear (35) utterances were also omitted:

32. Do you know *why they smell*? [BNC1994 DS KCX 5015]
33. A: I think like we could maybe go for less (.) but more special [. . .]
    B: why less? *Why less?* Then we'd just (.) you mean like healthier? [Spoken BNC2014: S2AX 749]
34. A: wasn't it that wasn't working?
    B: yeah (.) *why the?* it went really weird (.) I dunno what caused that [Spoken BNC2014: S682 955]
35. A: Who? Who?
    B: *Why [unclear]?*
    C: Because you just said you were gonna? [BNC1994 DS: KPL 357]

The number of valid instances after manual pruning was 82 in BNC1994 DS and 177 in Spoken BNC2014. In view of the different sizes of these two sources and the clausal nature of the *why*-fragments, the data were normalised per one million sentences in each of the corpora, resulting in a frequency of 134.3 in BNC1994 DS and 147.9 in Spoken BNC2014. The frequencies reveal a slight, though not significant, increase in productivity over the time span under analysis ($\chi^2(1)=0.43$, $p=0.512$).

4.2. Variables analysed

The null hypothesis in this chapter, as established in Section 2, was that the choice between canonical and enriched meanings was not influenced by linguistic factors. To either corroborate or reject this hypothesis, the data from the BNC corpora were analysed to determine the relationship between the binary dependent or response variable 'canonical/enriched meaning' (Section 4.2.1) and four independent variables: corpus, category of remnant, category mismatch between remnant and antecedent or correlate, and island violations between the remnant and the antecedent site (Section 4.2.2).

Some adjustments to the dataset were made to facilitate the implementation of the statistical model described in Sections 4.3 and 4.4 owing to the scarcity of examples in some of the levels. The variable 'category' thus combines information about the category of the remnant and about the existence of case mismatches between the remnant and the antecedent clause, and the original levels of the variable (fully nominal, pronominal; infinitival, *–ing*, *–ed*; adjectival, adverbial, prepositional, Small Clause) have been reduced to three (plus the case mismatch sub-levels): 'nominal', 'non-finite' and 'other'.

4.2.1. Dependent variable: 'Semantics'

The dependent variable 'semantics' encodes the meaning of the *why*-fragment as either (i) canonical, as in (36), or (ii) enriched, either by an added 'modal' meaning or by an added nuance of 'uniqueness', as in (37) and (38), respectively.

36. A: I know I felt guilty sort of sat inside but I was like—[. . .]
    B: *why guilty*? that's a curious word [Spoken BNC2014: SUPV 345]
37. A: I mean erm you've gotta pay the debt in the end whatever.
    B: Course you have. [unclear]
    C: *Why keep putting it off?* [BNC1994 DS: KBF 6316]
38. she'd go can you shake the lett- the rattle like the object in front of you shake it left to right and I was like well why do it left to right? *why not right to left?* [Spoken BNC2014: S5XD 3395]

The occurrence of canonical meanings in the data (179; 69.11 %) more than doubles that of enriched interpretations (80; 30.89 %).

4.2.2. Independent variables

(i) 'corpus', i.e. BNC1994 DS and Spoken BNC2014. Of the total number of instances retrieved, nearly a third (82; 31.66 %) belong to BNC1994 DS; the remaining two thirds (177; 68.34 %) belong to the 2014 edition.
(ii) 'category (of remnant)' controls for the category of the remnant. Three broad categories were identified: 'nominal',

which accounts for 38.61 % of the data (100 instances); 'non-finite', accounting for nearly half of the instances retrieved (118; 45.56 %), and 'other', which contains the remaining 41 (15.83 %).

- 'nominal': these remnants are either fully nominal ('nominal_case-NA': 88; 88 %), as in (39), or pronominal, where the pronominal remnant may show case match with the antecedent ('nominal_case-same': 5; 5 %), as in (40), or case mismatch ('nominal_case-mismatch': 7; 7 %), as in (41):

39. A: I've got to go up to Scotland and make recordings of randomers and I don't wanna do that
    B: *Why Scotland?* [Spoken BNC2014: SGUA 732]
40. A: Sarah [gap:name], Claire [gap:name] what do you reckon to her$_{\text{accussative}}$?
    B: *Why her*$_{\text{accussative}}$*?* [BNC1994 DS: KSV 3329]
41. A: I thought I$_{\text{nominative}}$ can't believe this.
    B: *Why me*$_{\text{accussative}}$*?* [BNC1994 DS: KBF 13138]

- 'non-finite': this category comprises remnants which are headed by bare infinitives, as in (42), and *–ing* and *–ed* verbal forms, as in (43) and (44), respectively:

42. He's getting better aren't you? *Why lie?* [BNC2994 DS: KBF 13215]
43. A: you can't be anywhere near it
    B: well then *why you going?* [Spoken BNC2014: SR5H 628]
44. A: Step on newsman as tyre is treaded?
    B: Well *why treaded?* I mean [BNC1994 DS: KE2 9781]

- 'other': this category includes the remaining types of remnants, i.e. adverbial phrases (45), adjective phrases (46), prepositional phrases (47) and Small Clauses (48):

45. mine asks when did Jesus in fact become Christ? *And why then?* [BNC1994 DS: KBX 1594]

46. why would you say wrong decision? *why wrong?* [Spoken BNC2014: SEKZ 2052]
47. A: well for her yes but
    B: *well why not for everybody* [Spoken BNC2014: S457 593]
48. it doesn't matter, don't worry about it, *why you upset?* [BNC1994 DS: KD7 465]

(iii) 'category mismatch' distinguishes remnants which are of a different category to that of their antecedent (i.e. category mismatch = 'yes') from those whose category is identical to that of their antecedent (i.e. category mismatch = 'no'), as shown in (49) and (50), respectively. Only 6 cases of mismatch (2.32 %) were attested in the data, 158 cases of category match (61 %), and 95 instances of informatively new remnants (36.68 %), as in (51). The latter are coded as 'NA'.

49. A: round two's coming [on one week's time]$_{\text{Prepositional Phrase}}$
    B: *why [not now]*$_{\text{Adverbial Phrase}}$*?* [Spoken BNC2014: SUWR 59]
50. A: why are they doing this [so early]$_{\text{Adverbial Phrase}}$? cos the election's in May isn't it? [. . .]
    B: probably but I mean *why [not now]*$_{\text{Adverbial Phrase}}$*?* [Spoken BNC2014: SPTQ 88]
51. it doesn't matter, don't worry about it, *why you upset?* [BNC1994 DS: KD7 465]

(iv) 'island violation' occurs when the remnant corresponds to either a complement or modifier of the NP antecedent, as illustrated in (52), or one of the two coordinates in a coordinated phrase, as in (53) (i.e. island violation = 'yes'). These cases, however, proved to be very rare in the database (8; 3.01 %), unlike remnants that do not occur in contexts of island violation (island violation = 'no'), as in (54), which account for 96.91 % of the instances retrieved (i.e. 251 cases).

52. A: the car that [an Essex boy] would drive would be a Ford Capri [. . .]
    B: mm *why suddenly Essex though?* [BNC1994 DS KD6 776]

53. A: I don't think [unfortunate and interesting] are the same thing
    B: *why unfortunate?* [Spoken BNC2014: SM6B 1234]
54. A: otherwise I've got to go up to Scotland and make recordings of randomers and I don't wanna do that
    B: *Why Scotland?* [Spoken BNC2014: SGUA 732]

4.3. Statistical analysis of the data

The revised list of variables, their levels and the number of instances per alternative are presented in Table 1, where either frequency or theoretical unmarkedness were the criteria used to establish the reference levels for each predictor.

Table 1: Summary of the dataset.

corpus		**semantics**		**island_violation**	
BNC1994 DS	82	canonical	179	yes	8
Spoken BNC2014	177	enriched	80	no	251
category		**category_mismatch**			
nominal_case-same	5	yes	6		
nominal_case-mismatch	7	no	158		
nominal_case-NA	88	NAs	95		
non-finite	118				
other	41				

To gauge the relative weights of the variables described in Section 4.2.2, a fixed-effects binomial regression model was fitted.[9] The analysis of potential (multi)collinearity in the model resulted in acceptable

9 The model was fitted with the functions glm() from the 'stats' package (R Core Development Team 2022) and 'lrm' from the 'rms' package (Harrell Jr 2022) using the statistical software R (R Core Development Team 2022).

values (i.e. 1.051–5.195), indicating medium but not potentially harmful collinearity.[10] Finally, backward stepwise elimination was used to find the model that best explains the variation in the data,[11] revealing that the category 'island violation' did not contribute significantly to the model. The findings demonstrated that the semantics of *why*-fragments (i.e. whether they convey a canonical or an enriched meaning) is sufficiently explained by the predictors 'corpus', 'category (of the remnant)' and 'category mismatch'.

The summary statistics for the model confirmed its good fit. The C-index was 0.745, which indicates acceptable discrimination and classification accuracy. The Nagelkerke R^2 value was 0.243, thus indicating a very good fit and a sufficient level of explained variance in the data.

In order to obtain a more detailed picture of the influence exerted on the variation by specifically significant predictors, Figures 1 to 3 contain the effects plots for each one,[12] where the y-axes show the predicted probabilities for each level's outcome, ranging from higher probability of a canonical interpretation (low on the scale) to higher probability of enriched meanings.

10 Potential (multi)collinearity was explored with the function 'vif' from the 'car' package (Fox and Weisberg 2019).

11 Backward stepwise elimination was carried out with the function 'step' from the 'MASS' package (Venables and Ripley 2002).

12 Function 'predictorEffects' from the 'effects' package (Fox and Weisberg 2019)—95 % error-bar confidence.

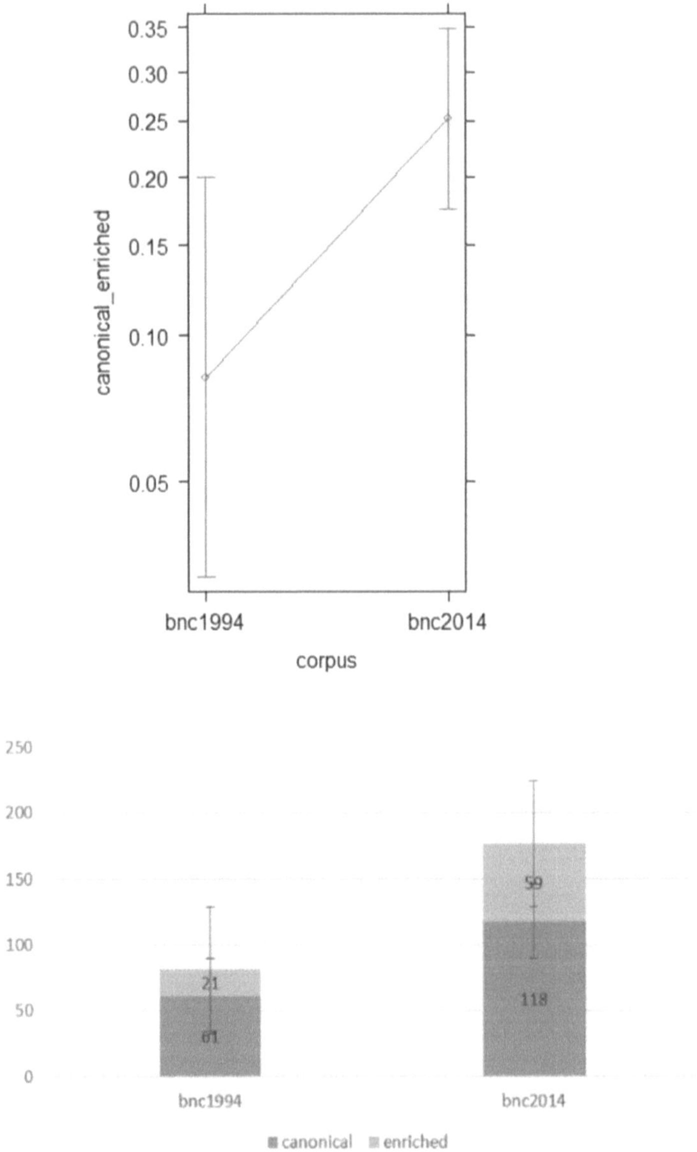

Figure 1. Effects plot and stacked barplot (95 % confidence interval) of the variables 'semantics' and 'corpus'.

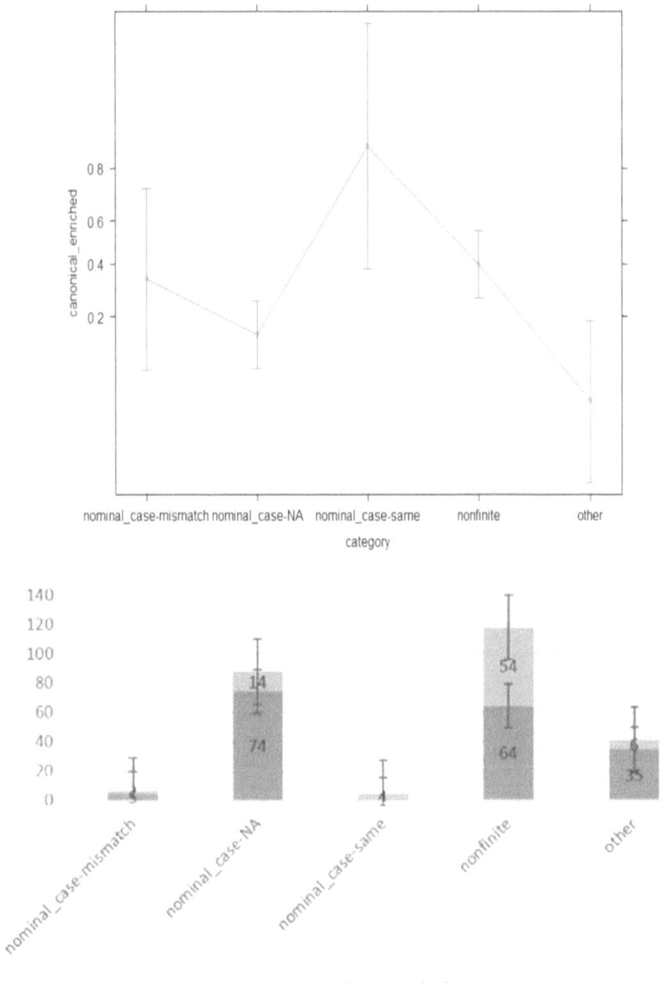

Figure 2. Effects plot and stacked barplot (95 % confidence interval) of the variables 'semantics' and 'category (of remnant)'.

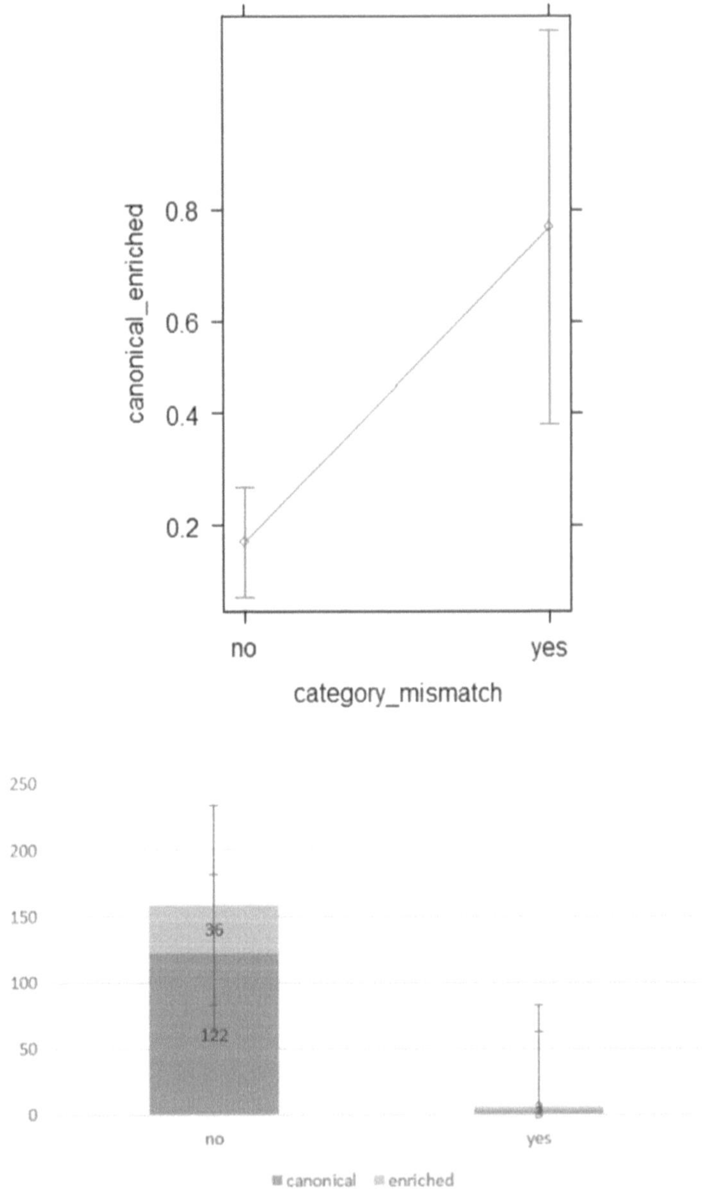

Figure 3. Effects plot and stacked barplot (95 % confidence interval) of the variables 'semantics' and 'category mismatch'.

4.4. Discussion of the results

The effects plots in Section 4.3 illustrate the probability trends of the variables that proved to be explanatory in the model: category (of remnant), category mismatch, and corpus.

While 'category (of remnant)' was not discarded during the backward-stepwise phase, its contribution to the model is very weak. This is shown not only by the *p*-values provided by the regression in Table 2, but also by the significant overlap among the different confidence bars (Figure 2). The only trend worth highlighting is a higher occurrence of canonical meanings in the category 'other'.

Table 2: Fixed-effects binomial regression coefficients (backward stepwise) [Signif. codes: 0 '***'; 0.001 '**'; 0.01 '*'; 0.05 '.'; 0.1 ' '; 1].

Coefficients	**Estimate**	**Std. Error**	**z value**	**Pr(>|z|)**	
(Intercept)	-1.7698	0.9543	-1.854	0.0638	.
corpus:bnc2014	1.3259	0.5503	2.409	0.01598	*
category:nominal_case-NA	-1.0314	0.9298	-1.109	0.26728	
category:nominal_case-same	2.4873	1.4577	1.706	0.08795	.
category:non-finite	0.2808	0.9251	0.304	0.76151	
category:other	-2.2878	1.1760	-1.945	0.05172	.
category_mismatch:yes	2.7665	0.9626	2.874	0.00405	**

As regards the variable 'category mismatch', Figure 3 above shows a significant preference for enriched meanings with novel remnants, i.e. remnants whose category is different from that of their correlates in the antecedent site. This finding is in keeping with the main tenet of Traugott and Trousdale's (2013) constructionalisation, which requires the creation of a (complex) sign with both a new form and a new meaning. Our *why*-fragments could be claimed to have demonstrated an incipient level of constructionalisation, as their enriched (new) meanings are associated with novel forms in the construction.

Finally, Figure 1 reflects an increase in the frequency of enriched meanings associated with *why*-fragments in the period 1990s–2010s. Specifically, the variable 'corpus' was found to be statistically significant in the model (p=.0159), and the effects plot shows a tendency for *why*-fragments to be more conventionalised the more recent they are.

5. Concluding remarks and issues for further research

The study shows that formal (syntactic design, acceptance of remnant types) and semantic/pragmatic (uniqueness/exclusiveness, modal interpretation) features are conventionalised in *why*-fragments, and that these expressions may therefore be classed as a type of construction distinct from complete *why*-sentences. To quote Boas (2013: 235),

> whenever it is not possible to predict all of the facts about the use, internal composition, combinatory potential, or meaning of the pattern under study to some independently motivated principles or already known construction(s), it may become necessary to propose a separate construction.

Based on Cognitive Construction Grammar theory, the analysis suggests that *why*-fragments and *why*-sentences may be interpreted as competing members of the same allostructional pair. The choice of one construction over the other depends on the enriched meaning intended by the speaker in a given situational context.

This chapter has explored the alternation between the canonical (i.e. equivalent to that of the corresponding complete *why*-sentences) and enriched (i.e. with an added modal meaning or nuance of uniqueness/exclusiveness) interpretations of *why*-fragment constructions in contemporary English based on evidence from spoken data retrieved from the BNC1994 DS and Spoken BNC2014 corpora. The statistical modelling of the data was based on a set of predictors compiled from the relevant literature, which included as independent variables corpus, category of remnants, attestation of category mismatches between fragments and their antecedent, and occurrence of the remnants' correlates in syntactic 'islands'. The data were analysed using a multivariable statistical technique that determined which predictors were significant in explaining the semantics of *why*-fragments.

Our case study shows that the timid (non-significant) increase in *why*-fragments revealed by the corpus data (normalised frequencies per 1 million sentences in BNC1994 DS: 134.3 and Spoken BNC2014: 147.9) is supported by both higher probability of the so-called enriched interpretation of *why*-fragments in the Spoken BNC2014 data than in examples from BNC1994 DS, and the preference for novel expressions in the fragments' remnants (i.e. for remnants not attested as such in the antecedent clauses) when the fragments have enriched meanings.

The acceptance of a cline between constructional changes that account for variations in the construction's form and/or interpretation, and Traugott and Trousdale's (2013) (radical) constructionalisation processes leading to constructions that are new both in form and in meaning is not free of controversy in Construction Grammar (see, among others, Flach 2020: 46–47 and Smirnova and Sommerer 2020: 10). This chapter does not attempt to describe the diachronic trend reflected by the data in a technical way but simply highlights a timid shift towards conveyance of enriched meanings, which is possibly closer to Smirnova and Sommerer's (2020: 18) theory of 'local node adjustment'.

The multivariate analysis of the BNC (spoken) data presented here sheds new light on the role of the linguistic variables with greater explanatory power in the alternation between canonical and conventionalised *why*-fragments. As a big-picture conclusion, the findings also confirm that linguistic variation and, in particular, processes of constructional change may be shaped and demonstrated by the application of statistical methods. Nevertheless, the picture is still far from complete. Further insights and understanding may be gained from incorporating into the model additional potential determinants of variation, data from varieties other than British English, examples from written English, and corroboration from other fragmentary constructions. These additions, which must be left for future research, would be helpful to test the validity of this chapter's findings concerning variation between canonical and conventional fragments in Present-Day English.

References

Akmajian, Adrian. 1984. Sentence Types and the Form-Function Fit. *Natural Language and Linguistic Theory* 2, 1–23.

Alves-Castro, Marian. 2020. 'Why not' and Other Patterns of Negative *Why*-Stripping. In López Ropero, Lourdes / Prieto García-Cañedo, Sara / Sánchez Fajardo, José Antonio (eds.), *Thresholds and Ways Forward in English Studies*. Alicante: Publicaciones de la Universidad de Alicante, 168–178.

Bhatt, Rajesh. 1998. *Argument-Adjunct Asymmetries in Rhetorical Questions*. Talk delivered at The 29th Annual Meeting of the North East Linguistic Society, University of Delaware.

BNC Consortium. 2007. *British National Corpus: XML Edition*. Oxford Text Archive.

BNC2014 User Manual = The British National Corpus 2014: *User Manual and Reference Guide (Version 1.1)* 2018. <http://corpora.lancs.ac.uk/bnc2014/doc/BNC2014manual.pdf>

Boas, Hans C. 2013. Cognitive Construction Grammar. In Hoffmann, Thomas / Trousdale, Graeme (eds.), *The Oxford Handbook of Construction Grammar*. Oxford: Oxford University Press, 233–252.

Bowie, Jill / Aarts, Bas. 2016. Clause Fragments in English Dialogue. In López-Couso, María José / Méndez-Naya, Belén / Núñez-Pertejo, Paloma / Palacios-Martínez, Ignacio M. (eds.), *Corpus Linguistics on the Move. Exploring and Understanding English through Corpora*. Leiden: Brill, 259–288.

Brezina, Vaclav / Hawtin, Abi / McEnery, Tony. 2021. The Written British National Corpus 2014—Design and Comparability. *Text & Talk* 41/5–6, 595–615.

Brezina, Vaclav / Platt, William. 2022. #LancsBox X 1.1.0 [Software Package].

Brinton, Laurel J. / Traugott, Elizabet Closs. 2005. *Lexicalization and Language Change*. Cambridge: Cambridge University Press.

Burnard, Lou. 2007. *BNC User Reference Guide*. <http://www.natcorp.ox.ac.uk/docs/URG/BNCdes.html>

Bybee, Joan L. 2013. Usage-Based Theory and Exemplar Representations of Constructions. In Hoffmann, Thomas / Trousdale, Graeme (eds.),

The Oxford Handbook of Construction Grammar. Oxford: Oxford University Press, 49–69.

Cappelle, Bert. 2006. Particle Placement and the Case for 'Allostructions'. *Constructions* SV1-7, 1–28. urn:nbn:de:0009-4-6839. <http://www.constructions-online.de>

COCA= The Corpus of Contemporary American English. Davies, Mark 2008-. *The Corpus of Contemporary American English* (COCA). Available online at <https://www.english-corpora.org/coca/>

Collins, Chris. 1991. Why and How Come. In Cheng, L. / Demirdache, H. (eds.), *More Papers on Wh-Movement. MIT Working Papers in Linguistics* 15, 31–45.

De Vaere, Hilde / Kolkmann, Julia / Belligh, Thomas. 2020. Allostructions Revisited. *Journal of Pragmatics* 170, 96–111.

Duffley, Patrick J. / Enns, Peter J. 1996. *Wh*-Words and the Infinitive in English. *Lingua* 98, 221–242.

Fernández, Raquel / Ginzburg, Jonathan / Lappin, Shalom 2007. Classifying Non-Sentential Utterances in Dialogue: A Machine Learning Approach. *Computational Linguistics* 33/3, 397–427.

Fernández-Pena, Yolanda. 2021. Towards an Empirical Characterisation and a Corpus-Driven Taxonomy of Fragments in Written Contemporary English. *RÆL, Revistœlectrónica de Lingüística Aplicada* 20/1, 136–154.

Flach, Susanne. 2020. Constructionalization and the Sorites Paradox. The Emergence of the *Into*-causative. In Sommerer, Lotte / Smirnova, Elena (eds.), *Nodes and Networks in Diachronic Construction Grammar*. Amsterdam/Philadelphia: John Benjamins, 45–67.

Fox, John / Weisberg, Sanford. 2019. *An R Companion to Applied Regression*. Thousand Oaks, CA: Sage.

Goldberg, Adele E. 1995. *Constructions: A Construction Grammar Approach to Argument Structure*. Chicago, IL: University of Chicago Press.

Goldberg, Adele E. 2006. *Constructions at Work: The Nature of Generalization in Language*. Oxford: Oxford University Press.

Goldberg, Adele E. 2013. Constructionist Approaches. In Hoffmann, Thomas / Trousdale, Graeme (eds.), *The Oxford Handbook of Construction Grammar*. Oxford: Oxford University Press, 15–31.

Goldberg, Adele E. 2019. *Explain Me This. Creativity, Competition, and the Partial Productivity of Constructions*. Oxford: Oxford University Press.

Gordon, David / Lakoff, George. 1971. Conversational Postulates. In *Papers from the Seventh Regional Meeting, Chicago Linguistic Society, April 16–18, 1971*. Chicago, IL: University of Chicago, 63–84.

Harrell Jr, Frank E. 2022. _rms: Regression Modeling Strategies_ . R package version 6.3-0. <https://CRAN.R-project.org/package=rms>

Heine, Bernd / Kaltenböck, Gunther / Kuteva, Tania. 2020. On the Status of *Wh*-exclamatives in English. *Functions of Language* 27/2, 207–233.

Hilpert, Martin. 2019. *Construction Grammar and its Application to English*. 2nd edition. Edinburgh: Edinburgh University Press.

Hoffmann, Thomas / Trousdale, Graeme. 2013. Construction Grammar: Introduction. In Hoffmann, Thomas / Trousdale, Graeme (eds.), *The Oxford Handbook of Construction Grammar*. Oxford: Oxford University Press, 1–12.

Huddleston, Rodney / Pullum, Geoffrey K. 2002 *The Cambridge Grammar of the English Language*. Cambridge: Cambridge University Press.

Hugou, Vincent. 2017. The WHX Construction (What the Hell…?) and Intensity. A Corpus-based Study. *Lexis. Journal in English Lexicology* 10, 1–30.

Johnson, David E. 1975. Why Delete Tense? *Linguistic Inquiry* 6/3, 481–489.

Kim, Jong-Bok / Abeillé, Anne. 2019. *Why*-Stripping in English: A Corpus-Based Perspective. *Linguistic Research* 36/3, 365–387.

Kim, Jong-Bok / Davies, Mark. 2019. English *What-With* Absolute Constructions: A Construction-Grammar Perspective. *English Language and Linguistics* 24/4, 637–666.

Leech, Geoffrey / Rayson, Paul / Wilson, Andrew. 2001. *Word Frequencies in Written and Spoken English: Based on the British National Corpus*. London/New York: Routledge.

Love, Robbie / Dembry, Claire / Hardie, Andrew / Brezina, Vaclav / McEnery, Tony. 2017. The Spoken BNC2014: Designing and Building a Spoken Corpus of Everyday Conversations. *International Journal of Corpus Linguistics* 22/3, 319–344.

Michaelis, Laura A. / Feng, Hanbing 2015. What Is This, Sarcastic Syntax? *Constructions and Frames* 7/2, 148–180.

Nakao, Chizuru / Yoshida, Masaya / Ortega-Santos, Ivan. 2012. On the Syntax of *Why*-stripping. In Arnett, Nathan / Bennett, Ryan (eds.), *Proceedings of the 30*th *West Coast Conference on Formal Linguistics*. Somerville, MA: Cascadilla, 270–280.

Nelson, Gerald / Wallis, Sean / Aarts, Bas. 2002. *Exploring Natural Language: Working with the British Component of the International Corpus of English*. Amsterdam/Philadelphia: John Benjamins.

Perek, Florent. 2021. Alternation-based Generalizations are Stored in the Mental Grammar: Evidence from a Sorting Task Experiment. *Cognitive Linguistics* 23/3, 601–635.

Pérez-Guerra, Javier / Fernández-Pena, Yolanda. 2022. *Why Why-Fragments? A Corpus-Based Constructional Analysis of their Form and Meaning*. Talk delivered at the CILC2022: 13th International Corpus Linguistics Conference, University of Bergamo.

Põldvere, Nele / Paradis, Carita. 2019. Motivations and Mechanisms for the Development of the Reactive *What-x* Construction in Spoken Dialogue. *Journal of Pragmatics* 143, 65–84.

Põldvere, Nele / Paradis, Carita. 2020. 'What and Then a Little Robot Brings It to You?' The Reactive *What-x* Construction in Spoken Dialogue. *English Language and Linguistics* 24/2, 307–332.

R Core Team. 2022. *R: A Language and Environment for Statistical Computing*. Vienna, Austria: R Foundation for Statistical Computing. <https://www.R-project.org>

Siemund, Peter. 2015. Exclamative Clauses in English and their Relevance for Theories of Clause Types. *Studies in Language* 39/3, 697–727.

Siemund, Peter. 2017. English Exclamative Clauses and Interrogative Degree Modification. In Napoli, Maria / Ravetto, Miriam (eds.), *Exploring Intensification: Synchronic, Diachronic and Cross-linguistic Perspectives*. Amsterdam/Philadelphia: John Benjamins, 209–230.

Smirnova, Elena / Sommerer, Lotte. 2020. Introduction. The Nature of the Node and the Network. Open Questions in Diachronic Construction Grammar. In Sommerer, Lotte / Smirnova, Elena (eds.), *Nodes and Networks in Diachronic Construction Grammar*. Amsterdam/Philadelphia: John Benjamins, 1–42.

Traugott, Elizabeth Closs / Trousdale, Graeme. 2013. *Constructionalization and Constructional Changes*. Oxford: Oxford University Press.

Van de Velde, Freek / De Smet, Hendrik / Ghesquière, Lobke. 2015. On Multiple Source Constructions in Language Change. In De Smet, Hendrik / Ghesquière, Lobke / Van de Velde, Freek (eds.), *On Multiple Source Constructions in Language Change*. Amsterdam/ Philadelphia: John Benjamins, 1–17.

Venables, W. N. / Ripley, B. D. 2002. *Modern Applied Statistics with S*. New York, NY: Springer.

Weir, Andrew. 2014. *Why*-Stripping Targets Voice Phrase. In Huang, Hsin-Lun / Rysling, Amanda / Poole, Ethan (eds.), *Proceedings of the* 43rd *Annual Meeting of the North East Linguistic Society*. Amherst, MA: GLSA, 235–248.

Weir, Andrew. 2017. But Write What? In LaCara, Nicholas / Moulton, Keir / Tessier, Anne-Michelle (eds.), *A Schrift to Fest Kyle Johnson*. Amherst, MA: University of Massachusetts, 401–408.

Yoshida, Masaya / Nakao, Chizuru / Ortega-Santos, Iván. 2014. The Syntax of Ellipsis and Related Phenomena. In Carnie, Andrew / Sato, Yosuke / Siddiqi, Daniel (eds.), *The Routledge Handbook of Syntax*. New York, NY: Routledge, 192–213.

Yoshida, Masaya / Nakao, Chizuru / Ortega-Santos, Iván. 2015. The Syntax of *Why*-Stripping. *Natural Language and Linguistic Theory* 33, 323–370.

Zaitsu, Anissa. 2018. *Why Make Sense of Silence? The Clausal Syntax of a Reduced Why-Question*. PhD, UC Santa Cruz.

Zaitsu, Anissa. 2020. Modality Force and Syntax in an Understudied Class of Reduced *Why*-Questions in English. *Glossa: A Journal of General Linguistics* 5/1, 1–37.

Part II
Case studies

ROSALÍA RODRÍGUEZ-VÁZQUEZ /
CLAUDIA DE LA IGLESIA SANJUÁN

The intonation of directive (in)subordinate *if*-clauses in American English: A corpus study

1. Introduction

One of the interests of Corpus Linguistics is the analysis of linguistic instances that somehow deviate, in terms of form, function, meaning or use, from the rules and expectations traditionally corresponding to those instances in a given language. So-called *fragments* are an example of a specific type of formal (i.e. syntactic) deviation, as they are characterised as structurally non-canonical but semantically felicitous constituents, that is to say, they are fully intelligible in the context where they are uttered. In other words, fragments are independent linguistic units which *prima facie* look incomplete but are nevertheless equivalent in propositional meaning, force and communicative function to a complete clause or sentence. Although fragments in written English have received some attention mainly from syntactic and communicative perspectives (Bowie and Aarts 2016; Merchant 2005; Morgan 1973; Stainton 2006), their description, analysis and classification in spoken English has been comparatively scarce. The present chapter aims at filling this research gap by analysing, describing and classifying the intonation contours of a specific group of fragments, namely directive insubordinate *if*-clauses, and comparing those to the intonation contours of subordinate conditional clauses.

The phenomenon of insubordination has been explored from syntactic, semantic and pragmatic perspectives. As Evans (2007) observes, insubordinate clauses respond to the 'conventionalized main clause use of what [...] appear to be formally subordinate clauses' (p. 367). According to Evans's (2007) theory regarding how insubordination is generated, the diachronic formation of insubordinate clauses follows four steps, from subordination proper, via the ellipsis of the main clause and the conventionalisation of the formally subordinate clause as a semantically main clause, through to the reanalysis of the resulting clause as a main clause with full meaning.

As a consequence of their evolution from dependent clauses to independent ones syntactically speaking, insubordinate clauses should be expected to be independent regarding their intonation contours, too. The analysis offered by the present study intends to shed some light on this precise issue by exploring the actual intonation realisation of the directive insubordinate and subordinate *if*-clauses found in the *Santa Barbara Corpus of Spoken American English* (henceforth *SBC*). In order to achieve this goal, the introduction offers a succinct review of the most recent research on the intonation of *if*-clauses, and delves into the objectives of the study. Section 2 deals with the specific methodology applied to analyse the spoken data retrieved from the *SBC*, while Section 3 explores the details of the analysis of the subordinate and insubordinate clauses found in the corpus with reference to their position in the utterance (i.e. initial, medial and final) and their illocutionary force (i.e. from less to more directive). Section 4 discusses the findings of the analysis regarding the previously mentioned variables. The conclusions of the study are offered in the fifth and last section.

1.1. Recent research on insubordinate if-clauses

As stated above, the research works that focus on the intonation contours of insubordinate *if*-clauses and their connection to the meaning and force of those clauses are not numerous. Two of the most rigorous studies dealing with the intonation characteristic of such clauses deal with Spanish *si*-clauses. In their examination of insubordinate *if*-clauses in Spanish, Elvira-García et al. (2017) highlight the fact that, in the existing literature, 'the formal elements that are usually considered to determine the degree of dependence of a construction are grammatical, syntactic, and pragmatic but not prosodic' (p. 30), which constitutes a salient research flaw, as syntactic events are very often reflected in the prosody of clauses and sentences.

There is no doubt that syntax is mirrored, in spoken language, by phrasing, which in turn materialises as a set of strategies used 'to mark syntactic non-final boundaries [. . . and] group together the parts of an utterance' (Elvira-García et al. 2017: 30). Those strategies are realised acoustically by means of pitch marks, lengthening and pauses. As pointed by Jun (2005), all languages seem to share the existence of specific prosodic units, called 'intonation phrases' (IPs), which are formed by complete utterances—the spoken equivalent to clauses and sentences in written language. A common intonation strategy displayed by a good number of languages to encode phrase boundaries inside an IP is the so-called 'continuation rise', realised as a rising tune—often accompanied by a pause or a segmental lengthening, normally described as a 'non-falling movement' (Elvira-García et al. 2017: 31). In accordance to this, the expected intonation configuration of a complex sentence is the division of the IP into two intermediate intonation groups (ip), where the first one typically describes a continuation rise[1]—no matter whether that first ip corresponds to the main or the subordinate clause—and the second one exhibits any of the possible nuclear configurations[2] in the language, as exemplified in Figure 1.

The existence of some predominant tonal movements to mark the boundaries of subordinate and main clauses (ips) in canonical instances of subordination entails that, in non-canonical cases, the intonation configuration of an IP must be analysed as a non-lexical marker of insubordination, i.e. intonation provides reliable clues to distinguish subordinate and insubordinate clauses. Elvira-García et al. (2017) conclude that 'if two clauses have the same lexical content but different degree of dependence, the only formal difference between them should lie in their prosody' (p. 33), and vice versa, 'changes in dependency imply changes in the intonational contour' (p. 43). In this regard, as Elvira-García et al. (2017) conclude that, in Spanish, insubordinate *if*-clauses tend to describe a falling intonation contour which ends in a

1 In spoken language, when a speaker wishes to indicate that they have not finished their turn—which sometimes corresponds to a complex sentence comprising two intermediate intonation phrases—, they may use a rising movement to make this explicit. Thus, in such cases, a continuation rise can be perceived just before the intonation boundary, right between the main clause and the subordinate clause.

2 Nuclear configurations, also called 'nuclear accents' or 'pitch accents', which can be found in any given language that uses intonation, are a set of possible combinations of high and low tones typically associated with a specific type of clause/sentence or with a certain illocutionary force.

low boundary, a configuration that may distinguish these clauses from subordinate *if*-clauses.

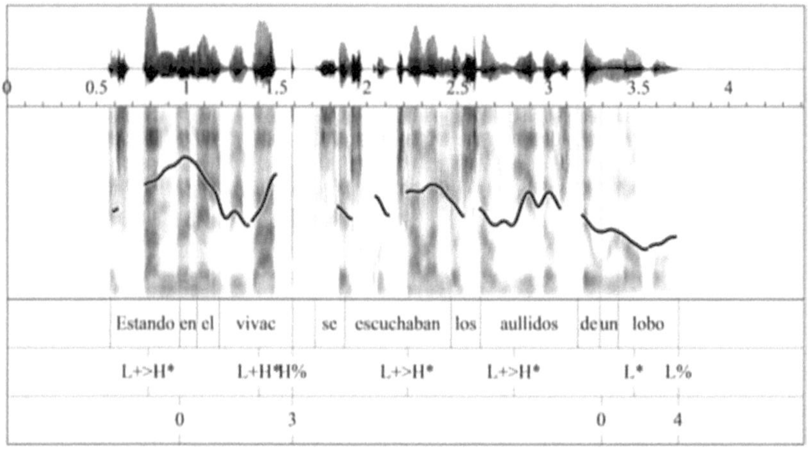

Figure 1: Continuation rise ((L)+H*H%) at the end of the subordinate clause and fall (L*L%) at the end of the main clause for the Spanish sentence *When they were at the vivac, they could hear a howling wolf* (in Estebas-Vilaplana et al. 2015).[3]

Along the same lines, Elvira-García (2019) offers an exploration of the prosody of elliptical and independent (i.e. insubordinate) '*si* + V' indicative clauses in Spanish. The author puts forward some relevant considerations regarding the intonation of these two types of *if*-clauses, insisting that 'intonation is the main cue listeners use in order to process an utterance as elliptical or insubordinate' (p. 241). In other words, a change in intonation will give rise to a change in meaning (Bolinger 1989), which entails that analysing the prosody of a sentence or clause will allow listeners to determine its meaning and illocutionary force and thus disambiguate between its potential meanings and pragmatic

3 The notation, as well as the intonation analysis provided, use the Tone and Break Index system (henceforth, ToBI) (Beckman and Ayers 1994), which comprises a number of symbols that facilitate the notation of intonation. These are L = low tone; H = high tone; * = pitch accent; + = leading or trailing tone; % = boundary tone, and – = phrase tone.

functions, if need be. In this regard, Elvira-García (2019) indicates that in Spanish, as in other languages, the intonation pattern of insubordinate *if*-clauses, typically describing a falling contour with a final low boundary tone, is used as a cue to indicate the type of speech act that it accomplishes, i.e. its prosody reflects its pragmatic function.

Turning to English, Kaltenböck's (2016) is the only study that provides a comprehensive analysis of the intonation of directive *if*- insubordinate clauses in British English (henceforth BrE). In intonation terms, his analysis concludes that the vast majority of insubordinate *if*-clauses display a prominent pattern involving a terminal contour, i.e. they describe a falling intonation pattern which finishes in a low boundary tone, which is the same contour reported by Elvira-García et al. (2017) and Elvira-García (2019) for Spanish. Thus, the use of certain predominant intonation contours and boundary tones for subordinate and insubordinate *if*-clauses does not seem to be capricious cross-linguistically; on the contrary, it mirrors the syntactic structure of clauses and sentences as well their meaning and pragmatic functions. In this regard, Kaltenböck (2016) introduces a very relevant consideration when he states that '[w]hile all insubordinate clauses are syntactically independent, only some of them—the more central cases—are also pragmatically independent' (p. 169). As will be observed in the present study, the overt inclusion of pragmatic considerations in a study of insubordinate clauses is paramount to grasping the reason for the emergence of a certain type of insubordinates as well as the intonation patterns used to mark them.

Along the lines of the existing research on insubordinate *if*-clauses, the main goal of this research work is to demonstrate that the intonation contours of this specific type of clauses in spoken American English (henceforth AmE) is more fixed than those of subordinate *if*-clauses, thus reinforcing the view that insubordinate *if*-clauses are independent, conventionalised fragments.

1.2. Objectives

In light of the scarcity of research works dealing with insubordinate *if*-clauses in varieties of English other than Standard BrE, the present study aims at checking whether Kaltenböck's (2016) conclusions remain valid in the case of spoken AmE. In order to reach a conclusion, the present study will analyse acoustically the terminal contours of insubordinate *if-* clauses in the *SBC* (249,000 words), will classify those contours according to the ToBI conventions for English (Beckman and Ayers 1997), and will compare the observed contours with those of canonical *if*-clauses in the same corpus. The types of directives analysed conform to Mato-Míguez's (2016) and Kaltenböck's (2016) taxonomy of directive insubordinate *if*-clauses, exemplified in utterances (1) through to (4), retrieved from the *SBC* (the tags between square brackets are the authors'):

1. If you need an additional piece. [offer] (SBC16a).[4]
2. I mean and they want you to. . . if you can help, you know, maybe grade paper or. . . [request] (SBC43).
3. if you—if you go over and have a look at the dining room. [order] (SBC29b).
4. But if you notice, there are no registers in here. [instruction] (SBC29a).

As can be observed in the above examples, in the majority of the directive insubordinate *if*-clauses in the *SBC*, the subject is 'you' and the tensed verb is a modal verb. Crucially for the purpose of this study, no verbal material can be retrieved from the conversation in which each of the clauses is uttered to fill the main clause slot, hence their status of insubordinate clauses. Moreover, given the conversational context in which they are uttered, they all have the illocutionary force of an indirect directive—i.e., a directive which is not expressed in the form of an imperative—on the part of the speaker. In turn, they are most probably expected to receive a response on the part of the listener. In Brown and Levinson's (1987) view, orders, requests, and offers constitute linguistic acts that threaten the listener's negative face, since they express the speaker's intrusion into the listener's freedom of action. In order to avoid or mitigate these face-threatening acts, participants in a conversation

4 The identification tags corresponding to examples extracted from conversations within the *SBC* where more than one instance of an *if*-clause was found have been added a letter so as to identify those examples as clearly as possible.

will put a number of strategies into practice, one of which is the substitution of straight imperatives by directive insubordinate *if*-clauses. In this regard, the insubordinate *if*-clauses under analysis here convey the expression of polite requests, offers and orders intended to soften the strong assertion that an imperative would imply. The analysis of the directive insubordinate *if*-clauses in the *SBC* will allow us to determine whether the intonation contours of insubordinate *if*-clauses are more fixed than those of subordinate *if*-clauses, as proven for Spanish and BrE, thus reinforcing the view of insubordinate *if*-clauses as prosodically and grammatically conventionalised fragments.

2. Methodology

2.1. Materials

The *SBC* (Du Bois et al. 2000–2005) contains 249,000 words of spoken AmE. It constitutes the most extensive corpus of AmE within the *International Corpus of English* (*ICE*). The *SBC* comprises sixty recordings of spontaneous spoken interaction on topics unrelated to one another recorded all throughout the United States. Regarding the speakers, they represent a wide variety of ages, genders, ethnic and socio-cultural backgrounds; it must be noted that such variables are not evenly distributed in the data analysed, a fact that remains unproblematic, as the afore-mentioned aspects were not taken into consideration in the analysis. The vast majority of the recordings correspond to spontaneous face-to-face conversation, although there are also some telephone conversations, lectures, sermons, meetings, etc. As for register, the majority are informal conversations. Nevertheless, some conversations are relatively formal and, as a consequence, show a higher degree of politeness strategies, either because of the occasion itself—a sermon, a university lecture, a conversation in court, a conversation with an attorney, a business meeting, a tour-guide explanation—or because of the fact that the people in those conversations had not met prior to the recorded conversation. The materials are not classified per text-type but the corpus offers summaries of the contents of each conversation as well as extralinguistic information about the participants in the exchange. Apart from the audios in .wav and .mp3 formats, transcriptions of all sixty recordings are provided as scripts.

2.2. Analytical procedure

The first step in the analysis of the relevant conversations in the *SBC* was to manually search for instances of the conjunction *if.* Once the relevant instances were extracted, a manual pruning process was carried out to discard repetitions and occurrences that did not introduce any clause. The remaining tokens were then filtered so as to be left with conditional clauses and insubordinate *if*-clauses expressing directive meaning. The *if*-clauses were classified according to their position in the utterance (i.e., initial, medial and final), and their force (i.e., offer, instruction, request, order).

Once the relevant audio fragments were located, the excerpts corresponding to each of those occurrences were cropped using GoldWave (GoldWave Inc. 2022), and the resulting files were made into plain text files (.txt). The files were annotated phonetically and intonationally using the Montreal Forced Aligner (McAuliffe et al. 2017) and PyToBI. (Domínguez et al. 2019), which automatically generated TextGrid files of each relevant token.[5] The resulting alignment was reviewed manually, and some minor corrections were made. The terminal contours of the insubordinate and subordinate *if*- clauses in the *SBC* were analysed using Praat (Boersma and Weenink 2021) with the Autosegmental Metrical (AM) model (Pierrehumbert 1980), a level-based approach that considers intonation to be a succession of high and low tones, anchored to prominent syllables (Figures 2 and 3). Finally, the observed contours (i.e., falling vs. rising)

for insubordinate and subordinate *if*-clauses were compared.

5 A TextGrid is a type of text file generated by means of a *Praat* script and used to annotate the analysis of an audio recording, thus complementing the acoustic information provided by spectrograms and oscillograms.

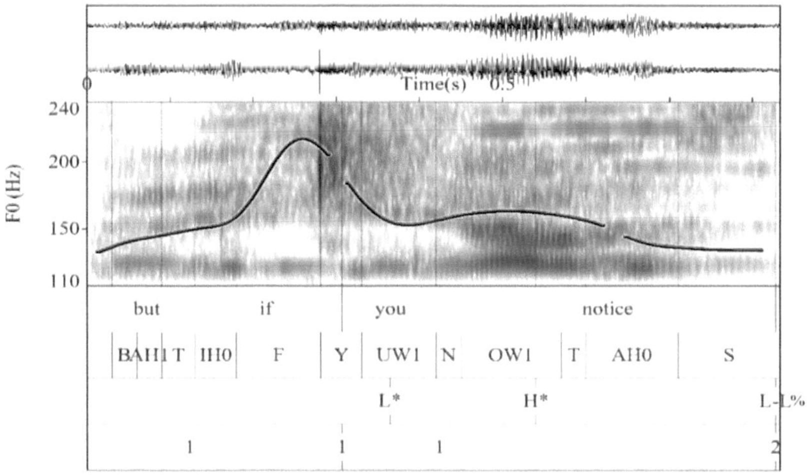

Figure 2: Spectrogram, oscillogram, orthographic transcription, SAMPA transcription, and ToBI annotation of the insubordinate directive *but if you notice* (SBC29a).[6]

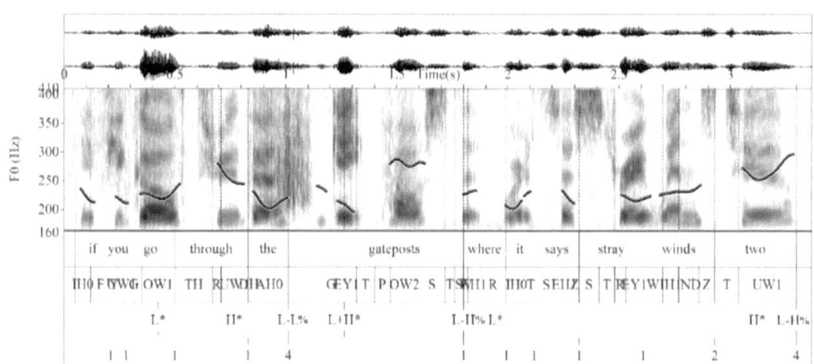

Figure 3: Spectrogram, oscillogram, orthographic transcription, SAMPA transcription, and ToBI annotation of the subordinate directive *if you go through the gateposts where it says stray winds two* (SBC56).

6 SAMPA is an acronym that stands for *Speech Assessment Methods Phonetic Alphabet.* It is a notation method that was developed as a workaround to create a phonetic script that computers would be able to read before they were programmed to process IPA symbols.

3. Analysis

A total of 47 *if*-clauses with directive meaning were found within the *SBC*—18 insubordinate and 29 subordinate (see Table 1).[7] Once this preliminary division was made, the *if*-clauses were further classified following two distinctive criteria, namely their position within the context of an utterance, i.e., initial, medial and final, and their illocutionary force (henceforth IF). All the utterances analysed were directives; besides, the IF was assigned to each of them using Yule's (1996), Mato-Míguez's (2016) and Kaltenböck's (2016) labels corresponding to four subtypes of directives, namely offer, instruction, request and order.

The following paragraphs showcase the results of the analysis with regard to two criteria, namely position within the utterance and IF.

3.1. Intonation contours by position within the utterance

The present section presents the analysis of the data regarding the intonation contours of insubordinate and subordinate *if*-clauses in relation to their position (initial, medial, final) within the utterance. The results extracted from the corpus, shown in Table 1, reveal that insubordinate *if*-clauses occur mostly in initial position (N=15) whereas subordinate *if*-clauses appear to be more evenly distributed between those being realised in initial (N=11) and final (N=15) positions. Conversely, those in medial position appear to be the least frequent cases in both insubordinate and subordinate *if*-clauses.

7 Given the fact that the total number of utterances (N=47) is relatively small compared to the magnitude of the original corpus, using raw numbers was deemed the most appropriate way to present the data.

Table 1: Distribution of (in)subordinate *if*-clauses regarding position within the utterance.

		Clause type	
		Insubordinate *if*-clauses	**Subordinate *if*-clauses**
Position	Initial	15 (83.33 %)	11 (37.93 %)
	Medial	1 (5.55 %)	3 (10.34 %)
	Final	2 (11.11 %)	15 (51.72 %)
	N	18 (100 %)	29 (100 %)

Regarding the insubordinate *if*-clauses retrieved from the corpus, their analysis with Praat (Boersma and Weenink 2021) and their annotation using ToBI (Beckman and Ayers 1997) conventions offer evidence that all insubordinate *if*-clauses with directive meaning display a falling contour regardless of their position. This entails that this is the default terminal contour in insubordinate *if*-clauses in spoken AmE.

As shown in Table 2, which provides a summary of insubordinate *if*-clauses contours as well as the contextual position of each clause and the clauses themselves where the accented word is in bold, there are three frequent terminal falling contours among insubordinate *if*-clauses, namely L-L%, H-L%, LL- (i.e., a fall from a low phrasal tone to a low boundary tone, a fall from a high to a low boundary and a falling phrasal tone, respectively), besides one instance of !H*+L (i.e., a downstep high pitch accent followed by a low trailing tone). The predominance of the L-L% terminal contour is further illustrated in clauses SBC04, SBC25a and SBC18, which correspond to insubordinate *if*-clauses that occur in initial, medial, and final position, respectively. These falling tonal movements tend to appear rather frequently; they start with a L* (i.e., a low pitch accent) and are followed by a progressive fall usually ending in L-L%. Additionally, there are three clauses which present a similar configuration containing a L* and followed by LL- which seem to occur in shorter clauses (N=2). Conversely, in the *SBC* there are eight utterances, namely SBC29a, SBC39, SBC01b, SBC12, SBC24, SBC26, SBC43 and SBC25a, where a different trend is shown, i.e., they start from a higher point in their F_0 and continue falling from that H*.

Table 2: Terminal contours of insubordinate *if*-clauses by position.

Conversation number	**Terminal contour**	**Position**	**Clause**
SBC04	L+H* L* L* L-L%	initial	*if you put it to them in a* **very** *simple way*
SBC29a	H* L-L%	initial	*but if you* ***notice****, there are no registers in here*
SBC39	!H*+L	initial	*if you've noticed that* ***before***
SBC46	L* LL-	initial	*If you just let that one kinda* ***heal***
SBC01b	L+H* H*+L L* L* LL-	initial	*If* ***you*** *wanna talk about somebody tired*
SBC18a	L* L-L%	initial	*if you want to let him* ***know***
SBC40	L* LL-	initial	*if anyone's interested in seeing what Perry looked like when he had his fourteen-foot* ***tail***
SBC29b	L* L* L* L-L%	initial	*if you—if you* ***go*** *over and have a look at the dining room*
SBC38a	L* L* L-L%	initial	*if you would right up this stairway when you get on the* ***balcony****, wait for me on the blue couches on the balcony please*
SBC01a	H* H*+L L* L-L%	initial	*if* ***you*** *would really get into it*
SBC12	H* L* L-L% L* H*+L H-L%	initial	***if*** *we remember our Chicano history*
SBC24	H*+L L* L-L%	initial	*now, if I can just get to the* ***next***
SBC26	H*+L H*!H*+L L-L%	initial	*and if we just be perfectly* ***honest*** *with each other*
SBC43	H*+L H-L%	initial	*if you can help, you know, maybe grade paper (. . .) do* ***something***
SBC53a	L* LL-	initial	*okay if I may look at* ***that***
SBC25a	H* L-L%	medial	*if you wanna meditate it on more- on it* ***more***
SBC18b	L* L-L%	final	*if you (. . .) if you wanna go ahead and* ***do*** *it*
SBC34	L* H-L%	final	*if we could turn the spider plant* ***around***

Subordinate *if*-clauses with directive meaning, on the other hand, present a wider array of possibilities. In Table 3, three recurring final tonal movements (L-L%, L-H% and LL-, i.e., a low fall towards a low boundary tone, a low phrasal tone followed by a high boundary tone, and a low phrasal tone, respectively) are displayed. Consistently with the fact that they are dependent clauses and in line with the observations made by Elvira-García et al. (2017) and Elvira-García (2019) for Spanish, and Kaltenböck (2016) for BrE, those occurring in initial and medial position show a rising contour as well as a wider range of variation in the type of pitch accent and overall pitch movement. There are six cases of initial and medial subordinate *if*-clauses where the pitch movement does not end in a boundary tone (%) but rather in a pitch accent (*), as in clause SBC21 (Table 3), which marks the continuation rising movement that non-final subordinates typically describe. Conversely, most subordinate *if*-clauses found in final position describe a falling pattern—predominantly, L* L-L%. Besides that, clauses in initial position tend to start their descent from a much higher point, as opposed to final clauses, which usually begin at a lower point. Thus, the position of the subordinate clause is key to determine the intonation pattern that it will be assigned. When they are produced in initial position, their pitch movement may be the expected L-H% (N=2), a pitch accent or, less frequently, L-L% (N=2). Conversely, when subordinate *if*-clauses are final, their contour consistently finishes in a L-L%, as observed in the existing literature on the topic.

Table 3: Subordinate *if*-clauses by position.

Conversation number	**Terminal contour**	**Position**	**Clause**
SBC09	H* L* L-L%	initial	*because if you* ***look*** *at it*
SBC10b	L*	initial	*if you wanna* ***join*** *us*
SBC13b	L+H* L*	initial	*if you don't* ***want*** *one*
SBC16a	H*+L	initial	*If you need an additional* ***piece***
SBC21	H*	initial	*if you could* ***get*** *them to me*
SBC31	L+H* H-L%	initial	*if you* ***want***

Continued

Table 3: *Continued*

Conversation number	**Terminal contour**	**Position**	**Clause**
SBC35b	L* L-L%	initial	*if you* ***wanna*** *get into something good*
SBC38b	L*+H L-H%	initial	*if you will, please, take a look at this picture taken during* ***construction***
SBC41	H* H*+L	initial	*if you wanna* ***do*** *that*
SBC52	H* L* L%	initial	*if you wanna be* ***fair*** *about it, spread it around the neighbourhood, don't just put them all*
SBC56	L+H* L-H% L* H* L-H%	initial	*If you go through the* ***gateposts****, where it says stray winds two, and just go through there and look to your left, there's a pasture*
SBC05	H* L-L%	medial	*if you wanna use* ***that***
SBC10a	L* LL-	medial	*if we can go ahead and* ***carry*** *on*
SBC16b	L*+H	medial	*if you* ***want***
SBC06	L* L-L%	final	*if you* ***want***
SBC08	L* L-L%	final	*if you want to get a drink of* ***water*** *or something like that*
SBC10c	!H* LL-	final	*if you don't* ***want***
SBC11	H* H+L* L* L* H%	final	***if*** *you want any*
SBC13a	H* L* L-L%	final	*if you'd like* ***that*** *tonight*
SBC14	L* L-L%	final	*if you want to direct it that* ***way***
SBC17a	!H*+L L-L%	final	*if you wish to, you know, have* ***dinner*** *with me*
SBC17b	H* L* L-L%	final	*if you wish to know my* ***phone*** *number*
SBC22	L+H* L-L%	final	*you can have her do it if you* ***want***
SBC25b	L* L-L%	final	*if you wanna read it* ***later***
SBC35a	L* L-L%	final	*or you can go upstairs if you* ***want***
SBC50	L* L-L%	final	*if you* ***want***
SBC53b	!H* L* L-L%	final	*if you'd like to* ***see*** *that*
SBC54	L* L* L-L%	final	*if you'd* ***like*** *them*
SBC58	L* L-L%	final	*You don't have to do that if you don't* ***want*** *to*

3.2. Intonation contours by illocutionary force

Illocutionary force (IFs) in this study is considered to feature within a continuum where the measuring yardstick is the degree of directiveness that each category has. Consequently, offers would be the clauses that carry the least directive meaning, followed by instructions, then requests and, lastly, orders, which convey the highest degree of directiveness. The data obtained from the *SBC* displayed in Table 4 show that requests (N=7) and instructions (N=5) are the most common options within insubordinate *if*-clauses, whereas offers (N=16) are the most frequent type in subordinate *if*-clauses.

Table 4: Utterance distribution regarding IF.

		Clause type	
		Insubordinate *if*-clauses	**Subordinate *if*- clauses**
Illocutionary force	Request	7 (38.88 %)	3 (10.34 %)
	Offer	4 (22.22 %)	16 (55.17 %)
	Instruction	5 (27.77 %)	4 (13.79 %)
	Order	2 (11.11 %)	6 (20.68 %)
	N	18 (100 %)	29 (100 %)

In the case of directive insubordinate *if*-clauses, the patterns produced by the speakers present some similarities, especially in orders (Table 5). On the one hand, the two instances of orders found in the corpus have an almost identical pattern, i.e., a low fall, as they begin at a L* (i.e., a low pitch accent) and continue descending towards low boundary tone –L-L%. As for offers and instructions, they show a wider range of variability than orders in the pitch movements preceding the final fall. Such is the case of utterances SBC01a, SBC25a, SBC29a or SBC04 (Table 5), which have preceding rising movements in them but end in the characteristic LL- or L-L%. Yet, those falling movements dwell in between mid falls and low falls, as in clauses SBC18a and SBC25a, which are offers, and in clauses SBC29a and SBC18b, which are instructions (Table 5). The first two are akin inasmuch as they display a H*+L H-L% (i.e., a high pitch accent with a trailing low tone, and a high phrasal tone continued by a low boundary tone) towards their end, whereas the other two present a slightly different configuration—H*+L L* L-L% (i.e., a bitonal pitch accent comprising a high pitch accent and a low trailing tone, a low pitch accent, and a falling phrase tone)—, highlighting that characteristic falling contour. On the other hand, most requests start from a H*, and the pitch movements vary albeit with some comparable cases such as utterances SBC12 and SBC43 or SBC01a and SBC24 from Table 5. Thus, there are some perceivable trends in their pitch movements before their predicted final fall that might be influenced by the degree of directiveness of each IF; orders seem to have a more fixed pattern while instructions and offers seem to increasingly progress in that internal pitch variation towards a greater fluctuation found in requests before the final fall. Overall, their terminal contour does not seem to be impacted by these preceding pitch movements. Indeed, as noted in the previous section, insubordinate *if*-clauses typically present either a L-L%, H-L% or LL-.

Table 5: Insubordinate *if*-clauses by IF.

Conversation number	Terminal contour	Illocutionary force	Clause
SBC01a	H* H*+L L* L-L%	request	*if **you** would really get into it*
SBC12	H* L* L-L% L* H*+L H-L%	request	***if** we remember our Chicano history*
SBC24	H*+L L* L-L%	request	*now, if I can just get to the **next***
SBC26	H*+L H*!H*+L L-L%	request	*and if we just be perfectly **honest** with each other*
SBC43	H*+L H-L%	request	*if you can help, you know, maybe grade paper (. . .) do **something***
SBC53a	L* LL-	request	*okay if I may look at **that***
SBC34	L* H-L%	request	*if we could turn the spider plant **around***
SBC01b	L+H* H*+L L* L* LL-	offer	*If **you** wanna talk about somebody tired*
SBC18a	L* L-L%	offer	*if you want to let him **know***

Table 5: *Continued*

Conversation number	**Terminal contour**	**Illocutionary force**	**Clause**
SBC40	L* LL-	offer	*if anyone's interested in seeing what Perry looked like when he had his fourteen-foot* ***tail***
SBC25a	H* L-L%	offer	*if you wanna meditate it on more- on it* ***more***
SBC04	L+H* L* L* L-L%	instruction	*if you put it to them in a* ***very*** *simple way*
SBC29a	H* L-L%	instruction	*but if you* ***notice****, there are no registers in here*
SBC39	!H*+L	instruction	*if you've noticed that* ***before***
SBC46	L* LL-	instruction	*If you just let that one kinda* ***heal***
SBC18b	L* L-L%	instruction	*if you (. . .) if you wanna go ahead and* ***do*** *it*
SBC29b	L* L* L* L-L%	order	*if you—if you* ***go*** *over and have a look at the dining room*
SBC38a	L* L* L-L%	order	*if you would right up this stairway when you get on the balcony, wait for me on the blue couches on the* ***balcony*** *please*

The classification of subordinate *if*-clauses with regard to their IF does not render any characteristic intonation contour in requests, offers, instructions and orders, especially because they display a wider range of variability than insubordinates. Orders and requests are a crisp example of that great disparity found in subordinate *if*-clause contours. The three requests found display various pitch movements, ranging from a single –H*– or a bitonal –H*+L– pitch accent to a descending contour, –LL-. Additionally, orders do present slight similarities inasmuch as three of them start with a H* (i.e., a high pitch accent) and end in L-L% (i.e., a low phrasal tone and a low boundary tone) (see clauses SBC17a, SBC52 and SBC17b in Table 6), but the other half follow different contours. Still there are some examples of similarities in instructions, which display a low fall configuration—L* L-L%—(see clauses

SBC25b and SBC06 in Table 6), and offers, which show either a low fall—L* L-L%—or a high or mid fall. In spite of this, it must be noted that instructions and offers follow the same variability trend explained in Section 3.1. above, which is more likely due to their position rather than to their IF. The same applies to orders and requests.

Table 6: Subordinate if-clauses by IF.

Conversation number	**Terminal contour**	**Illocutionary force**	**Clause**
SBC21	H*	request	*if you could* ***get*** *them to me*
SBC41	H* H*+L	request	*if you wanna* ***do*** *that*
SBC10a	L* LL-	request	*if we can go ahead and* ***carry*** *on*
SBC10b	L*	offer	*if you wanna* ***join*** *us*
SBC16a	H*+L	offer	*If you need an additional* ***piece***
SBC31	L+H* H-L%	offer	*if you* ***want***
SBC05	H* L-L%	offer	*if you wanna use* ***that***
SBC16b	L*+H	offer	*if you* ***want***
SBC08	L* L-L%	offer	*if you want to get a drink of* ***water*** *or something like that*
SBC10c	!H* LL-	offer	*if you don't* ***want***
SBC11	H* H+L* L* L* H%	offer	***if*** *you want any*
SBC13a	H* L* L-L%	offer	*if you'd like* ***that*** *tonight*
SBC14	L* L-L%	offer	*if you want to direct it that* ***way***
SBC22	L+H* L-L%	offer	*you can have her do it if you* ***want***
SBC35a	L* L-L%	offer	*or you can go upstairs if you* ***want***
SBC50	L* L-L%	offer	*if you* ***want***
SBC53b	!H* L* L-L%	offer	*if you'd like to* ***see*** *that*
SBC54	L* L* L-L%	offer	*if you'd* ***like*** *them*
SBC58	L* L-L%	offer	*You don't have to do that if you don't* ***want*** *to*
SBC09	H* L* L-L%	instruction	*because if you* ***look*** *at it*
SBC56	L+H* L-H% L* H* L-H%	instruction	*If you go through the* ***gateposts****, where it says stray winds two, and just go through there and look to your left, there's a pasture*

Table 6: *Continued*

Conversation number	**Terminal contour**	**Illocutionary force**	**Clause**
SBC06	L* L-L%	instruction	*if you **want***
SBC25b	L* L-L%	instruction	*if you wanna read it **later***
SBC13b	L+H* L*	order	*if you don't **want** one*
SBC35b	L* L-L%	order	*if you **wanna** get into something good*
SBC38b	L*+H L-H%	order	*if you will, please, take a look at this picture taken during **construction***
SBC52	H* L* L%	order	*if you wanna be **fair** about it, spread it around the neighbourhood, don't just put them all*
SBC17a	!H*+L L-L%	order	*if you wish to, you know, have **dinner** with me*
SBC17b	H* L* L-L%	order	*if you wish to know my **phone** number*

3.3. Summary

As the data put forward in this section show, there is not a clear pattern in any of the four categories of IFs regarding subordinate *if*-clauses nor the data are enough to draw definitive conclusions. In a similar vein, insubordinate *if*-clauses do not present a specific contour tied to requests, offers, instructions or orders. That fact notwithstanding, the data put forth in relation to their position show that initial insubordinate *if*-clauses, which add up to more than half of the total number of clauses, as well as medial and final are not influenced by such variable on their terminal contour. On the contrary, their terminal contours appear to be fixed as most of them end in L* L-L%. Additionally, the intonation contours of subordinate *if*-clauses are influenced by their position since initial and medial utterances may end in a pitch accent and not a boundary tone, while final subordinate *if*-clauses end in a falling contour. Despite the relatively small number of clauses retrieved, the results provide a preliminary sample of possible intonational and pragmatic behaviours in insubordinate and subordinate *if*-clauses with directive meaning as produced by AmE speakers.

4. Discussion of results

The previous section has presented the data according to two distinctive criteria, i.e., the position of the analysed clauses within the utterance where they occur and the illocutionary force of each one of those clauses. The present section discusses the results beginning with the most relevant aspects observed for insubordinate and subordinate *if*-clauses as classified by their position. It continues with highlights on their intonational behaviour regarding their IF and some insights on the previous analysis. Lastly, it discusses the significance of the results with regard to the objectives presented at the beginning of the study.

4.1. Clause position effect on if-clauses

One of the first aspects of the insubordinate *if*-clauses retrieved from the *SBC* highlighted in Section 3.1 is the high frequency with which they present a falling contour. Given that most of them occur in initial position, no predominant pattern can be linked with certainty to either of the other two positions, although all three instances of medial and final clauses end with L% (see Figures 4 and 5). The insubordinates occurring in initial position do present one dominant falling terminal contour that can be further divided into three –L-L%, H-L% and LL-. Beyond those terminal contours there are also three trends in the preceding pitch movements of initial insubordinate *if*-clauses that are worth noting. Firstly, those patterns that end in L-L% or H-L% tend to begin in a H*, then continue either up or downwards until their final fall. The second, typically, though not exclusively, applies to shorter clauses and is displayed as a global fall with the configuration L* LL-. Similarly, the third and most common pattern starts at a L* and continues descending towards that L-L%, which is also characterised as global fall (see

Figure 6). Overall, this stability in the intonation contours is indicative of the independent nature of the insubordinate *if*-clauses since a falling terminal contour usually signals a finished and closed sentence.

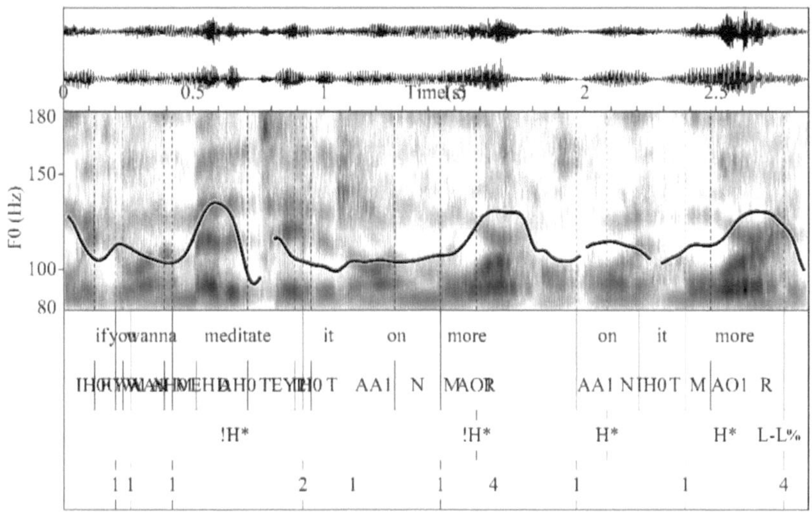

Figure 4: Medial insubordinate if-clause *if you wanna meditate it on more... on it **more*** (SBC25a).

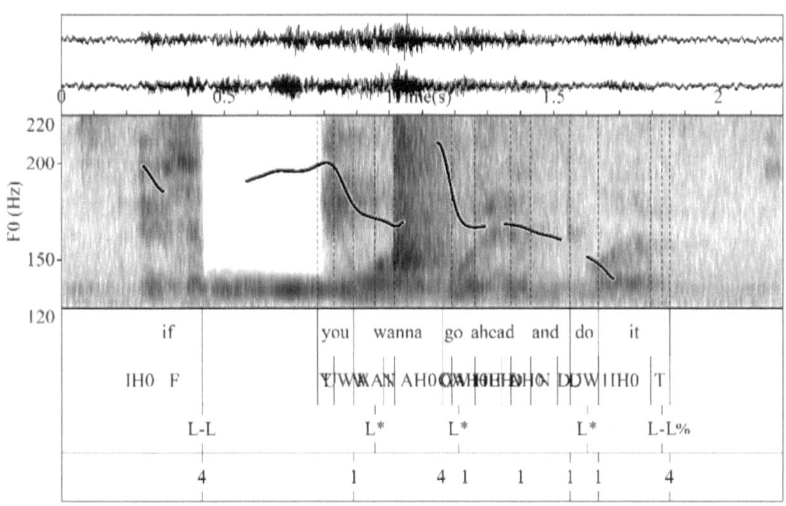

Figure 5: Final insubordinate if-clause *if you wanna go ahead and **do** it* (SBC18b).

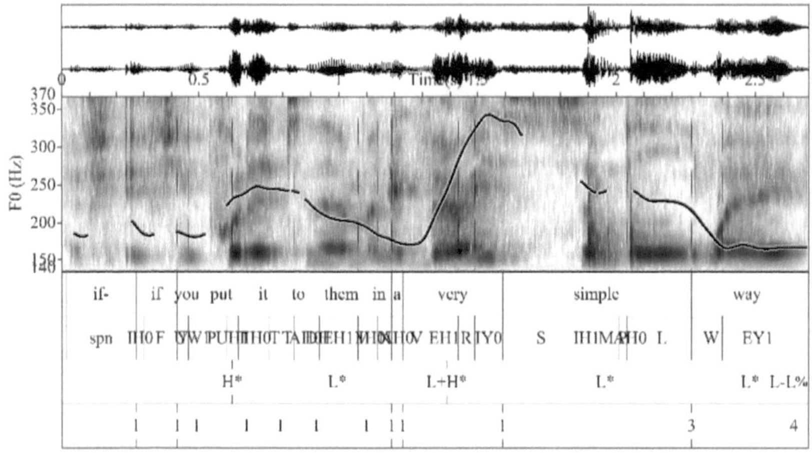

Figure 6: Initial insubordinate if-clause (L* L-L% configuration*) if you put it to them in a **very** simple way* (SBC04).

The analysed subordinate *if*-clauses present certain differences depending on their position within the utterance. Those in final position mostly end in L-L%, thus marking the final boundary of the clause. Conversely, those in initial and medial position range from ending in a pitch accent, such as H*, H*+L, L*, L*+H (Figure 7), to having a rising final contour—L-H% (Figure 8), as well as showcasing, albeit only in a few instances, a L-L% terminal contour. This proves that subordinate *if*-clauses are indeed connected to the context; a rising or unfinished pattern entails that the utterance continues as a whole beyond the *if*-clause, i.e., the continuation rise fulfils its function as an indicator of non-finality or continuation.

Thus, the observed tendency in insubordinate *if*-clauses to present a falling terminal contour indicates that this type of clause is fixed both grammatically and intonationally, as shown in the sample analysed in this chapter. Chiefly, those found in initial position are an example of that grammatical and intonational interconnection because, if they were not insubordinate clauses, they would be expected to show more intonational variability, as their subordinate counterparts do.

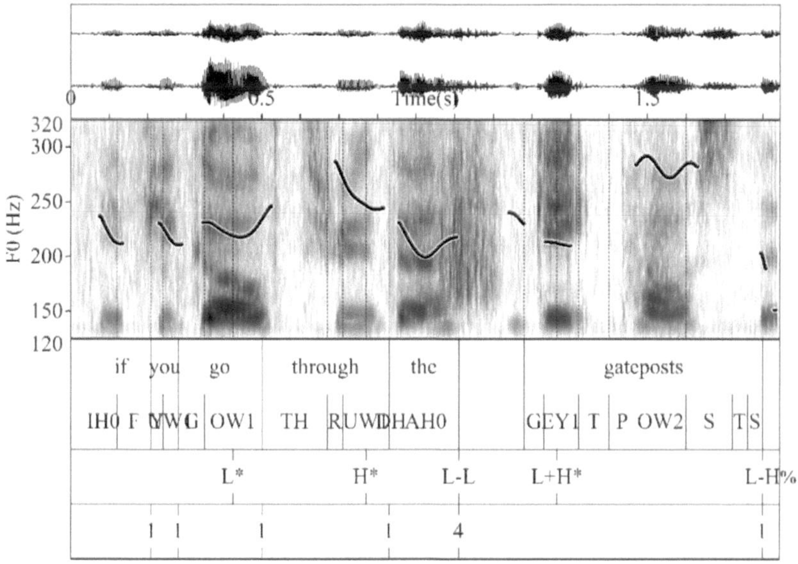

Figure 7: Initial subordinate *if*-clause (L+H* L-H% configuration) *if you go through the* ***gateposts*** (SBC56).

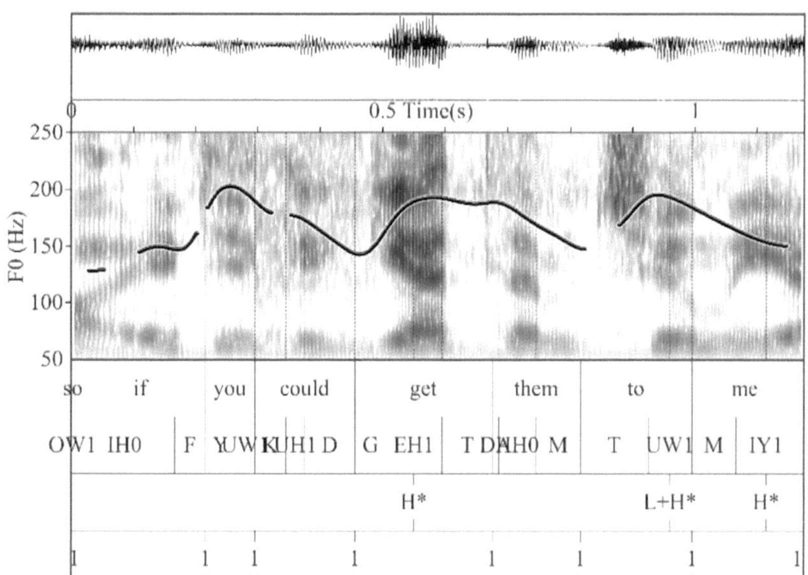

Figure 8: Initial subordinate *if*-clause (L+H* H* configuration) *if you could* ***get*** *them to me* (SBC21).

4.2. The Influence of IF in if-*clause intonation*

In Section 3.2, the distribution of insubordinate *if*-clauses depending on their illocutionary force was presented as being rather uneven since requests and instructions make up for most of the clauses. Despite that, an underlying trend related to this variable is found in each IF category when viewed as a whole. As noted in Section 3.2, the term *directive* represents a continuum whereby offers carry the least directive meaning and orders, the most directive meaning. This may be evinced by how fixed their intonation is depending on the IF of the clause.

Firstly, requests show the highest degree of variability within insubordinate *if*-clauses in their overall pitch movement as some of them start with H*, although they often end in a L%. They are followed, with regard to intonation variability, by offers and instructions, which sometimes depart from their frequent mid and low falls although, in general, they have rather fixed contours ending in L-L% or LL-. Lastly, orders show an almost identical contour, with a L* and L-L% as their dominant terminal contour. On the whole, this means that the more directive a clause is, the higher the degree of fixation of its intonation will be.

Such principle cannot be applied to subordinate *if*-clauses with directive meaning seeing that their intonation contours vary regardless of their IF, as described in Section 3.2. Certain orders present some minute similarities, which may be attributable to their position rather than their IF. Such is also the case for instructions, which show a L-L% in final position, as well as for six clauses classified as offers. In spite of that, seven other offers begin with H* and end in L-L% or contain one single pitch accent. In turn, requests present relatively disparate contours, demonstrating the diversity of subordinate *if*-clauses. Thus, this greater degree of variation in the pitch movement together with the occurrence of pitch accents at the expected end of the subordinate clause as well as the appearance of rising terminal contours evinces the subordinate nature of such utterances.

In summary, the analysis of the directive insubordinate and subordinate clauses in the *SBC* provides us with evidence to support the view that there is a predominant contour for insubordinate *if*-clauses in AmE, which confirms the findings attested by Kaltenböck (2016) for BrE. On the one hand, the falling terminal contour displayed by the vast majority of insubordinate *if*-clauses with directive meaning found in the *SBC* suggests that their intonation is much more fixed than that of their subordinate counterparts. Such contour typically ends in L-L% regardless of the position of the clause within the utterance. Conversely, the subordinate *if*-clauses retrieved from the *SBC* show that their position in the utterance affects their terminal contour. On the other hand, while the IF of the clauses does not impact the intonation of subordinate *if*-clauses, there is some evidence that the IF does have an influence on insubordinate *if*-clauses, although further research with a larger corpus must be conducted in order to reach more robust conclusions.

5. Concluding remarks

The present chapter has provided compelling evidence towards a comprehensive characterisation of the intonation contours of directive insubordinate *if*-clauses in a specific variety of English, namely AmE. More specifically, a comprehensive acoustic analysis of the terminal contours of directive insubordinate and subordinate *if*-clauses in the *SBC* has been conducted with the aim to determine whether there are any significantly salient differences in the predominant intonation contours used by AmE speakers when uttering directive subordinate clauses, on the one hand, and directive insubordinates, on the other. The existence of such differences, as proven for BrE in previous studies, would confirm the status of directive insubordinates as fragments inasmuch as they stand alone grammatically, semantically pragmatically, and also intonationally.

The analysis of the subordinate if-clauses with directive meaning found in the SBC renders a number of possible intonation contours depending on where the subordinate clause occurs with regard to the main clause. On the one hand, subordinate if-clauses occurring in initial and medial positions predominantly present a rising terminal contour—the so called 'continuation rise', typically used to indicate non-finality—, which is consistent with Kaltenböck's (2016) observations for BrE. On the other hand, the subordinate if-clauses found in final position describe a falling pattern, which, again, is consistent with the findings in BrE.

In the case of directive insubordinate if-clauses in the SBC, the intonation patterns produced by the speakers consistently conform to falling contours regardless of where the insubordinate clause occurs within the utterance. The very minor variations have to do with the type of fall, which is directly linked to the illocutionary force of directive (i.e. offer, instruction, request, order). In this regard, the close analysis conducted shows that the more directive a clause is, the higher the degree of fixation of its intonation will be.

In conclusion, the analysis of directive insubordinate and subordinate if-clauses in the SBC allows us to confirm that the intonation contours of insubordinate if-clauses are more fixed than those of subordinate if-clauses, as proven for Spanish and BrE, thus reinforcing the view of insubordinate if-clauses as prosodically and grammatically conventionalised fragments.

The research presented in this chapter requires a further exploration of the intonation of insubordinate clauses, in general, and insubordinate if-clauses, in particular. Given the size of the sample retrieved from the SBC, a larger corpus of spoken AmE should be analysed in order to check the statistical significance of the findings presented.

References

Beckman, Mary E. / Ayers, Gayle M. 1997. *Guidelines for ToBI Labelling.* ToBI Labelling Guidelines. Retrieved 9th April 2022, from https://www.ling.ohio-state.edu/research/phonetics/E_ToBI/

Boersma, Paul / Weenink, David. 2021. *Praat 6.2.23 Computer Software.* Amsterdam, Netherlands.

Bolinger, Dwight. 1989. *Intonation and Its Uses: Melody in Grammar and Discourse*. Stanford: Stanford University Press.

Bowie, Jill / Aarts, Bowie. 2016. Clause Fragments in English Dialogue. In López-Couso, María José / Menéndez-Naya, Belén / Núñez-Pertejo, Paloma / Palacios, Ignacio M. (eds.), *Corpus Linguistics on the Move: Exploring and Understanding English through Corpora*. Leiden: Brill, 259–288.

Brown, Penelope / Levinson, Stephen C. 1987. *Politeness: Some Universals in Language Usage*. Cambridge: Cambridge University Press.

Domíguez, Mónica / Roher, Patrick L. / Soler-Company, Juan. 2019. PyToBI: A Toolkit for ToBI Labeling under Python. *Proc. Interspeech 2019*, 3675–3676.

Du Bois, John W. / Chafe, Wallace L. / Meyer, Charles / Thompson, Sandra A. / Englebretson, Robert / Martey, Nii. 2000–2005. *Santa Barbara Corpus of Spoken American English Parts 1–4*. Philadelphia: Linguistic Data Corsortium.

Elvira-García, Wendy. 2019. Two Constructions, One Syntactic Form: Perceptual Prosodic Differences between Elliptical and Independent <si + V indicative> Clauses in Spanish. In Karin, Beijering / Gunther, Kaltenböck / Sansiñena, María S. (eds.), *Insubordination: Theoretical and Empirical Issues*. Berlin: De Gruyter Mouton, 240–264.

Elvira-García, Wendy / Roseano, Paolo / Fernández-Planas, Ana María. 2017. Prosody as a Cue for Syntactic Dependency. Evidence from Dependent and Independent Clauses with Subordination Marks in Spanish. *Journal of Pragmatics* 109, 29–46.

Estebas-Vilaplana, Eva / Gutiérrez, Yurema M. / Vizcaíno-Ortega, Francisco / Cabrera-Abreu, Mercedes. 2015. *Boundary Tones in Spanish Declaratives: Modelling Sustained Pitch. ICPhS15*. 18th International Congress of Phonetic Sciences, Glasgow.

Evans, Nicholas. 2007. Insubordination and Its Uses. In I. Nikolaeva (ed.), *Finiteness: Theoretical and Empirical Foundations*. Oxford: Oxford University Press, 366–431.

GoldWave Inc. 2022. *GoldWave 6.65 Computer Software*. Newfoundland, Canada.

Jun, Sun-Ah. 2005. Prosodic Typology. In S.-A. Jun (ed.), *Prosodic Typology: The Phonology of Intonation and Phrasing*. Oxford: Oxford University Press, 430–461.

Kaltenböck, Gunther. 2016. On the Grammatical Status of Insubordinate *If*-Clauses. In Kaltenböck, Gunther / Keizer, Evelien / Lohmann, Arne (eds.), *Outside the Clause: Form and Function of Extra-Clausal Constituents*. Amsterdam: John Benjamins, 341–377.

Mato-Míguez, Beatriz. 2016. *The Expression of Directive Meaning: A Corpus-Based Study on the Variation between Insubordinated If-Clauses, Imperatives and Conditionals in Contemporary Spoken British and American English.* Universidade de Santiago de Compostela: Unpublished PhD Dissertation.

McAuliffe, Michael / Socolof, Michaela / Mihuc, Sarah / Wagner, Michael / Sonderegger, Morgan. 2017. *Montreal Forced Aligner 2.0.0b4 Computer Software*. Montreal, Canada.

Merchant, Jason. 2005. Fragments and Ellipsis. *Linguistics and Philosophy,* 27, 661–738.

Morgan, Jerry L. 1973. Sentence Fragments and the Notion of 'Sentence'. In Kachru, Braj / Lees, Robert / Malkiel, Yakov / Pietrangeli, Angelina / Saporta, Sol (eds.), *Issues in Linguistics.* Urbana: University of Illinois Press, 719–751.

Pierrehumbert, Janet. 1980. *The Phonology and Phonetics of English Intonation.* Massachusetts Institute of Technology: Unpublished PhD Dissertation.

Stainton, Robert J. 2006. *Words and Thoughts: Subsentences, Ellipsis and the Philosophy of Language*. Oxford: Clarendon Press.

Yule, George. 1996. *Pragmatics*. Oxford: Oxford University Press.

ENCARNACIÓN ALMAZÁN-RUIZ /
AROA ORREQUIA-BAREA

A critical discourse analysis of 2020 US presidential debates

1. Introduction

The year 2020 began with the threat of a new disease. It did not take long for the disease to spread, and countries worldwide decreed a population lockdown to curb the spread of this disease, known as COVID-19[1]. The measures taken had health and social effects, as well as an impact on the global economy. Against this backdrop, the 2020 US presidential election took place.

The president at the time, Donald Trump, was seeking re-election, and his main opponent was the Democrat candidate, former Vice President Joe Biden. The two candidates endured one of the most intense election campaigns in US history in their quest for the White House, as evidenced by the two presidential debates on the 29th of September and the 22nd of October 2020.

Political discourse carries intentionality because, as Wilson (2005: 401) states, 'to have others believe you, do what you want them to do, and generally view the world in the way most favourable for your goals, you need to manipulate, or, at the very least, pay attention to the linguistic limits of forms of representation.' As a result, the language used by both politicians in their speeches in the presidential debates can be a remarkable object of study from a linguistic perspective.

1 COVID-19 is a disease caused by a new coronavirus that emerged in December 2019. The name stands for CoronaVirus Disease of 2019: https://time.com/5782284/who-name-coronavirus-covid-19/.

Given the exceptional circumstances in 2020, this research aims to make a comparative linguistic analysis of the presidential debates between the two contenders that year. The analysis will focus on lexical choice and the polarity of the words used, that is, Sentiment Analysis. For this reason, two research questions are posed:

RQ1.- What are the candidates' main linguistic differences regarding word choice when discussing the same topics?
RQ2.- What is the semantic orientation of the discourses?

This paper is organised as follows: Section 2 deals with the pillars of the research, namely, language, political discourse and presidential debates. Section 3 describes the corpus, the methodology, and the analytical framework used to analyse the data. Section 4 includes the results and the discussion. Finally, some conclusions are drawn.

2. Language, political discourse, and presidential debates

Since language is the primary human means of communication, it can become a powerful weapon when attempting to influence others' opinions. Presenting events in one way or another can have different effects on the communicative act. Given this feature of the language, it is manifest that how events are presented to the audience in the political setting can be crucial in determining the effect they have on the target audience.

As is known, the relationship between language and politics 'can be traced to classical Greek and Roman treatises on rhetoric' (Dunmire 2012: 735), indicating that the persuasive power of speech has always been noteworthy. Indeed, as Chilton (2004: 5) claims, it is hard to conceive of politics without considering the importance of language. Consequently, it is in the political domain where language acquires particular relevance because politicians, aware of the potential of language, use it intentionally to orient their discourse towards the objective they wish to achieve.

In this sense, Hashim (2015: 700) states that 'political discourse is not only about stating public propositions. It is about politics. It is about doing things with words.' Accordingly, politics constitute a wide realm to study the linguistic characteristics of discourse since it precisely exposes the power of words. Hence, 'linguistic options for representing the world are [. . .] central issues in political discourse', as Wilson (2005: 404) remarks.

However, defining political discourse appears to be a difficult task. Roughly speaking, as van Dijk (1997: 12) claims, it could be any spoken or written speech act concerning political professionals or political institutions. In this sense, Kenzhekanova (2015: 193) proposes that political discourse can be regarded as 'a collection of all speech acts, as well as public law, tradition and experience, which is determined and expressed in the form of verbal formations, content, subject and the addressee of which belongs to the sphere of politics.' In this broad context offered by the concept of political discourse, it is relevant and interesting to study the discursive strategies that politicians include to sway voters.

Politicians will likely employ discursive strategies to present the facts to the audience. Despite occurring in the same social and temporal context, the differences between ideologies and political actors may be discernible through the linguistic traces they leave in their speech. Similarly, when describing events and conveying to the public the decisions made on a certain issue, politicians try to balance the negative and the positive to mitigate the impact it might have on the audience (Chilton 2004: 40). This premise is a linguistic strategy that determines specific choices to be made. As Chilton (2004: 40–41) illustrates, politicians will employ the idea of unity, fraternity and patriotism to highlight the positive elements. The repetitive usage of the first-person plural personal pronoun is an outstanding example. On the other hand, they will try to minimise the negative aspects by using euphemisms or avoiding 'threatening referents.'

As a result, the meaning will not always be expressed explicitly. To appropriately interpret the politicians' message, it is, therefore, necessary to consider the conditions around it as well as what it intends to achieve. When analysing political language, the concepts of inference and implicature acquire particular relevance because they allow politicians 'to convey more than they say,' as Chilton points out (2004: 37). Besides, in one way or another, any declarative can be ambiguous and, as Edelman (1985: 10) suggests, it will be the context, the social situation and the listeners' previous knowledge that determine whether it is interpreted in one way or another.

Therefore, the main persuasive element of politicians is language. In politics, language is used to persuade the electorate as well as to argue for political decisions on a specific issue. According to McIntosh (2020), politicians can use language as a weapon to turn it into part of their power, provoking social divisions that can become real problems affecting coexistence in society.

Politicians use language to construct their own identity, one that attracts voters' attention. Scandals, provocations, insults or demeaning have been part of the agenda of far-right politics in the last few years. This anti-political correctness can be viewed as a sign of authenticity by the voters as it means that this type of politicians is willing to say what other politicians would not say (McIntosh 2020). However, most of these practices may have a completely different goal: to attract people's attention while unpopular decisions are being made (Wodak et al. 2021).

In the political context at issue, namely the election campaign for the presidency of the United States, television debates take on particular relevance. Firstly, in a democratic context, the debate is not only necessary but essential. As Coleman (2000: 1) states, a democracy that does not encourage and foster public deliberation of political matters would be unthinkable. Secondly, electoral campaigns provide an excellent opportunity for candidates to express their views and proposals to the people (Coleman 2000: 5). Thirdly, it cannot be overlooked that television has changed the way politicians reach the public, making it an excellent medium for reaching a wide audience and, hence, a huge number of potential voters (2000: 9).

The first televised debate in the United States occurred between Richard Nixon and John F. Kennedy in 1960 (Coleman 2000: 7). Since then, televised debates have served as an effective hook for catching voters. Certainly, these debates are essential not only for the American nation but also for the rest of the world, who also pay attention to these encounters between the two leading presidential candidates. The debates represent an excellent opportunity to know the candidates' ideas on various topics. Thus, political debates are a clear chance to discern politicians' language since language is never unintentional.

As previously mentioned, the 2020 election campaign was one of the most heated in US history not only because of the extraordinary circumstances the world was living in but also because Trump's rhetoric had been controversial during his whole term. Since Trump was elected President of the United States in 2016, his peculiar way of expressing himself in his political interventions has led to numerous studies (Abbas 2019; Lonsdale 2021; McIntosh 2020; Montgomery 2017; Wodak et al. 2021) that examine and analyse his discursive distinctiveness. As Lonsdale states, Trump's political discourse can be defined as fitting into the so-called populism. He is considered 'the populist par excellence', that is, to exemplify the populist communicative and leadership style (Oliver and Rahn 2016). His propaganda has been based on three main and related ideas: American greatness, the threat of a corrupt elite and the 'saviour' of America (Lonsdale 2021: 38), as will be shown in Section 4.1.

In fact, the debates were also a sample of his behaviour, particularly the first one. The media even described it as a 'hot mess, inside a dumpster fire, inside a train wreck'.[2] His continual interruptions and failure to respect the time limit for answering the questions made the moderator's role extremely difficult and it caused a format change[3] in the second debate, that of muting the microphones while they were answering.

3. Data and methods

3.1. Corpus description

The corpus consists of the transcriptions of the two debates constituting two sub-corpora within this study. The transcriptions were downloaded

2 In Jake Tapper's words, CNN's chief Washington correspondent. https://thehill.com/homenews/media/518879-cnns-jake-tapper-calls-debate-a-hot-mess-inside-a-dumpster-fire-inside-a-train/

3 https://www.bbc.com/news/election-us-2020-54366618

from the official website of the *Commission of Presidential Debates* (CPD)[4] This Commission is a non-profit organisation, funded in 1987, to guarantee that debates are celebrated as well as to organise and sponsor presidential debates, among other things. Its main purpose is to educate people about political matters and assist other countries where democracy is emerging.

Although three presidential debates were initially scheduled, only two were finally held, making the 2020 Presidential Campaign the one with the fewest debates since 1996. The first presidential debate was televised on the 29th of September. Chris Wallace, *Fox News Sunday* anchor, presented the event at Case Western Reserve University in Cleveland, Ohio. The second was planned for the 15th of October, but President Trump tested positive for COVID-19 on the 2nd of October and refused to do it remotely. Therefore, it was finally cancelled[5] and the third debate became the second. It was held on the 22nd of October and was moderated by Kristen Welker, *NBC News White House* reporter. Belmont University in Nashville, Tennessee, hosted the event[6].

The debates were led by a moderator who chose six topics for fifteen minutes each. According to the Commission, the debate format was divided into two-minute answers from each candidate to the question posed around each topic; followed by an open discussion for the rest of the fifteen minutes. Both parties had previously agreed to these rules though neither the candidates nor the Commission knew about the questions beforehand.

The first debate revolved around the following six topics: *Supreme Court, COVID-19, economy, race and violence, Trump-Biden record* and *election integrity*. Some of these topics were revisited in the second debate, while others were introduced for the first time. It centred on: *COVID-19, American families, race, climate change, national*

4 Transcriptions can be accessed at CPD: Debate Transcripts (debates.org).

5 Each candidate participated in town hall events separately but at the same time instead https://eu.usatoday.com/story/entertainment/tv/2020/10/15/trump-town-hall-nbc-faces-backlash-over-competing-biden-abc-town-hall/3661571001/.

6 There was also a debate between the vice presidential candidates (Mike Pence, from the Republican Party, and Kamala Harris, from the Democratic one) on the 7th of October.

security and *leadership*. The corpus amounts to 35,128 tokens and 5,036 types. The distribution of the corpus can be seen in Table 1.

Table 1: Distribution of the corpora.

Candidate	Debate	Tokens	Types	Total
Joe Biden	First	8,057	1,263	16,442
	Second	8,385	1,356	
Donald Trump	First	9,134	1,172	18,686
	Second	9,552	1,245	

3.2. Analysis procedure

Various digital tools were used since several aspects have been considered in the corpus analysis[7]. On the one hand, the text was analysed using the programming language *R* and *Sketch Engine* for corpus-based analysis. On the other hand, the software *Lingmotif* is used for Sentiment Analysis.

The linguistic analysis was carried out by means of the programming language *R*, which automatically analyses the text in terms of word frequency and retrieves lexical words (Fradejas Rueda 2019). Particularly, in this study, *R* was used to extract the most frequent words in each of the most important lexical categories, namely nouns, verbs and adjectives. The software *Sketch Engine* was also used to enrich this analysis because, among its functions, it allows the user to extract keywords, obtain frequent words and study concordances in detail (Kilgarriff et al. 2014).

In terms of Sentiment Analysis, the software *Lingmotif* (Moreno-Ortiz 2017) was employed to perform this type of analysis and to determine the orientation or polarity of the text. *Lingmotif* is a multi-platform application with a friendly GUI and supported by a comprehensive multilingual lexicon, which identifies words and multi-word

7 For the sake of clarity, the moderators' words have been deleted not to interfere with the analysis.

expressions with emotional content. It contains a manually annotated sentiment lexicon in English, consisting of over 28,000 words and more than 38,000 phrases. The application analyses any type of text, in terms of size and topic, identifying those words and multi-word expressions with emotional content stored in the lexicon and applying context rules to output several metrics (Moreno-Ortiz 2017).

Lingmotif provides different metrics, but for this study, the *Text Sentiment Score* (TSS) and the *Text Sentiment Intensity* (TSI) have been considered as they are meant to encapsulate the sentiment expressed in the text. The former provides an overview of the overall sentiment expressed within the text. In contrast, the latter details the proportion of sentiment-laden elements in relation to those that lack such emotional connotations in the text.

3.3. Analytical framework

This research makes use of the 'methodological' (Baker et al. 2008: 273) or even 'natural synergy' (Marchi and Taylor 2018: 1) of Corpus Linguistics and Critical Discourse Analysis. Sinclair refers to Corpus Linguistics and Discourse Analysis as 'the twin pillars of language research' and 'what unites them is [. . .] they both encourage the formulation of radically new hypotheses [and] the dimensions of pattern that they deal with are, on the whole, larger than linguistics is accustomed to' (Sinclair 2004: 11 quoted in Marchi and Taylor 2018: 1). Combining these two methods is advantageous for the study as the strengths of both of them can be exploited. Besides, they can overcome limitations that each one has separately by providing both quantitative and qualitative analysis (Marchi and Taylor 2018: 7).

On the one hand, Corpus Linguistics is considered a set of methods which is quantitative since it provides highly objective results and, therefore, reduces bias[8] (Ganzone and Santulli 2004: 353). Corpus Linguistics techniques, such as keywords or collocations, can be used

8 Certainly, human input is necessary for the decision-making process along the analysis, but the corpus queries allow the researcher to explore the text "free from any preconceived or existing notions regarding their linguistic or semantic/pragmatic content" (Baker et al. 2008: 277).

as an initial exploration of the corpus to detect salient patterns or lexis that can be analysed in more detail later through concordances (Stubbs 1994; Mautner 2007 quoted in Baker et al. 2008). Therefore, Corpus Linguistics helps see both patterns that the researcher has already thought of and others that were not so easy to find with the naked eye (Baker et al. 2008: 285).

However, a corpus-based analysis cannot account for interpretations of patterns in the text as it does not consider certain variables, such as the context of the data (Baker et al. 2008: 293). For this reason, it is necessary to combine Corpus Linguistics methods with Critical Discourse Analysis so that the researcher can explain the results obtained in the corpus based on a theoretical framework.

This issue is one of the most widespread criticisms of Corpus Linguistics, as many scholars regard the results obtained in a corpus-based analysis as 'decontextualised data' (Mautner 2007: 279 quoted in Baker et al. 2008). This objection can be overcome by combining Critical Discourse Analysis with Corpus Linguistics.

Critical Discourse Analysis (CDA henceforth), on the other hand, is described as a qualitative method that takes into account the examination of the contexts surrounding the text. Thus, the analysis extends beyond the results obtained from the text. CDA focuses on social wrongdoings and aims to evaluate the use people make of language in different contexts that reflect inequalities in social relationships, such as power, control or discrimination, among others (Baker et al. 2008: 280). Thus, context, surrounding circumstances and consequences play a crucial role in interpreting the text (Van Dijk, 2005 quoted in Baker et al. 2008). In this type of analysis, both the presence or absence of a certain linguistic pattern might have substantial implications and influence the overall findings (Baker et al. 2008).

Some of the most widespread criticism of CDA is the use of small corpora, which sometimes is not representative and even biased, as well as 'the scant to the linguistic data' (Widdowson 1995: 159, quoted in Garzone and Santulli 2004: 352). Therefore, mixing these two methods can provide more advantages than disadvantages, as the analysis is enriched by using the best tool of each approach. Additionally, combining the two methods and providing a thorough analysis can help overcome limitations and criticism.

As previously mentioned, Sentiment Analysis techniques are also used in this study. Sentiment Analysis (SA, henceforth) is becoming increasingly important in the fields of Computational Linguistics and Natural Language Processing (NLP) due to the rapid growth of the collaborative web and the vast amount of user-generated content that is available on the Internet and that can be very valuable for companies and organisations. SA constitutes a task of NLP, and as such, it consists of automatically processing opinionated texts and determining the sentiment or orientation contained in the text.

According to Liu, SA is 'the field of study that analyses people's opinions, sentiments, valuations, appraisals, attitudes, and emotions towards entities [...] and their attributes' (Liu 2012: 7). Thus, SA examines opinionated texts, that is, subjective texts in which people have expressed their perception or feelings about something. It classifies the text according to the polarity of its words and assigns positive, negative or neutral values to the words to later determine the overall sentiment of the text.

Two main approaches carry out this task: machine learning techniques and the lexical method. In the former, a set of tagged examples is used to train the algorithm. Then, its performance is evaluated against another set of tagged examples. These algorithms work well with datasets they have been trained for but they are not so accurate when the dataset is of a different nature. The lexicon-based approach uses a lexicon where words are listed according to the sentiment they carry. The task then consists of identifying such words and determining the polarity of such texts.

As previously stated, *Lingmotif* is based on lexicon (Moreno-Ortiz 2017). However, this approach does not come without problems. One recurrent problem dealing with lexical support is the general claim that the expression of sentiment seems to be domain-specific, which 'is in part a consequence of changes in vocabulary, [as] even the exact same expression can indicate different sentiment in different domains' (Pang and Lee 2008). If this is true, sentiment lexicons should be adapted, at least to a certain degree, for each domain. *Lingmotif* already includes several plug-ins that users can select and have a specific lexicon for such a domain, which makes it a helpful tool to analyse discourse.

4. Results

This section outlines the results obtained from two distinct analyses: lexical and sentiment analysis.

4.1. Lexical analysis

This section attempts to answer the first research question posed in Section 1:

> RQ1.- What are the candidates' main linguistic differences regarding word choice when discussing the same topics?

To answer this question, the results obtained in the keyword extraction and the frequency list retrieved by *Sketch Engine* have been considered. This analysis combines these two lists because both provide aspects relevant to how each politician uses the language. As is known, lexical choices are not randomly made, much less in political debates. Frequency lists provide information on the repeated use of the same lexical item. In contrast, keywords reveal the saliency of some terms that may not be noticed at first sight. These fundamental corpus linguistic tools facilitate the analysis of discourse construction, the presence of certain discourses as well as the comparison of different corpora (Baker 2006). Additionally, a close examination is carried out by analysing the concordances of the words retrieved by these two lists.

The selection process was the same for both keywords and frequent words. After *Sketch Engine* retrieved the fifty top words in each case, they were grouped according to topics (Baker et al. 2008: 278). Thus, we discarded some proper names which have no relevance for the groupings, such as 'Burisma' or 'Pelosi', in the case of keywords; and some general and grammatical words in the frequency list, such as 'people', 'president' or 'money'. Before making such decisions, concordances were checked to investigate the context in which the word appears and to determine whether they were relevant for the present study or not.

Keywords were extracted using Sketch Engine's default keyness score, that is, simple maths[9], which compares the relative frequency (per million) of a token in the focus corpus, that is, Trump's or Biden's, with the relative frequencies in the reference one, namely the default English Web 2020 (enTenTen20). For the frequent words, a stopword list was used to avoid the retrieval of grammatical words, which would create much noise in the results.

Keywords then reveal that both debates revolve around three common themes: *COVID-19, healthcare* and *race.* These three topics are motivated by the sections into which the debates were divided; in addition, they were also trendy topics during 2020. Nevertheless, apart from these common topics, others were also discussed in one debate or the other. In the first debate, there is another recurrent topic that emerged when asked about *Election integrity*. As is known, after his election defeat, Trump alleged that there had been political fraud.

The second debate also includes two other topics that are worth mentioning. The first one is *immigration.* No segment was devoted to this topic in the debate, but the anchor decided to ask them about it as part of the current national affairs. The second topic is *climate change.* Table 2 shows the most salient terms in each theme and the ones appearing in every debate.

9 For more information: https://www.sketchengine.eu/documentation/simple-maths/.

Table 2: Comparison of Biden's and Trump's keywords.

Debate	Topic	Biden	Trump
Both debates	**COVID-19**	COVID, panic, Wuhan, wherewithal, plexiglass, xenophobic, xenophobia, distancing	Fauci, xenophobic, ventilator, Moderna, Pfizer, mask, plexiglass, H1N1, spike, cubicle
	Healthcare	pre-existing, Obamacare, Bidencare, Medicare	Obamacare, Obama-Biden, pre-existing, socialised
	Race	African-Americans, insensitivity, Antifa, Klux, Floyd, suburb, Klan, supremacist, hoodie	Antifa, left-wing, African-Americans, superpredators
Only 1st debate	**Alledge political fraud**	Mail-in, ballot	Wastepaper, ballot, mailman, solicit, unsolicited
Only 2nd debate	**Immigration**	Maraud, disincentive, DACA, rapist	Cage, cartel, coyote, rapist
	Climate change	Fracking, pollute	Fracking, AOC[10], windmill, disservice, fume

As expected, the pandemic was the most recurrent topic during the debates as it did affect not only people's lives but also countries' economies, healthcare and even the act of voting. As the pandemic began in early 2020 and the debate took place in late September, the world was still struggling with this disease; the vaccines had not yet been released and the death toll was extremely high. A few days before the debates,

10 Trump specifically said "AOC plus three" referring to four Democratic congresswomen of colour: Alexandria Ocasio-Cortez (hence, AOC) and three of her colleagues (hence, "plus three"), namely, Ilhan Omar, Ayanna S. Pressley and Rashida Tlaib. They, among other people, were the ones promoting the Green New Deal. (For more information: https://www.nytimes.com/2020/10/23/us/elections/aoc-plus-three-plus-many-more-respond-after-trumps-debate-stage-attack.html).

the mortality rate in the US reached 200,000 fatalities, accounting for 20 % of all the deaths worldwide despite US inhabitants representing only 4 % of the world population[11].

Under these circumstances, it was to be expected that the word 'COVID' would be one of the most salient in Biden's corpus, as shown in Table 2. However, it is neither salient nor frequent in Trump's speech (8.5 vs 1.6)[12]. In contrast, Trump employs more general and abstract words to allude to the pandemic, such as 'disease' or 'plague', the latter being more informal and negative. In his discourse, avoiding calling the disease by its name can be interpreted as a euphemism, namely a way of belittling the importance of the disease. For him, it is irrelevant whether it is named one way or another, only that it is a disease.

Regarding this topic, some of the keywords in Trump's discourse related to the pandemic are vaccine names, 'Moderna' and 'Pfizer', as well as 'ventilator', 'mask' and 'spike'. Besides, 'Fauci' appears as a keyword since he was the director of the National Institute of Allergy and Infectious Disease (NIAID) and chief medical advisor to the president. Donald Trump uses all these words to emphasise his achievements during the pandemic.

(1) We got the gowns. We got the masks. We made the ventilators. You wouldn't have made ventilators. And now we're weeks away from a vaccine. (Trump, first debate).

(2) Dr Fauci said, "President Trump saved thousands of lives." Many of your Democrat Governors said, "President Trump did a phenomenal job." (Trump, first debate).

As (1) and (2) show, the Republican candidate's strategy was to depict himself as the saviour, as the solution to the problem that was occurring at the time and the protector of all the attacks that may threaten the American society. This approach is one of the characteristics of populist discourse. In this sense, Lonsdale (2021: 38) argues that Trump portrays himself as the source of all the positive things that have happened, presenting himself as 'the voice and saviour of the 'forgotten people' of America'.

11 https://time.com/5891101/us-coronavirus-deaths-200000/.

12 Normalised frequency (10,000) shows quantitative data as the corpora are not balanced.

However, the president's advisor's surname, 'Fauci', was not only used in the sense it appears in example (2). As previously mentioned, one of the arguments that Trump used to convince his voters is the existence of a corrupt and weak elite that is threatening traditional American values, one that he does not belong to as he is a successful businessman. Thus, he distances himself from failures. The elite can have different forms depending on the situation: the Democrats, the media, other countries, the establishment, the *Black Lives Matter* movement or even experts, such as Dr Fauci during the pandemic, as can be seen in (3).

(3) He [Dr Fauci] said very strongly, "Masks are not good." Then he changed his mind. He said, "Masks are good." (Trump, first debate).

The words 'Wuhan' and 'China' are also significant when talking about the pandemic. 'Wuhan' is a salient word in Biden's discourse, whereas 'China' is among the most frequent words in both debates. Although the frequency is similar (Biden 16.4 vs Trump 17.1), the remarkable aspect of this word is the use that each politician made of it.

As stated above, 'China' is part of such an elite that Trump believes to be threatening American values. Therefore, China constitutes a danger to the whole American society as it was the origin of COVID-19. Biden, on the other hand, refers to the country and international relationships when using this word (7.5 vs 2.4), as shown in examples (4) and (5).

(4) It's not my fault that it came here. It's China's fault (Trump, second debate).
(5) I'm going to rejoin Paris Accord and make China abide by what they agreed to. (Biden, second debate).

In terms of healthcare, as the politicians are in the middle of an election, they are proposing the health system they will implement. Specifically, as seen in Table 2, Joe Biden is advocating for 'Bidencare' as a replacement for the then-current healthcare system, commonly known as 'Obamacare'. Another prominent word in both discourses is 'pre-existing', which collocates with 'condition' to refer to people who have a previous medical condition when hiring health insurance. In this vein, 'socialized' is a term that collocates with 'medicine' and is used by Trump to refer to the model Biden is offering to the voters. It is worth noting that one of the main proposals of Bidencare[13] involves the

13 https://www.forbes.com/sites/advisor/2020/10/23/is-bidencare-the-new-obamacare/?sh=7473bbc152f9.

creation of a health insurance program managed by the federal government. Thus, instead of enrolling in a private insurance plan, Americans would have the option to enrol in a health insurance plan run by the federal government.

Racial politics is one of the most controversial and partisan issues in the US (Lonsdale 2021: 30). In the first debate, the two candidates mainly talked about events that happened during this year: George Floyd was killed by a police officer[14] and the subsequent wave of protests that took place all over the country[15]. The keywords reveal that both candidates refer to this community as the 'African-Americans' and mention some radical groups who have historically been against this community, such as 'Ku-Kux-Klan'.

On the other hand, Biden does refer to 'Floyd', the murder victim, as can be seen in example (6). Unexpectedly, there are no hits of this word in Trump's discourse, which can be interpreted as an attitude of disdain.

> (6) when Floyd was killed, when Mr. Floyd was killed, there was a peaceful protest in front of the White House. (Biden, first debate).

As previously mentioned, George Floyd's murder was followed by subsequent protests organised by the *Black Lives Matter* movement not only in the US but also all over the world. Some of these protests turned violent and became riots as the African-American community was not only facing another episode of police brutality but it was also one of the most afflicted by the pandemic, as Biden states in example (7).

> (7) You talk about helping African-Americans, one in 1000 African-Americans has been killed because of the coronavirus. (Biden, first debate).

It is noteworthy mentioning Trump's attitude to these social and racial issues. He adopted the so-called 'dog whistle technique' to avoid criticism. Thus, he does not mention Floyd's name and he uses the word 'black' to target a section of his electorate. In this sense, he can appeal to his voters' sentiments, gaining their support but also avoids criticism on behalf of Democrat voters so as to prevent them from voting

---

14 https://www.nytimes.com/2020/05/31/us/george-floyd-investigation.html

15 https://edition.cnn.com/2020/07/23/us/black-lives-matter-protests-continue/index.html

against him. Not only did he frequently use the word 'black' (8 vs 1.8) to refer to this community but he also trivialises the movement in the debates. As is known, the word 'black' has traditionally been considered offensive or even oppressive for a group of people. Trump portrays the protesters as one of those threats to American values, that is, as 'anti-American' (Lonsdale 2021: 38), as seen in example (8):

(8) [...] the first time I ever heard of Black Lives Matter, they were chanting, "Pigs in a blanket," [...] talking about our police. "Pigs in a blanket, fry them like bacon." I said, "That's a horrible thing." (Trump, second debate).

Making reference to stereotypes and depicting *Black Lives Matter* as 'trouble-making thugs wanting to cause trouble' (Lonsdale 2021: 32) are ways of polarising the discourse as they constitute an invalidation of the point of the protest.

Apart from these three common topics, the allegedly political fraud was also discussed as part of the *Election integrity* topic in the first debate. Remarkably enough, Trump already mentioned that this would happen after the elections, as example (9) shows:

(9) They sent out a thousand ballots. Everybody got two ballots. This is going to be a fraud like you've never seen. (Trump, first debate).

On the pretext that people had to vote via mail owing to COVID-19 circumstances, Trump used charges of political fraud as a weapon against his opponent. As is known, many American people avoided going to the polling station and exposing themselves. Trump's discourse contains highly noticeable lexical items related to this topic (see Table 2). In contrast, Biden's discourse has fewer occurrences of these words compared to Trump's. Specifically, the word 'ballot' is notably more frequent in Trump's corpus, with a count of 13.3 compared to Biden's count of 9.7. According to Biden, Trump was intentionally discussing this topic to influence the voters. In this regard, example (10) highlights the disparity in using the word 'vote' between Biden and Trump. Biden's repetition of the word (20 vs 4) emphasises the significance that Biden places on the act of voting. He highlights the value of voting by reiterating the word numerous times within a brief statement.

(10) And this is all about trying to dissuade people from voting because he's trying to conf-to scare people into thinking that it's not going to be legitimate. Show up and vote. You will determine the outcome of this election. Vote, vote, vote. (Biden, first debate).

In the second debate, apart from the three major topics, two very controversial topics during Trump's term were also discussed: *immigration* and *climate change*. As for the former, some of the keywords retrieved in Biden's corpus are 'maraud', 'disincentive', 'DACA' (*Differed Action For Childhood Arrivals*) and 'rapist'. In the case of Trump, some of the words found are: 'cage', 'cartel', 'coyote' and 'rapist'. In fact, 'cage' is not only a keyword but also one of the most frequent words in his discourse (5.89). However, no hits were found in Biden's. The immigration topic here is discussed from the perspective of the children who are separated from their parents when they get to the border.

Regarding the *climate change* topic, the word 'fracking' is a keyword of both candidates (See Table 2). The topic was discussed not only because of the effects climate change has on the environment but also due to Trump's withdrawal from the *Paris Accord*. Example (11) states it in his own words:

> (11) The Paris Accord, I took us out because we were going to have to spend trillions of dollars and we were treated very unfairly (Trump, second debate).

When combining corpus linguistics techniques with CDA, a close reading of the corpus can reveal outstanding aspects of qualitative corpus analysis. This technique made it possible to examine how each politician used language to convey their stance to the voters. In fact, the verbal confrontation between the two candidates was so notorious that it is well worth considering the data obtained in the corpus analysis regarding lexical usage.

Based on the lexical word lists retrieved by *R*, the close reading of the concordances shows how both candidates use opposing terms that make clear their clashing positions on the different topics discussed during both debates. It is remarkable that within the three main word categories, verbs, nouns and adjectives, there are contrasting terms that offer valuable insight into the stances adopted by each politician when examined within their contextual frameworks, as will be described in the following pages.

Despite the devastating consequences of the pandemic's global spread, Trump insists on positively presenting the facts and making optimistic predictions for the future. Biden, on the other side, is less optimistic in front of the audience but tries to be more realistic. In this regard, the following examples illustrate their perspectives:

(12) we're learning to live with it (Trump, first debate).
(13) he says that we're learning to live with it. People are learning to die with it. (Biden, first debate).

As observed, the verbs *live* and *die* are used to present the facts differently. While the Republican candidate believes that progress is being made and people are learning to coexist with the pandemic, Biden is more categorical in his response, arguing that they are not. Both certainly think that the people are learning, yet it is clear that they are dealing with different issues as the concepts of living and dying are semantically opposed.

As mentioned above, the pandemic had numerous economic consequences, as many countries worldwide imposed a lockdown on people and limited the economy to essential activities. As a result, educational institutions, restaurants and many other businesses were forced to close during the first months of the pandemic. The suspension of commercial activity led to a significant decline in countries' economies, and the United States was not the exception.

This fact was another bone of contention and confrontation in the presidential debates, as seen in the frequency of both verbs: 'open' (Biden 16.4; Trump 6.4) and 'close' (Biden 3.04; Trump 28.36). It is notable to observe the contrasting viewpoints of the two candidates with regard to their experiences during the challenging months of the pandemic, as the following examples show:

(14) He wants to shut down this country and I want to keep it open (Trump, first debate).
(15) And he'll close down the whole country. This guy will close down the whole country and destroy our country. (Trump, first debate).
(16) I'm going to shut down the virus, not the country. (Biden, second debate).

While Trump is committed to reopening businesses, Biden demands that they work and invest in opening businesses and schools safely for citizens, as shown in examples (17–19), demonstrating that not only are the policy positions opposed, but semantically opposite terms are used to present them:

(17) People want their places open. They want to get back to their lives. They'll be careful, but they want their schools open. (Trump, first debate).
(18) We have to open our country. We're not going to have a country. You can't do this. We can't keep this country closed. (Trump, second debate).
(19) Look, the way to open businesses is to give them the wherewithal to be able to open. (Biden, first debate).

Likewise, the discrepancy between the adjectives 'good' and 'bad' is notable evidence of the verbal disagreement and distinct opinions expressed by the two candidates. Both adjectives are more frequent in Trump's speech than in Biden's. The results of the corpus analysis reveal that the frequency of the adjective 'good', in its absolute[16] form, in Trump's speech is 11.2, while in Biden's, it is 7.09. On the other hand, in its absolute form, the frequency of 'bad' in Trump is 6.4, and in Biden, it is only 1.2. In this sense, Abbas (2019: 506) states that 'Trump often attempts to categorise people ideologically into positive (good) and negative (bad)', which could explain the higher frequency of these two adjectives in his discourse.

(20) We have a phenomenal nominee respected by all. Top, top academic, good in every way. (Trump, first debate).

In the context of the discussion on *COVID-19* and its consequences, example (21) takes place. In his speech, Trump states that even if he made the right decisions, the press would never acknowledge it; consequently, fake news makes Biden appear to have a better public image than he does.

(21) That's because of the fake news, [...]They give you good press, they give me bad press because that's the way it is, unfortunately. (Trump, first debate).

Likewise, he even claims that his administration has been resourceful enough, having obtained 'ventilators', 'masks' and 'gowns', as commented above. Therefore, Trump considers that his government has responded correctly, and not only have they done a good job, but a great job. As seen in the following example, when using the adjective 'great', he increases the scale between the adjectives 'good' and 'bad'.

(22) We've done a great job. (Trump, first debate).

16 The absolute form of an adjective refers here to its basic form, unlike the comparative and superlative forms.

Trump's critical discourse is evident and he goes beyond using the adjective 'good' in the superlative form. According to Lonsdale (2021: 38), Trump's propaganda has been based on American greatness, among other ideas. In his discourse, Trump has stressed that his government has worked to make the country greater and better. This strategy is particularly relevant as a pattern of his exaggerated discourse since he frequently uses them to state that everything in the country is working better than ever, regardless of the issue being discussed, as shown in (23).

(23) The greatest, before COVID came in the greatest economy in history, lowest unemployment numbers, everything was good. (Trump, first debate; economy).
We have the best testing in the world by far. (Trump, second debate; pandemic).
We have the best lowest number in carbon emissions. (Trump, second debate; climatic change).

The corpus results show that this linguistic strategy is much more frequent in Trump's speech (26.2) than in Biden's (4.9). The use of exaggerated expressions is clearly related to the discursive device of hyperbole, 'a powerful-ideological tool that can be used particularly by speakers and writers for acts of praising and criticizing' (Abbas 2019: 57). In this regard, Montgomery mentions 'discursive amplification' as another strategy used to achieve the same effect. According to the scholar, 'Trump has broken radically new ground by making statements in a form that leaves little room for turning up the discursive volume further' (2017: 262), as shown in (24).

(24) Because there is never been an administration or president who has done more than I've done in a period of three and a half years (Trump, first debate).
There has been nobody tougher on Russia than Donald Trump (Trump, second debate).

As mentioned above, he presents himself as the saviour and his greatness reflects in his great effort to do things well. He describes himself as one of the good people and, together with his administration, claims to be the only one capable of doing the right thing to solve the country's problems.

(25) But I'll tell you, Joe, you could never have done the job that we did. You don't have it in your blood. You could've never done that, Joe. (Trump, first debate)

His leading role is also shown in his discourse with the overuse of the personal pronoun 'I', though most politicians tend to use the inclusive 'we' to involve the audience in their speech. The corpus results show that the frequency of the pronoun 'I' in Trump's texts is significantly higher than in Biden's, 239.2 vs 147.2, respectively. A completely different picture is found with the pronoun 'we', whose frequency in Biden is 146.6 and 84.5 in Trump. According to McIntosh (2020: 16), most politicians tend to use discourse markers, such as *well* or *so* as fillers, when they are asked a question. However, it is worth mentioning that Trump does not follow this political convention; instead, he prefers to include the pronoun *I* in his answers.

4.2. Sentiment analysis

As mentioned above, how the speaker presents the facts and the word choice used to do it can make a difference in their tone and the polarity of their discourse. According to Chilton (2004: 40), politicians aim to balance negative and positive aspects in their communication to minimise adverse effects on their audience. Therefore, it is relevant to investigate the semantic orientation of the discourses and thus provide an answer to research question 2:

RQ2.- What is the semantic orientation of the discourses?

Lingmotif (Moreno-Ortiz 2017) is the tool used to perform the Sentiment Analysis to automatically determine the orientation of the texts. In general, the texts produced by Trump are more negative than those uttered by Biden. According to *Lingmotif*, Biden's first debate is classified as neutral and factual. As previously mentioned, the overall polarity of the text is calculated by means of the proportion of negative, positive and neutral words that appear in the text. *Lingmotif* shows that Biden's lexical items in the first debate are 3.9 % positive, 3.9 % negative and 12.5 % neutral. As can be seen, there is the same number of positive and negative items. This is the reason why, as shown in Figure 1, *Lingmotif* TSS result for Biden's first debate is neutral. Although Biden's speech is classified as neutral, it still contained negative language such as 'wrong' (7.4), 'die' (9.9), 'kill' (6.2), 'lie' (6.2), and 'problem' (6.2).

On the other hand, TSI calculates the proportion of words that carry sentiment and the ones that do not carry it. In this sense, the text is classified as factual as the numbers are similar.

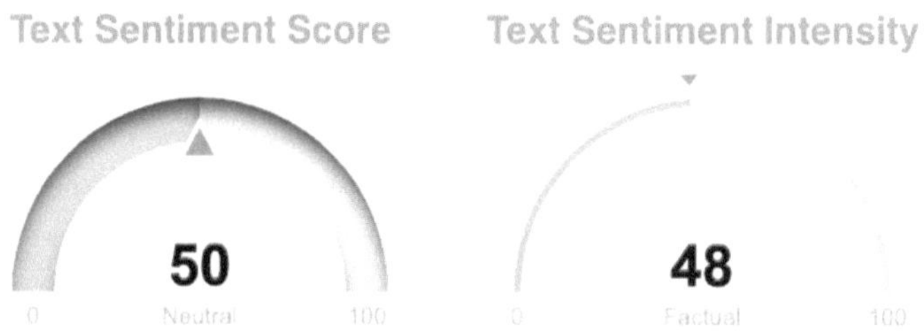

Figure 1: TSS and TSI results of Biden's first debate.

However, Trump's discourse in the first debate is classified as 'fairly negative' but also factual by *Lingmotif*, as Figure 2 illustrates.

Figure 2: TSS and TSI results of Trump's first debate.

According to *Lingmotif*, negative words such as 'wrong', 'problem', 'die', 'destroy', 'bad' or 'fraud', which have a high frequency in the corpus, make the tone negative, as the TSS result shows. Trump's lexical items are 3.9 % positive, 4.8 % negative and 15.4 % neutral. As can be seen, the quantity of negative words is higher in this corpus.

This result can be expected as some of the discussed topics were negative by nature: the pandemic, with words such as 'die'; the race topic, with words considered negative, such as 'racist' or 'crime'; or the election integrity topic with words such as 'fraud'. However, Trump uses other lexical items that are not topic-related but more general and that carry a negative connotation: the lemmas 'problem' (14.2) and 'bad' (13.1) as well as the words 'wrong' (10.9), 'radical' (8.7), 'destroy', (7.6), 'disaster' (6.5) or 'stupid' (3.3) (Hu and Liu 2004).

In the second debate, Biden's tone turned to be 'slightly negative', as the proportion of negative words is higher, 5.3 % of the lexical items are negative, 4.2 % are positive, and 13.5 % are neutral. The slight increase in negative words is what deemed this text as negative. Words such as 'death', 'dead', 'dangerous' or 'die', most related to the pandemic, make the text negative, as the topic itself is negative. Nevertheless, other items contribute to this negative sentiment: 'problem' (6), 'crime' (6), 'trouble' (4.8) or 'wrong' (3.5).

The TSI score is 'slightly intense' in this case, as can be seen in Figure 3. This indicates that there is a higher proportion of words carrying sentiment.

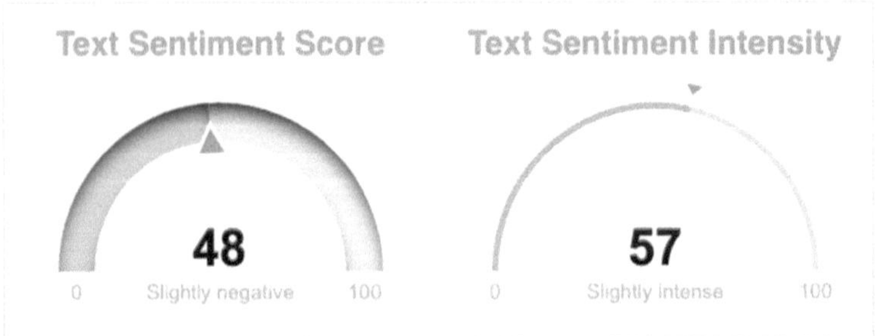

Figure 3: TSS and TSI results of Biden's second debate.

Trump's second debate is considered 'fairly negative' again since the corpus contains 5.3 % negative, 4.2 % positive words, and 13.5 %

neutral. The higher proportion of negative items reveals this negative aspect. 'Problem', 'disease', 'dying', 'fault' or 'horrible' are among the negative words that make this text have such orientation, according to *Lingmotif.* Additionally, other lexical items with such semantic polarity can also be found which are very frequent in the corpus: 'bad' (12.6), 'wrong' (12.6), 'racist' (4.1), 'disaster' (4.1), 'mess' (4.1) and 'terrible' (3.1).

However, this time, it is classified as 'fairly intense' in the TSI, as shown in Figure 4, as the sentiment-laden words are more numerous than the ones not carrying sentiment.

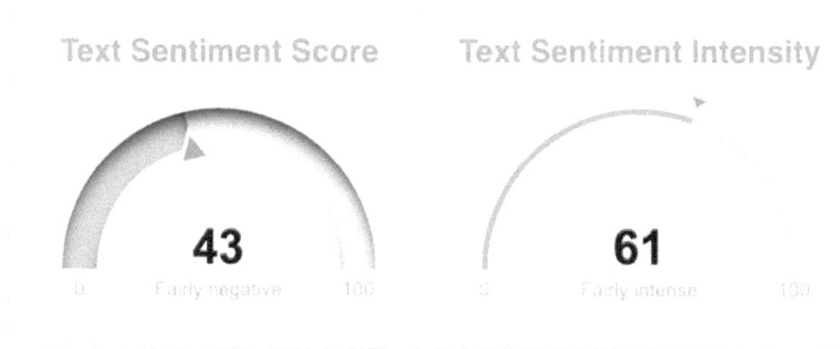

Figure 4: TSS and TSI results of Trump's second debate.

As expected, Trump's speech is often more negative because he is more categorical and tends to classify people as good and evil. He frequently presents himself as the saviour of all (see Section 4.1). In his opinion, the rest of the world is wrong and represents bad (Abbas 2019); therefore, the American people should vote for him and then all the nation's problems would be solved.

6. Conclusions

This corpus-based study analyses the 2020 presidential debates in the United States. The research is divided into two fundamental parts by combining Corpus Linguistics and Critical Discourse Analysis as methodological approaches. The findings have been shown in terms of word choice and sentiment analysis, which have allowed us to confirm that the discourse of both politicians is far from being alike. This fact highlights the power of language to influence the audience and to state the facts in one way or another.

The research questions posed in Section 1 have been addressed resulting in a comprehensive analysis that clearly reveals the striking differences between the two politicians and their ideologies. The comparison of the two candidates, as well as the two debates, has revealed uncovering meanings that cannot be seen at first sight.

RQ1 deals with the differences in word choice between the two contenders. The lexical choice appears crucial when politicians intend to influence electors and gain voters. Not only is their meaning important but also their semantic orientation. In political debates, politicians have the opportunity to convince the audience to vote for them in the next elections. Thus, they should take advantage of that moment to convey as much information as possible.

In terms of lexical choice, the two candidates deliberately select lexical items according to their ideology. For instance, it is remarkable to mention that Trump avoids using the words 'COVID' and 'Floyd' in a year that was marked by these events. At the same time, it is worth noting that Trump uses 'black', a historically offensive word, more frequently than Biden, who prefers the term 'African-American', more widely accepted. In the context of upcoming elections, politicians need to mobilise their own voters but at the same time, they cannot allow voters to alienate themselves. This is what Trump does in the above-mentioned topics. Thus, politicians attempt to address their electorate using sometimes hidden messages or references that only their political supporters will understand and, at the same time, prevent them from being criticised by other sections of the electorate. The dog whistle technique is widely used by populist politicians and Trump's discourse is a clear example of it since avoiding mentioning crucial words or using sentiment-laden ones is a clear trace of this technique.

As far as RQ2 is concerned, the differences in terms of sentiment analysis are not remarkable. Nevertheless, Trump's discourse in both debates is more negative than Biden's, with a very peculiar choice of words, as observed in the lexical analysis. This is a byproduct of his populist rhetoric as he tends to classify social actors as good or bad and to depict everything that is not related to him as 'bad' or negative. In short, the negativity of his speech is explained by the greater use of negative connotations, while Biden uses more neutral terms.

Language is the only weapon that politicians have to reach as many people as possible. Consequently, it is used as a means of persuasion for those still undecided. In this regard, language is weaponised and can foster the most inner divisions in society. As this study shows, the 2020 presidential debates are a clear example of how language influences people and how it can reveal underlying inequalities and power hierarchies. As is known, Trump's populist rhetoric caused societal divisions to the extent that his supporters decided to assault the Capitol after their disappointment with the election results (6th January 2021). Weaponised language has become a new kind of power in the political arena.

References

Abbas, Ali Haif. 2019. Super-Hyperbolic Man: Hyperbole as an Ideological Discourse Strategy in Trump's Speeches. *International Journal for the Semiotics of Law-Revue Internationale de Sémiotique Juridique* 32/2, 505–522.

Baker, Paul. 2006. *Using Corpora in Discourse Analysis. Using Corpora in Discourse Analysis*. London: Continuum. https://doi.org/10.1007/9781139764377.013

Baker, Paul / Gabrielatos, Costas / Khosavinik, Majid / Krzyżanowski, Michał / McEnery, Tony / Wodak, Ruth. 2008. A Useful Methodological Synergy? Combining Critical Discourse Analysis and Corpus Linguistics to Examine Discourses of Refugees and Asylum Seekers in the UK Press. *Discourse & Society* 19/3, 273–306. https://doi.org/10.1177/0957926508088962.

Chilton, Paul A. 2004. *Analysing Political Discourse: Theory and Practice.* London: Routledge.

Coleman, Stephen. 2000. *Televised Election Debates. International Perspectives*. New York: St Martin's Press.

Dunmire, Patricia L. 2012. Political Discourse Analysis: Exploring the Language of Politics and the Politics of Language. *Language and Linguistics Compass* 6/11, 735–751.

Edelman, Murray. 1985. Political Language and Political Reality. *PS: Political Science & Politics* 18/1, 10–19.

Fradejas Rueda, José Manuel. 2019. Cuentapalabras. Estilometría y Análisis de Textos Con R Para Filólogos. http://www.aic.uva.es/cuentapalabras.

Garzone, Giuliana / Santulli, Francesca. 2004. What can Corpus Linguistics Do for Critical Discourse Analysis? In Partington, Alan / Morley, John / Haarman, Louann (eds.), *Corpora and Discourse*. Bern, Oxford: Peter Lang.

Hashim, Safair Safwat Mohammed / Suhair, Safwat. 2015. Speech Acts in Political Speeches. *Journal of Modern Education Review* 5/7, 699–706.

Hu, Minqing / Liu, Bing. 2004. Mining and Summarizing Customer Reviews. In *KDD '04: Proceedings of the Tenth ACM SIGKDD International Conference on Knowledge Discovery and Data Mining*, 168–77. Association for Computing Machinery. https://doi.org/10.1145/1014052.1014073.

Kenzhekanova, Kuralay Kenzhekankyzy. 2015. Linguistic Features of Political Discourse. *Mediterranean Journal of Social Sciences* 6/6 S2, 192–199.

Kilgarriff, Adam / Baisa, Vít / Bušta, Jan / Jakubíček, Miloš / Kovář, Vojtěch / Michelfeit, Jan / Rychlý, Pavel / Suchomel, Vít. 2014. The Sketch Engine: Ten Years On. *Lexicography* 1/1, 7–36. https://doi.org/10.1007/s40607-014-0009-9.

Liu, Bing. 2012. *Sentiment Analysis and Opinion Mining*. Morgan & Claypool Publishers.

Lonsdale, Thomas. 2021. To What Extent Had Trump Used George Floyd as a Campaigning Tool? A Critical Discourse Analysis of Trump's Twitter in its Political Context. *Annual Review of Education, Communication and Language Sciences* 18/1, 26–47.Marchi, Anna / Taylor, Charlotte (eds.). 2018. *Corpus Approaches to Discourse: A Critical Review*. London: Routledge. https://doi.org/10.4324/9781315179346.

Mautner, Gerlinde. 2007. Mining Large Corpora for Social Information: The Case of Elderly, *Language in Society* 36/1, 51–72.

McIntosh, Janet. 2020. Introduction: The Trump Era as a Linguistic Emergency. In McIntosh, Janet / Mendoza-Denton Norma (eds.), *Language in the Trump Era: Scandals and Emergencies*. Cambridge: Cambridge University Press.

Montgomery, Martin. 2017. Post-Truth Politics? Authenticity, Populism and the Electoral Discourses of Donald Trump. *Journal of Language and Politics* 16/4, 619–639. https://doi.org/10.1075/jlp.17023.mon

Moreno-Ortiz, Antonio. 2017. Lingmotif: A User-Focused Sentiment Analysis Tool Lingmotif: Una Herramienta de Análisis de Sentimiento Enfocada En El Usuario. *Procesamiento del Lenguaje Natural* 58/1, 133–140.

Oliver, J. Eric / Rahn, Wendy M. 2016. Rise of the Trumpenvolk: Populism in the 2016 Election. *The ANNALS of the American Academy of Political and Social Science* 667/1, 189–206.

Pang, Bo / Lee, Lilian. 2008. Opinion Mining and Sentiment Analysis. *Foundations and Trends in Information Retrieval*, 2/1–2, 1–135.

Sinclair, John. 2004. *Trust the Text: Language , Corpus and Discourse*. London: Routledge.

Stubbs, Michael. 1994. 'Grammar, Text, and Ideology: Computer-assisted Methods Linguistics of Representation'. *Applied Linguistics* 15/2, 201–223

Van Dijk, Teun A. 1997. What is Political Discourse Analysis. *Belgian Journal of Linguistics* 11/1, 11–52.

Van Dijk, Teun A. 2005. *Discourse and Racism in Spain and Latin America*. Amsterdam: Benjamins.

Widdowson, Henry. 1995. Discourse Analysis: A Critical View. Language and Literature 4/3:157–172

Wilson, John. 2005. Political Discourse. In Schiffrin, D. / Tannen, D. / Hamilton, H. E. (eds.), *The Handbook of Discourse Analysis*. Oxford: Blackwell Publishers Ltd, 398–415.

Wodak, Ruth / Culpeper, Jonathan / Semino, Elena. 2021. Shameless Normalisation of Impoliteness: Berlusconi's and Trump's Press Conferences. *Discourse & Society* 32/3, 369–393.

CARMEN GREGORI-SIGNES

Who's friends with the victim? A corpus-based stylistic approach to the analysis of the TV series The Killing[1]

1. Introduction

Although television crime fiction is one of the most proliferating genres nowadays, many of its features are still understudied. Most research on fictional drama has focused on the offender, the detective, or the plot, thus relegating the victim of murder to second place in the literature. This research proves that the functional role of the victim in the development of the narrative plot is worth being further investigated.

The fictionalisation of crime has been a popular genre since the Middle Ages. In China, crime fiction started already during the Song Dynasty (960–1279). In the western world, the father of crime fiction is thought to be Edgar Allan Poe with *The Murders in the Rue Morgue,* a short story published in 1841, while on television *Telecrime* (BBC, 1938–1939) is acknowledged as the first televised crime mystery series. Cawelti (2004: 364) categorises the detective story as one of the most important popular myths of modernity, one that causes endless fascination to contemporary audiences. Nowadays, one of the most popular genres on network TV is crime-related programming (cf. Moody 2003).

Crime fiction (cf. Rezpka and Horsley 2010; Akrivos and Antoniou 2019) has often been perceived as the result of applying established

1 This contribution is part of a larger project (NewsGen PID2019-110863GB-I00) in which I study how the texts construct the identity of women who have been victims of crime.

formulae. Nevertheless, Allan et al. (2020) argue that in the past twenty years structuralist semiotics and narratology have exonerated detective fiction's moral dubiousness by paying attention to its form rather than its content. These theories underline that the textuality, plotting and epistemological enquiry of detective fiction provides a model for narrative itself. Their proposal advocates for authors to steer away from conventional accounts of crime fiction and enhance the non-conforming and innovative features that are 'more than just a reworking of pre-existing formulae' (Allan et al. 2020: 3). In that spirit, their introduction to the volume encourages theoretical and methodological innovation in future reflections on the current state of crime fiction criticism.

Along those lines, this chapter ventures into one of the least travelled routes in academic accounts of crime fiction: a linguistic analysis of the function and presence of victim-naming in the dialogues of televised Murder Mystery Series (MMS), in which the victim is a woman, taking as a case in point the cult TV series *The Killing* (AMC 2011–2014). MMS is here understood in the terms specified by Gregori-Signes as 'an umbrella term for drama and comedy crime, detective and procedural genres whose plot revolves around solving the mystery of a murder rather than other types of crime (e.g., mugging, blackmail, rape, etc.) (2020: 34).' Victim-naming is one of the stylistic devices used to construct the victim of murder, and one that still remains unexplored in televised crime-fiction. As is the case with vocatives in natural conversation, my contention is that variations in naming serve to establish characters' identities (cf. Formentelli 2019: 27) and status within the fictional world (Chierichetti 2021) of television series, while also reinforcing the central plot of solving the murder case.

There is a relatively vast amount of research on written crime fiction (Reilly 1980; Priestman 1990; Gregoriou 2007; Dutta-Flanders 2017; Akrikos and Antoniou 2019; Allan et al. 2020a, 2020b; Perce 2021) but not so much on televised crime fiction. In fact, in their introduction to the *Routledge Companion to Crime Fiction,* Allan et al. state that crime TV series deserve to be treated comprehensively, since they 'have arguably become the most significant manifestation of crime fiction' (2020a, 2020b: 5). Within the categories of characters (cf. Bednarek 2011; Gregoriou 2011) in crime fiction (Todorov 1966), the (discursive) role of the victim of murder is one of the least examined. Most of the literature on fictional crime drama has been devoted to the study of offenders or detectives rather than victims of crime (Gregoriou 2007; Gregoriou 2011; Binder 2021). The victim of murder has often been deemed the least important role (Wright 1946: 40) or even been dismissed as negligible in some studies (Gregory-Klein 1995; Malmgren 2010), become almost invisible (Binder 2021) and said to disappear during the course of the investigation, as the detective gains ascendancy over the criminal or offender (Gregory Klein 1995; Binder 2021). In her essay, Bolin (2018: 21) contends that while many murder stories have women as victims, it is not the victim herself but rather her memory that takes the role of a distinct character. Mills (2020), following Pyrhönen (1999), concludes that the victim is one piece of a puzzle, and a necessary point of contact between detective and crime (Pyrhönen 1999: 132). Knight (2004: 87–8) also argues that 'in the context of post-war fiction, the victim has some wealth and authority'. Other studies on fictional victims have paid attention to features such as gender, race (cf. Bednarek 2011) and other behavioural characteristics (cf. Rader et al. 2015). Rader, Rhineberger-Dunn and Vasquez (2015) used a statistical approach to study how demographic factors (e.g., gender, race, age), incident-related factors (location, crime type, relationship with offender), and behavioural factors (drug use, alcohol use, sexual promiscuity etc.) predict victim blaming, in 124 episodes of 7 different crime TV dramas. Pedro-Mustieles (2020) victim-blaming in the series YOU and claims that the series perpetuates a gendered ideology that assigns responsibility for the violence perpetrated against them upon women on the grounds of their sexuality. Menti (2019) applied corpus methodologies to study crime and criminals and the gender of the victims in the BBC's *Sherlock* and American CBS's *Elementary.* Palomino-Manjon (2022) described how victims of gender violence are appraised in the TV series *Westworld,* while Rosca (2021) compared the most frequent phrasal verbs used in police investigative work in two television crime series.

Central to the present research were Gregori-Signes' (2020) and Tabbert's work (2013, 2015, 2016). Tabbert (2016) analysed victim-naming strategies in German and English newspapers (cf. also Maruenda-Bataller 2021; Santaemilia-Ruiz 2021) and concluded that naming is an essential textual tactic to construct and determine the way audiences view victims (Tabbert 2016: 80). Gregori-Signes (2020) analysed victim-naming choices for Laura Palmer, the 17-year-old girl murdered in the series *Twin Peaks*. Her investigation traced the distribution (cf. Biber 1989) of the presence of the victim in the whole series both in quantitative and qualitative terms. These two studies coincide in pointing out the adequacy of applying corpus linguistic techniques (Fischer-Starcke 2010) in their analyses, since these techniques may help find non-obvious patterns that derive from the use of victim-naming forms (Kenney 2002) that otherwise would be difficult to discern.

The methodology followed to analyse the function of the victim in the dialogues of the first two seasons (cf. Table 1) of the TV series *The Killing* combined the methods exposed in Tabbert (2016) and Gregori-Signes (2020). The first two seasons may be considered a corpus since they feature a closed narrative within the overall series. At the end of the second season, the murder of Rosie Larsen is solved, while the series progresses to explore new murder cases involving different victims. Although some corpus linguists may contend that a corpus of this size may be insufficient to make generalisable claims, McIntyre and Walker (2019: 112) argue that corpus-based stylistics 'necessitates a less prototypical definition of a corpus' since the objective may not be to make generalisable claims but to gain insights into text style. Consequently, one single text, or even a poem can be (O'Halloran 2007). McIntyre/Walker allege that 'by exploring the possibilities of subjecting the target text itself to corpus analysis' (2019: 111), we can better understand the stylistic choices made in the text. The authors label the practice of 'treating the target text as a corpus in its own right' (2019: 111) as *corpus-based stylistics*'. Applying a corpus-based methodology, this analysis examined the frequency and distribution of victim-naming terms throughout the text and among various different characters in the first two seasons of the cult TV series *The Killing*.

Results proved that victim-naming choices function as a plot propeller which lends coherence and continuity to the primary plotline, while also emphasising for the audience the relevance of the characters in the fictional world. In this sense, the results obtained suggest the convenience of relying on corpus-based techniques for the analysis of individual television series or a selection of seasons within the series (cf. Gregori-Signes et al. 2021), as is the case here. Using corpus-based techniques helped provide textual justification of the function of victim-naming as a propeller of the plot and an indicator of the status of the different characters within the internal fictional world of the series (e.g., Sara Linden, the main protagonist, has the highest number and range of victim referring terms).

The main hypothesis underlying the study was that the victim should prove pivotal to the narrative plot, both in quantitative and qualitative terms. One potential method of verifying this hypothesis could be to examine the varied victim-naming forms employed by the characters in the dialogues (Kozloff 2000). I further hypothesised that the closer the relationship with the victim, the higher the quantitative number of victim-related terms the character would use. Likewise, the stronger the relationship with the victim, the higher the internal status of the character in the fictional world.

The present paper is structured as follows. Section 2 includes a brief introduction to the TV series *The Killing*. Section 3 reviews some relevant contributions on naming and forms of address. Section 4 exposes the methodology by describing the target corpus, the methodological framework and the procedure applied in the analysis. Sections 5 and 6 comprise the analysis and results obtained. Finally, Section 7 is dedicated to the conclusions and suggestions for further research.

As known, the analysis of TV series can be approached, mainly, from 3 broad perspectives: production, reception and product (Bednarek 2018). However, and due mainly to space restrictions, the present study focuses exclusively on the dialogues, that is, the verbal component, as opposed to other multimodal elements such as sound, music and image (cf. Bednarek 2018).

2. The Killing

There are not many examples of television series that have become cult phenomena, marking the canon by which the rest of the series of that subgenre will be judged, as has been the case of *Forbrydelsen* (DR 2007–2012), the series that marked the path of rebirth of Nordic noir and the rise of Scandinavian series. *The Killing,* its American adaptation, is the object of analysis of the present paper.

As argued by Bolin (2018) and LeBor (2020), many examples of crime fiction rely on murdered women and girls as a story engine, partly because dead women seem to have been an easy plot device in the history of MMS. *Twin Peaks* is often cited as the series that started it all, and it is no secret to anyone who followed the critics, that *The Killing* has been classified in the press as the heir of *Twin Peaks*. Both storylines revolve around two seventeen-year-old girls found dead in the water, Laura Palmer (*Twin Peaks*) wrapped in plastic and Rosie Larsen (*The Killing*) in the boot of a sunken car. Both were at the same time liked and envied in their school, worked in a casino, got involved in a prostitution network and left behind video tapes and voice messages.

The main characters in *The Killing* can be classified as belonging to three sets of categories: investigators, family and friends; and the community (cf. Gregori-Signes 2020). Sarah Linden and Stephen Holder are the two main detectives in charge of solving the murder of the teenager Rosie Larsen. Her family is formed by Stan, the father; Mitch, the mother; Aunt Terry and her two younger brothers, Tommy and Denny. The third group, the community, would include as its main protagonists councilman Darren Richmond, who is running for mayor and his two main campaign advisors, Jamie Wright, and Gwen Eaton. Rosie Larsen's body was found in the trunk of a car registered under Richmond's campaign.

3. Naming choices for the victim of murder

Terms of address, or vocatives, have been the object of study in sociolinguistics (Ervin-Tripp 1969; Trudgill 1983; Braun 1988) and anthropology, as well as in linguistics since the 1950s (Bratt Paulston 2008; Chaika 1982; Keshavarz 2001), their interest evolving mainly from the fact that they reflect not only grammatical differences, but also nearness or remoteness in social relations (Brown and Gilman 1968: 253–60). Rodríguez-Martín points out, when analysing the TV series *Breaking Bad* (AMC 2008–2013), that 'terms of address are the linguistic manifestation of a number of social factors that shape the linguistic behaviour of interlocutors and their relationship' (2021: 55). Terms of address also vary according to the interlocutor and therefore may provide information about 'who the speaker believes he is, who he believes the addressee is, what he thinks their relationship is, and what he thinks he is doing by saying what he is saying' (Parkinson 1985: 1). Thus, the linguistic forms that speakers use to name others can mirror the complex social relations of individuals in a speech community, and, by extension, the relationship between the characters of a television series.

Van Leeuwen (2008: 42) distinguishes between *functionalisation* and *identification*. Functionalisation occurs when social actors are referred to in terms of an activity or in terms of something they do, for instance, an occupation or role (e.g., a journalist); or by a noun which denotes a place or tool closely associated with an activity (e.g., pianist or chairperson). Identification occurs, according to van Leeuwen (2008), when social actors are defined, not in terms of what they do, but in terms of what they, permanently or unavoidably, are (e.g., a woman). Van Leeuwen (2008: 42) describes three types of identification. The first, *relational* identification, is realized by a closed set and would represent individuals in terms of their personal relationship or work relations. The second, *classification*, is done in terms of social major categories such as age, class, gender. The third one, *physical* identification, focuses on the character's physical characteristics.

Forms of address can take many forms (Biber et al. 1999; Leech 1999; Culpeper 2001; McCarthy and O'Keeffe 2003; Formentelli 2019) such as endearments (*dear*), family terms (*Daddy*), familiarisers (*dude*), familiarised first names (*Katie*), full first names (*Dianne*), title and surname (*Miss Lorte*), honorifics (*Ma'am*), nicknames (*you reds*), and even elaborated nominal structures such as *those of you who want to bring your pets along*. Following Jeffries (2010) and Tabbert (2013) I use the term *naming* as a broader category which includes those forms that are used to refer to, describe, name or label someone. Jeffries (2010) contends that naming includes several linguistic practices such as (1) choosing a noun over another to indicate a referent, (2) constructing pre- /postmodified noun phrases which further describe the referent and (3) using nominalisation. In particular, the present analysis focuses on the variations in *victim-naming* (cf. Tabbert 2016) choices or forms used by the characters (Gregori-Signes 2020; Chierichetti 2021), to refer to the victim of murder, *Rosie Larsen*, in the dialogues of the TV series *The Killing*.

Particularly relevant for this research is Tabbert's (2013, 2015, 2016) analysis on how victims, murders, offenders and crimes are constructed in the British and German Press. For Tabbert, naming choices are 'part of a mosaic where different linguistic elements combine to construct offenders and victims based on ideological views of them' (2016: 43). Tabbert's (2016) analysis resorts to labelling theory and to criminological and sociological theories. Her research interest lies in how society creates deviance by 'making rules, applying them to particular people and labelling them as outsiders' (Becker 1966: 9, cited in Tabbert 2016: 44). As for the victims, Tabbert indicates that they are constructed linguistically 'partly by how they are named and described in noun phrases' (2016: 45). Tabbert (2016: 75) groups victim-naming into 5 different categories: social system (family, mother), gender (woman, man), victimhood status or role in investigation (victims, body), age (children, pupil), profession (investors) and other (people). The objective of the present study differs from Tabbert's (2016), first, because the data is televised fiction in the form of dialogue, which is substantially different from news reports. Secondly, because although I also analysed noun phrases (e.g., *my daughter*), my main focus was on the victim's first name and surname, which Tabbert excludes from her study precisely because she is not interested in such forms of address (2016: 77–78). In the present work, this decision is quantitatively justified, since the combinations FN (first name) and FN+S (first name + surname) are the most frequent victim-naming forms in the data. In this respect, van Leeuwen (2008: 41) claims that *nomination* is typically realised by proper nouns, which can be *formal* (surname only, with or without honorifics), *semiformal* (given name and surname), or *informal* (given name only). Additionally, van Leeuwen (2008: 46–47) states that while proper names, possessive pronouns and nouns personalise social actors, abstract nouns can sometimes yield to *abstraction* (poor, black, unskilled, Muslim) or *objectivation.* The latter can be expressed by a metonymical reference in the form of *spatialisation* (e.g., substituting 'Australians' by 'Australia' in *Australia was bringing in about 70.000 migrants a year*); *utterance autonomisation* (e.g., *This concern, the report noted, was reflected in surveys*) which lends a kind of impersonal authority to the utterances; and *instrumentalisation*, by which social actors are represented by reference to the instrument with which they carry out the action, as in *A 120mm mortar shell slammed into Sarajevo's marketplace*. Finally, *somatisation* represents social actors by means of reference to a part of their body.

In real life, the rules for uses of first names and surnames as well as titles are regulated by social convention and are considered common ground (Ridley 2016). Using appropriate forms of address during interactions requires considering both the status of the participants and the context of the situation. Other factors such as discursive dominance and power or audience orientation can also influence the selection of a particular form of address (cf. Labov 2001; Garofalo 2016; Sharma 2018). However, the focus in this research is not on how social status and power may affect the discursive dominance of one or another character (cf. del Saz-Rubio and Gregori-Signes 2013), but on how through naming choices the characters express their relation to the victim. It is precisely this aspect, the use of referring terms to name a character who is not alive, and consequently cannot take an active part in the interaction, that is still understudied in the field of telecinematic discourse. The naming system offers a powerful tool for constructing dialogue and can be exploited to emphasise specific aspects of a victim's personality (Clark 1992; Jeffries 2010). This can be particularly relevant in murder narratives, where the use of specific names and labels can play an important role in shaping the story and highlighting themes. The lexical choice of a naming term over another creates a 'map' (Fowler 1991: 82) which attributes values, while reflecting and influencing relations (Carter and Simpson 1989) within and outside the fictional world.

4. Methodology

4.1. Research objectives

Using a combination of qualitative and quantitative techniques, the analysis of the first two seasons of *The Killing* focused on the discursive role of victim-naming. The hypotheses were 1) that the number of references to the victim should be sufficient to presuppose its centripetal role in the development of the narrative plot of the series; 2) that variations in victim-naming choices in the form of first name and surname, and other noun phrases (e.g., *the little girl*) may vary not only according to the setting, intimacy and social distance but also according to the activity type (e.g., interrogating possible suspects) and status of the speakers involved in it.

4.2. Corpus

The corpus for this study comprises the first two seasons of *The Killing* (cf. Table 1) at the end of which the murder of *Rosie Larsen* is solved. The character names and allocation of turns were identified by watching the videos for each episode. Individual corpora for each relevant character were created for comparison purposes, as illustrated in Table 2 below.

Table 1: The Killing dates of release (Wikipedia).

	Originally released			
Season	Episodes	First released	Last released	Network
1	13	April 3, 2011	June 19, 2011	AMC
2	13	April 1, 2012	June 17, 2012	

Table 2: Subcorpora of the most relevant characters.

	CHARACTER	TYPES	TOKENS
POLICE	Sarah Linden	2084	19709
	Stephen Holder	2094	15201
FAMILY	Stanley Larsen	862	5585
	Mitch Larsen	609	3307
	Terry	668	3273
	Jasper (ex-boyfriend)	214	525
	Sterling (best friend)	223	660
	Belko (close family friend)	354	1375
	Tommy (brother)	228	667
	Denny (brother)	251	682

Table 2: *Continued*

COMMUNITY	Darrell Richmond	1377	7261
	Jamie	1185	5279
	Gwen Eaton	1016	5729

4.3. Corpus-based stylistics

McIntyre and Walker (2019: 314) claim that corpus linguistics analytical techniques are particularly valuable in corpus-based stylistics to identify patterns in texts and validate or invalidate intuitions about individual texts (cf. Stubbs 2005; O'Halloran 2007). Corpus linguistics adopts an empirical approach to the analysis of linguistic data that makes use of computer technologies to analyse computerised collections of text (corpora). The investigation usually focuses on language use and typicality (repeated patterns) and may combine quantitative with qualitative analysis. Quantitative information includes the analysis of frequent words or combinations of words, while qualitative analysis usually proceeds via concordancing. However, the application of corpus linguistic techniques to the analysis of TV series (Bednarek 2018; Chierichetti 2021) still remains an area of limited research..

The linguistic analysis of victim-naming in *The Killing* used the tools *Word lists, Concordances, File view* and *Plot* as provided by the freely available online concordancer Antconc (version 4.0.1) created by Laurence Anthony. The creation of the subcorpora for each character was assisted by Piao's Multilingual Concordancer (2012), which facilitated the extraction of xml annotated subcorpora. *Word/frequency* lists include all the words in the corpus ordered by frequency. Words are counted in terms of types and tokens. Token refers to the total number of words in the corpus and type to the number of different words. Grammatical words (e.g., articles, prepositions) usually obtain the highest frequency since they occur more repeatedly than content words (Baker 2006: 53). The *concordance* tool gives every contextual occurrence of the search pattern, which can be explored using the *File view* tool. The File tool shows the text of individual files and, therefore, allows you to investigate in more detail the results generated in other tools of AntConc (Anthony 2022). The *Plot* tool shows concordance search results plotted in a ‘barcode’ format (see Image 1 below). This allows you to see the position where search results appear in the target texts.

4.4. Procedure

The procedure involved first an exploration of the whole corpus to obtain the number of types and tokens using Antconc 4.0.1. The verbal corpus of the first two seasons of *The Killing* contains 5834 types and 97520 tokens. It comprises the dialogues as uttered by the characters, without annotations or tags. In order to check if the victim was recurringly named in the dialogues, a manual exploration of the wordlist ensued. After grammatical words (*the, in* etc.), the victim’s first name *Rosie* was the most frequent word (see Table 3 below), proving therefore the high presence of the victim’s name in the dialogues in quantitative terms. I then proceeded to explore the concordances for First name (FN) and First name and Surname (FN+S). The File tool allowed me to examine the co-text, i.e., the words surrounding the search term, around the concordances obtained for *Rosie/ Rosie Larsen*. This exploration resulted in the identification of various referring terms such as 'my baby' and the deictic pronoun ‘she’(e.g., Rosie was different. She was curious) However, the primary focus remained on FN, FN+S and other Noun Phrases. The use of the deictic pronoun was not further examined since it is mainly used to avoid repetition.

The use of the Plot tool played a crucial role in demonstrating the centrality of the victim to the narrative development. This tool facilitated the quantitative analysis of occurrences of FN/FN+S across the entire corpus, as well as for each individual character (see Table 4 below). Consequently, naming choices were classified into 3 different subtypes:

(a) Combinations of FN and/or FN+S. These appear in subject, object or complement position (e.g., as subject in *Rosie promised to bring us biking at the docks* or as object in *You think I killed Rosie?*).
(b) Genitive constructions with the FN/ FN+S (*Rosie’s body*); *Rosie’s teacher*; *Rosie Larsen’s death.*
(c) Other Noun phrases (henceforth NPs) which were used to refer to the victim (e.g., *my daughter, the dead girl*).

Each concordance was manually scrutinised and classified accordingly. Finally, the subcorpus of the character Sarah Linden, the main detective in charge of the case, was explored in detail, since quantitatively she mentions the victim more often than any other character. Each example drawn from Linden's lines was classified according to one of the five categories (cf. Tabbert 2016; Gregori-Signes 2020) listed below:

1. Utterances referring to the story of the crime or the victim herself, in order to reconstruct the crime, e.g., [. . .] *if you saw this girl, Rosie Larsen, in the basement Friday night.*
2. Utterances which mention Rosie as a murder case or investigation, e.g., *[. . .] to prove she was involved in Rosie Larsen's murder.*
3. Utterances which mention Rosie as a body, e.g., *Rosie's body was found.*
4. Utterances which describe the victim's personal profile, e.g., *Rosie was sneaking out during school.*
5. Utterances which mention the victim's personal possessions (*What about Rosie's burner-phone records?*) or relationships (*Rosie's teacher*).

Further patterns in the use of the victim's FN and FN+S by Linden were explored taking into account the concept of *style-shifting*, which Labov (2001: 87) defined as 'both adaptation to different audiences and different degrees of audio-monitoring.' Firstly, I proceeded to quantify the interactions of Linden with other characters searching the data with regular expressions, then classified style variation according to activity type and audience-orientation (cf. Sharma 2018).

5. The centrality of victim-naming in the narrative plot

The starting point to identify different names for the victim was to obtain and examine the wordlist. After the category of grammatical words, the first most frequent word was *Rosie*. The search for *Rosie/Rosie Larsen* gave a total of 401 hits distributed in four different forms, as illustrated in Table 3 below. As mentioned above, this outcome was the first signal of the centrality of the victim as a potential conversational topic. A further manual scrutiny revealed that were two possible combinations to introduce the victim as the topic: a) FN or FN+S in subject, object or complement position (*Rosie/ Rosie Larsen*); b) FN and S in objective or subjective genitive constructions (*Rosie's backpack, Rosie Larsen's murder).*

Table 3: Total number of hits for Rosie/ Rosie Larsen.

Rosie	260
Rosie Larsen	36
Rosie's	74
Rosie Larsen's	31
TOTAL	401

As exposed in Table 3 above, the most frequent victim-naming term was the victim's FN, *Rosie,* as object, subject or complement or as part of a genitive construction (*Rosie's*). Genitive constructions amounted to a total of 105 cases. In this category, I also included those examples in which Rosie Larsen functioned as premodifier of a noun [*det. Article+ Rosie Larsen + noun*], *e.g., the Rosie Larsen files*. The latter were found to belong to the lexico-semantic field of CRIME: *case* (5 hits), *murder* (6 hits), *murder case* (2), *files, film* (1 hit each).

The distribution of the four patterns (cf. Table 3 above) that contain the victim's FN and FN+S, as shown in Image 1 below, indicates that the victim is evenly dispersed throughout the corpus, and therefore recurrently present in the dialogues.

Image 1. Dispersion plot for the presence of the victim in the dialogues

The subsequent step examined the number of mentions by the key characters involved in the murder case. Table 4 below illustrates the results obtained for each character. These were classified as belonging to one of the following three categories (cf. Gregori-Signes 2020): Rosie's family and (close) friends, the police and the community (represented by the politician Richmond and his co-workers).

Table 4: Types and Tokens, and victim-naming terms for the main characters.

		Rosie	**RLarsen**	**Rosie's**	**RLarsen's**
POLICE	Sarah Linden	79	18	25	6
	Stephen Holder	32	4	13	4
	Lieutenant Oakes	2	0	3	0
FAMILY & FRIENDS	Stanley Larsen (father)	59	0	0	0
	Mitch Larsen (mother)	13	0	0	0
	Terry (aunt)	12	0	0	0
	Jasper (boyfriend)	6	0	0	0
	Sterling (best friend)	10	0	0	0
	Belko (close family friend)	10	0	0	0
	Tommy (bro)	5	0	0	0
	Denny (bro)	7	0	0	0
COMMUNITY	Darrell Richmond (politician)	0	1	0	4
	Jamie Wright (team member)	0	3	0	0
	Gwen Eaton (team member)	0	2	0	0

Table 4 above illustrates that Rosie's family and friends, who were close to her, never used her full name. Rosie was their daughter, sister, niece and girlfriend. On the contrary, the politician and his team refrained from using the victim's FN only, and opted for the semiformal *Rosie Larsen*. This choice suggests a certain level of detachment from the murder case and from the victim herself, since if evidence were to emerge suggesting that they had a relationship with the victim it could potentially have devastating consequences for their political careers. Genitive constructions *Rosie's* and *Rosie Larsen's* were used to talk about her relationship with other characters (*Rosie's teacher*), her possessions (*Rosie's backpack*) and to express other types of relations, such as to mention parts of her dead body (*Rosie's detox*), some aspect of her life (*Rosie's voicemail*), and even to refer to her murderer (*Rosie's killer*). The outcomes coincide partly with Tabbert's (2016) naming strategies for victims and with Gregori-Signes' (2020) reported use of FN and FN+S in *Twin Peaks*, although, in general, victim-naming patterns in the form of NPs are more varied in *The Killing* than in *Twin Peaks* (cf. Gregori-Signes 2020).

A manual exploration of the concordances and co-text around *Rosie/ Rosie Larsen* revealed the presence of other NPs that referred to the victim. Following Tabbert's (2016: 75) core dimensions along which victims can be constructed, victim-naming forms were listed and classified in 4 different categories, as illustrated in Table 5 below. In the examples, the numbers in parentheses (e.g., (20) for *your daughter*) indicate the frequency of co-occurrences for each of the collocations that appeared more than once.

Table 5: Core categories of victim-naming terms (adapted from Tabbert 2016: 76).

Category	**Victim-naming NPs**
(1) Social system	that Larsen girl (1) The/ Larsen girl (22), my daughter (20), my baby girl (2), my little girl, our girl, your niece, your girlfriend, their daughter, his daughter, your daughter (20), a great kid
(2) Gender + age	a little girl, that sweet little girl, that pretty little girl, your 17-year-old niece, that dead 17 year old girl, a 17 year old senior.
(3) Victimhood status or role in the investigation	the murder of Seattle teen Rosie Larsen, the murder of local high school teen Rosie Larsen, the murder victim, the dead girl (2) the Larsen case (3), the Rosie Larsen case, Rosie Larsen's body, good little dead girl, was a bad little live girl
(4) Profession	A student of your husband's, a 17-year-old senior, a maid

As can be inferred from Table 5, there is some overlap between categories. Therefore, some cases could be classified as belonging to more than one category. For example, *that dead 17-year-old girl* could be said to identify the victim both in terms of gender and age, and as a victim of murder. For practical purposes, nevertheless, each example has been assigned to only one dimension. The most abundant NPs that describe the victim are those classified under the category (1) *social system*. Within those, the most numerous labels are relational identifications (van Leeuwen 2008) of the victim in terms of her personal kinship (*my daughter*) and terms of endearment (*my baby girl)* which describe a sense of relationality, of belonging to the same family and therefore 'anchor the victim in a family system' (Tabbert 2016: 54), e.g., *The Larsen girl*. These instances are almost always, using van Leeuwen's terminology, (2008) *possessivated*, as in e.g., *their daughter* and confirm that Rosie Larsen is part of a circle of people who are affected by her death (Shapland and Hall 2007: 179).

In category (2), gender + age, the examples with the word *girl* are the most numerous. When accompanied by determiners such as 'a' and 'that', these NPs can create a certain distance as in *a girl*, or *that* in *that pretty little girl. Little*, *sweet* and *pretty* are examples of appraisement (van Leeuwen 2008: 45). They indicate sensitivity towards the victim who is often subjectively identified as a child (*my baby girl*), vulnerable, and naïve. Other labels such as *Seattle teen Rosie Larsen*, which appear on the TV news, serve the purpose of *spatialising* (van Leeuwen 2008) the victim. In this case, the murdered girl and her family lived in Seattle.

The category victimhood (3) includes examples that itemise the victim as a murder case (*the Rosie Larsen case*). A great deal of those refer to the description of the victim's body (*Larsen's tissue*). Others use a possessive NP structure [Rosie Larsen's +X], to talk about how the parts of her body were affected by the criminal act (e.g., *fingerprints, hands, nails*) or how the act of murder was carried out.

Finally, even though it is a singular occurrence, it is worthwhile to take note of the irony present in Detective Holder's comment: *So, good little dead girl was a bad little live girl*. This utterance introduces the idea that the victim may have had an inappropriate behaviour. This is labelled by Cameron and Frazer (2000: 29) as the 'whore' category, which is a plot thread implicitly sustained during the whole two seasons (e.g., *I'm not sure what Rosie Larsen would be doing in a place like this*). The ambiguity surrounding the character of the victim and whether she is a 'good' or a 'bad' *girl* is a common theme in many crime shows that feature young women as victims (e.g., *Twin Peaks, Mare of Easttown, Top of the Lake, True Detective*). This uncertainty is typically left unsolved until the end of the series. In some cases, this category is related to the victim's profession (4) or occupation. As for *Rosie*, close to the end of the investigation, the plot reveals that she was working in the casino as a maid, not as a prostitute.

In general terms, the function of FN and S is be to act as a topic marker or initiator of information about both the victim and the crime act. After identifying the victim through FN, FN+S or a NP, subsequent information is largely introduced using the deictic pronoun *she* in order to avoid repetition. There were 405 examples of *she* in utterances which were either about the victim's private live, or about the reconstruction of the crime or a mixture of the two. For example, Linden says: *A girl with dreams. Her teacher said she wanted to see the world. Wanted something more than what she had. So, why was she hanging out in a dusty construction site in some crap casino in the middle of the night?* In the first part of her turn, Linden would be talking about the victim's personal traits, while in the second part (from *So* onwards) *she* is used to refer to the day in which the crime was committed.

Furthermore, the examination of the patterns that emerged from the victim-naming choices signal a reciprocal relationship between the status of the characters as primary or secondary, and the quantity and variety of victim-naming labels they used. The highest number and variety of referring terms (45 %) is by members of the police, specially by Linden and her partner Holder, the detectives in charge of the investigation. Linden mentions of the victim amount to 32 % of total number of victim's mentions in the dialogues, followed by Holder's, with 13,2 % of the total number. This indicates their involvement with the case of murder and with making justice for the victim. As such, the main detective Linden suspended her wedding, sacrificed her relationship with her boyfriend and lost her son temporarily to her father, all for the sake of solving the crime. In the next section, I analyse victim-naming choices by Sarah Linden, the detective, in order to test the emerging patterns that would indicate how victim-naming helped establish the relationship between Linden (the character that mentions the victim more frequently) and the victim both for the characters and the audience.

6. Detective Sarah Linden's victim-naming strategies

Sarah Linden is a homicide detective with Seattle Police Department, a single Mum and a loner. At the beginning of the series, she wants to start living a normal life separated from the distressing events of her job, leave Seattle, move to Sonoma, California, and get married. But when Rosie Larsen is killed, she gets too involved in the murder and decides to stay until it is solved. As illustrated in Table 6 below, Linden's preference to refer to the victim is her FN, *Rosie*, which amounts to 33 % of the total number of times for *Rosie* and 34 % of the cases of *Rosie's* in the whole corpus. The prevalence for the use of her first name, informal (van Leeuwen 2008), coincides with the preference of the victim's family (cf. Table 4 above). This denotes her involvement with the case and her concern about the victim.

Table 6: Use of victim's first name by Linden.

Rosie	79/260
Rosie Larsen	18/36
Rosie's	25/74
Rosie Larsen's	6/31

Depending on the context and activity type Linden is involved in (e.g, interrogating possible suspects, finding information about the victim), her uses of FN/FN+S vary. As can be observed in Table 7 below, the analysis of the data prompted me to classify examples into five different activity types and patterns in Linden's victim-naming choices.

Table 7: Context sensitive use of victim-naming.

Activity type	*example*
(1) Reconstructing the crime	.. the key to Ahmed's apartment. He probably let Rosie into the apartment that night. Rosie Larsen was inside the Wapi Eagle casino the night. . .
(2) Victim as a murder case/ investigation	You have to drop charges and reopen the Rosie Larsen case. The killer's still out there.
(3) Victim as a body	Blood's a match to Rosie's type.
(4) Victim's personal profile	Rosie had everything. She had a family who loved her [. . .]
(5) Victim's personal possessions or relationships	Would you mind if I look through Rosie's room, Mr. Larsen?

As demonstrated in Table 4 above, Linden surpasses the other characters in both the number of NPs and combinations of FN+ S used to refer to the victim. When taking into account activity type and audience-orientation, distinct patterns emerged.

The exchanges between the victim's parents and Linden are brief conversations primarily focused on Linden's enquiries about their daughter's habits and routine. In these situations, Linden refers to the victim predominantly with the personal pronoun *she* followed by *your daughter*. A qualitative analysis of all their conversations reveals that Linden uses *Rosie* in relation to four activities: when enquiring about possible relationships with men, about her use of drugs, when asking about the victim's real father (*Even if Rosie wasn't your child? Who was Rosie's father?*) and to ask about a possession (*Did Rosie have a lockbox at home?*). These are aspects of the victim's private life that some may perceive as reflecting an inadequate behaviour on her part. Linden uses the NP "your daughter" predominantly, accounting for 9 out of 20 instances (45%) in which it is used in the narrative. Similarly, the victim's father utilizes 'my daughter' in 16 out of 20 of the total cases in which "my daughter" appears. The resting 4 are used by her mother. By consistently referring to Rosie as someone's loving daughter the detective demonstrates both a sensibility towards the family and a recognition that Rosie is more than just a regular police case.

In her interactions with Holder, she employs the highest number of FN references: a total of 36 (out of 79), that is 45 %. During the activity *reconstructing the day of the crime*, Linden uses informal *Rosie.* Two distinct types of utterances arise in this case: (a) those whose content reconstructs the day of the murder (*Bennet could've never let Rosie in. He's on tape at the dance at 11:20. And that storeowner saw Rosie at the apartment at 10:00*) and (b) those that give personal information about the victim's life, habits, or personality traits. However, the latter are somewhat associated with her murder. For example, the utterance *Rosie had secrets. She went all over the city with that camera*, talks about a habit that she had but also suggests a possible connection with her murder. Likewise, when talking about the victim's personal possessions, personal relations or profile (*Rosie was scared and alone*), Linden's preference is *Rosie/Rosie's*, thus denoting interest towards things that mattered to the victim (*Rosie's backpack*) in her everyday life but may also provide information on her whereabouts or her murder. All in all, it seems that Linden's use of her first name is mostly connected with her function as the main detective: i.e. reconstruct and solve the murder case.

Linden's use of semiformal *Rosie Larsen* is again connected to the reconstruction of the crime. She chooses to do so primarily when she talks to characters who are less familiar with the victim or are enquired because they may have knowledge involving the crime, e.g., the school janitor (*. . .to know is if you saw this girl, Rosie Larsen, in the basement Friday night),* one of the suspect's wife (*Rosie Larsen was a student of your husband's?*), the principal of the school (What was the extent of Mr. Ahmed's relationship with *Rosie Larsen*). Linden also uses FN+S when talking to a possible suspect, for example the politician Richmond. The use of her full name, *Rosie Larsen,* would reflect her role as a detective, identifying the victim as a unique citizen with a name and a surname. That is, it is not a *Rosie* or a *Ms. Larsen*, it is *Rosie Larsen.* FN+S also prevails when she talks about the murder case as such (*. . .Carlson's off our backs until we solve Rosie Larsen's murder*).

7. Conclusions

The present study aimed to achieve two primary objectives. First, it sought to establish the quantitative centrality of the vicitm in the narrative plot of the TV series The Killing by analising the frequency and distribution of victim-naming terms within the two first season of the series. Secondly, once the centrality of the victim was confirmed, the analysis delved into how the characters employed different victim-naming labels. The results confirmed that the use of victim-naming served as a device to give coherence and continuity to the main narrative, to help the audience distinguish between primary and secondary characters and to introduce information related to the victim and to the modus operandi of the murderer and the crime itself .

The analysis applied corpus-based stylistic techniques and used the concordancer Antconc to facilitate both quantitative and qualitative exploration. The results indicated the recurrent presence of the victim in the dialogues first because, after grammatical words the most frequent word was *Rosie* the first name of the victim. The exploration of the co-text surrounding FN and FN+S lead to the discovery of other NPs (*my daughter, my baby*) and examples in which the victim was referred to through the deictic pronoun *she*. The total number of combinations of FN + S, other NPs and the instances of the pronoun *she*, confirmed that references to the victim were statistically significant. Additionally, using the Plot tool to explore the dialogues revealed that the victim's name was consistently dispersed across the whole corpus. This has the effect of continuously reminding the audience of the victim's significance in the plot. The results coincide with previous studies indicating that the main narrative thread of the TV series focuses on revealing to the audience both, how the victim was murdered and the motives behind the murder. However, until the murder is solved, the information on the murder is usually intertwined with the characterisation of the victim as an individual, including details about her personality, her relationship with her family and friends, and her aspirations.

Underlying the whole analysis was the intention to prove the adequacy of a corpus-based stylistics (McIntyre and Walker 2019) methodology for the analysis of the presence of the victim in the narrative plot of MMS. This approach to text analysis argues that the application of corpus methods can give valuable information about the text that would be difficult to obtain through other means. In fact, using corpus tools to explore the first two seasons of *The Killing* confirmed such claims by providing textual objective justification of the centrality of the victim in the dialogues, as demonstrated by a variety of context sensitive victim-naming choices. A possible continuation of this project would be to investigate whether this pattern, which coincides with Gregori-Signes's (2020) findings on Twin Peaks, is common to other TV series and to other types of crimes. It would also be interesting to contrast verbal indications for the victim with other multimodal aspects that may accompany them.

References

Akrivos, Dimitris / Antoniou, Alexandros K. (eds.) 2019. *Crime, Deviance and Popular Culture*. Palgrave Studies in Criminal Culture.

Allan, Janice et al. 2020a. Introduction. New Directions in Crime Fiction Scholarship. In Allan, Janice et al. (eds.), *The Routledge Companion to Crime Fiction*. Routledge, 1–9

Allan, Janice et al. 2020b. *The Routledge Companion to Crime Fiction*. Routledge.

Anthony, Laurence. *AntConc* (4.0.) 2022. Tokyo, Japan, Waseda University. Available from https://laurenceanthony.net/software.html.

Baker, Paul. 2006. *Using Corpora in Discourse Analysis*. Continuum.

Becker, Howard S. 1966. *Outsiders: Studies in the Sociology of Deviance*. The Free Press.

Bednarek, Monika. 2011. The Stability of the Televisual Character: A Corpus Stylistic Case Study. In Piazza, Roberta / Bednarek, Monika / Rossi, Fabio (eds.), *Telecinematic Discourse: Approaches to the Language of Films and Television Series*. John Benjamins, 185–204.

Bednarek, Monika. 2018. *Language and Television Series. A Linguistic Approach to TV Dialogue*. Cambridge University Press.

Biber, Douglas. 1989. A Typology of English Texts. *Linguistics* 27/1, 3–44. https//doi.org/10.1515/ling.1989.27.1.3.

Biber, Douglas et al. 1999. *Longman Grammar of Spoken and Written English.* Longman.

Binder, Sabrine. 2021. *Women and Crime in Past-Transitional South African Crime Fiction*. Costerus New Series Online.

Bolin, Alice. 2018. *Dead Girls: Essays on Surviving an American Obsession.* Harper Collins Publishers.

Bratt Paulston, Christin. 2008. Pronouns of Address in Swedish: Social Class Semantics and a Changing System. *Language in Society* 5/3, 198–216. https://doi.org/10.1002/9780470758434.ch13.

Braun, Friederike. 1988. *Terms of address: Problems of Patterns and Usage in Various Languages and Cultures*. Contributions to the Sociology of Language 50. Mouton de Gruyter.

Brown, Roger / Gilman, Albert. 1968. The Pronouns of Power and Solidarity. In Fishman, Joshua A. (ed.), *Readings in the Sociology of Language.* Mouton and Co. N.V. Publishers, 252–275. http://dx.doi.org/10.1515/9783110805376.252,

Cameron, Deborah / Frazer, Elizabeth. 2000. On the Question of Pornography and Sexual Violence: Moving Beyond Cause and Effect. In Cornell, Drucill (ed.), *Feminism and Pornography.* Oxford University Press, 240–53.

Carter, Ron / Simpson, Paul (eds.) 1989. *Language, Discourse and Literature.* Unwin Hyman.

Cawelti, John G. 2004. *Mystery, Violence and Popular Culture*. The University of Wisconsin Press.

Chaika, Elaine. 1982. *Language the Social Mirror.* Rowley, MA: Newbury House.

Chierichetti, Luisa. 2021. *Diálogos de serie; Una Aproximación a la Construcción Discursiva de Personajes Basada en Corpus.* Linguistic Insights 279. Peter Lang.

Clark, Kate. 1992. The Linguistics of Blame: Representations of Women in *The Sun's* Reporting of Crimes of Sexual Violence. In Toolan, Michael (ed.), *Language, Text and Context: Essays in Stylistics.* Routledge, 208–226.

Culpeper, Jonathan. 2001. *Language and Characterisation*. Routledge. https//doi.org/10.4324/9781315839349.

del Saz-Rubio, Milagros/ Gregori-Signes Carmen. 2013. Facework Strategies and the Achievement of Multiple Goals in a Court Martial Cross-Examination in the Film *A Few Good Men*. *Language and Dialogue* 3/3, 341–370.

Dutta-Flanders, Rhemi. 2017. *The Language of Suspense in Crime Fiction. A Linguistic Stylistic Approach*. Palgrave Macmillan.

Ervin-Tripp, Susan M. 1969. *Sociolinguistics. Advances in Experimental Social Psychology,* 4. Academic Press, 91–165.

Fischer-Starcke, Bettina. 2010. *Corpus Linguistics in Literary Analysis: Jane Austen and her Contemporaries*. Continuum.

Formentelli, Maicol. 2019. What's in a Vocative? Address(ing) Creativity in English Film Dialogue. *Studi Italiani di Linguistica Teorica e Applicata*, XLVIII, 27–49.

Fowler, Roger. 1991. *Language in the News: Discourse and Ideology in the Press*. Routledge.

Garofalo, Giovanni. 2016. Jura o promete decir la verdad sobre lo que se le pregunte? La práctica de la prueba como actividad interaccional en un juicio del Tribunal del Jurado, *Orillas rivista d'ispanistica* 5, 1–24.

Gregoriou, Christiana. 2007. *Deviance in Contemporary Crime Fiction*. Palgrave Macmillan.

Gregoriou, Christiana. 2011. *Language, Ideology and Identity in Serial Killer Narratives*. Routledge.

Gregori-Signes, Carmen. 2020. Victim-Naming in the Murder Mystery TV Series *Twin Peaks:* A Corpus Stylistic Study. *SERIES, International Journal of TV Serial Narratives* 6/2, 33–46. https://doi.org/10.6092/issn.2421-454X/11218

Gregori-Signes, Carmen / Fuster-Márquez Miguel / Maruenda-Bataller, Sergio (eds.) 2021. *Discourse, Dialogue and Characterisation in TV Series*. Comares.

Gregory Klein, Kathleen. 1995. *The Woman Detective: Gender and Genre*. University of Illinois Press.

Jeffries, Leslie. 2010. *Critical Stylistics. The Power of English*. Palgrave Macmillan.

Kenney, J. Scott. 2002. Victims of Crime and Labelling Theory: A Parallel Process? *Deviant Behaviour: An Interdisciplinary Journal* 23/3, 235–265.

Keshavarz, Mohammad Hossein. 2001. The Role of Social Context, Intimacy, and Distance in the Choice of Forms of Address. *International Journal of the Sociology of Language* 148, 5–18. https://doi.org/10.1515/ijsl.2001.015

Knight, Stephen. 2004. *Crime Fiction 1800–2000*. Palgrave Macmillan.

Kozloff, Sarah. 2000. *Overhearing Film Dialogue*. University of California Press.

Labov, William. 2001. The Anatomy of Style-Shifting. In Eckert, Penelope / John Rickford (eds.), *Style and Sociolinguistic Variation,* Cambridge University Press, 85–108.

LeBor, Adam. 2020. Too Many Women are Being Murdered. Why Crime Writers Need to Move on from Serial Femicide. https://thecritic.co.uk/too-many-women-are-being-murdered/ [accessed May 2021]

Leech, Geoffrey. 1999. The Distribution and Function of Vocatives in American and British English. In Hasselgard, Hilde / Oksefjel, Signe (eds.), *Out of Corpora: Studies in Honour of Stig Johanson.* Rodopi, 107–18.

Malmgren, Carl. 2010. The Pursuit of Crime: Characters in Crime Fiction. In Rzepka, Charles J. / Horsley, Lee (eds.), *A Companion to Crime Fiction.* Wiley-Blackwell, 152–163.

Maruenda-Bataller, Sergio. 2021. The Role of News Values in the Discursive Construction of the Female Victim in Media Outlets: A Comparative Study. In Fuster-Márquez, Miguel et al. (eds.), *Exploring Discourse and Ideology through Corpora.* Peter Lang, 141–166.

McCarthy, Michael / O'Keeffe, Anne. 2003. What's in a Name? Vocatives in Casual Conversations and Radio Phone-In Calls. In Leistyna, Pepi / Meyer, Charles F. (eds.), *Corpus Analysis: Language Structure and Language Use,* 153–85. Rodopi.

McIntyre, Dan / Walker, Brian. 2019. *Corpus Stylistics*. Edinburgh University Press.

Menti, Archontoula. 2019. The Representation of Crime and Criminals in the TV Series *Sherlock* and *Elementary:* A Corpus Study. In Akrivos, Dimitris/ Antoniou, Alexandros K. (eds.), *Crime, Deviance and Popular Culture.* Palgrave Macmillan, 42–73.

Mills, Rebecca. 2020. Victims. In Allan, Janice et al. (eds.), *The Routledge Companion to Crime Fiction*. Routledge, 149–159.

Moody, Nickianne. 2003. Crime in Film and on TV. In Priestman, Martin (ed.), *The Cambridge Companion to Crime Fiction*. Cambridge University Press, 227–243. https://doi.org/10.1017/CCOL0521803993.

O'Halloran, Kieran. 2007. A Corpus-assisted Literary Evaluation. *Corpora* 2/1, 33–63.

Palomino-Manjón, Patricia. 2022. Savior or Villain? A Corpus Stylistic Approach to the Linguistic Construction of Victim-Survivors of Sexual Violence in *Westworld*. Atlantis, 44/2, 65–87, https://doi.org/10.28914/Atlantis-2022-44.2.04

Parkinson, Dilworth B. 1985. *Constructing the Social Context of Communication: Terms of Address in Egyptian Arabic*. Mouton de Gruyter.

Pedro-Mustieles, Dina. 2020. Usurping the Victim's Trauma Narrative: Victim-Blaming And Slut-Shaming On Season 1 of *You*. *Revista de Estudios Norteamericanos* 24, 159–179. http://dx.doi.org/10.12795/REN.2020.i24.08

Perce, Dana (ed.) 2021. *Towards a Theory of Whodunits. Murder Rewritten*. Cambridge Scholars.

Piao, Scott / Andrew Wilson / Tony McEnery. 2002. A Multilingual Corpus Toolkit. In *AAACL 2002 Conference*. Indianapolis, Indiana, USA. Conference.

Priestman, Martin. 1990. *The Cambridge Companion to Crime Fiction*. Cambridge University Press,1990.

Pyrhönen, Heta. 1999. *Mayhem and Murder: Narrative and Moral Problems in the Detective Story*. University of Toronto Press.

Rader, Nicole E. / Rhineberger-Dunn Gayle M./ Vasquez, Lauren. 2015. Victim Blame in Fictional Crime Dramas: An Examination of Demographic, Incident-Related, and Behavioural Factors. *Women and Criminal Justice* 0, 1–21.

Reilly, John M. (ed.) 1980. *Twentieth-Century Crime and Mystery Writers*. Macmillan.

Ridley, Peter J. 2016. *A Pragmatic View of Proper Name Reference*. PhD Thesis. King's College.

Rodríguez-Martín, Gustavo. 2021. 'Walter', 'Walt', 'Mr. White', or 'Bitch': The Stylistic Use of Terms of Address in *Breaking Bad*.

In Gregori-Signes, Carmen/ Fuster-Márquez, Miguel/ Maruenda-Bataller, Sergio (eds.), *Discourse, Dialogue and Characterisation in TV Series*. Comares, 135–148.

Rosca, Andreea. 2021. *Phrasal Verbs through the Lens of Cognitive Linguistics. A Study of Adverbial Particles in British and American Varieties through TV Crime Series*. PUV: IULMA.

Rzepka, Charles J. / Horsley, Lee (eds.) 2010. *A Companion to Crime Fiction*. John Wiley & Sons.

Santaemilia-Ruiz, José. 2021. News Values as Evaluation. Main Naming Practices in Violence Against Women News Stories in Contemporary Spanish Newspapers: *El País* vs. *El Mundo* (2005–2010). *Research in Corpus Linguistics* 9/2, 90–113.

Shapland, Joanna / Hall, Matthew. 2007. What Do We Know about the Effects of Crime on Victims? *International Review of Victimology* 14, 175–217.

Sharma, Devyani. 2018. Style Dominance: Attention, Audience and the 'real me'. *Language and Society* 47, 1–31. https://doi.org/10.1017/S0047404517000835.

Stubbs, Michael. 2005. Conrad in the Computer: Examples of Quantitative Stylistic Methods. *Language and Literature* 14/1, 5–24. https//doi.org/10.1177%2F0963947005048873.

Tabbert, Ulrike. 2013. *Crime through a Corpus: The Linguistic Construction of Offenders, Victims and Crimes in the German and UK Press*. PhD Thesis, University of Huddersfield. Retrieved from http//eprints.hud.ac.uk/id/eprint/18078/.

Tabbert, Ulrike. 2015. *Crime and Corpus. The Linguistic Representation of Crime in the Press*. John Benjamins.

Tabbert, Ulrike. 2016. *Language and Crime. Constructing Offenders and Victims in Newspaper Report*. Palgrave Macmillan.

Todorov, Tzvetan. 1966. *The Typology of Detective Fiction*. BookCrime and Media.

Trudgill, Peter. 1983. *Sociolinguistics: An Introduction to Language and Society*. Penguin.

Van Leeuwen, Teun. 2008. *Discourse and Practice: New Tools for Critical Discourse Analysis*. Oxford University Press.

Wright H. Willard. 1946. The Great Detective Stories. In Howard Haycraft (ed.), *The Art of the Mystery Story: A Collection of Critical Essays. Simon and Schuster*, 33–70.

TV Series

Borgen (DR, 2010-)
Breaking Bad (AMC 2008–2013)
Bron/Broen (Nimbus Film 2011–2013)
Mare of Eastown (2021)
Telecrime (BBC, 1938–1939)
Top of the Lake (2013)
True Detective (2014-)
Twin Peaks (1990–1991)

IGNACIO M. PALACIOS-MARTÍNEZ /
PALOMA NÚÑEZ-PERTEJO

The role of age in the Twitter discourse of British rappers and singers*

1. Introduction

Age, gender, social class, and ethnicity have traditionally been seen as significant sociolinguistic variables in the study of language. In particular, the role that age plays in language use has received extensive attention (Holmes 1992; Eckert 1997; Cheshire 2006; Meyerhoff 2006; Barbieri 2008; Tagliamonte 2012, 2016, among others). Indeed, there is an intrinsic correlation between age and language production; the way in which speakers express themselves varies according to the age of the individual, given that language is an inherent part of one's personality and identity (Coupland and Coupland 1995).

When addressing issues relating to the notion of age, we should bear in mind that it is a broad concept, and has a variety of different interpretations. Thus, Eckert (1997) and Cheshire (2006) make a distinction between chronological age (the age that a person has attained as measured from their birth to a specific point in time), biological age (the individual's degree of maturity), and social age (based on certain life events, such as marriage). Since biological and social age are to some extent abstract and hence difficult to measure, in our study we will focus mainly on chronological age, but without ignoring

* We are grateful to the Spanish State Research Agency and the European Regional Development Fund (grants no. PID2020-114604GB-I00 & PID2021-122267NB-I00), and the Regional Government of Galicia (grants no. ED431B 2021/02 & ED431B 2023/03).

the influence that the other two types of age may have on language development.

When considering chronological age, the following stages in a person's life are generally distinguished (Eckert 1997): (i) childhood; (ii) adolescence; (iii) young adulthood; (iv) middle age; and (v) old age. In the case of (i), it evidently takes children some time to acquire a language of their own, and in terms of complexity and use this will gradually come to resemble that of their primary caretakers and the speakers around them. However, it is also widely accepted that children develop sociolinguistic competence from an early age. By contrast, adolescents and young speakers have not only acquired a language but are also generally seen to be agents of language change and innovation (Eckert 1997; Stenström et al. 2002; Tagliamonte 2016); they use language as a means of reinforcing their identity both as individuals and as a group, and thus to distinguish themselves from both adults and children. As Eckert (1997: 163) notes, 'adolescence is the focus of development of the social use of the vernacular, and in general is seen as the time when linguistic change from below is advanced'. Young adults, however, tend to converge with the norms of standard language use when they join the labor market and have children of their own, that is, when they begin the transition towards middle age. Finally, whereas middle-aged speakers have been observed to show concern for the status and the role that participants play in the communicative exchanges as well as with the standard conventions of language, more elderly speakers, whose speech has been the least studied of all, seem to be less conservative (linguistically speaking) here, and show less concern for such issues (Holmes 1992; Eckert 1997; Tagliamonte 2012).

In light of this, our main purpose here is to study the role of age in Twitter discourse with special reference to the interactions of British rappers and pop stars with their fans and followers in this social media. This paper is organized as follows. First, we review the main studies that have considered the age factor with reference to language use on Twitter (Section 2). Following this we set out the aims of our own study and describe the methodology used (Sections 3 and 4, respectively). Section 5 goes on to present and discuss the findings, by means of a comparison between the language of young adults and more mature speakers in Twitter interactions, this on the basis of a number of relevant features of language use. The paper closes with some reflections and concluding remarks on the findings together with suggestions for further research (Section 6).

2. Age in Twitter discourse

As mentioned above, age has been addressed extensively in relation to off-line communication, yet the same cannot be said of digital genres such as Twitter (Herring 1996, 2001; Crystal 2001; Yus 2011; Zappavigna 2012; Squires 2016), where far fewer studies focused on the age variable are available. It is this gap in the literature that the current paper aims to fill. The absence of research here is generally accounted for as a result of the difficulties in controlling for the age variable within the context of social media activity, especially in terms of drawing contrasts with traditional corpora, ethnographic, experimental, and sociolinguistic studies where, in most cases, it is possible to obtain a complete profile of each speaker, including their age. With regard to Twitter, although the site provides a potentially huge amount of linguistic data, it is often difficult to obtain a full picture of those people who post tweets, in that the information available about such users might be wholly fictitious or, in the best-case scenario, restricted to a photograph, a pseudonym, and a very brief synopsis of their life and occupation. This issue will be addressed further in Section 4 on our methodology.

Most existing studies that deal with the age factor on Twitter have sought to classify users according to different age groups, in that such information might be of use for the purposes of marketing, advertising and for mass-media companies interested in building up customer profiles so as to cater more effectively for their needs and interests. Thus, the American company Statista, in a report published in April 2021 and based on addressable ad audiences, reveals that the 25–34 age group includes the most frequent users of this social media site (38.5 % of total users), followed by the 35–49 age cohort (20.7 %). Almost 60 %

of Twitter users, then, are reported to be speakers between the ages of 25 and 49. Fewer users are recorded for the age groups 18–24 and +50, both of these groups representing around 17 % of total users. Finally, only 6.6 % of teenagers seem to favor this microblogging platform, and are generally observed to prefer more attractive alternatives to Twitter, such as Snapchat, YouTube, TikTok and Instagram, results obtained in this case on the basis of a survey carried out by the AmeriSpeak panel consisting of online and telephone interviews with parents and teens from March 7 to April 10, 2018 (Anderson and Jingjing 2018).

In what follows we will review those studies of Twitter (or similar microblogging platforms) which have gone beyond the mere classification of users according to different age groups and which have sought to establish the extent to which the age of tweet posters can be predicted based on an examination of the language used.

Two main groups of studies can be distinguished here: the first is mainly concerned with generating data on the age of the individual posters through the use of algorithms and other computational tools; the second group, however, explores the language used in these interactions, and draws conclusions accordingly. In the current study, we will tend towards this latter approach.

Within the first group of papers, Morgan-López et al. (2017) investigate the validity of linguistic and metadata features, both separately and taken together, in predicting the age of Twitter users. The study is more interested in exploring and testing the robustness of the methodology used than in issues relating to how members of different age groups use language. The approach taken was to collect birthday announcement tweets from the Twitter search API, this for a period of about four months; the authors concluded that the study of linguistic and Twitter handle features (tweets, retweets, replies, hashtags, trending topics, etc.), in combination, is a more effective procedure for predicting the age of users than Twitter metadata or linguistic features alone. They also found strong similarities in the way teenagers and young adults use language on Twitter and Facebook. However, the group of adults over 25 turned out to be the most challenging in their model in terms of age prediction.

In a similar vein, Nguyen, Gravel, Trieschnigg and Meder (2013) investigated age prediction of Dutch Twitter users through manual and automatic (algorithmic) instruments, the former apparently being more reliable than the latter. The results revealed that younger users tend to employ stylistic modifications, such as word lengthening and capital letters, a greater use of 1st and 2nd person pronouns (they talk more about themselves) and chat language, while older users tend to write longer tweets and use conventional expressions in turns that convey support or well-wishing (e.g., *enjoy*, *thanks*, *take care*, *wish*, etc.), and also use the 1st person plural pronoun *we* more frequently.

By turn, Rao, Yarowsky, Shreevats and Gupta (2010) explored four latent user attributes on Twitter, namely gender, age, regional origin and political orientation, this by means of an array of a stacked support vector machine (SVM) that employs different algorithms for classification of data referred to the target audience, in this case, the language users. In the case of the age attribute, they made a binary distinction between users below or above 30 years, and looked for initial seed topics such as 'baby boomers' and 'young moms' in the user description field. This seed sample was then expanded by adding all the followers and crawling their profiles. The age groups were then established by manually consulting the profile that many of these users had posted on sites such as *MySpace*, *LinkedIn,* blogs and homepages that the users themselves provided, along with their Twitter profile. For the analysis of the data, three main models were used: sociolinguistic-feature models, Ngram-feature models, and a stacked model that agglutinates the results from the previous two. Regarding the age attribute, the Ngram-feature model worked better than the sociolinguistic one, but the stacked model performed better still. The findings of this study revealed that the use of emoticons was similar for both age groups, while alphabetic character repetition was 30 % more frequent in younger Twitter users than older ones.

The study by Flekova, Ungar and Preoţiuc-Pietro (2016) can be classified within the second group of papers, in that they analyzed two samples of around 5,000 Twitter users according to writing style, this by considering four main features: *surface*, that is, length of tweets in words and characters, and the length of words in relation to the lexical density of the tweet; *readability*, measured in terms of average word and sentence lengths, and the number of syllables per sentence; *syntax*, that is, information on parts of speech (POS) and its arrangement in the posts with special attention to the measurement of the ratio of each POS; and, finally, *style*, measured in terms of the proportion of elongation of sounds (*Wooow!),* the presence of words with numbers (*good n8*), the ratio of hapax legomena and the frequency of hedges and abstract words. The main conclusions indicated that Twitter users' writing styles correlate with both age and income, and that all the features (except readability) show a stronger relationship with age than with income.

Nishimura (2015) focuses on how men and women of different ages express themselves through blogging, with special attention to the use of emoticons. The data here were collected from a large blogging site (*Japan Blog Village*), which contains subcategories based on the author's age, gender and blog topic. Regarding the role of age, the findings were not conclusive: while younger women were found to use emoticons significantly more frequently than members of other groups, older men used more emoticons than younger men, and older women tended to use more than their younger and older male counterparts.

From the review of these studies, it seems clear that any analysis involving the age of Twitter users will pose serious methodological issues, no matter whether the approach is automatic or manual. In the present study we will seek to control for this variable in a novel way, by looking at Twitter exchanges involving a number of recognized singers and artists, these representing either younger or more mature users. We hypothesize that all of these users, in their posts and exchanges with other Twitter users, will approximate to one group or the other in terms of age, in that a correlation should exist between the age variable and their tastes in music. Hence, it might be expected that followers and fans of artists such as Elton John or Phil Collins will be older than those who follow Berwin or Backroad Gee, for example. Furthermore, this seems to be supported by reports on the demographics of some of the followers of the singers selected.[1] We are aware, however, that such a criterion is not free from potential problems, but we believe it may provide some insights into differences in the use of language on this microblogging platform in relation to the age factor.

1 See, for example,<https://starngage.com/app/global/influencers/eltonjohn>.

3. Aims

This study seeks to establish the extent to which the age factor plays a role in Twitter discourse. As noted above, Statista's 2021 report clearly shows that the 25–34 age group comprises the most frequent users of this social media site. Thus, one of our aims here is to see how the language used by these young adults on Twitter differs from that employed by more mature adults. To this end, we aim to explore how the age differences between the two groups are reflected in their linguistic expression. Ultimately, we intend to test whether the variable of age plays a significant role in Twitter, as has been reported in the case of off-line communication. In keeping with the findings of similar studies that looked at off-line communication (Stenström et al. 2002; Palacios 2011; Tagliamonte 2016), we will assume that younger users will be more informal, will make greater use of vernacular forms and slanguage, and will resort more often than their older counterparts to a variety of distinctive features of Twitter communication. Our findings, then, will either confirm or nullify these assumptions.

Although our interest here is purely linguistic, the findings we report are also of potential interest to anyone involved in commerce, advertising, or marketing that seeks to address age-specific customers on social media platforms more effectively.

4. Methodology

Twitter users tend to include their first name(s), location, and a brief biography in their profiles; gender and age, however, are not obligatory fields, and are frequently omitted.

With this in mind, and for the purposes of this paper, we have 'controlled' for the age variable by contrasting the Twitter posts involving the accounts of three young British rappers and songwriters (all in their twenties), whose stage names are Berwyn, Backroad Gee and Enny, with a similar sample of Twitter posts drawn from the accounts of three older, well-known British musical artists, Elton John, Phil Collins and Samantha Fox, who were all born in the 1950s and 60s (see Table 1 below). The accounts of the three rappers were chosen because, in exchanges with their fans and followers, their language can be regarded as representative of youth talk; in addition, they are very popular among British teenagers and young adults, are prominent in *Top of the Pops* lists, and are considered to genuinely embody current British rap music.[2] Turning to the three more mature artists, they are representative of a middle-aged generation and of a more traditional type of modern music, with a more international profile, a fact that may account for the presence in their Twitter interactions of posters from a wide range of countries, who at times use their own native language instead of English. In this respect, all non-English tweets were removed and not considered for the analysis.

All six artists chosen share a common origin: they are from or were raised in London, and they all have a strong attachment to the city. This circumstance was taken into account so as to make the two groups of singers as comparable as possible.

2 See, for example, <https://guap.co/ones-to-watch-2021/>; <https://www.darkusmagazine.com/post/the-mobo-awards-announce-their-2021-nominees>.

Table 1: General background and biographical information on the six artists.

Artist's name	Stage name	Twitter name	Age	Gender	Origin & background	Followers & achievements	Period covered
Enitan Adepitan	Enny	Enny (@ annyintegrity)	27	female	Nigerian origin, born and raised in Thamesmeads, South East London.	9,579 followers. Her song 'Peng Black Girls' has over a million views on YouTube. In 2021 she was nominated for the *Female Artist of the Year* award.	2020–2021
Not available	Back Road Gee	BackRoad Gee	25	male	Congolese background, and raised in London.	12,200 followers. His song 'Party Popper' has over 2 million views on YouTube.	2020–2022
Berwyn Du Bois	Berwyn	BERWYN@ berwynberwyn_	25	male	Trinidadian origin, based in East London from the age of 9.	2,218 followers. He was placed third on the BBC's *Sound of 2021* list. Also nominated for *Best Newcomer* at the MOBO Awards.	2020–2022
Elton John	Elton John (original name Reginald Kenneth Dwight)	@eltonofficial	75	male	Born in Pinner, Harrow, Greater London (12 miles from Charing Cross).	1.1 million followers. One of the most successful singers in the history of popular music; a career lasting over 50 years; 32 albums and more than 300 million copies sold.	December 2021
Phil Collins	Phil Collins (original name Philip David Charles Collins)	@PhilCollinsFeed	71	male	Born and raised in West London (Chiswick, Hounslow, Middlesex).	192,500 followers. British drummer, songwriter, actor and singer. He was the drummer and singer with the band *Genesis*.	2021
Samantha Fox	Samantha Fox (original name Samantha Karen Fox)	@SamFoxCom	56	female	Born in London.	75,400 followers, international singing artist, songwriter and all-around entertainer. Former actress and model.	2020–2021

Our search was mainly restricted to a two-year period, 2020 and 2021, since we were aimed at analyzing recent data, and includes a total of 10,000 posts, although occasional tweets from 2019 and 2022 do appear in the sample selected. The length of the posts varies considerably, from only one word to forty-five, although the mean length of the tweets is 10 words, the whole sample of data used amounting to ca. 100,000 words. Not all the accounts considered are equally active, and the numbers of tweets and retweets vary greatly from one to another. Elton John's account, for example, is extremely active and for this reason our analysis was restricted to the period of one month, December 2021. Nevertheless, we compiled samples of a similar size in each case, with the aim of having sufficient data to be in a position to arrive at sound conclusions.

The analysis focused on the posts uploaded by these six artists to their Twitter accounts, as well as all responses by their fans and followers. Although all the posts were considered together, the two groups of tweets were kept apart as this could provide additional details of interest for the interpretation of some linguistic features. The tweets uploaded by the artists themselves correspond to one third of the total, while all the rest, that is, two thirds of the whole sample, represent the responses and comments made by the participants to the original artists' posts. However, messages that the six artists retweeted were not considered, since it was difficult to verify the original authorship of these, and this might have distorted the findings; alterations to the original tweets might also have been made, which could have brought about changes in their interpretation.

The topics debated in the posts of both groups include the release of new songs and records, merchandising and advertising, fans' reactions to and comments on songs, concerts, shows and interviews, and sports (football in particular). However, the younger users often seem to be more politically aware and introduce issues with a more social dimension, such as the situation in Africa (Congo, Ghana and Nigeria in particular), racism, labor conditions, London transport problems, poverty in some parts of London, women inequality, etc.

In a previous study (Palacios and Núñez 2022), one which sought to show the potential of Twitter as a data source for the study of the language of teenagers and young adults, a total of 56 grammar and discourse features were identified in the posts of several artists and rappers in exchanges with their fans. These language features were subsequently grouped into three main categories, which will also be used in the current study:

(i) **Morphosyntactic**: lack of 1st and 3rd person subjects, common use of nominal vocatives, *was/were* variation, lack of copula BE and/or HAVE, vernacular negatives, etc.
(ii) **Lexical**: tendency to incorporate words from other languages and even from other varieties of English (i.e., Jamaican English), high frequency of items relating to music and drugs, overuse of clipped forms, etc.
(iii) **Features typical of Twitter discourse**: emoji, word lengthening, use of capitals to express emphasis or anger, abbreviations common in net communication, etc.

Our analysis will be mainly qualitative, although some figures and numbers will also be provided in some cases to illustrate some of our findings.

5. Main findings

5.1. Introduction

In light of the above, Tables 2, 3 and 4 below include all of the 56 features considered (morphosyntactic, lexical, and characteristic of Twitter discourse, respectively). Due to space limitations, we cannot deal with each of these features in detail. The ones selected for further study in the following sections of this paper are highlighted in bold, these being the most distinctive and interesting from a linguistic perspective. The symbol √ in the following tables indicates that a feature in question is found in the language of a specific group, and the symbol X indicates that it is not.

Table 2: Morphosyntactic features.

Morphosyntactic Features	**Young adults**	**Mature adults**
1. Omission of subjects (mainly 1st and 3rd person): e.g. Also, just heard myself on radio 1 for the first time[3] (Berwyn 27/01/2020)	√	√
2. Use of address terms	√	√
3. *Was/were* variation: Enny & Simz!! Wish I *was* in the UK for this one! (Enny 30/07/2021)	√	X
4. Lack of copula HAVE: Been a huge fan since the 70s, thanks for all the great music! (Phil Collins 12/02/2021); seen this? (BackRoad Gee 24/10/2022)	√	√
5. Lack of copula BE: we good innit? (BackRoad Gee 20/10/2022)	√	X
6. Lack of agreement between subject and verb: Rafi Camino *Love* this! (Samantha Fox 11/07/2021)	√	√
7. *Ain't* (representing *are/am/is not* and *has/have not)*: gassed *aint* even the word (Berwyn 05/01/2021)	√	X
8. Double negatives: I will *not* ever *NOT* listen to PC (Phil Collins 10/09/2021)	√	√
9. Third person singular negative *don't*: You're both Congolese as well this *don't* help (BackRoad Gee 28/02/2022)	√	X
10. Negative vernacular forms as response tokens (*nope, noh, naaa*): Is he dropping the album or *na*? (BackRoad Gee 15/01/2022)	√	X
11. *So* as intensifier	√	√
12. *Very* as intensifier	X	√
13. *Real/ly* as intensifier	X	√
14. Positive semantic prosody adjectives as intensifiers	√	X
15. *Fucking* as intensifier	√	√
16. *Bloody* as intensifier	√	√
17. *Truly* as intensifier	X	√
18. *Absolutely* as intensifier	X	√
19. *Proper* as intensifier	√	√
20. *Totally* as intensifier	X	√

3 All the examples given have been transcribed as in the original. No changes have been introduced.

Table 2: *Continued*

Morphosyntactic Features	**Young adults**	**Mature adults**
21. *Pretty* as intensifier	X	√
22. *Super* as intensifier	√	√
23. *Mega* as intensifier	√	X
24. Plural of animate nouns with *-dem*: Leave di people pikney *dem* alone man wth (Enny 18/05/2021)	√	X
25. *Man* as a pronoun: See footnote 7.	√	X
26. *Bare* expressing quantification: high numbers. Can't wait to show you what I've got *bare* things cominggg for you (Enny 27/07/2021)	√	X
27. Use of invariant tags, particularly *innit*: Congo wasn't ur choice *innit*? (BackRoad Gee 23/10/2022)	√	X

Table 3: Lexical features.

Lexical Features	**Young adults**	**Mature adults**
28. Use of Jamaican words: *ends, peas, yardie, allow it…*	√	X
29. Words connected with music: *banger, stem, bootleg, bubble* (a type of dance), *grime, riddim/riddum, vibe, bar, sega-a* (style of music traditional in Mauritius), *NDUBZ*, (a band from London), *hook* (catchy part of a song)	√	X
30. Words undergoing semantic change: *wicked, sick, hard, cold, dope*…	√	X
31. Words denoting a pejorative meaning: *wasteman, gasman, roadman, rent boy, hollow man* ('bad rapper')	√	X
32. Words connected with drugs: *crack, peng, bizzle, plug*, and marginal sectors: change your *plug* (BackRoad Gee 15/10/2022)	√	X
33. Lexical items connected with technology, videogames: *Play Station 4, Wizard, Wizzie, GTO…*	√	X
34. Clippings/ reduced forms: Wow, beautiful and honest, keep trusting in *yrself, yr fab* x (Berwyn 18/06/2021)	√	√
35. Abbreviations typical of net language (Twitter slang): *bizzle* (billiards + puzzle)	√	√

Continued

Table 3: *Continued*

Lexical Features	**Young adults**	**Mature adults**
36. Loans from other languages	√	X
37. Slanguage: *slang, dirty, vogue, vague, proxy, gassed* ('overwhelmed'), and small words like *bot* 'stupid', *peng* ('attractive', also refers to 'marihuana'), e.g., Who the fuck unfollowed me. I was *gassed* to be on 6k followers now I'm bk to 5,999 kmt (BackRoad Gee 10/12/21)	√	√

Table 4: Features typical of Twitter discourse.

Features typical of Twitter	**Young adults**	**Mature adults**
38. Pictures	√	√
39. Gifs	√	√
40. Memes	√	√
41. Photos	√	√
42. Videos	√	√
43. Exclamations	√	√
44. Emoji	√	√
45. Emoticons: Sing MORE of that stuff!!!*:)* (Samantha Fox 15/09/2021)	√	√
46. Non-standard orthography, simulating spoken language/ oralisation: Bought tickets last year *b4* lockdown (Phil Collins 22/01/2021)	√	√
47. Lengthening of words: Washington DC come *onnnnnnnnn* (Phil Collins 20/10/2021)	√	√
48. Leaving spaces between letters (letter spacing) for 'loud and clear': I . . . superman. You . . . Rocketman! (Elton John 22/ 11/22)	√	√
49. Repeated punctuation marks (*?!,,,*): The great*!!!!* Phil*!!!* (Phil Collins 22/02/2021)	√	√
50. Use of capitals to intensify a message or part of a message: Because of all that *SO GOOD AFRICAN VIBE*! (Phil Collins 01/04/2021)	√	√

Table 4: *Continued*

Features typical of Twitter	**Young adults**	**Mature adults**
51. Repetition of words to express emphasis: *Please please please please please please* make it to where I can come see y'all and come to Dallas!! (Phil Collins 15/04/2021)	√	√
52. Use of numbers (cardinal and ordinal) instead of words: *4* sure (BackRoad Gee 21/12/2021)	√	√
53. Minimal punctuation: No but listen to plenty o song by genesis and Phil brilliant songs Phil stay safe take care (Phil Collins 19/02/2021)	√	√
54. Putting pairs of words together: *WELLDONE* SIR ELTON *WE LOVEYAAAA* (Elton John 24/12/2021)	√	√
55. Word/phrase emphasis by means of asterisks which may also represent swear words: Boris Johnson is Still a *F***ing C****' is the only choice for xmas number one (Elton John 22/ 12/2021)	√	√
56. Use of small clauses: So excited!! (Phil Collins 12/02/ 2021); no surprise (Elton John 18/12/2021)	√	√

Once the data were all pruned by removing incomplete and meaningless posts as well as those in languages other than English, the resulting samples were manually analyzed and organized into two main groups. The first of these comprised those features present in both young and mature adults' posts, hence showing no or very few differences in use, such as the high occurrence of clippings and abbreviations, and *so*, *fucking* and *bloody* as intensifiers, etc. The second group included those features that can be regarded as exclusive to young adults since they were not found at all in the posts of more mature users; that is the case, for example, of *man* as a pronoun or the presence of invariant tags such as *innit*. The classification of the different grammar features under one group of users or another was then provided on the attestation of each of these features in their respective posts.

In what follows, a full description of the features under scrutiny is provided. Thus, Sections 5.2.1 and 5.2.2 deal with nominal vocatives and intensifiers, respectively, while adjectives undergoing semantic change, abbreviations typical of net language and loans from other languages are the focus of Sections 5.3.1, 5.3.2 and 5.3.3. Finally, features characteristic of Twitter discourse, such as exclamations and emoji, are discussed in Sections 5.4.1 and 5.4.2.

5.2. Morphosyntactic features

5.2.1. Nominal vocatives

Differences are observed regarding the use of nominal vocatives between the two groups of posters in terms of the following parameters: (i) frequency; (ii) type of vocative; (iii) items selected; and (iv) mode of use.

(i) Frequency: Nominal vocatives have a greater overall frequency in tweets by young adults. So, as an example, if we compare the figures recorded in BackRoad Gee with those in the Elton John account, we find a total of 83 tokens in the case of the former versus 14 in the latter. This means that the frequency of this feature in the posts extracted from the BackRoad Gee's account is almost six times higher than that observed in Elton John. This seems to be the general trend in the rest of the data analyzed of the posters for each group. Moreover, this is in line with what has been found in general conversation (Palacios 2018).

(ii) Type of vocative: The group of nominal vocatives generally referred to as 'familiarizers', e.g., *man*, *mate*, *dude*, *you guys, dawg (dog)*, that is, address terms that serve to foster solidarity and reinforce bonds between participants in exchanges (Leech 1999; Biber et al. 2021), are more common in young adults (1), while 'endearments' (terms of endearment) such as *darling*, *baby*, *love*, *king*, *queen*, *honey* (2), and honorifics (*sir, madam*) are used more frequently by the mature users (3). As a way of illustration, in the posts extracted from the BackRoad Gee account, we find only 3 tokens as terms of endearment (*baby*, repeated twice, and *baby girls*) and 3 as honorific (*sir* on 3 occasions), while the remaining 77 are familiarisers with a prevalence of *man* and *bro*. In the case of Elton John, out of a total of 14 vocatives, 5 of them are honorifics (*sir*), 1 is a term of endearment (*darling*), and all the rest, that is, 8 tokens, are familiarisers, with a prevalence, on this occasion, of *man* and *mate*. By contrast, taboo or offensive vocatives such as *bitch, idiot* and *bastard* are very unusual in both groups, especially among adult users (4). Whereas such offensive address terms are quite common in the language of teenagers and young adults in everyday conversation (Palacios 2018, 2021; Palacios and Núñez 2022), in the Twitter accounts here their frequency is very limited. This may have to do with the regulations imposed by this platform, which specifically indicate that hate and foul language should be avoided, with the threat that an account might otherwise be suspended.[4]

(1) A: Unbelievably proud.
B: Vice versa *dude* (Enny 30/07/21).[5]
(2) Hope it's not long before you are touring there, sign of the times *hun*[6] xx (Phil Collins 8/10/2021).
(3) *Sir* any news on the Ireland dates? (Phil Collins 20/10/21).
(4) Mercury nominated *bitch* TT🏆 (Berwyn 22/07/21).

The familiarizers *man* and *mate* are common among mature users, but to a lesser degree. Note how in some cases *man* has lost its gender reference and cannot only be used to refer to a male addressee, but also to a female one.

(5) Yesssss *mate*, well done *guys* (Elton John 17/12/2021).
(6) *Man*, what he would have had to say about all this (Phil Collins 09/10/20).
(7) also back up your fucking phone *man* (Enny 17/10/21).

Apart from being a vocative, *man* also occurs in some posts of young adults as a 1st or 3rd person singular pronoun,[7] as in the following.

(8) TOMORROW. 7PM. GRM PREMIERE… MAN SAID GRM PREMIERE (Berwyn 27/04/2021). GRM=Grime and Rap Music.

---

4 <https://help.twitter.com/en/rules-and-policies/twitter-rules>.

5 For each example, the account from which it was extracted is given together with the date of collection. This information is provided for anyone interested in tracing the examples and replicating the study.

6 Short abbreviation for *honey*.

7 *Man/mandem* as a pronoun is quite common in *Multicultural London English* and has been explored quite extensively in the literature (Cheshire 2013; Adams 2018; Hall 2019; Palacios 2018, 2022).

As is the case in general speech (Leech 1999; Biber et al. 2021; Palacios 2018), these vocatives tend to appear more often in final position (1), (2) and (4), although some examples are also found in initial position, such as in (3) and (6), and even in middle position (5). The position of these address terms is not random, in that it is closely related to their pragmatic function: while in initial position they tend to act as attention-getters or even indicate the person to whom the post is addressed, those in final position have more of an interpersonal function and serve to express comradeship and the reinforcement of bonds among participants in the exchanges (Palacios 2018).

(iii) Items used:[8] Young adults are very fond of nominal vocatives like *bro, pal, fam, crew, g (god/gangsta), dick, people, boss*, *fella*, *baba*, unlike their adult counterparts who prefer other terms, some of which of a more formal nature, such as *genius, legend, love, folks, you guys, (sexy) sweetheart, baby, (my) dear, chaps, bugger, darling, sweetie, honey/hunney, sir, buddy, dude, (you) boy(s), lad(s), girl, Master, king, queen, buster, prat, peeps*, as well as some euphemistic forms like *b*****d, t**t, p*ss*.

(9) send it to me *bruh*, you want to enjoy alone (BackRoad Gee 23/12/21).
(10) Lool *fam* what a typo (Enny 24/04/21).
(11) Hi *legends* (Elton John 21/12/2021).
(12) Stay safe *peeps* (Phil Collins 22/01/2021).

(iv) Mode of use: While mature adults mainly use these forms to address their idols (13), and only very rarely to address one another (with the exception of *(you) guys*) (16), young adults use them in both ways, as in (14), (15) and (17).

8 Most of these forms can be found with different spellings; for example, *bae* and *babe* for *baby*, *luv* for *love*, *bwoyy* for *boy, sista* and *sis for sister, buster for bastard, famm* for *fam, mandem* for *man.* It is with *brother* that we find the greatest variation (*bro, broo, broski, bruh, bruv, bruddah, brethren*), possibly because it is by far the most frequently used among young posters. Word lengthening is also frequent with these address terms, e.g., *Whatever you say mannnn* 🤷‍♂(BackRoad Gee 28/02/2022).

(13) That was lovely *darling*💪🤘👌 (Samantha Fox 29/12/2021).
(14) Pay me first *bro*, before I teach u (BackRoad Gee 11/12/2021).
(15) Too much talent my *bro* love it my *g* keep creating (BackRoad Gee 19/05/2021).
(16) I had a few tears at Elton's first solo line as I lost my Grandma this year but *you guys* definitely deserve a 4th number one with this (Elton John 17/12/2021).
(17) So excited for *you guys* to hear her in full this Friday!! (Berwyn 22/09/2020).

Notice how two vocatives are sometimes registered in the same post, as in (15), where we have *my bro* and *my g* preceded by the possessive, which serves to reinforce the sense of community, comradeship and peer-group strengthening, something which has been noted elsewhere as especially prevalent in Twitter interactions (Zappavigna 2012). Emoji may also accompany these vocatives, as in (13), which, as we will see below, often emphasize the meaning of the tweet or add an additional tone of humor, surprise, sarcasm, etc.

5.2.2. Intensifiers

So as an intensifier is the most common form in both groups of users, together with *proper, super* and *absolutely*, although the latter three in smaller numbers.

(18) THIS WOULD GO *SO* HARD BRUV 🔥🔥🔥🔥🔥🔥 (BackRoad Gee 15/01/2022).
(19) I'm *so* proud of you (Elton John 31/12/2021).
(20) I love Phil Collins, *proper* decent guy (Phil Collins 22/06/2021).
(21) *Super* proud to be Aussie right now (Elton John 20/12/2021).
(22) The concert was *absolutely* brilliant and for the first time in 46 years I was 25 again (Phil Collins 10/10/2021).

Bloody and *fucking* (*fucken, focking, facking*) as intensifiers are also found in the expression of both young and mature adults, although the former use them more frequently, as has also been found in off-line communication (Palacios and Núñez 2012; Núñez and Palacios 2014). As an example, in the posts of young adults, a total of 11 tokens of *fucking* as intensifier are recorded whereas this number is restricted to only 3 in the case of mature adults. In comparing *bloody* and *fucking*, we also found that *fucking* is by far the more common, and occurs with a greater number of word classes (adjectives, adverbs, verbs, nouns).

(23) Still sounding *bloody* great (Phil Collins 30/01/2021).
(24) So *fucking* pretty (Enny 06/05/2021).

Some euphemistic variants of these two intensifiers are also attested, such as the following:

(25) Let's *fxxking* get this (BackRoad Gee 15/01/2022).

Very, *really*, *pretty, truly* and *totally* are not found in the sample of young posters, whereas they are relatively common in the tweets of more mature adults. By turn, *mega* occurs only in the language of young adults. These findings are just partially in keeping with the literature on off-line communication (Tagliamonte 2008; Palacios and Núñez 2012; Núñez and Palacios 2014), where the intensifiers *really* and *pretty* are very frequent in teen talk while *very* is clearly declining in use.

(26) *Pretty* rare I wasn't even sure I still had this (Samantha Fox 07/07/2021).
(27) Thank you for the update and the circumstances are *totally* understandable (Phil Collins 08/10/2021).

It is also worth noting that mature adults make use of a wide variety of adjectives involving positive semantic prosody with an intensifying value, e.g., *massive*, *superb*, *fantastic, great, wonderful, awesome, amazing, brilliant, incredible, immense, huge, gorgeous, fabulous, lovely, terrific, cute, adorable*. A total of 98 tokens are registered in our sample. These are used mainly by fans and followers to compliment their respective artists.

(28) *Massive* respect to you and wishing you all the best with the rest of the tour (Phil Collins 07/12/2021).
(29) *Superb* song and video, is it on iTunes yet, Sam? (Samantha Fox 15/09/2021).
(30) *Wonderful* woman (Samantha Fox 07/06/2021).

5.3. Lexical features

5.3.1. Adjectives undergoing semantic change

In the expression of young adults, we find a total of 20 lexical items that have undergone a process of 'amelioration', that is, a word with a negative sense that develops a positive one (Traugott and Dasher 2001). This applies mainly to adjectives such as *cold, icy, hard, wicked, sick, mad, greezy, crazy/cray, bad, heavy, dope, smooth, tight*, as well as to some nouns, e.g., *shit.*

(31) Can't believe I wasn't following you. Just bumped 6,008 to 6,009. Keep killing it, your sound is *sick*! (BackRoad Gee 10/12/2021).
(32) *Mad* jam!!! (BackRoad Gee 18/12/2021).
(33) Some real *shit* from the heart and soul (Berwyn 28/04/2021).

Thus, in the previous examples the posters describe the music of BackRoad Gee and Berwyn in very positive terms, despite using words which traditionally convey negative connotations, such as *mad, sick* and *shit.* This phenomenon has also been reported as common in off-line communication in the language of teenagers (Stenström et al. 2002; Palacios 2016; Tagliamonte 2016).

5.3.2. Abbreviations typical of net language

As expected, both mature and young adults employ abbreviations of this type, although they are far more common in the latter group, where they include a higher number and a wider variety of swear words such as *fuck, bitch, bastard, motherfucker*. Apart from differences in frequency of use here, 59 tokens in the set of young adults versus a total of 41 examples in that of more mature ones, the two groups of posters also differ in some of the abbreviations used, as shown in the following table; those which appear in both groups have been highlighted. The use of lower and upper case also seems to alternate freely in these forms, e.g., *lol/LOL, wtf/WTF*. See Tables 5 and 6 below.

Table 5: Abbreviations typical of net language used by young adults.

Abbreviation	**Young adults**
ak	ass kisser
asap	as soon as possible
asf*[9]	as fuck
bk	Back
brb	Be right back
btw	by the way
dkm	Don't kill me
DPMO*	Don't piss me off!
FASHO*	for sure
fr*	for real
GTFOH*	Get the fuck out of here
IDGAF*	I don't give a fuck
idk	don't know
ikdr*	I don't know damn right
ikr*	I know right
ilsm*	I love you so much
kmft*	kiss my fucking teeth
kmt*	kiss my teeth
lfb*	little fat bitch/bastard/buddy
mco	Laughing my cats off
lol	laughing out loud
mf*	motherfucker
MIA*	missing in action
nf	not funny
ngll*	not gonna lie
nmn	Never mind
OG	Oh God!
omds/oms	Oh my days!

9 The asterisk next to an abbreviation indicates that it is not included in Crystal's *Glossary of Netspeak and Textspeak*. The fact that this work was published in 2004 may account for the high number of abbreviations with no entry in this mini dictionary of common internet terms.

Table 5: *Continued*

Abbreviation	Young adults
Omfg	Oh my fucking god
plz/pls	please
ppl*	people
smh*	shaking my head
stfu	Shut the mouth fuck up
SYM*	Shout your mouth
tbh*	to be honest
tf	the fuck
tktv*	you know the vibe
ty*	thank you
tysm*	thank you so much
wsp*	What's up
wtf	what the fuck
wth	what the hell/heck
yh*	Yeah
YP	Yes, please

Table 6: Abbreviations typical of net language used by mature adults.

Abbreviation	Mature adults
atm	at the moment
be	Baby
DM	direct message
ffs*	for fuck's sake
fr	for real
GC	group chat
goat*	greatest of all times
HBD/HBTU	Happy birthday!
ICYMI*	In case you missed it
idk	I don't know
ILY	I love you

Continued

Table 6: *Continued*

Abbreviation	Mature adults
IMO	in my opinion
lmao	laughing my ass off
lol	laughing out loud
OG*	old gangsters
OMF*	Oh my fuck
OMG	Oh my god
pm	private message
Re	with reference to
sm*	so much
sos*	Sorry
tbd*	to be decided/to be declared
Xoxo	kisses and hugs

The tendency to be quick and concise in the use of language may be the reason for the adoption of most of these acronyms, which can be grouped into five main categories: (i) those which serve to convey quick responses or reactions to previous messages, e.g., *lol, lmao, nf, dkm, sos, kmt*; (ii) exclamations such as *OG, wtf, wth, ffs, omd(s)*; (iii) discourse markers which help to provide cohesion and to organize the information included in posts, and which in some cases can be seen as fixed formulae, e.g., *IMO, pz, asap, btw*; (iv) other terms associated with Twitter communication, such as *DM, pm, re, GC, brb, bk*, etc.; (v) reduced versions of nominal vocatives or address terms, e.g., *ak, lfb, be, mf.* In most cases these short forms are created with the initials of the words they represent, although they can also stand for a full sentence, e.g., *ilsm, IDGAF, SYM, GTFOH.* Most of these acronyms are also found in other social media and digital genres such as Instagram, Facebook, TikTok, etc.

5.3.3. Loans from other languages

The use of loan words from other languages, mainly Latin (*ad-libs*), Old Persian (*baba*), Arabic (*fiya, marhaba, inshallah*), French (*petit meme, ressemble*), German (*doppelgänger*), Nigerian (*igbo, abeg*) and Spanish (*holla*), is restricted in our data to posts by young adults. There are several reasons for this. First, the three rappers selected, although having spent most of their life in London, all have their origins in other countries, as noted above. Thus, Enny is Nigerian, and BackRoad Gee and Berwyn have Congolese and Trinidadian backgrounds, respectively. This may explain why these artists and their followers incorporate in their interactions terms connected with these language environments. Second, teenagers and young adults are generally very open to the introduction of lexical borrowing from other languages in their everyday communication (Drange 2002, 2009; Palacios 2011; Drange et al. 2014). Third, all three of these young artists are very active in social media and in the use of technology, exhibiting in some cases an interest in music, art, design and fashion, areas of knowledge which naturally lead to the incorporation into their lexicons of a wide array of terms from different languages. Here are some examples from the samples selected:

(34) 😅 this guy needs to come do my *ad-libs*[10] (BackRoad Gee 20/12/2021).
(35) That's your *doppelgänger* ak (BackRoad Gee 28/02/22).
(36) *Marhaba*[11] brother (BackRoad Gee 23/02/22).
(37) So pretty *c'est petit même* (Enny 06/05/21).
(38) The air smells like a warm summers night… I'm Praying for a peaceful summer for real we know how the streets get. Value life man *abeg*[12] (Enny 31/03/21).
(39) Your song titles are *fiyaaaah*[13] too (BackRoad Gee 17/08/21).
(40) *Oga*[14] rest (Backroad Gee 26/07/22).

10 Also 'ad libitum', from Latin. A term used in musical notation to indicate that a performer is given the freedom to vary the notes or tempo; in jazz it typically means to improvise freely.
11 Greeting in Arabic.
12 'Please', used in West-Africa, Nigerian pidgin.
13 *Fiya* is an Arabic/Muslim girl name meaning 'powerful'.
14 *Oga* is a Nigerian pidgin word which means 'senior' or 'boss'.

5.4. Features characteristic of Twitter discourse

5.4.1. Exclamations

A very common feature of Twitter posts is that users openly express their feelings and emotions towards other events and their own life experiences, and also towards other users. This explains why exclamations play such an important role in this type of discourse.

We find a high frequency of exclamations at the beginning of posts in both user groups, a total of 59 equally distributed in the two groups, although they are employed differently. Thus, young adults tend to make more use of exclamations of a religious (*amen, inshallah, Jesus, blood of Jesus, hallelujah, god damnit, damn, my goodness, Oh my days, Oshe*) and an onomatopoeic nature (*brr, haha, wow, yeeh, woi, phew, woah, che-ching, whew*).

(41) *Cha-chiiiiiiiiiiing* What a wonderful sight Love seeing this. Congrats M'aam. (Enny 03/08/2021).

(42) If live shows have shown me anything... white men sing Peng Black Girls from their core *Omds* ('Oh my days'; Enny 26/11/21).

By contrast, mature adults tend to favor other exclamations, such as *yikes, dammit, wo(w)!, ahh, ohh, uh, Yay, whottwoot!*

(43) *Wow*! I saw you & your son in Vegas....what an incredible performance! (Phil Collins 22/01/2021).

(44) *aaaah* elton that's so excitinggg!! (Elton John 18/12/2021).

In both user groups it is very frequently the case that posters use letter lengthening, as in (41) and (44), to sound more emotional or to convey a higher degree of personal involvement. Exclamation marks are not always used, although at times we in fact find several of them used repeatedly, as in (44). Although, as noted above, they are often placed in initial position, exclamations may also stand alone as a response to a previous message.

(45) *Haha* (Backroad Gee 05/07/22).

5.4.2. Emoji

The *Oxford English Dictionary* defines this term as of Japanese origin, meaning 'a small digital image or icon used to express an idea, emotion, etc., in electronic communications' (*OED* s.v. *Emoji* n.). Although this definition provides quite an accurate description of what an emoji is, from our analysis we observe that the use of emoji entails far more than this, in that they perform different roles and serve a wide array of pragmatic functions in this type of discourse.

Emoji are considered to be distinctive features of Twitter and other digital discourses (Herring 1996; Yus 2011; Zappavigna 2012; Squires 2016) and have been extensively studied from a variety of perspectives relating to their discourse and pragmatic functions (Herring and Dainas 2020; Wiese and Labrenz 2021; Yus 2021), their semantic meaning and interpretation (Jones and Hafner 2012), and the impact that sociolinguistic variables such as age, gender, race, and cultural context have on their use (Nishumira 2015; Albawardi 2018; Herring and Dainas 2020; López Rúa 2021; Miltner 2021). Others (Parkwell 2019; Zappavigna and Logi 2021) have considered emoji in terms of the social semiotic dimension, exploring how they are used in their functional context and how they behave as semiotic resources in combination with the co-text in which they are found. Rodrigues et al. (2018) have also compiled a database of emoji and emoticons, including the evaluative meanings given by users to a total of 238 stimuli, 85 emoticons, and 153 emoji. The study involves a new perspective, in that it introduces the views of real users in the analysis, rather than restricting itself to interpretations made by researchers.

Due to space limitations, in the present study we will simply describe our preliminary findings here, but we also note that the use of emoji merits further, independent study; indeed, in a future study we will focus specifically on their pragmatic functions and on their role in Twitter discourse.

In our present analysis of the use of emoji, no major differences of use are identified between the two user groups on Twitter. The differences that we have found tend to have more to do with the topics discussed and with the selection of specific emoji than with their broad pragmatic function (see Section 4 on methodology). The topics debated in the posts of both groups have a bearing on some of the emoji used as already pointed out by other scholars (Zappavigna and Logi 2021).

At the syntactic level, emoji are found at the beginning of the clause (46), in the middle (47), at the end (48), and even on their own as a single turn (49). However, end position is the most common. In this respect, we can draw a parallel with nominal vocatives, which may also occupy all these positions in the clause.

(46) 🤲 DONT EVER STOP MY BRO (BackRoad Gee 18/12/2021).
(47) I'm loving all the videos 🕺 🤯 u lot proper understand the assignment ❤️ 🙌 ▒ (BackRoad Gee 26/11/2021).
(48) Great show 🙌 (Berwyn 18/06/2021).
(49) _💎💎💎 (Berwyn 24/01/2022).

Emoji can be repeated, or used in combinations of more than one. This contributes to the reinforcement of the multimodal nature of this type of discourse.

(50) Your energy bro 🔥🔥🔥 (BackRoad Gee 07/12/2021).
(51) Long awaited 🔥🔥❤️🥺 (BackRoad Gee 15/01/2022).

The combination of emoji may also help to express different ideas or feelings simultaneously. So, for example, in (52) the poster wishes merry Christmas to their favorite star and, at the same time, sends him their love.

(52) Season greetings to you and yours 🎄🎅❤️ (BackRoad Gee 25/12/21).

There is no real limit as to the number of emoji that may occur together, and it is also common to find variation in the use of different colors with the same emoji. At times this may even become a kind of game as if users were playing with emoji with humorous or aesthetic purposes in mind. Some posters combine apparent non-related emoji or make use of the same one but with different colors; see the hearts in (54).

(53) Congratulations, Phil Collins! Well deserved ❤️👏▒👏▒👏▒👏▒ 🥇🎶🎤🎹 (Phil Collins 28/02/2020).
(54) This was absolutely stunning 🎶🤩💜💚💙 (Berwyn 17/06/20).
(55) The UK artist we have been waiting for yaaaas brother tell our stories. You got me emotional in my feelings 🔥🎼👊▒💫🤗❤️. mercury (Berwyn 17/8/21)

Face expressions such as laughing, crying, begging, expressing surprise, joy or worry (🤔,🥳, 😂,😧), hearts (❤️❤️), hands praying or clapping (👏, 🙏), clenched fists (✊ ▒), fingers crossed (🤞), musical notes (🎶🎼), flowers (🌹), flexed biceps (💪), fire (🔥), Christmas tree (🎄), birthday cake (🎂), diamonds (💎), four-leaf clover (🍀), crowns (👑) and flags of different nationalities are amongst the most frequent in both groups of posters, with some differences between them Thus, those that represent a clenched fist, fire, bombs and collisions occur more frequently in the accounts of younger adults.

In our analysis we find emoji playing different pragmatic functions, which may even overlap. Here are the most notable:

(i) Banter:

(56) I take my man out he paying 🔥😛❤ 💯 (Enny 11/12/21).

The female poster in (56) refers to the fact that she is going out with her partner for a meal and is forcing him to pay for it.

(ii) Solidarity:

(57) Your energy bro 🔥🔥🔥 (BackRoad Gee 07/12/2021).
(58) Great show 🙌 (Berwyn 18/06/2021)

This is a very common use of emoji in the samples selected, with fans and followers expressing their support for their idols with these visual resources.

(iii) Irony:

(59) Bruhhh even got the same lips I cba 😂😂😂😂😂😂😂😂 (BackRoad Gee 01/03/2022).

Here BackRoad Gee sends a general post in which he proudly declares he looks like a Manchester United player. Several responses from other posters follow, in which they make fun of him for this comment.

(iv) Emotional: This function is very closely related to the following one, in that the posters express a high degree of emotion, often combining emoji with exclamations and/or capital letters.

(60) your sound is sick! 🔥🔥🔥 (BackRoad Gee 10/12/2021).
(61) WE LOVE YOU YOO❤ 🙌 ▒ (BackRoad Gee 19/11/2021).
(62) The UK artist we have been waiting for yaaaas brother tell our stories. You got me emotional in my feelings. 🔥🎼👊▒🔄🤗❤#mercury (Berwyn 17/08/2021).

(v) Intensification: Emoji here simply convey an added value to what posters express with words.

(63) Love your new music bro 💪💯 (BackRoad Gee 09/12/2021).

(vi) Iconical: Here emoji fulfil a multimodal function which helps to make the message more direct and clearer, or represent a word, concept or feeling.

(64) This is cold 🥶🥶🥶broski (BackRoad Gee 09/12/2021).
(65) HAPPY BIRTHDAY 🎈🎂🥳 MY G 👊(BackRoad Gee 17/12/2021).
(66) My❤belongs to you (Phil Collins 24/05/2019).

(vii) Symbolic: This function is closely related to the previous one, since emoji here function as symbols, e.g., rockets to represent Elton John, the 'rocket man', a reference to one of his best-known songs; flags to illustrate different countries, an egg for Easter, the sun, the earth, the rainbow.

(67) Tonight is the night 🚀 (Elton John 25/06/2020).
(68) Is there any plans for Scotland? 🏴󠁧󠁢󠁳󠁣󠁴󠁿 (Phil Collins 11/05/2021).

The above descriptions of the functions of emoji in the expression of young and mature adults is not exhaustive. Other functions could be added, such as those of mitigating and clarifying an utterance, expanding or illustrating textual content, negotiating meaning, closing a turn, behaving as punctuation marks, etc. Indeed, this list might be far longer, which underlines the need for an independent study of the issue.

6. Conclusions and suggestions for further research

Although this is a preliminary analysis, we believe that age is an important variable to be considered not only in off-line but also in online communication and digital genres, with Twitter as a case in point here. This study seems to bear out our initial assumptions, although it is clear that further evidence is required. As observed above in Section 5, our findings confirm those of previous studies (Nguyen et al. 2013; Flekova et al. 2016) in relation to those features of Twitter discourse which are most frequent in the tweets of young speakers, such as word lengthening, the use of capitals, the brevity of tweets, a high proportion of nominal vocatives, especially familiarizers, loan and swear words, vernacular negatives, *man* as a pronoun, slanguage, etc. In contrast, there are also some features that are more closely associated with the posts of mature adults, who tend to use some specific intensifiers *(very, absolutely, truly, pretty*) more often, and resort very frequently in their posts to a wide array of adjectives expressing positive semantic prosody with an intensifying value (e.g., *massive, wonderful, awesome, brilliant*). Something similar applies, for example, to emoji, which seems to be highly conditioned by the topics discussed in the tweets exchanged, and which differ greatly from young to more mature adults, the former being more highly concerned, at least apparently, with political and social issues.

We have identified differences in the use of language between young and mature adults at the three levels analyzed: morphosyntactic (nominal vocatives and intensifiers), lexical (use of loanwords, items used to effect a semantic shift, abbreviations), and Twitter discourse (exclamations and emoji). Such differences were not restricted to a higher or lower frequency in one group of users over the other, but also involved the selection of particular items and the role that these played in the use of language.

Methodological issues should also be addressed with care when accounting for the real effects of the age of speakers in Twitter discourse. Our approach to controlling for this variable, by closely analyzing and comparing the language used in 5,000 posts extracted from the accounts of three young rappers in their interactions with their followers and fans, with equivalent Twitter samples of more mature posters, is a useful way of attaining a high degree of certainty as to the age of posters, although there is still no absolute guarantee that participants in the interactions in each age-defined group can be definitively classified as belonging to that particular age group. However, we believe that it can provide some insights into the phenomenon, and as such may open up new paths of analysis, especially ones that serve as complementary to other, automatic instruments of analysis.

Finally, and given that our study has been mainly qualitative in nature, a further necessary step is to complement our findings with more quantitative data. Many questions remain to be addressed in further research, including the use of non-standard grammar, oralization, non-standard spellings, multimodality, etc., all of which have the potential to enrich our understanding of language as used in digital genres and the age variable.

References

Adams, Zoe K. 2018. "I don't know why man's calling me family all of a sudden": Address and Reference Terms in Grime Music. *Language and Communication* 60, 11–27.

Albawardi, Areej H. 2018. *Digital Literacy Practices of Saudi Female University Students*. PhD Thesis. Reading: University of Reading.

Anderson, Monica / Jiang, Jingjing. 2018. *Teen Social Media and Technology 2018 Report.* Pew Research Center.

Barbieri, Federica. 2008. Patterns of Age-Based Linguistic Variation in American English. *Journal of Sociolinguistics* 12/1, 57–88.

Biber, Douglas / Johansson, Stig / Leech, Geoffrey N. / Conrad, Susan / Finegan, Edward. 2021. Grammar of Spoken and Written English. Amsterdam/Philadelphia: John Benjamins.

Cheshire, Jenny. 2006. Age and Generation-Specific Use of Language. In Ammon, Ulrich / Dittmar, Norbert / Mattheier, Klaus / Trudgill, Peter (eds.), *Sociolinguistics: An Introductory Handbook of the Science of Language and Society*. Berlin: Mouton, 1552–1563.

Cheshire, Jenny. 2013. Grammaticalisation in Social Context: The Emergence of a New English Pronoun. *Journal of Sociolinguistics* 17/5, 608–633.

Coupland, Nikolas / Coupland, Justine. 1995. Discourse, Identity and Aging. In Nussbaum, Jon F. / Coupland, Justine (eds.), *Handbook of Communication and Aging Research*. Mahwah, New Jersey: Lawrence Erlbaum Associates, 79–103.

Crystal, David. 2001. *Language and the Internet*. Cambridge: Cambridge University Press.

Crystal, David. 2004. *A Glossary of Netspeak and Textspeak*. Edinburgh: Edinburgh University Press.

Drange, Eli-Marie D. 2002. Teenage Slang in Norway. In Breivik, Leiv Egil / Hasselgren, Angela (eds.), *From the Colt's Mouth … and Others': Language Corpora Studies. In Honour of Anna-Brita Stenström*. Amsterdam/New York: Rodopi, 71–80.

Drange, Eli-Marie D. 2009. Anglicisms in the Informal Speech of Norwegian and Chilean Adolescents. In Stenström, Anna-Brita / Jørgensen, Annette Myre (eds.), *Youngspeak in a Multilingual Perspective*. Amsterdam/Philadelphia: John Benjamins, 161–175.

Drange, Eli-Marie D. / Hasund, Ingrid Kristine / Stenström, Anna-Brita. 2014. Teenagers' Swearing by Mother in English, Spanish and Norwegian. *International Journal of Corpus Linguistics* 19/1, 29–59.

Eckert, Penelope. 1997. Sex and Gender Differences in Variation. In Coulmas, Florian (ed.), *The Handbook of Sociolinguistics*. London: Blackwell, 151–167.

Flekova, Lucie / Ungar, Lyle / Preoţiuc-Pietro, Daniel. 2016. Exploring Stylistic Variation with Age and Income on Twitter. *Proceedings of the 54*th *Annual Meeting of the Association for Computational Linguistics*. Volume 2: Short Papers. Berlin: Association for Computational Linguistics, 313–319.

Hall, David. 2019. The Impersonal Gets Personal: A New Pronoun in Multicultural London English. *Natural Language and Linguistic Theory* 38/3, 117–150.

Herring, Susan C. (ed). 1996. *Computer-Mediated Communication*. Amsterdam/ Philadelphia: John Benjamins.

Herring, Susan C. 2001. Computer-Mediated Discourse. In Schiffrin, Deborah / Tannen, Deborah / Hamilton, Heidi E. (eds.), *Handbook of Discourse Analysis*. Oxford: Blackwell, 612–634.

Herring, Susan C. / Dainas, Ashley R. 2020. Gender and Age Influences on Interpretation of Emoji Functions. *ACM Transactions on Social Computing* 3/2, 1–26.

Holmes, Janet. 1992. *An Introduction to Sociolinguistics*. London: Longman.

Jones, Rodney H. / Hafner, Christoph A. 2012. *Understanding Digital Literacies*. London: Routledge.

Leech, Geoffrey. 1999. The Distribution and Function of Vocatives in American and British English. In Hasselgård, Hilde / Oksefjell, Signe (eds.), *Out of Corpora: Studies in Honour of Stig Johansson*. Amsterdam: Rodopi, 107–120.

López Rúa, Paula. 2021. Men 😂 and Women ❤ on Twitter: A Preliminary Account of British Emoji Usage in Terms of Preferred Topics and Gender-Related Habits. *Language@internet* 19, article 3.

Meyerhoff, Miriam. 2006. *Introducing Sociolinguistics*. London/ New York: Routledge.

Miltner, Kate M. 2021. One Part Politics, One Part Technology, and One Part History: Racial Representations in UNICODE 7.0 Emoji Set. *New Media Society* 23/3, 515–534.

Morgan-López, Antonio A. / Kim, Annice E. / Chew, Robert F. / Ruddle, Paul. 2017. Predicting Age Groups of Twitter Users Based on Language and Metadata Features. *PLoS ONE* 12/8, e0183537. https://doi.org/10.1371/journal.pone.0183537

Nguyen, Dong / Gravel, Rilana / Trieschnigg, Dolf / Meder, Theo. 2013. "How old do you think I am": A Study of Language and Age in Twitter. *Proceedings of the Seventh International AAAI Conference on Weblogs and Social Media* 7/1, 439–448.

Nishimura,Yukiko. 2015. A Sociolinguistic Analysis of Emoticon Usage in Japanese Blogs: Variation by Age, Gender and Topic. *Selected Papers of Internet Research 16*: *The 16th Annual Meeting of the Association of Internet Researchers*. Retrieved from: http://spir.aoir.org.

Núñez, Paloma / Palacios, Ignacio. 2014. *That's Absolutely Crap, Totally Rubbish*. The Use of the Intensifiers *Absolutely* and *Totally* in the Spoken Language of British Adults and Teenagers. *Functions of Language* 21/2, 210–237.

Palacios, Ignacio. 2011. The Language of British Teenagers. A Preliminary Study of Its Main Grammatical Features. *Atlantis* 33/1, 105–126.

Palacios, Ignacio. 2016. Describing Teen Talk across Languages. A Preliminary Corpus-Based Study. In Spiegel, Carmen / Gysin, Daniel (eds.), *Jugendsprache in Schule, Medien und Alltag*. Frankfurt am Main: Peter Lang, 395–410.

Palacios, Ignacio. 2018. "Help me move to that, blood". A Corpus-Based Study of the Syntax and Pragmatics of Vocatives in the Language of British Teenagers. *Journal of Pragmatics* 130, 33–50.

Palacios, Ignacio. 2021. Taboo Vocatives in the Language of London Teenagers. *Pragmatics* 31/2, 250–277 (published online 18/ 11/ 2020).

Palacios, Ignacio / Núñez, Paloma. 2012. He's Absolutely Massive. It's a Super Day. Madonna, She Is a Wicked Singer. Youth Language and Intensification: A Corpus-Based Study. *Text & Talk. An Interdisciplinary Journal of Language, Discourse & Communication Studies* 32/6, 773–796.

Palacios, Ignacio / Núñez, Paloma. 2022. Teenagers and Social Networking. Twitter as a Data Source for the Study of the Language of London Teenagers and Young Adults. In Groff, Cynthia/ Hollington, Andrea / Hurst-Harosh, Ellen / Nassenstein, Nico / Nortier, Jacomine / Pasch, Helma / Yannuar, Nurenzia (eds.), *Global Perspectives on Youth Language Practices*. Berlin: Mouton de Gruyter, 85–104.

Parkwell, Corinna. 2019. Emoji as Social Semiotic Resources for Meaning-Making in Discourse: Mapping the Functions of the Toilet Emoji in Cher's Tweets about Donald Trump. *Discourse, Context & Media* 30/2, 100307. https://doi.org/10.1016/j.dcm.2019.100307

Rao, Dellp / Yarowsky, David / Shreevats, Abhishek / Gupta, Manaswi. 2010. Classifying Latent User Attributes in Twitter. *Proceedings of the 2nd International Workshop on Search and Mining User-Generated Contents*, 37–44.

Rodrigues, David L. / Prada, Marilia / Gaspar, Rui / Garrido, Margarida / Lopes, Diniz Lopes. 2018. Lisbon Emoji and Emoticon Database (LEED): Norms for Emoji and Emoticons in Seven Evaluative Dimensions. *Behavior Research Methods* 50/1, 392–405. https://doi.org/10.3757/s13428-017-0878-6

Squires, Laurel. 2016. *English in Computer-Mediated Communication: Variation, Representation, and Change*. Berlin: Mouton.

Statista. 2021. <https://www.statista.com/statistics/283119/age-distribution-of-global-twitter-users/>

Stenström, Anna-Brita / Andersen, Gisle / Hasund, Ingrid. 2002. *Trends in Teenage Talk: Corpus Compilation, Analysis and Findings*. Amsterdam/Philadelphia: John Benjamins.

Tagliamonte, Sali. 2008. So Different and Pretty Cool! Recycling Intensifiers in Toronto, Canada. *English Language and Linguistics* 12/2, 361–394.

Tagliamonte, Sali. 2012. *Variationist Sociolinguistics: Change, Observation, Interpretation.* Malden/Oxford: Wiley-Blackwell.

Tagliamonte, Sali. 2016. *Teen Talk: The Language of Adolescents.* Cambridge: Cambridge University Press.

Traugott, Elizabeth Closs / Dasher, Richard B. 2001. *Regularity in Semantic Change.* Cambridge: Cambridge University Press.

Wiese, Heike / Labrenz, Annika. 2021. Emoji as Graphic Discourse Markers. In Van Olmen, Daniël / Šinkūnienė, Jolanta (eds.), *Pragmatic Markers and Peripheries.* Amsterdam/Philadelphia: John Benjamins, 277–300.

Yus, Francisco. 2011. *Cyberpragmatics. Internet-Mediated Communication in Context.* Amsterdam/Philadelphia: John Benjamins.

Yus, Francisco. 2021. Pragmatics, Humour and the Internet. *Internet Pragmatics* 4/1, 1–11.

Zappavigna, Michele (ed.) 2012. *Discourse of Twitter and Social Media: How We Use Language to Create Affiliation on the Web.* New York: Continuum.

Zappavigna, Michele / Logi, Lorenzo. 2021. Emoji in Social Media Discourse about Working from Home. *Discourse, Context & Media* 44, 100543. https://doi.org/10.1016/j.dcm.2021.100543

GEMA ALCARAZ-MÁRMOL / JORGE SOTO-ALMELA

A contrastive corpus-assisted study of the portrayal of Afghan women in the Twitter discourse during the 2021 Taliban takeover

1. Introduction

Social networks have become a space where users express their feelings, attitudes and opinions about what is happening in the world and how they perceive it, sharing these ideas with other users. This study takes as its starting point the Taliban's return to power, an event in Afghanistan's recent history that was widely commented on the social network Twitter during the summer of 2021. To understand the current situation in Afghanistan, and how it came to be, we must go back to 1978, when Daouh Khan's government ended and the so-called Saur Revolution began, a communist-style revolution supported by the former USSR. At the same time, the United States was training and financing the so-called mujahideen in an attempt to prevent the installation of a communist regime in the country. These Islamic fundamentalists declared war on the newly formed communist government, which collapsed in 1992 after the USSR's final demise. The country was then plunged into a civil war until 1996, when the Taliban seized power.

The Taliban regime's rise to power was a brutal setback for women's rights. The burqa was imposed, and women were denied fundamental rights such as the right to formal education and public life. In addition, their right to health care was curtailed because they could not be treated by male doctors. They were also denied the right to work and leisure. Women were thus relegated to the domestic sphere, under the guardianship of their male relatives, with no possibility of leading an independent life.

After five years of Taliban government, in September 2001 the United States suffered the biggest terrorist attack of all time on the Twin Towers in New York and the Pentagon. Following this event, then US President George W. Bush declared war on the Afghan Taliban and invaded the country with the support of NATO forces, turning it into an international conflict that involved European countries, including Spain. The so-called International Security Assistance Force (ISAF), led by the United States, occupied Afghan territory. They overhauled all the country's institutions (army, police, judicial, educational and health systems), thus initiating a process of democratization and restoring some of the rights taken away from women during the years of Taliban rule.

However, Taliban forces never disappeared from the country and the conflict lasted until the summer of 2021, when the US withdrew the last troops, handing over full responsibility to the Afghan government, whose president left the country on 15th August. The day after, the Taliban army announced that it had taken the capital, Kabul, and thus regained control of the country. It was then announced that people would have until 31st August to try to leave the country, as the borders would be closed on that day. Thousands of Afghans tried to flee the country for fear of reprisals, especially women, who during the democratic period had become part of the country's working, academic and social life, even occupying positions of responsibility. During those two weeks, from 15th to 31st August, the return to power of the Taliban in Afghanistan was one of the worldwide trending topics on Twitter, where thousands of users commented on the event.

In this chapter, we analyze the Twitter discourse about this conflict and particularly we aim to explore and contrast through semantic preference as a collocational phenomenon how Afghan women were portrayed in tweets posted in Spain and the United States during this 17-day period. We will focus on the lemmas *mujer/woman* and their semantic preference in Twitter discourse during this conflict. For the study of semantic preference, we will explore the different collocates of *mujer/woman* and classify them into semantic categories that will be compared to find out whether there exist differences or similarities between the Twitter discourse in Spain and the United States with respect to the Taliban takeover of Kabul in August 2021.

2. Women in social media discourse analysis

It is beyond doubt there exists a vast increase of social media use nowadays. In fact, Shulman (2017: 215) states that social media are the society's 'newest stage', where laypeople share their thoughts and talk about different topics. Indeed, social media constitute one of the main ways of communication and space for discussion on almost every topic (Mautner 2005), becoming a channel for public sentiment, offering a better understanding of public opinion (McGregor 2019). In this sense, Twitter has become one of the most relevant social networks for the diffusion of information, and where users expose personal or public events, give their opinion or just share their viewpoints on a range of current affairs. In this line, Giachanou and Crestani (2016: 1) claim the value of tweets as a source of opinion as they can be used for 'a variety of applications that require understanding the public opinion about a concept'.

In the last years, the pandemic provoked by the Sars-Covid19 virus (Abdo et al. 2020; Wicke and Bolognesi 2021), the climate change (Anderson and Huntington 2017; Veltri and Atanasova 2017), recent international conflicts (Klausen 2015; Tenenboim 2017), social movements (Giorgi et al. 2022) and different political issues such as the rise of populism (Breeze 2020) or the 2020 US presidential election (Chen et al. 2022) have arisen as hot or trending topics which are discussed by millions of users. All of them have been of great interest to the public and this has been demonstrated, as each of these issues has generated a huge number of tweets, the analysis of which from different perspectives has provided data on the attitude of public opinion towards these issues.

Social networks have also served as spaces for the representation of different groups such as the Muslim or Asian community (Alcántara-Pla and Ruíz-Sánchez 2017; Melbourne et al. 2021) or migrants and refugees (Mullo et al. 2021; Bozdag and Smets 2017). Women have also been a topic for discussion on social media. Several studies explore how women are represented in spaces that have traditionally been occupied mostly by men, such as politics (Fuchs and Schäfer 2020; Ncube and Yemurai 2020), sports (Hull 2016; Adá 2019) or video games

(Manzano-Zambruno and Paredes-Otero 2019). The results of these studies show how social networks somehow reinforce stereotypes of women as caregivers, sexual objects, subordinate and far from leadership positions, even leading to invisibilization in some cases.

For instance, Fuchs and Schäfer (2020) explore what it is said about four female Japanese politicians in social media. The researchers combine quantitative and qualitative methods to analyze how these four women are portrayed in Twitter. They conclude that many users conceive those politicians as sexual objects or reduce them to their role of mothers. In the same line, Ncube and Yemurai (2020) observe how female candidates to 2018 Election in Zimbabwe were not taken seriously by Twitter users, whose discourse pointed to portraying women candidates as irrelevant in the election race. A similar picture is found in sports. Hull (2016) and Adá (2019) explore how social media deal with female sport. They remark the invisibilization of sports women in Twitter through gender stereotypes and evidencing discrimination. It can be observed that sports sources and their users underestimate achievements in female sports or even ignore them. Women are undervalued when it comes to video games. This field also replicates gender stereotypes, which are accepted and even supported by social media users. A study by Manzano-Zambruno and Paredes-Otero (2019) shows that women who are involved in this field are harassed and discriminated. This is extremely common in social media which, far from avoiding stereotypes, reproduce and sustain them.

Thus, as well as users, women are also objects of opinion in Twitter. Movements such as the 8M strikes or Metoo have had women as protagonists, generating millions of tweets. These events have been of interest to scholars. Hassan et al. (2019) compiled about 1 million tweets on the MeToo phenomenon. Likewise, Reyes-Menéndez et al. (2020) analyzed more than 31,000 tweets from a corpus-assisted discourse approach. Both studies highlight the polarization in the emotions and reactions of users towards this movement, finding an unconditional and devoted support or a strong rejection.

Other studies such as Field et al. (2019) and Idoiaga et al. (2022) focus on the representation of women as victims, while at the same time users claim the figure of the man as a powerful being, despite the fact that he is the perpetrator of many abuses against women. Social networks have also been identified as a tool for the reinforcement of women's identity as human beings with rights. In this sense, Molpeceres and Filardo-Llamas (2020) and Sampietro et al. (2020) carried out studies from a multimodal perspective, where both text and other elements of digital discourse such as emojis were explored. These scholars observe that there is a construction of a common identity through the creation of lemmas and certain expressions, as well as the use of certain emojis. All of this belongs to a series of discursive strategies that show an identity discourse in social movements with women as protagonists.

Piñeiro-Otero and Martínez-Rolán (2021) claim that social platforms are a hostile space for women, as they perpetuate inequality and the patriarchal order. These authors attribute this fact to the disinhibiting nature of the anonymity found in networks. Their study consists of an analysis of how people talk about or interact with 50 highly visible women in different spheres such as politics, science, culture and business. Their results show that up to 25 % of posts about these women constitute hate speech. They claim that 'as well as becoming hostile spaces for women purely because they are women, social media platforms have also fostered new, virulent forms of sexism such as gendertrolling' (2021: 3). In this line, Villar-Aguilés and Pecourt (2021) explore this phenomenon by focusing on the hashtag #Stopfeminazis. Their analysis reflects how the practice of gender-trolling is carried out through different communicative strategies. The most direct is the insult, although they also find other forms of expression such as sarcasm, defamation or even threats in some cases.

Manne (2017) affirms that many of these insults and threats reveal a sexist attitude, linking women's value to sexual practice. This type of cyberviolence against women is also studied by Bonet-Martí (2020). The author examines the discourse against women in 250 tweets posted between March and April 2020. In this case, the most common way of gender-trolling consisted of attacking women's physical aspect, age and psychological condition. They are seen as an interest group and fundamentalists against men. They were also portrayed as taking advantage because they are women, using their gender to get more rights and money than men.

These studies confirm that social networks are a double-sword weapon, being a platform for discrediting and attacking gender equality, but at the same time for supporting the feminist cause through the so-called cyberfeminism. For instance, Esposito and Sinatora (2021) conducted a multimodal investigation compiling a corpus from Facebook and Instagram. They adopted a critical discourse framework to analyze posts published by different women-supporting groups from the Middle East between 2011 and 2019. They explore the different linguistic and visual strategies to promote emancipatory discourse for women. In this line, most studies about cyberfeminism focus on Twitter (Dixon 2014; Baer 2016; Larrondo-Ureta and Orbegozo-Terradillos 2021). In fact, Barker-Plummer and Barker-Plummer (2017) considered the hashtag as a tool of feminist discursive activism, something which may promote 'agenda building events with worldwide impact' (2017: 3). Thus, they studied the hashtag #YesAllWomen and noted that it helped create collective identity as gender-rights supporters and also validated and spread protest. Talbot and Pownall (2022) explored how #AcademicTwitter became a channel to promote feminism. They compiled almost 600 tweets containing that hashtag. The researchers adopted a reflexive thematic analysis approach to establish semantic codes. Their analysis revealed that this hashtag served female scholars to reclaim women's rights and advocate for equality in the Academia and other contexts. In a similar tone, Palomino-Manjón (2022) analyzed the hashtag #WhyIDidntReport from a corpus-assisted discourse perspective. She mostly identified keywords and collocations which were linked to denouncing sexual violence and to the fight for women's rights, opposing to patriarchal ideology.

3. Understanding semantic preference

The extended unit of meaning model proposed by Sinclair is where the notion of semantic preference first emerged (Sinclair 1996; Sinclair 1998). This model includes semantic preference as well as collocation, colligation, and semantic prosody, to which Stubbs (2001: 64) refers as 'four types of co-occurrence relations in extended lexico-semantic units'. Although the focus of our study will be on semantic preference, it must be highlighted that semantic preference and semantic prosody are closely related, and that defining the former requires a comparison with the latter. Accordingly, these phenomena have been described as 'two distinct yet interdependent collocational meanings' (Xiao and McEnery 2006: 107) or 'two types of the same collocational phenomenon' (Bednarek 2008: 121).

Nonetheless, semantic preference and semantic prosody have different scopes, with the former having a narrower scope. Thus, semantic prosody refers to a broader semantic group and is typically classified as negative/unpleasant or positive/pleasant, whereas semantic preference refers to 'the habitual collocation of lexical items with linguistic expressions that belong to certain semantic fields' (Bednarek 2008: 120). Semantic preference, which 'involves collocation with semantic subsets of different degrees of generality' (Bednarek 2008: 129) has been found to go beyond these abstract categories of negative/positive semantic prosodies. As a result, semantic preference may be determined by the lexical items that appear alongside a word and frequently share semantic characteristics that can be sorted into distinct semantic subsets or categories.

Stubbs (2002) and Partington (2004) both highlight that semantic preference results from the semantically connected collocates of a given node word. In this line, Xiao and McEnery (2006) claim that semantic preference is a feature of the collocates. Several authors, including Stubbs (2001) and Whitsitt (2005), give instances of words that frequently appear with items from particular semantic categories, demonstrating that the collocates of a word can help to define its meaning, as semantic preference is precisely a collocational meaning. For example, the adjective *large* frequently appears with terms that imply size and quantity (Stubbs 2001), and the verbs *alleviate* and *relieve* exhibit a preference for words that describe discomfort or symptoms like backache, cramping, swelling, or bruising (Whitssit 2005).

Regarding its characteristics, it has been found that semantic preference is context-, genre-, and domain-dependent (Partington 2004; Hoey 2005). When the collocates of a particular node vary from genre to genre, this form of preference—often referred to as genre preference—occurs. For instance, depending on whether they appear in news articles or scientific publications, the collocates surrounding a node word may change. Additionally, it has been found that word class, meaning, and colligation (syntactic patterning) all interact with semantic preference. As a result, the semantic preference of a word may change depending on its grammatical category. Different semantic preferences may come from the literal and metaphorical meanings of a lexical item (Bublitz 1996).

Semantic preference has been investigated using methodologies that combine corpus-based approaches with manual examinations or intuitions of the researchers. It is the analyst who chooses how to interpret, label, and classify the collocates semantically, according to Bednarek (2008: 122), who claims that semantic preference is '(relatively objectively) observable by looking at corpus data'. In order to identify and define the semantic preference of *mujer* and *woman*, our study uses corpus analytic techniques before classifying their many collocates based on their semantic similarity. The term 'collocate' is frequently used in relation to semantic preference; however, it is important to note that collocate here means 'word co-occurring with the node item'.

4. Methodology

4.1. Corpus description and procedure

The corpus consists of two sub-corpora: a corpus of Spanish tweets posted in Spain (ES Corpus) and a corpus of English tweets posted in the United States (US Corpus). Both corpora contain all the tweets published between 15 August and 31 August 2021 (17 days), respectively coinciding with the beginning of the Taliban takeover of Kabul and the closure of Afghan borders after the completion of the evacuation process of international troops. Retweets and comments are not included in our corpus. For corpus compilation, we used the tool Twitter API v2 - Developer platform with Academic Research Access and selected the start and end dates mentioned above. As a query to obtain the tweets related to the conflict, we used the hashtag *#Afganistán* for Spanish and *#Afghanistan* for English and the keywords *Afganistán* for Spanish and *Afghanistan* for English.

The number of tweets, tokens and types in each sub-corpus is specified in Table 1. As can be seen, the US Corpus contains three times as many tweets and words as the ES Corpus. As a result, the number of types is also higher in the US Corpus. The average number of daily tweets posted during this conflict in Spain was 304.29 tweets and, in the US, it was 941.94 tweets. This may be interpreted as a sign of the conflict being more attention-grabbing in the US compared to Spain. All the tweets were pasted into a txt. file that was subsequently processed with the corpus analysis tool WordSmith 6.0 (Scott 2012).

Since semantic preference is a collocational phenomenon, we studied the behavior of the lemmas *mujer* and *woman* in an L5-R5 window of collocates. With these lemmas serving as the node words, our overarching objective is to shed light on the depiction of women within social media discourse, thereby contributing to the existing body of literature on this trending topic, as previously outlined.

In line with Stubbs (2001) and Partington (2004), semantic preference will be explored through co-occurrence. In fact, Bednarek (2008) points out that in order to study this phenomenon, the researcher must first use corpus analysis tools and then classify and label the different collocates into semantic categories. This procedure was applied to our work, where the collocates were classified ad hoc in a bottom-up approach, i.e., the semantic categories were not pre-established, but emerged from the detailed analysis of the collocates.

Table 1: Corpus description in number of tweets, tokens and types.

	ES Corpus	**US Corpus**
No. of tweets	5,173	16,013
No. of tokens	209,446	624,617
No. of types	15,238	25,463

In this research we focused on lemmas and content words. As for lemmas, all inflectional forms of verb tenses, as an example, were counted as a single lemma. This is the case for the verb *proteger* in Spanish, which would include the inflectional forms *protegido*, *protegida*, *protegidos*, *protegidas*, *protegiendo*, *protegen*, etc., or the verb *fight* in English, which would include, among others, the forms *fighting* or *fought*. However, derivative words were considered to be different lemmas, such as, for example, *protección* or *protection*. As for content words, a stop-list was used to eliminate all grammatical words - articles, conjunctions, prepositions—because they do not contribute to the construction of the semantic preference.

5. Data analysis

In this section the results of the study will be presented in a contrastive way, that is, by comparing the results obtained from the analysis of the two corpora. We will examine the semantic preference of the lemmas *mujer* and *woman*, as these appear to be the most common lemmas used to portray the Taliban's takeover of Kabul on Twitter. Indeed, both *mujer* and *woman* appear in the top ten most frequently used lemmas in our corpora: *mujer* (825 hits, 0.39 %) is the third most frequent word in the ES Corpus, and *woman* (1,437 hits, 0.23 %) is the eighth one in the US corpus.

Both the lemma *mujer* and *woman* seem to show a semantic preference for three semantic categories, namely empowerment, mistreatment and benevolence-empathy. As far as the first subset is concerned, in both corpora, collocates related to female empowerment are common, representing the awareness, both individually and collectively, that women have the power to be masters of their own actions, to take action and, in short, to lead their lives. Thus, as we can see in Table 2, in the ES Corpus we find 21 lemmas (205 occurrences, 0.09 %) that express empowerment, such as *derecho*, *libertad*, *defender*, *feminista* or *valiente*. *Right* is also the most frequent collocate in the US Corpus, where we find 19 lemmas with a total of 261 occurrences (0.04 %), as shown in Table 3. Other empowerment lemmas in the US Corpus are *fight*, *freedom*, *brave*, *equal* or *feminist*. It is also observed that ten of the lemmas are shared by both corpora: *derecho/right*, *libertad/freedom*, *feminista/feminist*, *valiente/brave*, *libre/free*, *igual/equal*, *lucha/fight*, *igualdad/equality*, *voz/voice* and *respeto/respect*. Women's empowerment in this conflict can be exemplified in the following tweets:

(1) #Afganistan | Colectivos feministas se han concentrado este viernes en la Plaza Federico Moyua bajo el lema "Los *derechos de las mujeres* afganas son asunto de todas" (20/08/2021)

(2) Junt_s en #Almendralejo por la libertad del pueblo de #Afganistán, los *derechos y libertades de las mujeres* y personas LGBTIQ+ afganas, y los #DerechosHumanos. La Comunidad Internacional no puede volver a mirar hacia otro lado, como lo hizo con el pueblo español en el franquismo. (20/08/2021)

(3) #Afghanistan Where's Kamala? I thought she was so passionate about *women's rights*. (18/08/2021)

(4) @DrGJackBrown Afghan women are like most women in the world. Afghan *women fight* for injustice and inequalities. Guess that's why men fear them.

Table 2: Empowerment collocates in the ES Corpus.

Lemma	Total	TL	TR	L5	L4	L3	L2	L1		R1	R2	R3	R4	R5
Derecho	89	70	19	11	3	56	0	0		0	1	6	7	5
Libertad	19	17	2	4	0	12	1	0		0	0	0	0	2
Defender	18	17	1	6	1	10	0	0		0	0	0	0	1
Feminista	8	2	6	1	1	0	0	0		5	1	0	0	0
Valiente	8	2	6	2	0	0	0	0		6	0	0	0	0
Libre	7	0	7	0	0	0	0	0		0	5	1	1	0
Igual	7	1	6	1	0	0	0	0		0	5	0	0	1
Lucha	7	2	5	0	0	2	0	0		0	0	0	0	5
Igualdad	7	7	0	0	1	5	1	0		0	0	0	0	0
Salir	5	0	5	0	0	0	0	0	M	0	0	0	5	0
Feminismo	5	2	3	1	1	0	0	0	U	0	0	0	0	3
Respeto	3	3	0	0	0	3	0	0	J E	0	0	0	0	0
Luchar	3	0	3	0	0	0	0	0	R	1	0	2	0	0
Protestar	3	0	3	0	0	0	0	0		2	0	0	0	1
Voz	3	2	1	2	0	0	0	0		0	0	0	0	1
Denuncia	3	0	3	0	0	0	0	0		0	0	0	3	0
Respetar	2	2	0	2	0	0	0	0		0	0	0	0	0
Reclamar	2	2	0	0	2	0	0	0		0	0	0	0	0
Armado	2	0	2	0	0	0	0	0		0	0	0	0	2
Arma	2	0	2	0	0	0	0	0		0	0	0	0	2
Capaz	2	0	2	0	0	0	0	0		0	0	0	2	0
	205	129	76	30	9	88	2	0		14	12	9	18	23

Table 3: Empowerment collocates in the US Corpus.

Lemma	Total	TL	TR	L5	L4	L3	L2	L1		R1	R2	R3	R4	R5
Right	92	28	64	4	3	8	13			6	34	1	12	11
Fight	49	21	28			20	1			5	7		13	2
Freedom	32	8	24	1		2	5					14	4	6
Brave	27	27	0		4	17	5	1						
Equal	6	5	1	3		2						1		
Feminist	6	1	5		1								4	
Voice	6	6	0			6								
Courageous	5	4	1			1		3			1			
Free	5	3	2	1	1		1		**W**		1	1		
Liberal	5	5	0		1		3	1	**O**					
Respect	5	5	0				1	4	**M**					
Liberty	4	2	2			2			**A N**	2				
Progress	4	3	1			3							1	
Street	4	1	3				1					1	2	
Powerful	3	0	3									3		
Empower	2	2	0				2							
Equality	2	2	0				2							
Heroic	2	1	1					1				1		
Revolutionary	2	2	0		2									
	261	126	135	9	12	61	34	10		13	43	22	36	19

Another label that seems to characterize L5-R5 *mujer/woman* collocates is mistreatment. This category includes negative lemmas that imply treating a person badly, cruelly or unfairly. In this case, those who suffer mistreatment are Afghan women and this is reflected in the Twitter discourse in Spain through lemmas such as *sufrir*, *violencia*, *miedo*, *maltratar* or *odio*. In the ES Corpus, a total of 38 lemmas (137 occurrences, 0.06 %) related to mistreatment were found. In the case of Twitter discourse in the US, *suffer*, *abandon*, *slaughter*, *rape* and *violence* stand out as the most frequent collocates out of a total of 37 (188 occurrences, 0.03 %). The top 10 collocates of mistreatment can be found in Table 4 for the ES Corpus and Table 5 for the US Corpus. There are numerous lemmas that appear in both corpora: *sufrir/suffer*, *violencia/violence*, *miedo/fear*, *asesinar/kill*, *atrapar/trap*, *abandonar/*

abandon, and *opresión/oppression*, among others. The cruel or unjust treatment towards Afghan women can be seen in these tweets:

(5) Dónde están las feministas? No he visto en los medios de comunicación ni una palabra sobre el burka que tienen que llevar de nuevo *las mujeres en Afganistán, que sufrirán* de nuevo y serán sometidas. (18/08/2021)

(6) #mujeresafganas La *violencia sexual contra #mujeres* y #niñas se generaliza en el conflicto e incluso se utiliza como táctica de #guerra. Si lo mejor que puedes aportar son tuits que denotan misoginia, eres un impresentable retrógrado. Eso no es libertad de expresión ni opinable. (16/08/2021)

(7) Amazing that our first female @VP was the last person in the room when @ POTUS decided to *abandon Afghan women* and girls to the Taliban. Civil rights for Afghan women are evidently something else 46 didn't want to hand down to his successors. (17/08/2021)

(8) Dear @POTUS, not sure if you're aware or not, but there's folks gettin beheaded, innocent *women being slaughtered and abused*, 20 years worth of deaths, and fighting hard for peace for the people of #Afghanistan and you sided with the #Taliban. #Traitor (25/08/2021)

Table 4: Top 10 Mistreatment collocates in the ES Corpus.

Lemma	**Total**	**TL**	**TR**	**L5**	**L4**	**L3**	**L2**	**L1**		**R1**	**R2**	**R3**	**R4**	**R5**
Sufrir	16	11	5	1	1	1	8	0		1	0	0	3	1
Violencia	14	13	1	0	7	6	0	0		0	0	0	0	1
Miedo	8	6	2	2	1	3	0	0		0	2	0	0	0
Maltratar	5	0	5	0	0	0	0	0	**M**	3	0	1	1	0
Odio	4	4	0	0	0	4	0	0	**U**	0	0	0	0	0
Asesinar	4	0	4	0	0	0	0	0	**J**	3	0	0	0	1
Atrapar	4	0	4	0	0	0	0	0	**E R**	4	0	0	0	0
Abandonar	3	3	0	0	0	3	0	0		0	0	0	0	0
Someter	3	0	3	0	0	0	0	0		1	0	0	0	2
Opresión	3	2	1	0	0	2	0	0		0	0	0	1	0

Table 5: Top 10 Mistreatment collocates in the US Corpus.

Lemma	Total	TL	TR	L5	L4	L3	L2	L1	WOMAN	R1	R2	R3	R4	R5
Suffer	15	7	8			3	4			4		1		3
Abandon	13	13	0	3		4	2	4						
Slaughter	13	3	10			3					3		6	1
Rape	12	2	10					2			3	2	4	1
Violence	12	10	2		4		6						2	
Kill	10	4	6	1	2		1			1	1	3	1	
Fear	8	3	5		1	1	1			1		2		2
Die	7	2	5				2			1	2		1	1
Escape	7	0	7							3		1	3	
Oppression	7	6	1			2	2	2						1

Among the *mujer/woman* collocates we can identify a third category that includes lemmas conveying benevolence or empathy with Afghan women. Words implying sympathy and goodwill towards women are common in both corpora. The Twitter discourse echoes that women are victims of the conflict, innocent, vulnerable and therefore should be supported and protected. In fact, in the ES Corpus this category is represented by 9 lemmas (40 occurrences, 0.01 %) and headed by collocates such as *apoyo*, *pobre*, *protección* or *solidaridad*. In the case of the US Corpus, the category of Benevolence-empathy seems to be more prominent in the Twitter discourse with 16 lemmas and 292 occurrences (0.04 %). The most frequent collocates are *innocent*, *protect*, *help*, *need* and *support*. In Tables 6 and 7, it can be observed, once again, that there are words that are repeated in both corpora, regardless of the country and language: *apoyo/support*, *pobre/poor*, *solidaridad/solidarity*, *proteger/protect* and *ayudar/help*. Support and empathy with women are shown in the following tweets:

(9) Esta tarde nos concentrábamos en #Hontalbilla en *apoyo a las mujeres* y niñas afganas, gracias a las mujeres de Hontalbilla que no dejan pasar la ocasión de mostrar la dignidad y solidaridad de una parte de la España vaciada. #AfghanWomen #Afganisthan #AfganistanWomen #Afganistan (20/08/2021)

(10) @DonutsComeme 🤣 Es que no se que se nos ha perdido en #Afganistan 20 años, 🤔PETROLEO!!! *Pobres mujeres* y niños afganos… De los que

están en España pues bueno, que se jodan. Haz turismo invadiendo un país, es barato y te pagan la estancia… 🤦 Vendımos democracia a un monstruo (16/08/2021)

(11) @KamalaHarris we need to *protect these Afghan women*! How do we launch refugee programs to bring these women to the US and protect them!!! #WomenSupportingWomen #AfghanWomen (17/08/2021)

(12) To any Afghan era vet who might see this, thank you. You deserve better than this but know my gratitude remains unending. US Lord have *mercy on the women* and girls of #Afghanistan. (15/08/2021)

Table 6: Benevolence-empathy collocates in the ES Corpus.

Lemma	**Total**	**TL**	**TR**	**L5**	**L4**	**L3**	**L2**	**L1**	**MUJER**	**R1**	**R2**	**R3**	**R4**	**R5**
Apoyo	7	7	0	2	1	4	0	0		0	0	0	0	0
Pobre	7	7	0	0	0	0	1	6		0	0	0	0	0
Protección	5	5	0	0	0	1	4	0		0	0	0	0	0
Solidaridad	5	5	0	0	0	5	0	0		0	0	0	0	0
Proteger	4	4	0	0	0	4	0	0		0	0	0	0	0
Ayudar	4	4	0	0	0	3	1	0		0	0	0	0	0
Refugio	2	2	0	0	0	2	0	0		0	0	0	0	0
Apoyar	2	2	0	0	0	2	0	0		0	0	0	0	0
Ayuda	4	4	0	2	2	0	0	0		0	0	0	0	0
	40	40	0	4	3	21	6	6		0	0	0	0	0

Table 7: Benevolence-empathy collocates in the US Corpus.

Lemma	Total	TL	TR	L5	L4	L3	L2	L1	WOMAN	R1	R2	R3	R4	R5
Innocent	79	16	63	3	1	3	2	7			63			
Protect	52	39	13	3	2	12	21	1		2		2	7	2
Help	43	30	13		6	8	11	5		4	5			4
Need	32	17	15	14	2	1				6	1	1	5	2
Support	27	24	3	3	4	9	8					1		2
Care	21	20	1	3	1	12	4						1	
Mercy	7	5	2			5								2
Empathy	5	5	0	4		1								
Victim	5	5	0				5							
Vulnerable	5	4	1				3	1						1
Donate	3	1	2			1								2
Poor	3	3	0			1	2							
Pray	3	3	0			3								
Solidarity	3	3	0			3								
Assistance	2	2	0	2										
Rescue	2	0	2								1	1		
	292	177	115	32	16	59	56	14		12	70	5	13	15

Finally, we will compare the relative percentage that each category represents in the Twitter discourse of the countries under analysis. As evidenced in Figure 1, the category of Empowerment holds a dominant position in the ES Corpus, constituting 24.85 %, whereas the category of Benevolence-empathy carries the most substantial percentage in the US Corpus, coming to 20.32 %. The most prominent disparity between the two nations is predominantly observed in the Benevolence-empathy category, with a difference of more than 15 points. Indeed, whereas the ES Corpus fails to reach 5 %, this specific category constitutes over 20 % of the US Twitter discourse. Lesser variations are discerned in the categories of Empowerment (approximately a 7-point difference) and Mistreatment (a difference of 3.5 points), which indicates a parallelism in the Twitter discourse concerning the conflict in both nations. This is observed not merely in the percentage of occurrences, which seems to display minor fluctuations in these two categories, but also in the collocates utilized within the Spanish and US tweets, as our foregoing analysis has revealed.

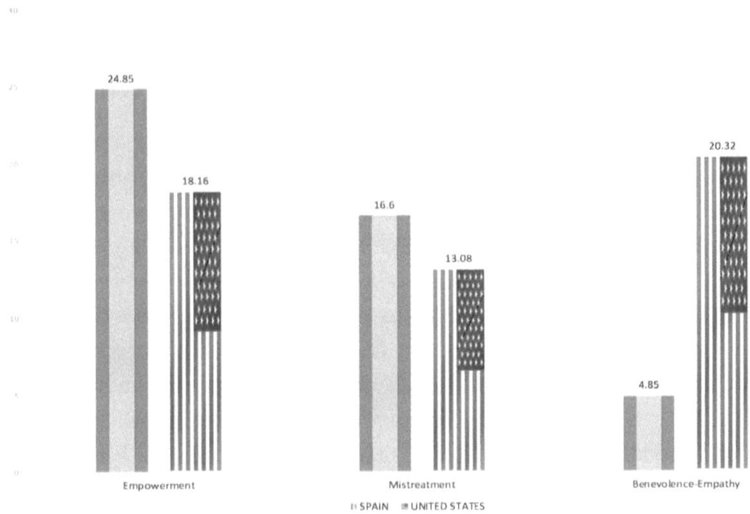

Figure 1: Percentage of each subset in the ES Corpus and in the US Corpus.

6. Discussion and conclusions

The analysis of the data has proved that in both the ES Corpus and the US Corpus the lemmas *mujer* and *woman*, respectively, are among the top 10 frequent words when it comes to commenting on Twitter about the Taliban takeover of Kabul. This shows that the figure of women takes center stage in an apparently warlike discourse or discourse of confrontation between the Taliban and US troops.

The study of semantic preference has resulted in three categories that contribute to the portrayal of women as (1) victims of the conflict, (2) beneficiaries of benevolence and empathy, and (3) fighters and activists for their rights and freedoms. The image of women as unjustly treated victims is perhaps the most predictable in a context of invasion and war. Indeed, women and children have traditionally been seen as the most fragile and vulnerable in war. In our corpora, women and children are not so much mentioned as women and girls, presumably because it is the Taliban who are in power, known for their sexist and oppressive ideology towards women. Hence, the word *woman* stands out as she is the sufferer of their policies.

The suffering and subjugation of women triggers a sense of empathy in the Western world, which sees itself as the benevolent society that must protect, help, care for and rescue women from the Taliban takeover. The results of this study indicate that the lemmas related to this benevolent and rescuing attitude constitute the most abundant category in the US Corpus.

The representation of women as victims and the benevolence of a more civilized society (the US in this case) has also been analyzed in other studies on print media such as the one carried out by Jiwani (2009: 729), who claims that Afghan women are represented as 'quintessential innocent victims requiring rescue'. According to Abu-Lughod (2013) and Macdonald (2006), the 'rescue motif' has been a constant feature of colonial discourse, with the Taliban in this case being the colonizers, invaders, conquerors and subjugators, and the Americans, the liberators and rescuers.

The study of women's representation in online media has, according to Karimullah (2020), a long tradition in Western political discourse on the Middle East. Indeed, after 9/11, the media began to pay more attention to the situation of women in Afghanistan, highlighting that Taliban restrictions were largely imposed on urban women (in Kabul, for example) and that oppression towards women was less before the Taliban took over (Hirschkind and Mahmood 2002).

As Al-Hejin (2015) points out, the discourse of benevolence and empathy in social networks, which is much more prevalent in the US than in Spain, can reinforce some stereotypes. For some authors, such as Abu-Lughod (2013), this representation of women as victims, as in need of protection and help, is a consequence of the perception of women by the elites of the Western world, especially in this case, as can be seen in the results of the US Corpus. For example, Al-Hejin (2015) uses corpus-assisted discourse analysis to explore how news discourse contributes to the creation of subjectivities through the construction of discursive worlds (e.g., 'Middle East' and the 'Muslim world') and the subjects that occupy them (e.g., 'Muslim man and Muslim woman'). By analyzing frequent lexical patterns, Al-Hejin (2015) identifies how positive and negative associations are discursively formed around women and men, and how these are distinct, portraying women as passive, needy and violated subjects, as opposed to men, who are the ones who act, fight and defend. In addition, Sjoberg and Whooley (2015) observe that the media narratives used in various political and media discourses have in common the use of the situation of women as a barometer of the success of westernization, liberalization and democratization of a territory. In this case, the fact that women are mistreated reflects the lack of westernization and democratization. Mhajne and Whetstone (2017) also analyze news stories about women's political activism and social media posts by Egyptian women activists. The results suggest that these news stories focus on women as beings in need of protection, ignoring or minimizing women's activist and political roles.

This image of women as objects, victims of mistreatment and in need of help from the Western world, contrasts with the category of women as agents who fight for their rights and freedoms, denounce, take to the streets and protest. This category, which highlights the figure of women as fighters and empowered women, is the most numerous in the ES Corpus. Our results are in line with the study conducted by Tabazo and Mustafa-Awad (2022), who analyzed a corpus of English digital news about Jordanian women. Their results reveal that, while the image of oppressed women still exists, women are increasingly portrayed as empowered, fighting for their rights. This image of women as agents of change for society can also be found in Salehi et al. (2020), who conclude from their study that Iranian women no longer see themselves, or are seen, as victims but as promoters of feminism, using social networks and other media as a tool to do so.

Our study has revealed, through the exploration of semantic preference, that the lemma *mujer/woman* is accompanied by collocates that reflect this apparently opposing but compatible double strand of victimization and empowerment in the representation of Afghan women on Twitter during the Taliban takeover of Kabul. As future research lines, it would be interesting to extend the comparison of this type of discourse to non-Western countries, to determine whether the semantic preference remains the same or differs. Another interesting issue to explore is how women are portrayed in other conflicts such as the Ukrainian one, it being a European territory, as opposed to Middle East countries such as Afghanistan.

References

Abdo, Muhammad / Alghonaim, Ali / Essam, Bacem. 2020. Public Perception of COVID-19's Global Health Crisis on Twitter Until Weeks After the Outbreak. *Digital Scholarship in the Humanities* 36/3, 509–524. https://doi.org/10.1093/llc/fqaa037

Abu-Lughod, Lila 2013. *Do Muslim Women Need Saving?* Harvard: Harvard University Press.

Adá, Alba 2019. Invisibilización de la Mujer Deportista en el Twitter de los Medios Deportivos. *Comunicación y Género* 2/1, 33–46. https://dx.doi.org/10.5209/CGEN.64460

Alcántara-Plá, Manuel / Ruiz-Sánchez, Ana. 2017. The Framing of Muslims on the Spanish Internet. *Lodz Papers in Pragmatics* 13/2, 261–283.

Al-Hejin, Bandar. 2015. Covering Muslim Women: Semantic Macrostructures in BBC News. *Discourse & Communication* 9/1, 19–46.

Anderson, Ashley / Huntington, Heidi. 2017. Social Media, Science, and Attack Discourse: How Twitter Discussions of Climate Change Use Sarcasm and Incivility. *Science Communication* 39/5, 598–620. https://doi.org/10.1177/1075547017735113

Baer, Hester. 2016. Redoing Feminism: Digital Activism, Body Politics, and Neoliberalism. *Feminist Media Studies* 16/1, 17–34. https://doi.org/10.1080/14680777.2015.1093070

Barker-Plummer, Bernadette / Barker-Plummer, Dave. 2017. Twitter as a Feminist Resource: #YesAllWomen, Digital Platforms, and Discursive Social Change. *Emerald Studies in Media and Communication* 14, 91–118.

Bednarek, Monika 2008. Semantic Preference and Semantic Prosody Re-examined. *Corpus Linguistics and Linguistic Theory* 4/2, 119–139.

Bonet-Martí, Jordi 2020. Análisis de las Estrategias Discursivas Empleadas en la Construcción de Discurso Antifeminista en Redes Sociales. *Psicoperspectivas* 19/3, 1–12. https://dx.doi.org/10.5027/psicoperspectivas-vol19-issue3-fulltext-2040

Bozdag, Cigdem / Smets, Kevin. 2017. Understanding the Images of Alan Kurdi with "Small Data": A Qualitative, Comparative Analysis of Tweets about Refugees in Turkey and Flanders (Belgium). *International Journal of Communication* 11, 4046–4069.

Breeze, Ruth. 2020. Exploring Populist Styles of Political Discourse in Twitter. *World Englishes* 39, 550–567. https://doi.org/10.1111/weng.12496

Bublitz, Wolfram. 1996. Semantic Prosody and Cohesive Company: Somewhat Predictable. *Leuvense Bijdragen* 85, 1–32.

Chen, Emily / Deb, Ashok / Ferrara, Emilio. 2022. #Election2020: The First Public Twitter Dataset on the 2020 US Presidential Election. *Journal of Computational Social Science* 5, 1–18. https://doi.org/10.1007/s42001-021-00117-9

Dixon, Kitsy. 2014. Feminist Online Identity: Analyzing the Presence of Hashtag Feminism. *Journal of Arts and Humanities* 3/7, 34–40.

Esposito, Eleonora / Sinatora, Francesco. 2021. Social Media Discourses of Feminist Protest from the Arab Levant: Digital Mirroring and Transregional Dialogue. *Critical Discourse Studies* 19/5, 502–522. https://doi.org/10.1080/17405904.2021.1999291

Field, Anjalie / Bhat, Gayatri / Tsvetkov, Yulia. 2019. Contextual Affective Analysis: A Case Study of People Portrayals in Online #MeToo Stories. *Proceedings of the Thirteenth International AAAI Conference on Web and Social Media,* 13, 158–169.

Fuchs, Tamara / Schäfer, Fabian. 2020. Normalizing Misogyny: Hate Speech and Verbal Abuse of Female Politicians on Japanese Twitter. *Japan Forum* 33/4, 553–579. https://doi.org/10.1080/09555803.2019.1687564

Giachanou, Anastasia / Crestani, Fabio. 2016. Like It or Not: A Survey of Twitter Sentiment Analysis Methods. *ACM Computing Surveys* 49/2, 1–41. https://doi.org/10.1145/2938640

Giorgi, Salvatore / Guntuku, Sarath / Himelein-Wachowiak Mckenzie / Kwarteng, Amy / Hwang, Sy / Rahman, Muhammad / Curtis, Brenda. 2022. Twitter Corpus of the #BlackLivesMatter Movement and Counter Protests: 2013 to 2021. *Proceedings of the Sixteenth International AAAI Conference on Web and Social Media,* 1228–1235.

Hassan, Naeemul / Mandal, Manash / Bhuiyan, Mansurul / Moitra, Aparna / Ahmed, Syed. 2019. Can Women Break the Glass Ceiling? An Analysis of #MeToo Hashtagged Posts on Twitter. *IEEE/ACM International Conference on Advances in Social Networks Analysis and Mining*, 653–656.

Hirschkind, Charles / Saba Mahmood. 2002. Feminism, the Taliban, and the Politics of Counter-Insurgency. *Anthropological Quarterly* 75/2, 339–54.

Hoey, Michael. 2005. *Lexical Priming. A New Theory of Words and Language*. London: Routledge.

Hull, Kevin. 2016. An Examination of Women's Sports Coverage on the Twitter Accounts of Local Television Sports Broadcasters. *Communication & Sport* 5/4, 471–491. https://doi.org/10.1177/2167479516632520

Idoiaga, Nahia / Berasategui, Naiara / Beloki, Nekane / Belasko, Maitane. 2022. #8M Women's Strikes in Spain: Following the Unprecedented Social Mobilization through Twitter. *Journal of Gender Studies* 31/5, 639–653. https://doi.org/10.1080/09589236.2021.1881461

Jiwani, Yasmin. 2009. Helpless Maidens and Chivalrous Knights: Afghan Women in the Canadian Press. *University of Toronto Quarterly* 78/2, 728–744.

Karimullah, Kamran. 2020. Sketching Women: A Corpus-based Approach to Representations of Women's Agency in Political Internet Corpora in Arabic and English. *Corpora* 15/1, 21–53.

Klausen, Jytte. 2015. Tweeting the Jihad: Social Media Networks of Western Foreign Fighters in Syria and Iraq. *Studies in Conflict & Terrorism* 38/1, 1–22. https://doi.org/10.1080/1057610X.2014.974948

Larrondo-Ureta, Ainara / Orbegozo-Terradillos, Julen. 2021. Hashtivism's Potentials for Mainstreaming Feminism in Politics: The Red Lips Revolution Transmedia Narrative. *Feminist*

Media Studies 22/5, 1139 1162. https://doi.org/10.1080/14680777.2021.1879197

Macdonald, Myra. 2006. Muslim Women and the Veil: Problems of Image and Voice in Media Representations. *Feminist Media Studies* 6/1, 7–23.

Manne, Kate. 2017. *Down Girl: The Logic of Misogyny*. Oxford: Oxford University Press.

Manzano-Zambruno, Laura / Paredes-Otero, Guillermo. 2019. El Periodismo de Videojuegos desde una Perspectiva y de Género. Las Periodistas Especializadas ante el Acoso y la Discriminación en España dentro de las redes sociales. *Compolíticas* 1, 84–98.

Mautner, Gerlinde. 2005. Time to Get Wired: Using Web-Based Corpora in Critical Discourse Analysis. *Discourse & Society* 16/6, 809–828. https://doi.org/10.1177/0957926505056661

McGregor, Shannon. 2019. Social Media as Public Opinion: How Journalists Use Social Media to Represent Public Opinion. *Journalism* 20/8, 1070–1086. https://doi.org/10.1177/1464884919845458

Melbourne, Oliver / Chen, Emily / Ferrara, Emilio. 2021. Pictures as a Form of Protest: A Survey and Analysis of Images Posted During the Stop Asian Hate Movement on Twitter. *IEEE 18th International Conference on Mobile Ad Hoc and Smart Systems (MASS)*, 667–668. https://doi.org/10.1109/MASS52906.2021.00100

Mhajne, Anwar / Crystal Whetstone. 2017. The Use of Political Motherhood in Egypt's Arab Spring Uprising and Aftermath. *International Feminist Journal of Politics* 20/1, 54–68.

Molpeceres, Sara / Filardo-Llamas, Laura. 2020. Llamamientos Feministas en Twitter: Ideología, Identidad Colectiva y Reenmarcado de Símbolos y la Huelga del 8M y la Manifestación Contra la Sentencia de "La Manada". *Dígitos. Revista de Comunicación Digital* 6, 55–78. https://doi.org/10.7203/rd.v1i6.181

Mullo, Alex / Falconí, Franklin / Balseca, Johana. 2021. El Discurso del Prosumer y la Representación del Fenómeno Migratorio Venezolano en Redes Sociales de la Prensa de Ecuador. *Discurso & Sociedad* 15/2, 408–438.

Ncube, Gibson / Yemurai, Gwatisira. 2020. Discrimination Against Female Politicians on Social Media: An Analysis of Tweets in the Run-up to the July 2018 Harmonised Elections in Zimbabwe. *International Sociology Reviews* 35/5, 59–76.

Palomino-Manjón, Patricia. 2022. Feminist Activism on Twitter: The Discursive Construction of Sexual Violence and Victim-survivors in #WhyIDidntReport. *Journal of Language Aggression and Conflict* 10/1, 140–168. https://doi.org/10.1075/jlac.00049.pal

Partington, Alan. 2004. “Utterly Content in Each Other’s Company”: Semantic Prosody and Semantic Preference. *International Journal of Corpus Linguistics* 9/1, 131–156.

Piñeiro-Otero, Teresa / Martínez-Rolán, Xabier. 2021. Say It to my Face: Analysing Hate Speech Against Women on Twitter. *Profesional de la información* 30/5, 1–16. https://doi.org/10.3145/epi.2021.sep.02

Reyes-Menéndez, Ana / Saura, Jose Ramón / Thomas, Stephen. 2020. Exploring Key Indicators of Social Identity in the #MeToo Era: Using Discourse Analysis in UGC. *International Journal of Information Management* 54, 102–129. https://doi.org/10.1016/j.ijinfomgt.2020.102129

Salehi, Asiyeh / Sebar, Bernadete / Whitehead, Dean / Hatam Nahid /Coyne, Elisabeth / Harris Neil. 2020. Young Iranian Women as Agents of Social Change: A Qualitative Study. *Women’s Studies International Forum* 79, 1–7.

Sampietro, Agnese / Calvo, Dafne / Campos-Domínguez, Eva. 2020. Los Emojis del 8M: Su Uso en Twitter Durante las Movilizaciones Feministas de 2019. *Dígitos. Revista de Comunicación Digital* 6, 137–158. https://doi.org/10.7203/rd.v1i6.170

Scott, Michael. 2012. WordSmith Tools [Version 6.0.]. Available at http://www.lexically.net/wordsmith/downloads/

Shulman, David. 2017. *The Presentation of Self in Contemporary Social Life*. Lafayette: Sage Publishing.

Sinclair, John. 1996. The Search for Units of Meaning. *Textus* 9/1, 75–106.

Sinclair, John. 1998. The Lexical Item. In Edda Weigand (ed.), *Contrastive Lexical Semantics*. Amsterdam: John Benjamins, 1–24.

Sjoberg, Laura / Whooley, Jonathon. 2015. The Arab Spring for Women? Representations of Women in Middle East Politics in 2011. *Journal of Women, Politics and Policy* 36/3, 261–284.

Stubbs, Michael. 2001. On Inference Theories and Code Theories: Corpus Evidence for Semantic Schemas. *Text* 21/3, 437–465.

Stubbs, Michael. 2002. Two Quantitative Methods of Studying Phraseology in English. *International Journal of Corpus Linguistics* 7/2, 215–244.

Tabaza, Duaa / Mustafa-Awad, Zahara. 2022.Within and Beyond Stereotypes of Arab Women: A Corpus-based Approach to Jordanian Women's Portrayal in English Digital News. *Journal of International Women's Studies* 23/1, 367–385.

Talbot, Catherine / Pownall, Madeleine. 2022. "If Your Institution Refuses to Provide What You Need, Create It Yourself": Feminist Praxis on #AcademicTwitter. *Feminism & Psychology* 32/1, 101–118. https://doi.org/10.1177/09593535211052234

Tenenboim, Ori. 2017. Reporting War in 140 Characters: How Journalists Used Twitter During the 2014 Gaza–Israel Conflict. *International Journal of Communication* 11, 3497–3518.

Veltri, Giuseppe / Atanasova, Dimitrinka. 2017. Climate Change on Twitter: Content, Media Ecology and Information Sharing Behaviour. *Public Understanding of Science* 26/6, 721–737. https://doi.org/10.1177/0963662515613702

Villar-Aguilés, Alicia / Pecourt, Juan. 2021. Antifeminismo y Troleo de Género en Twitter. Estudio de la Subcultura Trol a Través de #STOPfeminazis. *Teknokultura. Revista de Cultura Digital y Movimientos Sociales* 18/1, 33–44. http://dx.doi.org/10.5209/TEKN.70225

Whitsitt, Sam. 2005. A Critique of the Concept of Semantic Prosody. *International Journal of Corpus Linguistics* 10/3, 283–305.

Wicke, Philipp / Bolognesi, Marianna. 2021. Covid-19 Discourse on Twitter: How the Topics, Sentiments, Subjectivity, and Figurative Frames Changed Over Time. *Frontiers in Communication* 6/65, 1–20. https://doi.org/10.3389/fcomm.2021.651997

Xiao, Richard / McEnery, Tony. 2006. Collocation, Semantic Prosody, and Near Synonymy: A Cross-Linguistic Perspective. *Applied Linguistics* 27/1, 103–129.

STEFANIA M. MACI / CHERUBINO DI LORENZO /
CATELLO VOLLONO

All together now: Disentangling Beatles' song titles in medical research articles*

1. Introduction

The purpose of article titles in science is that of synthetically introducing the topic the research article (RA) will deal with and, at the same time, making that topic interesting. Not only do they allow the reader to locate relevant content, but also they are used for indexing purposes (cf. Sala 2013) and are indicative of a publication's strengths and informativity (Giannoni 2013), which seems to be prevalent in most biomedical journals (Sisó 2009).

There are guidelines as to how construct an RA title; nevertheless, creating an RA title is not simple. It seems that long and complex titles have become even longer and more complex, as scientific fields mature (White and Hernandez 1991; cf. also Giannoni 2013). However, given that titles constitute the most concise statement of an article's content, and that they are heavily used by information retrieval systems, titles should be as informative as possible (Giannoni 2013), which has traditionally been determined on the basis of the number of substantives an article has (Yitzhaki 1997). Lewison and Hartley (2005) report an average of around 13 words per title in articles, notes and reviews from British biomedical journals published from 1981–2001, with variability generally ranging from 11 (Wang and Bai 2007) to 15 (Soler 2007), and even to 18

* Authors' contribution: Maci conceived, designed, planned, and managed the study, acquired data, interpreted the results, drafted the manuscript, and critically reviewed it for important intellectual content. De Lorenzo and Vollono conceived the study, supervised the data analysis, and the interpretation of results.

words (Jacques and Sebire 2010). As Sala (2013) claims, RA titles are referential and informative because they concisely lead to the RA's investigation. In this regard, they are seen as an anticipatory device because they are "front matter and summary matter" (Swales 2003: 179). They are also a text in miniature, one which provides information as well as an initial introduction (Haggan 2004: 294). This is the reason why 'they are expected to contain recognizable key terms and expressions on the basis of which the reader can measure the correspondence of the propositional content in the title to his/her own interests or search criteria' (Sala 2013: 223). In this respect, titles may be indicative of the text style and register of the whole RA or of the type of RA investigation applied (Sala 2013). For this reason, the relationship between a title's linguistic and semantic aspects and content complexity in RA texts have also been studied (White and Hernandez 1991). In addition, Sala (2013) explains that titles are relevant for the initial cognitive representation of the whole text they represent (Heurley 1994) while, at the same time, guiding its interpretation: they are, in other words, the criterion against which to measure the RA's degree of informativeness and relevance (Ganier 1999).

It remains unclear how the structure of an RA title influences its readership and impact, but certainly a poorly chosen title makes a paper difficult to discover or discourages its readership, thus reducing the paper's impact (Fox and Burns 2015). In this regard, Goodman (2000: 915, in Giannoni 2013) claims that 'there is evidence that doctors sometimes make clinical decisions from the titles of journal articles'. While there is an effort to achieve a close integration between empirical research and pedagogical advice (Lewison and Hartley 2005), when it comes to titles, 'recommendations of scientific journal editors [. . .] are largely based on their personal experiences' (Paiva et al. 2012: 509) and are therefore subjective (Giannoni 2013).

Although the title structure tends to reflect disciplinary and/or editorial preferences (Soler 2011; Giannoni 2013), Hudson (2016) shows that the structure of titles depends on other variables, namely:

(i) title length—which is directly proportional to the number of authors in almost all disciplines (and the most recent papers have more authors than papers published earlier);
(ii) the use of colons and question marks—which tends to decline with increasing author numbers (cf. also Hartley 2005b, 2007);

(iii) thc numbcr of paper citations—which is higher when the titles are shorter and lower when paper have question marks, and yet lower when they use question marks.

Notwithstanding, titles are part of the publishing environment they serve, although '[t]he trend is undoubtedly for journals to become more like newspapers' with the double purpose of readability and trying to grab people's attention' (Smith 2000: 915). Indeed, titles have a persuasive purpose: they codify meaning *and* attract the reader's attention, to such an extent that they can even affect an RA's citational status or impact factor in the long run (Whissell 1999; Wang and Bai 2007: 389; Sala 2013). Furthermore, titles can also have an implicit promotional function for authors: with a persuasive and promotional type of discourse (Sala and Consonni 2019) they can disclose information about the author's persona, the author's way of conceiving and conducting research as well as the author's place in the academic community (Sala 2013).

All this, together with the 'publish or perish' pressure (Wilson 1942: 197) characterizing, in particular, the medical community, as well as the relevance of the Impact Factor (which, in some cases, can be more relevant than the research itself; cf. Callaham et al. 2010; Mavrogenis et al. 2018; Wheatley 2018) has necessitated the elaboration of strategies to increase the number of citations. A strategy seems to be the quotation of popular song titles to attract more readers. To the best of our knowledge, there has been hardly any analysis of medical RA titles constructed with popular groups' or singers' song titles. Indeed, only Rijkers (2017) has described their use, showing that Bob Dylan (cf. the article by Michaels and published in 2014 on *The Guardian* website, available at https://www.theguardian.com/music/2014/sep/29/swedish-scienti sts-bet-bob-dylan-lyrics-research-papers) and Beatles song titles are used particularly, also probably on the basis that researchers "who used Beatles and Dylan quotes would by now be close to retirement, as they might have been teenage fans when the Beatles and Dylan were scoring most of their hits" (Rijkers 2017: 85) or because "the Beatles and Dylan are a sophisticated type of music and as such get noticed by "sophisticated scientists" when they are at an age ready to publish scientific articles" (Rijkers 2017: 86). Gornitzki, Larsson and Fadeel (2015: h6505) too, in showing that Bob Dylan song titles have become more and more popular as RA titles since 1990, suggest that this popularity may be due to the fact that "the young and radical students of the 1960s who listened to Dylan ended up as medical doctors and scientists", while Brown et al. (2015) show that this is true not only for medical doctors, but also for meteorologists and climate impact scientists.

However, Beatles' song titles seem to be used more frequently than Bob Dylan ones, despite the fact that Bob Dylan was awarded the Nobel Prize for literature in 2017. Considering that, apart from Rijkers (2017), no one else has ever investigated Beatles song titles, in the following sections we will try to show the extent to which Beatles song titles are used in medical RA titles to attract readers and to explain why researchers do so.

2. Methods

As described above, titles are used by information retrieval systems (Giannoni 2013). Indeed, in any retrieval system, fields normally used for indexing are author's title, abstract, journal title and journal type. One of the most popular retrieval systems is PubMed®. PubMed® is a free resource supporting the search and retrieval of biomedical and life sciences literature with the aim of improving health—both globally and personally, it has a database comprising more than 33 million citations and abstracts of biomedical literature from MEDLINE, life science journals, and online books (https://pubmed.ncbi.nlm.nih.gov/about/).

In order to identify titles constructed from Beatles songs, we followed these steps:

1. We checked *The Beatles Bible* (www.beatlesbible.com/songs) to see all Beatles songs listed by singer (McCartney, Lennon, Starr, Harrison), for a total of 207 songs; we were only interested in songs written by The Beatles, and not in those where they had covered others' work. For example, Beatles' cover versions of classics, such as *Besame mucho* by Velázquez-Skylar, were excluded from further analysis.
2. We used PubMed®/MEDLINE as a search interface with advanced filters (i.e. *search title*), given that this search engine

uses a stop-word list consisting of commonly found terms which are not included in a search. Next to the exact song title, we also found numerous title variations.

3. We excluded song titles where it was difficult to unequivocally attribute such a title to a specific song. For example, the RA title *Birthday*, which could apparently refer to the Beatles song, actually referred to 'festchrifts' in honour of some scholar on the occasion of his/her birthday—and for this reason it was excluded; the search of *A day in the life* yielded 544 results (comprising exact titles and extended titles), and it was virtually impossible to establish a direct link to the song: therefore, the exact title was considered only; *Michelle* was found in more than 47,000 titles, but it was linked to it the name of a person interviewed/ involved in the RA, and, thus, cannot in any possible way be linked to the Beatles song.
4. Song titles consisting of a general term or expression, such as *Yes it is*, were checked manually for the context in which they were used. In most cases the publications were not considered for investigation.

The search resulted in 546 titles constructed with Beatles song titles or having an intertextual connection to them.

Based on Sala (2013), we used an integrated model to analyze RA titles and assess the efficiency of several alternative structures, including factors and criteria from other research (White and Hernandez 1991; Haggan 2004; Hartley 2007; Eyrolle et al. 2008).

This model examines such strategies on three levels:

- the textual level (distinguishing between nominal, compound, and full-sentence constructions), from which it is possible to measure the degree of informativeness found in titles (Swales 1990; Fortanet et al. 1998; Soler 2007; Sisó 2009);
- the sentence level, especially at the level of syntactic relations between nominal, verbal, and prepositional phrases (differentiating between topic, bi-head, and focal titles) (Wang and Bai 2007);
- the lexical level, accounting for the presence of specialized and domain-specific lexis, through which to measure the specificity of titles and their gate-keeping function, in that specialized lexis

> determines the degree of text accessibility and appeal (Hartley 2005a, 2007).

The application of such a model to our corpus allowed us to: (1) determine which title typology is best for RAs, (2) discuss its prototypicality in relation to the disciplinary epistemology that underpins medical research, and (3) account for the possible degree of variation in titling practices over time.

3. Results and discussion

The search of RA titles constructed with Beatles song titles with PubMed® yielded 546 titles in medical publications, and a total of 55 different songs were quoted, as can be seen in Table 1, below:

Table 1: Breakdown of publication titles constructed with Beatles' songs.

Beatles song title	***Publication titles constructed with Beatles songs***	%
A day in the life	91	16.66
All together now	86	15.75
With a little help from my friends	62	11.35
Here comes the sun	31	5.67
Ticket to ride	28	5.12
A hard day's night	24	4.39
Come together	22	4.02
We can work it out	17	3.11
Bad Boy	14	2.56
Run for your Life	14	2.56
Twist and shout	14	2.56
Hello Goodbye	12	2.19
Magical mystery tour	11	2.01
All you need is love?	9	1.64
Fixing a hole	9	1.64

Table 1: *Continued*

Beatles song title	***Publication titles constructed with Beatles songs***	%
Getting better	8	1.46
Good night (sleep tight)	8	1.46
When I'm sixty-four	6	1.09
Eight days a week	5	0.91
Help!	5	0.91
Hold me tight	5	0.91
Yellow submarine	5	0.91
A taste of honey	4	0.73
Across the universe	4	0.73
Helter-Skelter	4	0.73
Ask me why	3	0.54
Can't buy me love	3	0.54
Come and get it	3	0.54
Here, there and everywhere	3	0.54
Matchbox	3	0.54
While my guitar gently weeps	3	0.54
Yes, it is	3	0.54
Golden slumbers	2	0.36
I want to hold your hand	2	0.36
Please, please me	2	0.36
The fool on the hill	2	0.36
Octopus's Garden	1	0.18
Acts naturally	1	0.18
Baby it's you	1	0.18
Carry that weight	1	0.18
Cry baby Cry	1	0.18
Day Tripper	1	0.18
Dear Prudence	1	0.18
Dig it	1	0.18
Eleonor Rigby	1	0.18
Free as a bird	1	0.18

Continued

Table 1: *Continued*

Beatles song title	***Publication titles constructed with Beatles songs***	%
Glass Onion	1	0.18
Honey don't	1	0.18
Lady Madonna	1	0.18
Little child	1	0.18
Lucy in the sky with diamonds	1	0.18
PS: I love you	1	0.18
Rock and Roll Music	1	0.18
Where have you been all my life?	1	0.18
With love from me to you	1	0.18
TOTAL	***546***	***100***

The top Beatles song titles employed to construct RA titles are: *A day in the life* (16.6 % of all publications); *All together now* (15.75 %); *With a little help from my friends* (11.35 %); *Here comes the sun* (5.67 %); *Ticket to ride* (5.12 %); *A hard day's night* (4.39 %); *Come together* (4 %); *We can work it out* (3.11 %); *Bad Boy* (2.56 %); *Run for your Life* (2.56 %); *Twist and shout* (2.56 %); *Hello Goodbye* (2.19 %); and *Magical mystery tour* (2 %), which overall correspond to 78 % of all Beatles quotations.

As can be seen in Graph 1, below, Beatles quotations have gradually augmented over the years, with a peak in 2002, and then a gradual rise up to 2021 (with a drop in 2022, due to the fact that the research ended in January 2022).

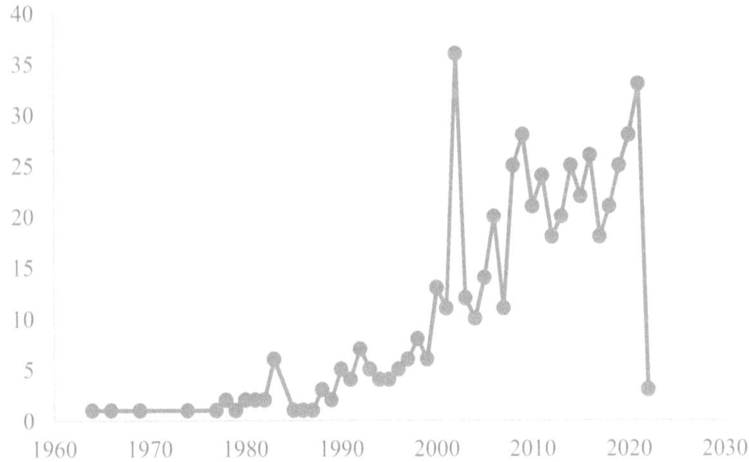

Graph 1. Breakdown of Beatles quotations in publications over time.

The academic journals that have more titles constructed with Beatles song titles (Table 2, below) are the *Journal of the American Academy of Physician Assistants*, where we find 26 quotations of *A day in the life*; *Nature*, where there are overall 10 Beatles title quotations (*All together now*, *Bad Boy*, *Come together*, *Run for your Life*); *Nursing Standard* which has 19 publications constructed with Beatles song titles (*All together now*, *A day in the life*, *A hard day's night*, *Day Tripper*, *Getting better*, *Help!*, *Ticket to ride*), and *Nursing Times* which has 51 publications with Beatles quotations in their titles (*All together now*, *A day in the life*, *A hard day's night*, *Eight days a week*, *Hello Goodbye*, *Help!*, *Here comes the sun*, *Ticket to ride*, *We can work it out*, *With a little help from my friends*), with an overall preference for the following songs: *All together now* (4 journals); *A day in the life* (3 journals); *A hard day's night; Come together*; *Help!*; and *Ticket to ride* (2 journals).

Table 2: Breakdown of most frequent Beatles song titles across academic journals.

Journal Title	**# titles**	**Song title**
Journal of the American Academy of Physician Assistants	26	*A day in the life*
Nature	10	*All together now* *Bad Boy* *Come together* *Run for your Life*
Nursing Standard	19	*All together now* *A day in the life* *A hard day's night* *Day Tripper* *Getting better* *Help!* *Ticket to ride*
Nursing Times	51	*All together now* *A day in the life* *A hard day's night* *Eight days a week* *Hello Goodbye* *Help!* *Here comes the sun* *Ticket to ride* *We can work it out* *With a little help from my friends*

Table 3 shows the breakdown of the top medical fields where Beatles song titles are used. As can be seen, (medical) *practice, nursing* (activity), *healthcare* and *microbiology* are the domains where Beatles song titles are mostly quoted. Overall, however, almost 50 % of the titles constructed with Beatles songs are found in 9 medical fields, in a time span from the 1980s to the 2020s, except for the nursing field, where titles constructed in this way have been used ever since the 1960s.

Table 3: Breakdown of top fields with titles constructed with Beatles songs.

Field		*# Beatles song titles*	%	*Time range*
Practice		*83*	30.51	1991–2020
	Subfield			
	practice—association of physicians	*35*	*12.86*	2002–2019
	practice—long-term care	*1*	*0.36*	2020
	practice—nursing	*35*	*12.86*	1998–2005
	practice—palliative care	*2*	*0.73*	2000–2008
	practice—physician	*5*	*1.83*	1991–2020
	practice—surgery	*4*	*1.47*	1998–2005
	practice—dentistry	*1*	*0.36*	2009
Nursing		*57*	20.95	1966–2021
Healthcare		*38*	13.97	1986–2021
Microbiology		*32*	11.76	2001–2022
Biology		*15*	5.51	1993–2021
Cardiology		*13*	4.77	2001–2021
Genetics		*13*	4.77	1983–2018
Neurology		*12*	4.41	2005–2021
Education		*9*	3.3	1994–2021
TOTAL		**272**	**100**	

Among the top titles used in the various fields, *A day in the life* is the most quoted Beatles song title with 35 hits in both *practice* and *nursing*, while *All together now* is particularly present in *nursing* (13 hits) and *healthcare* (12 occurrences).

We did not analyze the impact that songs can have when compared to the geographical distribution of authors' affiliations as this information may be distorted: the decision to construct a publication title with a Beatles'= song may also depend on what the academic journal stylesheet or publication guidelines allow. Furthermore, an author may have a different geographical origin from the geographical distribution of her/his affiliation—which might imply cultural variables. In addition, although 281 (51.4 %) publications are by one single author, 221

(45.4 %) publications are co-authored (the remaining ones are anonymous): in the latter case, co-authors do not necessarily have the same affiliation. Similarly, we decided not to analyze the authors' gender distribution because, culturally, gender is a fluid notion and, in the case of co-authored publications, what title to use might be a team decision.

Ten authors tend to always publish their contributions (23 in total; 18 editorials and 5 RAs) with titles reproducing Beatles song titles, which seems to be a personal preference/style.

When we come to the type of article published which quotes a Beatles song title, we could detect that the most common types of publications (that is, RAs, editorials and commentaries, reports and clinical trials, popularized articles and personal notes) are, obviously, also those where Beatles song titles are most quoted. As can be seen in Table 4, below, the three most frequently quoted song titles are: *A day in the life* (81 quotations altogether), *All together now* (45 quotations), *With a little help from my friends* (39 quotations).

Table 4. Breakdown of the type of publication with reference to Beatles songs.

Type of article	#	*Top Beatles song titles quoted*
Personal note	153	*A day in the life* (55 quotations)
		Ticket to ride (18 quotations)
		A hard day's night (14 quotations)
Research Articles	138	*With a little help from my friends* (30 quotations)
		All together now (26 quotations)
		A day in the life (26 quotations)
Editorials and commentaries	112	*All together now* (15 quotations)
		Here comes the sun (10 quotations)
		Come together (8 quotations)
Reports & clinical trials	13	*With a little help from my friends* (9 quotations)
		Ticket to ride (7 quotations)
		Twist and shout (3 quotations)
Popularized articles	10	*All together now* (4 quotations)

Not all types of publications have been here reported, as the remaining publications cannot be reconciled to a common prototypical category; furthermore, not all Beatles song titles are indicated in Table 4, because in most cases there was only one single quotation.

If a publication entitled *A day in the life* may be intuitively understood as a type of article which is actually the scholar's personal note or report of a typical day in the profession, in all other cases, the presence of a quotation from a Beatles song title could not be accounted for. For this reason, a more in-depth investigation has been necessary.

As Sala (2013) claims, titles can be classified based on: (1) the textual perspective, on the basis of which it will be possible to measure their level of informativeness (Fortanet et al. 1998; Swales 2003; Soler 2007; Sisó 2009); (2) the sentence viewpoint, to examine how information is packed in order to produce a recognizable and effective meaning; and (3) the lexical level to measure the degree of accessibility and referential transparence in RA titles.

More precisely, from a textual viewpoint (level of informativeness), titles can be:

(a) Full-sentence titles (cf. Haggan 2004; Soler 2007), i.e. those titles whose structures are syntactically complete and semantically self-standing (declarative/declaratory; interrogative titles), as in the following examples (our emphasis here and there):

   (1) *Run for* your *life* . . . at a comfortable speed and not too far.
   (2) Biology's *bad boy* is back
   (3) *All you need is love*?

(b) Compound titles (informative), i.e, titles whose formulations comprise two parts (phrases, clauses or full sentences), usually separated by a colon or a corresponding punctuation mark (Sisó 2009: 30), also called hanging (Day 1994) or colonic titles (Hartley 2005b). The two parts are logically interconnected, mutually clarifying and organized in theme-rheme sequences, where the first part establishes the given information and the second modifies, specifies, articulates or frames it through the introduction of new informative material. These patterns, as specified by Swales and Feak (1994), represents the type problem-solution, general-specific, topic-method, and major-minor, all clusters, as can be seen in the following examples:

(4) *Here comes the sun*: recognition of UV-damaged DNA.
(5) *All together now.* Operational challenges to a practice in an integrated delivery system.

(c) Nominal titles, i.e. titles whose formulations contain neither a finite nor a conjugated verb and consist of a single verbless text segment (non-finite verbal forms such as gerunds, participles, to + infinitives):

(6) **Getting** around (on four wheels) *with a little help from my friends.*
(7) Sphingosine-1-Phosphate as the Lymphocyte's *Ticket* ***to Ride*** and **Survive**
(8) ***Fixing*** *a hole* where the Ras gets in.
(9) *A day in the life*

The analysis carried out at the sentence level helped us to understand how information is packaged. In this case, titles have been classified as:

(a). Topic titles, i.e. titles formed with a single nominal group or including a modifying possessive, partitive or relational genitive element, when this qualifies the noun phrase itself rather than modifying its semantic relation to other phrases or cotextual elements, as in the following cases (our emphasis here and there):

(10) *The matchbox sign*
(11) *The magical mystery tour* **of** health insurance.
(12) The similarity **of** life *across the universe.*

(b). Bi-head titles (cf. Wang and Bai 2007), or correlates, are those composed of two noun phrases correlated by the conjunction 'and' (in some cases 'or'), like the examples below:

(13) IL-22 **and** inflammation: leukin' through *a glass onion*
(14) Some further comments on aseptic processing guidance, **or** *the fool on the hill*: Parenteral Drug Association.

(c) Focus titles are those formulations where the noun phrase (i.e. the topic) is followed by a disambiguating post-modifying element (i.e. focus), be it a prepositional phrase or a to + infinitive clause, which further articulates the semantic relationship between the noun phrase and its lexical cotext, as can be seen in the following instances:

(15) A "*Yellow Submarine*" **in** Dermoscopy.
(16) *A day in the life*: a night **to remember**.

From a lexical perspective, titles can be:

(a). titles with specialist lexis (expressions which presuppose and require domain-specific competence on the part of the reader to be recognized):

(17) Are ***GOLD*en** *slumbers* drug induced?
(18) *Helter-skelter*-like **perylene polyisocyanopeptides**.

(b) titles using 'language as mention'. This term broadly refers to all those 'markedly non-specialized items' which appear to be borrowed from other (non-specialized) situational contexts or registers, and inserted in the wording of the title for their cognitive impact. This strategy can be realized through the use of metaphors and figurative language, actual quotations (if stylistically marked), or clashing registers. These language-as-mention strategies, which Hartley (2007: 559) defines as 'attractors', are possibly intended as popularizing resources, in the sense established by Dubois (1985) (i.e. not as the influence of media or popular discourse but as interpretation facilitating devices for the processing of a text), meant to clarify or help represent the meaning of the title and, as a consequence, of the associated publication.

(19) A **"Yellow Submarine"** in Dermoscopy.
(20) Here comes the **sun**: medical professionalism and the implications of the sunshine act for gastroenterology practice.

While in (19) there is a clear indication of the mention stylistically marked with inverted commas, in (20) *sun* is a rhetorical trope as it acts as a pun to indicate the SUNSHINE Act issued to provide more transparent relations between physicians and medical devices or pharmaceutical manufacturers.

Clearly, as the analysis is on three different levels, the categories can overlap. Indeed, as can be seen in the examples above, the title *A 'Yellow Submarine' in Dermoscopy* is at the same time a nominal, focus title which uses language as mention.

The analysis of titles at the level of informativeness is summarized in Tables 5, 6 and 7, below.

As can be seen, Table 5 indicates the degree of informativeness represented in titles:

Table 5: Breakdown of textual informativeness.

Type of titles	#	%
Full-sentence titles	27	4.95
Compound titles	313	57.32
Nominal titles	206	38.09
Total	**546**	**100**

Apparently, data suggest that compound titles (57.32 %) and nominal titles (38.09 %) are preferred. In the case of compound titles, they are normally formed with the song in the thematic position, followed by a colon, introducing the 'real' title of the contribution which illustrates the topic that is being dealt with by the publication.

Table 6: Breakdown of sentence informativeness.

Type of titles	#	%
Topic titles	192	35.16
Bi-headed titles	15	2.74
Focus titles	339	62.08
Total	**546**	**100**

The analysis at the sentence level measures the way in which information is packaged. As can be seen in Table 6, above, titles are primarily focus ones (62.08 %): the topic of the title, normally the Beatles song title, is followed by the 'real' title acting as a disambiguating post-modifying element, the focus, which creates a semantic bridge between the Beatles song title and the RA co-text.

In Table 7, below, we can see the degree of accessibility and referential transparency in RA titles. The classification made by Sala (2013) is based on titles containing specialized lexis vs titles containing markedly non-specialized items.

Table 7: Breakdown of lexical informativeness.

Type of titles	#	%
Titles with specialized lexis	16	2.93
Titles with both specialized and non-specialized lexis	78	14.28
Titles with both specialized and 'language as mention'	7	1.28
Titles with non-specialized lexis	413	75.64
Titles with 'language as mention'	32	5.86
Total	**546**	**100**

In all the cases represented in Table 7, above, titles are constructed with one Beatles song. Intuitively, the song title introduces the 'real' title which may have specialized language used in the field under investigation. Interestingly, however, 75.64 % of titles are constructed with no specialized language; in only 5 % of titles does the Beatles song title form what Sala (2013) calls 'language as mention', i.e. 'markedly non-specialized items' which appear to be borrowed from the song itself and stylistically marked with actual quotations. In any case, the presence of a Beatles song title, be it stylistically marked or not, is intended to act as an attractor (Hartley 2007: 559): a popularizing resource meant to clarify or help represent the meaning of the title and, as a consequence, the associated publication.

The level of informativeness has been put in relation to titles' meaning-making. In other words, we have semantically investigated whether the level of informativeness has an autonomous meaning or whether the meaning of the title could be understood only in relation to the research article's content. Indeed, we detected that some titles quote a Beatles song title, as in *Come together*, and apparently do not refer to anything in particular: the meaning of the title can be understood only after reading the publication, which becomes the context creating the semantic reference point via which to understand the title.

In this case, we have divided titles into 'allusive' vs 'informative'. Allusive titles are those quoting a Beatles song title and whose meaning cannot be understood; informative titles are those which offer an explicit meaning (Table 8, below).

Table 8. Allusive vs informative titles.

Allusive vs informative titles	#	%
allusive	211	38.64
informative	335	61.35
Total	**546**	**100**

Roughly 61 % of titles are informative and almost 39 % are allusive.

All allusive and informative titles, simply by referring to a Beatles song title, belong to the category defined by Hartley (2007: 96) as 'Titles that bid for attention by using startling or effective openings'.

Informative titles have thus been further investigated, following Hartley (2007), to understand the implied meaning of the part of the title acting as a disambiguating post-modifying element (if analysed as a focus title) or as the rhematic part modifying, articulating, and specifying the Beatles song title (if analysed as a compound title). The categories applied by Hartley (2007) are:

(i) announcing titles, that is titles that announce the general topic dealt with within the publication, as in (21) below:

> (21) *Ticket to ride:* export of proteins to the Plasmodium falciparum-infected erythrocyte.

(ii) thematizing titles, that is titles that particularize the theme dealt with in the publication, as in (22):

> (22) *It's Been a Hard Day's Night* and I've Been Working Like a Dog: Workaholism and Work Engagement in the JD-R Model.

(iii) titles posing the controlling rcscarch question, as in (23):

(23) *Run for your life*: can exercise be used to effectively target GLUT4 in diabetic cardiac disease?

(iv) titles answering the paper's research questions, as in (24);

(24) *A hard day's night*. The harmful effects of shift work.

(v) methodological approach titles, that is titles that put emphasis on the methodology applied, as in (25):

(25) *All together now*: experimental multispecies biofilm model systems

(vi) titles indicating guidelines or a comparison, as shown in (26), below;

(26) Dietary Intervention for Glucose Tolerance In Teens (*DIG IT*): Protocol of a randomized controlled trial using health coaching to prevent youth-onset type 2 diabetes.

(vii) mystifying titles, i.e. titles that attract but do not carry meaning per se, if not linked to the research context, as in (27), below;

(27) Getting around (on four wheels) *with a little help from my friends*.

(viii) titles indicating the author's position or direction in a topic, as in (28):

(28) *Here comes the sun:* new policies will bring better times ahead for the nephrology specialty.

Data indicate that titles can be classified as shown in Table 9, below:

Table 9: Types of informative titles.

Type of title	#	%
i. announcing a general subject	161	48.05
ii. theme particularizing	70	20.89
iii. posing a research question	11	3.28
iv. answering a research question	46	13.73

Table 9: *Continued*

Type of title	#	%
v. perspectivizing methodologies	6	1.79
vi. suggesting guidelines	14	4.17
vii. mystifying	6	1.79
viii. indicating the author's position	21	6.26
Total	**335**	**100**

As can be seen, informative titles forming our corpus are mainly constructed to announce the general subject (48 %), particularize the subject (21 %) or offer answers to the research questions. Informative titles, therefore, seem to be either *indicative* of the research topic, or *conclusive*, when they anticipate the research results in the title.

Given that both allusive and informative articles may contain a Beatles song title, the latter seems to have the anchorage function as defined by Barthes (1968). Every Beatles song title has a meaning in the context of the Beatles song it is linked to. However, when the title is linked to different related texts, it acquires polysemous related meanings. Seen in this way, such possibilities for multiple interpretations are limited when titles and texts are anchored. In the case of allusive titles (be they nominal titles—185 hits, or topic titles—190 hits), the meaning is anchored by the relationship existing between the title and the content of the research publication; in the case of informative titles, anchorage is offered by the relation the Beatles song title has to the second part of the RA title, in particular in the case of compound titles (295 hits) and focus titles (315 occurrences).

This is particularly relevant in cases in which:

- the title thus constructed is created by modifying an existing Beatles title, as shown in (29):

  (29) *Good Night, Sleep Tight*, Bed Bugs Continue to Bite

  where not only the original title 'Good Night, Sleep Tight' but also the common-sense 'Good Night, Sleep Tight, don't let Bed Bugs Bite' is modified to acquire meaning amplification when connected to the research content. Indeed, the article is not about bugs in mattresses, which may cause difficulties with sleeping, but rather about a completely different medical topic: the case of a child who presented with sleep-related rhythmic movement disorder, diagnosed because he also had attention-deficit issues;

- the function of the title is to offer feedback or comment on a previously published paper, as in (30) below:

(30) '*Help! I need somebody*': getting timely assistance in clinical practice

which is a comment on a paper entitled 'The "go-between" study: a simulation study comparing the 'Traffic Lights' and 'SBAR' tools as a means of communication between anaesthetic staff', both of them published in the 71(7) issue of *Anesthesia* in 2015, and thanks to which the article entitled 'The "go-between" study' published a correction in the following issue;

- the reference is external to the publication and linked to a new context, as in the following examples:

(31) Come and *get IT*
(32) *Here comes the sun*
(33) *Twist and shout*
(34) *Here Comes the SUN* (Part 2): Standardization of Uveitis Nomenclature for Disease Classification Criteria

Where, in (31), 'IT' refers to Information Technology; in (32), 'sun' refers to the Sunshine Act regulating the relations between medics and the pharmaceutical industry to make them more transparent; in (33), the title is a comment on an article entitled 'Mutations in TWIST, a basic helix-loop-helix transcription factor' and, by creating a pun, refers to the basic helix-loop-helix transcription factor, called TWIST, seen as a candidate for Saethre-Chotzen syndrome; in (34), 'SUN' is the acronym for Standardization of Uveitis Nomenclature.
There is, in particular, one case that is worth noting. A 2008 publication entitled *Here comes the sun* created a semantic link the title and the general topic of public health. In 2010, the same link is again dealt with in a slightly modified title, which appears to

be longer but also a development of the topic dealt in the 2008 article: the title *Here comes the sun (and the rain, wind and snow)* refers to the study carried out by the author showing the impact climate change has on public health.

Although not frequently used, these strategies are employed in both allusive and informative titles, as can be seen in Table 10, below, which indicates that 18.31 % of titles modify the Beatles title, and 2.56 % comment on a previous article

Table 10: Breakdown of allusive vs. informative titles.

Type of article	**Modifying a Beatles song title**		**Commenting on a previous article**	
allusive	18	3.29 %	4	1.9 %
informative	82	15.01 %	12	3.57 %
Total	**100**	**18.31 %**	**16**	**2.93 %**

These titles clearly bid for attention by using startling or effective openings.

3. Conclusion

The purpose of this paper has been to understand the reason why Beatles song titles are used as titles for medical research publications. Through a corpus-assisted investigation of journals or disciplines, we have focused on current practices in the creation of medical titles which use a Beatles song title. As claimed by Rowley-Jolivet and Carter-Thomas (2005: 45), "By analysing how language is used [...] and heightening awareness of its specific and contextually motivated features, applied linguistics has an important role to play in helping scientific researchers participate more effectively in the discourse practices of their field."

We have seen that titles which use a Beatles song title are a form of 'language as mention', even though the mention is not stylistically singled out: by quoting a Beatles song title, the author of the publication clearly creates an attention-seeking device with startling effect. Such a strategy does not seem to depend on a particular point in time, a particular journal, or a particular Beatles song title. These titles are puns that create an anchorage, either with the content of the published research, if allusive, or with the second part of the title, if informative. The former titles are nominal titles; they can turn into informative titles if they appear in a personal note section (as in the case of *A day in the* life). The latter titles, if created as compound or focus titles, exploit a startling effect to attract the readership to the second part of the title, which disambiguates or focuses information on a field topic. Informative titles, by announcing a general topic or presenting the research question, are *indicative* in the sense that they indicate the research angle from which the readership must position; by answering the research question, they are *conclusive* in that they anticipate the research results in the title itself. As these titles carry research information, the Beatles element in the title is appealing and entices the reader to stop and read the research.

In all cases, as explained by Fairclough (1993: 141), this contributes to reconstructing boundaries in social practices and generating new hybrid promotional genres, which, as sustained by Bhatia (1997: 191), are exploited to introduce innovations and achieve more communicative purposes. Scientific articles attract by informing, and titles have a retrieval function. With these titles, what is important is the surprise value of information rather than information per se.

References

Barthes, Roland. 1968. *Elements of Semiology.* Hill and Wang, New York.

Bhatia, Vijay. 1997. Genre-Mixing in Academic Introductions. *English for Specific Purposes* 16/3: 181–195.

Brown, Sally, Aplin, Karen L., Jenkins, Kathie, Mander, Sarah, Walsh, Claire, Williams, Paul D. 2015. Is there a rhythm of the rain? An analysis of weather in popular music. *Weather* 70, 198–204.

Callaham, Michael / Wears, Robert L. / Weber, Ellen. 2010. Journal Prestige, Publication Bias, and Other Characteristics Associated with Citation of Published Studies in Peer-Reviewed Journals. *JAMA* 287/21, 2847–2850.

Day, Robert A. 1994. *How to Write and Publish a Scientific Paper*. Cambridge: Cambridge University Press.

Dubois, Betty Lou. 1985. Popularization at the Highest Level: Poster Sessions at Biomedical Meetings. *International Journal of the Sociology of Language* 56, 67–84.

Eyrolle, Hélène, Virbel, Jacques, Lemarié, Julie. 2008. Effects of Incomplete Correspondence between Document Titles and Texts on Users' Representations: A Cognitive and Linguistic Analysis Based on 25 Technical Documents. *Applied Ergonomics* 39, 241–246.

Fairclough, Norman. 1993. Critical Discourse Analysis and the Marketization of Public Discourse: The Universities. *Discourse & Society* 4/2, 133–168.

Fortanet, Inmaculada / Posteguillo, Santiago / Coll, Juan F. / Palmer, Juan C. 1998. Linguistic Analysis of Research Article Titles: Disciplinary Variations. In Vázquez, Ignacio / Guillén, Ignacio (eds.), *Perspectivas Praguietices en Linguistica Aplicada*. Zaragoza: Anubar, 443–447.

Fox, Charles W. / Burns, C. Sean. 2015. The Relationship between Manuscript Title Structure and Success: Editorial Decisions and Citation Performance for an Ecological Journal. *Ecology and Evolution* 5/10, 1970–1980.

Ganier, Franck. 1999. *Le traitement cognitif: déterminant de la conception de documents procéduraux*. PhD diss., Université de Bourgogne.

Giannoni, Davide. 2013. Whose Genre Awareness? The Case of Medical Titles. In Bernadette O'Rourke / Nicola Bermingham / Sara Brennan (eds.), *Opening New Lines of Communication in Applied Linguistics. Proceedings of the 46th Annual Meeting of the British Association for Applied Linguistics*, 5–7 September 2013. Edinburgh: Heriot-Watt University, 151–159.

Gornitzki, Carl / Larsson, Agne / Fadeel Bengt 2015. Freewheelin' Scientists: Citing Bob Dylan in the Biomedical Literature. *British Medical Journal* 351, h6505.

Haggan, Madeline. 2004. Research Paper Titles in Literature, Linguistics and Science: Dimensions of Attraction. *Journal of Pragmatics* 36/2, 293–317.

Hartley, James. 2005a. To Attract or to Inform: What Are Titles for? *Journal of Technical Writing and Communication* 35/2, 203–213.

Hartley, James. 2005b. Improving That Title: The Effects of Colons. *European Science Editing* 31, 45–47.

Hartley, James. 2007. Planning That Title: Practices and Preferences for Titles with Colons in Academic Disciplines. *Library and Information Science Research* 29, 553–568.

Heurley, Laurent. 1994. *Traitement de textes procéduraux. Etude de psycholinguistique cognitive des processus de éproduction et de compréhension chez des adultes non-experts.* Diss., Universit de Bourgogne.

Hudson, John. 2016. An Analysis of the Titles of Papers Submitted to the UK REF in 2014: Authors, Disciplines, and Stylistic Details. *Scientometrics* 109, 871–889.

Jacques, Thomas S. / Sebire, Neil J. 2010. The Impact of Article Titles on Citation Hits: An Analysis of General and Specialist Medical Journals. *Journal of the Royal Society of Medicine Short Reports* 1/2, 1 5.

Lewison, Grant / Hartley, James. 2005. What's in a Title? Numbers of Words and the Presence of Colons. *Scientometrics* 63/2, 341–356.

Mavrogenis, Andreas F. / Panagopoulos, Georgios N. / Megaloikonomos, Panayiotis D. / Panagopoulos, Vassilis N. / Mauffrey, Cyril / Quaile, Andrew / Scarlat, Marius M. 2018. Scientific Misconduct (Fraud) in Medical Writing. *Orthopedics* 41/2, e176–e183.

Michaels, Sean. 2014. Swedish Scientists Sneak Bob Dylan Lyrics into Articles as Part of a Long-Running Bet. *Guardian Online*. Retrieved November 20, 2017, from: http://www.theguardian.com/music/2014/sep/29/swedish-cientists-bet-bob-dylan-lyrics-resea rch-papers

Paiva, Carlo Eduardo / da Silveira, Nogueira Lima / João, Paulo / Sakamoto, Bianca Ribeiro Paiva. 2012. Articles with Short Titles Describing the Results Are Cited More Often. *Clinics* 67/5, 509–513.

Rijkers, Ger T. 2017. Tell Me Why Bob Dylan and the Beatles Song Titles Are Used in Biomedical Literature. *Webology* 14/2, 78–89. Available at: http://www.webology.org/2017/v14n2/a159.pdf

Rowley-Jolivet, Elizabeth / Carter-Thomas, Shirley. 2005. The Rhetoric of Conference Presentation Introductions: Context, Argument and Interaction. *International Journal of Applied Linguistics* 15/1, 45–70.

Sala, Michele. 2013. Language Change in Legal Research Article Titles. In Poppi, Franca / Cheng, Winnie (eds.), *The Three Waves of Globalization: Winds of Change in Professional, Institutional and Academic Genres*. Newcastle upon Tyne: Cambridge Scholars Publishers, 222–243.

Sala, Michele / Consonni, Stefania. 2019. Titles in Medicine and Science Popularization. In: Bondi, Marina / Cacchiani, Silvia / Cavalieri, Silvia (eds.), *Communicating Specialized Knowledge: Old Genres and New Media*. Newcastle upon Tyne: Cambridge Scholars Publishers, 16–32.

Sisó, Mercedes Jaime. 2009. Titles or Headlines? Anticipating Conclusions in Biomedical Research Article Titles as a Persuasive Journalistic Strategy to Attract Busy Readers. *Miscelànea* 39, 29–54.

Smith, Richard. 2000. Informative Titles in the BMJ. *British Medical Journal* 320/7239, 915.

Soler, Viviana. 2007. Writing Titles in Science: An Exploratory Study. In *English for Specific Purposes* 26/1, 90–102.

Soler, Viviana. 2011. Comparative and Contrastive Observations on Scientific Titles Written in English and Spanish. *English for Specific Purposes* 30/2, 124–137.

Swales, John M. 1990. *Genre Analysis: English in Academic and Research Settings*. Cambridge, UK: Cambridge University Press.

Swales, John M. 2003. *Genre Analysis: English in Academic and Research Settings*. Shanghai: Shanghai Foreign Language Education Press.

Swales, John / Feak, Cristine. 1994. *Academic Writing for Graduate Students*. Ann Arbor: The University of Michigan Press.

Wang, Yan / Bai, Yongquan. 2007. A Corpus-Based Syntactic Study of Medical Research Article Titles. *Syntax* 35/3, 388–399.

Wheatley, Danys. 2018. Writing Scientific and Medical Papers Clearly. *The Anatomical Record*. Available at: https://onlinelibrary.wiley.com/doi/abs/10.1002/ar.23860.

Whissell, Cynthia. 1999. Linguistic Complexity of Abstracts and Titles in Highly Cited Journals. *Perceptual and Motor Skills* 88, 76–86.

White, Arden / Hernandez, Nelda. 1991. Increasing Field Complexity Revealed through Article Title Analyses. *Journal of the American Society for Information Science* 42, 731–734.

Wilson, Logan. 1942. *The Academic Man: A Study in the Sociology of a Profession*. New York: Oxford University Press.

Yitzhaki, Moshe. 1997. Variation in Informativity of Titles of Research Papers in Selected Humanities Journals: A Comparative Study. *Scientometrics* 38, 219–229.

Notes on contributors

Gema Alcaraz Mármol holds a PhD in English Studies from the University of Murcia (Spain). She currently works as an Associate Professor and Researcher at the Department of Modern Philology at the University of Castilla-La Mancha, where she teaches Foreign Language Methodology and Communicative Skills in Foreign Language. Her main research interests are Corpus Linguistics, Discourse Analysis and L2 Vocabulary.

Encarnación Almazán-Ruiz got her PhD in English Linguistics at the University of Granada (Spain). She currently works as an assistant professor at the University of Jaén, teaching in both Graduate and Postgraduate programs. Her research interests include Corpus Linguistics, Discourse Analysis, Digital Linguistics and implementing innovative teaching approaches in the EFL classroom. Dr Almazán-Ruiz has published several papers in the field, with a particular focus on analysing political discourse and researching the effectiveness of the Flipped classroom approach for teaching English grammar.

F.Co Mario Barcala Rodríguez is a computer engineer (1999) and doctorate in computing (2010) from the University of A Coruña (Spain). He is been working and researching for more than 20 years in collaboration with different teams of linguists, on different topics related to corpus linguistics and computational linguistics. In 2015 he created NLPgo Technologies, S.L., for the use of technology to solve problems proposed by linguists.

Claudia de la Iglesia Sanjuán holds a BA in Foreign Languages and an MA in Advanced English Studies from the University of Vigo (Spain). Her research interests include phonetics and phonology, language variation and sociolinguistics. In her BA and MA dissertations, she dealt with the realisation and production of specific segmental and suprasegmental features of English by Spanish-Galician bilingual university students of English. She is currently working on her PhD thesis, which deals with accent distinction and attitudes towards varieties of English by university students of English.

Cherubino Di Lorenzo (MD, PHD) is a Clinical Neurologist and Researcher at Department of Medico-Surgical Sciences and Biotechnologies of Sapienza University of Rome (Polo Pontino, Latina, Italy) active in the field of neurogenetics, neurophysiology, and nutraceutical and nutritional treatments in different neurological conditions, in particular headaches. In 2020 he coordinated the Italian Study Group for the use of ketogenic diet in headache clinical practice, publishing clinical recommendations. At present, he is also the medical advisor of Italian Cephalalgic Alliance (Al.Ce.), the Italian association of patients with headache, Editor of the patient's association bulletin 'Cefalee Today', and president of Eupraxia Association, that aims to promote the culture of health and wellness in all its aspects and scientific research in health.

Eva M.ª Domínguez Nova is a Research Associate at the *Instituto da Lingua Galega*, a research centre of the University of Santiago de Compostela (Spain). Her research focuses mainly on the area of computational linguistics for Galician and Spanish. Regarding the former, she coordinates the linguistic part of the *Corpus de Referencia do Galego Actual* (CORGA) and she is responsible for the linguistic resources used by the XIADA tagger in the annotation of this corpus. In relation to Spanish, she is currently collaborating in the ESLORA project, a corpus for the study of oral Galician Spanish.

Maricel Esteban-Follonosa holds a PhD in Languages, Literatures, Cultures and their Applications from the University of Valencia (Spain). She also holds three BAs: in German Philology from the University of Valencia, in Media Studies from the C.E.U. San Pablo, and in Hispanic Studies from the Universitat de València. Her research focuses on contrastive linguistics, discourse analysis and applied linguistics, especially in the area of teaching German as a foreign language.

Yolanda Fernández-Pena is Lecturer in the Department of English, French and German at the University of Vigo (Spain). Yolanda's research focuses on the linguistic variation of verb number agreement with complex collective subjects in Late Modern and Present-Day English, the syntactic characterisation of fragments in Present-Day English and the provision of agreement morphology and overt subjects in L2 English. She is the author of the monograph *Reconciling synchrony, diachrony and usage in verb number agreement with complex collective subjects* (Routledge, 2020).

Giovanni Garofalo is Full Professor of Spanish Language and Translation in the Department of Languages, Literatures, and Comparative Cultures at the University of Bergamo (Italy). He is a member of CERLIS (Research Centre on Specialized Languages at the University of Bergamo), of the CORPLING research group (Corpus Linguistics, Developments, and Applications) at the University of Valencia, and a Collaborating Professor in the EDAP (Academic and Professional Discourse Studies) research group, led by Professor Estrella Montolío, at the University of Barcelona. Additionally, he is the director of the panel 'Discourse, Literary Analysis, and Corpus' of AELINCO (Spanish Corpus Linguistics Association). His main research interests encompass corpus-assisted specialized discourse analysis, and his most recent publications focus on communication in legal, touristic, and political contexts; the language of appraisal in judicial texts; and the discursive construction of gender.

Luisa González-Romero holds a PhD in English Philology and is Associate Professor at the University of Huelva (Spain), where she teaches courses on English syntax and theoretical linguistics. She has been a member of different research groups and has participated in several R&D projects. Her main areas of research are contrastive grammar English-Spanish and corpus linguistics.

Carmen Gregori-Signes is an Associate Professor at the University of Valencia (Spain). She has been a research visitor in several universities (Nottingham University, Birmingham University, Iowa University, Cambridge University, Università degli studi di Bergamo, Swansea University, Queen Mary University, George Mason University). She was a founding member and vicepresident of the Association EDISO

(*Estudios de Discurso y Sociedad*) for four years. Her publications and presentations include papers on multimodal and media discourse analysis, applied linguistics and language education. Her most recent research focuses on discourse analysis, media discourse, corpus linguistics and corpus stylistics. She is the director of the research group CORPLING: Corpus Linguistics: developments and applications—CORPLING (GIUV2018-425).

Stefania M. Maci (PhD, Lancaster University, UK) is Full Professor of English Language at the University of Bergamo (Italy), where she is the coordinator of the MA in Digital Humanities and Director of CERLIS (Research Centre on Specialized Languages). Her research is focused on the study of the English language in academic and professional contexts, with particular regard to the analysis of tourism and medical discourses. Recent publications include: the monographs Evidentiality in the genre of medical posters (2022) and English Tourism Discourse (2020); the co-edited volumes Corpus Linguistics and Translation Tools for Digital Humanities (2022), The Routledge Handbook of Scientific Communication (2022); Metadiscourse in Digital Communication (2021); and the papers 'Data triangulation using Sketch Engine and WMatrix: Ketogenic diet on Twitter' (2022); 'The narrative of the anti-vax campaign on Twitter' (2021); and 'Parents' narrative about congenital heart diseases' (2019).

Antonio Moreno Ortiz is an Associate Professor in the Department of English, French, and German Philology at the University of Malaga (Spain), where he is currently Head of Department. His research focuses on Computational Linguistics, Corpus Linguistics, and Language Technologies, including the development of software and resources for Natural Language Processing and Digital Humanities. He has participated in numerous national and international research and development projects related to language engineering. Within these projects, he has developed computational tools for corpus management, ontology and terminology management. In the private sector, he has worked for multinational companies such as Harper-Collins, Sandvik Group, and Ubisoft. He has led three R&D projects funded by the Spanish National Plan and two within the FEDER Andalusia Operational

Program, resulting in tangible outcomes in the form of applications and resources in the field of Language Technologies, including registered software: BNC Indexer, OntoTerm, Sentitext, Lingmotif.

Paloma Núñez-Pertejo is Associate Professor of English Linguistics at the University of Santiago de Compostela (Spain) and a member of the VLCG (Variation, Linguistic Change and Grammaticalization) Research Unit. Her main research interests include grammaticalization processes in the history of English, with special reference to the development of the aspectual system and English intensifiers. She has published in international journals and volumes, mainly on verb categories and on youth language and intensification. Between 2005 and 2013 she served on the Editorial Committee of *Folia Linguistica* (Mouton), and currently sits on the Advisory Board of *Atlantis*, the official journal of the *Spanish Association for English and American Studies* (AEDEAN).

Aroa Orrequia-Barea is a lecturer at the University of Cádiz (Spain), where she obtained her PhD in English Philology. Her research interests include Corpus Linguistics, which she applies to various topics such as Semantics, Discourse Analysis, Computational Linguistics, and Sentiment Analysis. She is currently working on a critical discourse analysis of trendy media topics, specifically political speeches. Dr Orrequia-Barea has authored several publications that focus on analysing political speeches, particularly those related to the Brexit process.

Ignacio M. Palacios-Martínez obtained his PhD in English in 1992 from the University of Santiago de Compostela (Spain). Since 1995 he has been working, first as an Associate Professor and now as a Full Professor, in the English and German Department of the same university. He is the coordinator of the SPERTUS research group and the principal investigator of a research project, funded by the Spanish Ministry of Science and Innovation, concerned with the description of English in social media from theoretical and applied perspectives. He was also Head of the University's Modern Language Centre between 2007 and 2010 and Secretary of the Spanish Association of Anglo-American Studies (AEDEAN) from 2004 to 2009.

Javier Pérez-Guerra is Full Professor of English Linguistics at the University of Vigo (Spain), where he coordinates the LVTC (Language Variation and Textual Categorisation) research group. He has been the Principal Investigator of competitive research projects on topics such as information packaging in the clause, multidimensional approaches to register variation, the study of grammatical variation between Modern and Present-day English from corpus-based empirical perspectives, and the impact of performance preferences and ease of processing on the design of grammars.

Rosalía Rodríguez-Vázquez is Associate Professor of English Linguistics and Director of the Language and Cognition Lab at the University of Vigo (Spain). She obtained a PhD in Phonology and Music from the University of Edinburgh and worked as a research fellow at the Structures formelles du langage research lab (CNRS) in Paris and the MARL and CLaME labs (NYU) in New York. Her research interests include phonetics and phonology, and the interface phonology-metrics-music. She has published a good number of articles and book chapters, as well as the monograph *The Rhythm of Speech, Verse and Vocal Music: A New Theory* (Bern: Peter Lang).

Paula Santalla Del Río (PhD) is a Lecturer at the University of Santiago de Compostela (Spain). Her research focuses on the fields of natural language processing, linguistic engineering and corpus linguistics, for both corpus development and exploitation. She is currently collaborating in a research project for the development of an annotated spoken corpus of Galician Spanish (ESLORA).

Jorge Soto Almela earned his PhD in Translation and Interpreting from the University of Murcia (Spain). Presently, he serves as a lecturer within the Department of English Studies at the University of Alicante. His scholarly pursuits primarily revolve around the exploration of corpus linguistics, with a particular emphasis on its application to specialized domains and translation. Dr. Soto-Almela's research is showcased in several prestigious, high-impact journals and he has participated in numerous international conferences.

Catello Vollono (MD, PhD, Catholic University, Rome, Italy) is a neurologist at Fondazione Policlinico Universitario Agostino Gemelli IRCCS - Catholic University of Rome (Italy). He has 25 years of experience in medical practice and in clinical and neurophysiological research. Having qualified in Medicine from 'Seconda Università degli Studi di Napoli', and residency in Neurology from the 'Catholic University' of Rome, he began his career as a neurologist in Ospedale Pediatrico Bambino Gesù of Rome. Since 2011 is neurologist at Fondazione Policlinico Universitario Agostino Gemelli of Rome. His major research activities involved the basic mechanisms of primary headache, epilepsy, and sleep disorders, in both experimental and clinical settings, and translating this knowledge into better management. Dr Vollono is author or co-author of more than 150 full papers indexed in PubMed, investigator in several international trials in headaches and epilepsy disease, teacher in residency courses of Neurology and Child Neuropsychiatry, member of various editorial board of international peer review journal, member of International Headache Society (IHS), Società Italiana per lo studio delle Cefalee (SISC), Società Italiana Neurologia (SIN), Società Italiana Neurofisiologia Clinica (SINC), Lega Italiana Contro l'Epilessia (LICE).

Linguistic Insights

Studies in Language and Communication

This series aims to promote specialist language studies in the fields of linguistic theory and applied linguistics, by publishing volumes that focus on specific aspects of language use in one or several languages and provide valuable insights into language and communication research. A cross-disciplinary approach is favoured and most European languages are accepted.

The series includes two types of books:

- Monographs – featuring in-depth studies on special aspects of language theory, language analysis or language teaching.
- Collected papers – assembling papers from workshops, conferences or symposia.

Each volume of the series is subjected to a double peer-reviewing process.

Vol. 1 Maurizio Gotti & Marina Dossena (eds)
Modality in Specialized Texts. Selected Papers of the 1st CERLIS Conference.
421 pages. 2001. ISBN 3-906767-10-8 · US-ISBN 0-8204-5340-4

Vol. 2 Giuseppina Cortese & Philip Riley (eds)
Domain-specific English. Textual Practices across Communities and Classrooms.
420 pages. 2002. ISBN 3-906768-98-8 · US-ISBN 0-8204-5884-8

Vol. 3 Maurizio Gotti, Dorothee Heller & Marina Dossena (eds)
Conflict and Negotiation in Specialized Texts. Selected Papers of the 2nd CERLIS Conference.
470 pages. 2002. ISBN 3-906769-12-7 · US-ISBN 0-8204-5887-2

Vol. 4 Maurizio Gotti, Marina Dossena, Richard Dury, Roberta Facchinetti & Maria Lima
Variation in Central Modals. A Repertoire of Forms and Types of Usage in Middle English and Early Modern English.
364 pages. 2002. ISBN 3-906769-84-4 · US-ISBN 0-8204-5898-8

Editorial address:

Prof. Maurizio Gotti Università di Bergamo, Dipartimento di Lingue, Letterature e Culture Straniere Piazza Rosate 2, 24129 Bergamo, Italy
Fax: +39 035 2052789, E-Mail: m.gotti@unibg.it

Vol. 5 Stefania Nuccorini (ed.)
Phrases and Phraseology. Data and Descriptions.
187 pages. 2002. ISBN 3-906770-08-7 · US-ISBN 0-8204-5933-X

Vol. 6 Vijay Bhatia, Christopher N. Candlin & Maurizio Gotti (eds)
Legal Discourse in Multilingual and Multicultural Contexts.
Arbitration Texts in Europe.
385 pages. 2003. ISBN 3-906770-85-0 · US-ISBN 0-8204-6254-3

Vol. 7 Marina Dossena & Charles Jones (eds)
Insights into Late Modern English. 2nd edition.
378 pages. 2003, 2007.
ISBN 978-3-03911-257-9 · US-ISBN 978-0-8204-8927-8

Vol. 8 Maurizio Gotti
Specialized Discourse. Linguistic Features and Changing Conventions.
351 pages. 2003, 2005.
ISBN 3-03910-606-6 · US-ISBN 0-8204-7000-7

Vol. 9 Alan Partington, John Morley & Louann Haarman (eds)
Corpora and Discourse.
420 pages. 2004. ISBN 3-03910-026-2 · US-ISBN 0-8204-6262-4

Vol. 10 Martina Möllering
The Acquisition of German Modal Particles. A Corpus-Based Approach.
290 pages. 2004. ISBN 3-03910-043-2 · US-ISBN 0-8204-6273-X

Vol. 11 David Hart (ed.)
English Modality in Context. Diachronic Perspectives.
261 pages. 2003. ISBN 3-03910-046-7 · US-ISBN 0-8204-6852-5

Vol. 12 Wendy Swanson
Modes of Co-reference as an Indicator of Genre.
430 pages. 2003. ISBN 3-03910-052-1 · US-ISBN 0-8204-6855-X

Vol. 13 Gina Poncini
Discursive Strategies in Multicultural Business Meetings.
2nd edition. 338 pages. 2004, 2007.
ISBN 978-3-03911-296-8 · US-ISBN 978-0-8204-8937-7

Vol. 14 Christopher N. Candlin & Maurizio Gotti (eds)
Intercultural Aspects of Specialized Communication. 2nd edition.
369 pages. 2004, 2007.
ISBN 978-3-03911-258-6 · US-ISBN 978-0-8204-8926-1

Vol. 15 Gabriella Del Lungo Camiciotti & Elena Tognini Bonelli (eds)
Academic Discourse. New Insights into Evaluation.
234 pages. 2004. ISBN 3-03910-353-9 · US-ISBN 0-8204-7016-3

Vol. 16 Marina Dossena & Roger Lass (eds)
Methods and Data in English Historical Dialectology.
405 pages. 2004. ISBN 3-03910-362-8 · US-ISBN 0-8204-7018-X

Vol. 17 Judy Noguchi
The Science Review Article. An Opportune Genre in the Construction of Science.
274 pages. 2006. ISBN 3-03910-426-8 · US-ISBN 0-8204-7034-1

Vol. 18 Giuseppina Cortese & Anna Duszak (eds)
Identity, Community, Discourse. English in Intercultural Settings.
495 pages. 2005. ISBN 3-03910-632-5 · US-ISBN 0-8204-7163-1

Vol. 19 Anna Trosborg & Poul Erik Flyvholm Jørgensen (eds)
Business Discourse. Texts and Contexts.
250 pages. 2005. ISBN 3-03910-606-6 · US-ISBN 0-8204-7000-7

Vol. 20 Christopher Williams
Tradition and Change in Legal English. Verbal Constructions in Prescriptive Texts.
2nd revised edition.
216 pages. 2005, 2007. ISBN 978-3-03911-444-3.

Vol. 21 Katarzyna Dziubalska-Kolaczyk & Joanna Przedlacka (eds)
English Pronunciation Models: A Changing Scene.
2nd edition. 476 pages. 2005, 2008. ISBN 978-3-03911-682-9.

Vol. 22 Christián Abello-Contesse, Rubén Chacón-Beltrán,
M. Dolores López-Jiménez & M. Mar Torreblanca-López (eds)
Age in L2 Acquisition and Teaching.
214 pages. 2006. ISBN 3-03910-668-6 · US-ISBN 0-8204-7174-7

Vol. 23 Vijay K. Bhatia, Maurizio Gotti, Jan Engberg & Dorothee Heller (eds)
Vagueness in Normative Texts.
474 pages. 2005. ISBN 3-03910-653-8 · US-ISBN 0-8204-7169-0

Vol. 24 Paul Gillaerts & Maurizio Gotti (eds)
Genre Variation in Business Letters. 2nd printing.
407 pages. 2008. ISBN 978-3-03911-681-2.

Vol. 25 Ana María Hornero, María José Luzón & Silvia Murillo (eds)
Corpus Linguistics. Applications for the Study of English.
2nd printing. 526 pages. 2006, 2008. ISBN 978-3-03911-726-0

Vol. 26 J. Lachlan Mackenzie & María de los Ángeles Gómez-González (eds)
Studies in Functional Discourse Grammar.
259 pages. 2005. ISBN 3-03910-696-1 · US-ISBN 0-8204-7558-0

Vol. 27 Debbie G. E. Ho
Classroom Talk. Exploring the Sociocultural Structure of Formal ESL Learning.
2nd edition. 254 pages. 2006, 2007. ISBN 978-3-03911-434-4

Vol. 28 Javier Pérez-Guerra, Dolores González-Álvarez, Jorge L. Bueno-Alonso & Esperanza Rama-Martínez (eds)
'Of Varying Language and Opposing Creed'. New Insights into Late Modern English.
455 pages. 2007. ISBN 978-3-03910-788-9

Vol. 29 Francesca Bargiela-Chiappini & Maurizio Gotti (eds)
Asian Business Discourse(s).
350 pages. 2005. ISBN 3-03910-804-2 · US-ISBN 0-8204-7574-2

Vol. 30 Nicholas Brownlees (ed.)
News Discourse in Early Modern Britain. Selected Papers of CHINED 2004.
300 pages. 2006. ISBN 3-03910-805-0 · US-ISBN 0-8204-8025-8

Vol. 31 Roberta Facchinetti & Matti Rissanen (eds)
Corpus-based Studies of Diachronic English.
300 pages. 2006. ISBN 3-03910-851-4 · US-ISBN 0-8204-8040-1

Vol. 32 Marina Dossena & Susan M. Fitzmaurice (eds)
Business and Official Correspondence. Historical Investigations.
209 pages. 2006. ISBN 3-03910-880-8 · US-ISBN 0-8204-8352-4

Vol. 33 Giuliana Garzone & Srikant Sarangi (eds)
Discourse, Ideology and Specialized Communication.
494 pages. 2007. ISBN 978-3-03910-888-6

Vol. 34 Giuliana Garzone & Cornelia Ilie (eds)
The Use of English in Institutional and Business Settings. An Intercultural Perspective.
372 pages. 2007. ISBN 978-3-03910-889-3

Vol. 35 Vijay K. Bhatia & Maurizio Gotti (eds) Explorations in Specialized Genres.
316 pages. 2006. ISBN 3-03910-995-2 · US-ISBN 0-8204-8372-9

Vol. 36 Heribert Picht (ed.)
Modern Approaches to Terminological Theories and Applications.
432 pages. 2006. ISBN 3-03911-156-6 · US-ISBN 0-8204-8380-X

Vol. 37 Anne Wagner & Sophie Cacciaguidi-Fahy (eds)
Legal Language and the Search for Clarity / Le langage juridique et la quête de clarté.
Practice and Tools / Pratiques et instruments.
487 pages. 2006. ISBN 3-03911-169-8 · US-ISBN 0-8204-8388-5

Vol. 38 Juan Carlos Palmer-Silveira, Miguel F. Ruiz-Garrido & Inmaculada Fortanet-Gómez (eds)
Intercultural and International Business Communication. Theory, Research and Teaching.
2nd edition. 343 pages. 2006, 2008. ISBN 978-3-03911-680-5

Vol. 39 Christiane Dalton-Puffer, Dieter Kastovsky, Nikolaus Ritt & Herbert Schendl (eds)
Syntax, Style and Grammatical Norms. English from 1500–2000.
250 pages. 2006. ISBN 3-03911-181-7 · US-ISBN 0-8204-8394-X

Vol. 40 Marina Dossena & Irma Taavitsainen (eds)
Diachronic Perspectives on Domain-Specific English.
280 pages. 2006. ISBN 3-03910-176-0 · US-ISBN 0-8204-8391-5

Vol. 41 John Flowerdew & Maurizio Gotti (eds)
Studies in Specialized Discourse.
293 pages. 2006. ISBN 3-03911-178-7

Vol. 42 Ken Hyland & Marina Bondi (eds)
Academic Discourse Across Disciplines.
320 pages. 2006. ISBN 3-03911-183-3 · US-ISBN 0-8204-8396-6

Vol. 43 Paul Gillaerts & Philip Shaw (eds)
The Map and the Landscape. Norms and Practices in Genre.
256 pages. 2006. ISBN 3-03911-182-5 · US-ISBN 0-8204-8395-4

Vol. 44 Maurizio Gotti & Davide Giannoni (eds)
New Trends in Specialized Discourse Analysis.
301 pages. 2006. ISBN 3-03911-184-1 · US-ISBN 0-8204-8381-8

Vol. 45 Maurizio Gotti & Françoise Salager-Meyer (eds)
Advances in Medical Discourse Analysis. Oral and Written Contexts.
492 pages. 2006. ISBN 3-03911-185-X · US-ISBN 0-8204-8382-6

Vol. 46 Maurizio Gotti & Susan Šarcevic' (eds)
Insights into Specialized Translation.
396 pages. 2006. ISBN 3-03911-186-8 · US-ISBN 0-8204-8383-4

Vol. 47 Khurshid Ahmad & Margaret Rogers (eds)
Evidence-based LSP. Translation, Text and Terminology.
584 pages. 2007. ISBN 978-3-03911-187-9

Vol. 48 Hao Sun & Dániel Z. Kádár (eds)
It's the Dragon's Turn. Chinese Institutional Discourses.
262 pages. 2008. ISBN 978-3-03911-175-6

Vol. 49 Cristina Suárez-Gómez
Relativization in Early English (950-1250). the Position of Relative Clauses.
149 pages. 2006. ISBN 3-03911-203-1 · US-ISBN 0-8204-8904-2

Vol. 50 Maria Vittoria Calvi & Luisa Chierichetti (eds)
Nuevas tendencias en el discurso de especialidad.
319 pages. 2006. ISBN 978-3-03911-261-6

Vol. 51 Mari Carmen Campoy & María José Luzón (eds)
Spoken Corpora in Applied Linguistics.
274 pages. 2008. ISBN 978-3-03911-275-3

Vol. 52 Konrad Ehlich & Dorothee Heller (Hrsg.)
Die Wissenschaft und ihre Sprachen.
323 pages. 2006. ISBN 978-3-03911-272-2

Vol. 53 Jingyu Zhang
The Semantic Salience Hierarchy Model. The L2 Acquisition of Psych Predicates
273 pages. 2007. ISBN 978-3-03911-300-2

Vol. 54 Norman Fairclough, Giuseppina Cortese & Patrizia Ardizzone (eds)
Discourse and Contemporary Social Change.
555 pages. 2007. ISBN 978-3-03911-276-0

Vol. 55 Jan Engberg, Marianne Grove Ditlevsen, Peter Kastberg & Martin Stegu (eds)
New Directions in LSP Teaching.
331 pages. 2007. ISBN 978-3-03911-433-7

Vol. 56 Dorothee Heller & Konrad Ehlich (Hrsg.)
Studien zur Rechtskommunikation.
322 pages. 2007. ISBN 978-3-03911-436-8

Vol. 57 Teruhiro Ishiguro & Kang-kwong Luke (eds)
Grammar in Cross-Linguistic Perspective.
The Syntax, Semantics, and Pragmatics of Japanese and Chinese.
304 pages. 2012. ISBN 978-3-03911-445-0

Vol. 58 Carmen Frehner Email – SMS – MMS
294 pages. 2008. ISBN 978-3-03911-451-1

Vol. 59 Isabel Balteiro
The Directionality of Conversion in English. A Dia-Synchronic Study.
276 pages. 2007. ISBN 978-3-03911-241-8

Vol. 60 Maria Milagros Del Saz Rubio
English Discourse Markers of Reformulation.
237 pages. 2007. ISBN 978-3-03911-196-1

Vol. 61 Sally Burgess & Pedro Martín-Martín (eds)
English as an Additional Language in Research Publication and Communication.
259 pages. 2008. ISBN 978-3-03911-462-7

Vol. 62 Sandrine Onillon
Pratiques et représentations de l'écrit.
458 pages. 2008. ISBN 978-3-03911-464-1

Vol. 63 Hugo Bowles & Paul Seedhouse (eds)
Conversation Analysis and Language for Specific Purposes. 2nd edition.
337 pages. 2007, 2009. ISBN 978-3-0343-0045-2

Vol. 64 Vijay K. Bhatia, Christopher N. Candlin & Paola Evangelisti Allori (eds)
Language, Culture and the Law.
The Formulation of Legal Concepts across Systems and Cultures.
342 pages. 2008. ISBN 978-3-03911-470-2

Vol. 65 Jonathan Culpeper & Dániel Z. Kádár (eds)
Historical (Im)politeness.
300 pages. 2010. ISBN 978-3-03911-496-2

Vol. 66 Linda Lombardo (ed.)
Using Corpora to Learn about Language and Discourse.
237 pages. 2009. ISBN 978-3-03911-522-8

Vol. 67 Natsumi Wakamoto
Extroversion/Introversion in Foreign Language Learning. Interactions with Learner Strategy Use.
159 pages. 2009. ISBN 978-3-03911-596-9

Vol. 68 Eva Alcón-Soler (ed.)
Learning How to Request in an Instructed Language Learning Context.
260 pages. 2008. ISBN 978-3-03911-601-0

Vol. 69 Domenico Pezzini
The Translation of Religious Texts in the Middle Ages.
428 pages. 2008. ISBN 978-3-03911-600-3

Vol. 70 Tomoko Tode
Effects of Frequency in Classroom Second Language Learning. Quasi-experiment and stimulated-recall analysis.
195 pages. 2008. ISBN 978-3-03911-602-7

Vol. 71 Egor Tsedryk
Fusion symétrique et alternances ditransitives.
211 pages. 2009. ISBN 978-3-03911-609-6

Vol. 72 Cynthia J. Kellett Bidoli & Elana Ochse (eds)
English in International Deaf Communication.
444 pages. 2008. ISBN 978-3-03911-610-2

Vol. 73 Joan C. Beal, Carmela Nocera & Massimo Sturiale (eds)
Perspectives on Prescriptivism.
269 pages. 2008. ISBN 978-3-03911-632-4

Vol. 74 Carol Taylor Torsello, Katherine Ackerley & Erik Castello (eds)
Corpora for University Language Teachers.
308 pages. 2008. ISBN 978-3-03911-639-3

Vol. 75 María Luisa Pérez Cañado (ed.)
English Language Teaching in the European Credit Transfer System. Facing the Challenge.
251 pages. 2009. ISBN 978-3-03911-654-6

Vol. 76 Marina Dossena & Ingrid Tieken-Boon van Ostade (eds)
Studies in Late Modern English Correspondence. Methodology and Data.
291 pages. 2008. ISBN 978-3-03911-658-4

Vol. 77 Ingrid Tieken-Boon van Ostade & Wim van der Wurff (eds)
Current Issues in Late Modern English.
436 pages. 2009. ISBN 978-3-03911-660-7

Vol. 78 Marta Navarro Coy (ed.)
Practical Approaches to Foreign Language Teaching and Learning.
297 pages. 2009. ISBN 978-3-03911-661-4

Vol. 79 Qing Ma
Second Language Vocabulary Acquisition.
333 pages. 2009. ISBN 978-3-03911-666-9

Vol. 80 Martin Solly, Michelangelo Conoscenti & Sandra Campagna (eds)
Verbal/Visual Narrative Texts in Higher Education.
384 pages. 2008. ISBN 978-3-03911-672-0

Vol. 81 Meiko Matsumoto
From Simple Verbs to Periphrastic Expressions:
The Historical Development of Composite Predicates, Phrasal Verbs, and Related Constructions in English.
235 pages. 2008. ISBN 978-3-03911-675-1

Vol. 82 Melinda Dooly
Doing Diversity. Teachers' Construction of Their Classroom Reality.
180 pages. 2009. ISBN 978-3-03911-687-4

Vol. 83 Victoria Guillén-Nieto, Carmen Marimón-Llorca & Chelo Vargas-Sierra (eds)
Intercultural Business Communication and Simulation and Gaming Methodology.
392 pages. 2009. ISBN 978-3-03911-688-1

Vol. 84 Maria Grazia Guido
English as a Lingua Franca in Cross-cultural Immigration Domains.
285 pages. 2008. ISBN 978-3-03911-689-8

Vol. 85 Erik Castello
Text Complexity and Reading Comprehension Tests.
352 pages. 2008. ISBN 978-3-03911-717-8

Vol. 86 Maria-Lluisa Gea-Valor, Isabel García-Izquierdo & Maria-José Esteve (eds)
Linguistic and Translation Studies in Scientific Communication.
317 pages. 2010. ISBN 978-3-0343-0069-8

Vol. 87 Carmen Navarro, Rosa Ma Rodríguez Abella, Francesca Dalle Pezze & Renzo Miotti (eds)
La comunicación especializada.
355 pages. 2008. ISBN 978-3-03911-733-8

Vol. 88 Kiriko Sato
The Development from Case-Forms to Prepositional Constructions in Old English Prose.
231 pages. 2009. ISBN 978-3-03911-763-5

Vol. 89 Dorothee Heller (Hrsg.)
Formulierungsmuster in deutscher und italienischer Fachkommunikation. Intra- und interlinguale Perspektiven.
315 pages. 2008. ISBN 978-3-03911-778-9

Vol. 90 Henning Bergenholtz, Sandro Nielsen & Sven Tarp (eds)
Lexicography at a Crossroads. Dictionaries and Encyclopedias Today, Lexicographical Tools Tomorrow.
372 pages. 2009. ISBN 978-3-03911-799-4

Vol. 91 Manouchehr Moshtagh Khorasani
The Development of Controversies. From the Early Modern Period to Online Discussion Forums.
317 pages. 2009. ISBN 978-3-3911-711-6

Vol. 92 María Luisa Carrió-Pastor (ed.)
Content and Language Integrated Learning. Cultural Diversity.
178 pages. 2009. ISBN 978-3-3911-818-2

Vol. 93 Roger Berry
Terminology in English Language Teaching. Nature and Use.
262 pages. 2010. ISBN 978-3-0343-0013-1

Vol. 94 Roberto Cagliero & Jennifer Jenkins (eds)
Discourses, Communities, and Global Englishes
240 pages. 2010. ISBN 978-3-0343-0012-4

Vol. 95 Facchinetti Roberta, Crystal David, Seidlhofer Barbara (eds)
From International to Local English – And Back Again.
268 pages. 2010. ISBN 978-3-0343-0011-7

Vol. 96 Cesare Gagliardi & Alan Maley (eds)
EIL, ELF, Global English. Teaching and Learning Issues
376 pages. 2010. ISBN 978-3-0343-0010-0

Vol. 97 Sylvie Hancil (ed.)
The Role of Prosody in Affective Speech.
403 pages. 2009. ISBN 978-3-03911-696-6

Vol. 98 Marina Dossena & Roger Lass (eds)
Studies in English and European Historical Dialectology.
257 pages. 2009. ISBN 978-3-0343-0024-7

Vol. 99 Christine Béal
Les interactions quotidiennes en français et en anglais.
De l'approche comparative à l'analyse des situations interculturelles.
424 pages. 2010. ISBN 978-3-0343-0027-8

Vol. 100 Maurizio Gotti (ed.)
Commonality and Individuality in Academic Discourse.
398 pages. 2009. ISBN 978-3-0343-0023-0

Vol. 101 Javier E. Díaz Vera & Rosario Caballero (eds)
Textual Healing. Studies in Medieval English Medical, Scientific and Technical Texts.
213 pages. 2009. ISBN 978-3-03911-822-9

Vol. 102 Nuria Edo Marzá
The Specialised Lexicographical Approach. A Step further in Dictionary-making.
316 pages. 2009. ISBN 978-3-0343-0043-8

Vol. 103 Carlos Prado-Alonso, Lidia Gómez-García, Iria Pastor-Gómez & David Tizón-Couto (eds)
New Trends and Methodologies in Applied English Language Research. Diachronic, Diatopic and Contrastive Studies.
348 pages. 2009. ISBN 978-3-0343-0046-9

Vol. 104 Françoise Salager-Meyer & Beverly A. Lewin Crossed Words. Criticism in Scholarly Writing?
371 pages. 2011. ISBN 978-3-0343-0049-0.

Vol. 105 Javier Ruano-García
Early Modern Northern English Lexis. A Literary Corpus-Based Study.
611 pages. 2010. ISBN 978-3-0343-0058-2

Vol. 106 Rafael Monroy-Casas
Systems for the Phonetic Transcription of English. Theory and Texts.
280 pages. 2011. ISBN 978-3-0343-0059-9

Vol. 107 Nicola T. Owtram
The Pragmatics of Academic Writing.
A Relevance Approach to the Analysis of Research Article Introductions.
311 pages. 2009. ISBN 978-3-0343-0060-5

Vol. 108 Yolanda Ruiz de Zarobe, Juan Manuel Sierra & Francisco Gallardo del Puerto (eds)
Content and Foreign Language Integrated Learning. Contributions to Multilingualism in European Contexts 343 pages. 2011. ISBN 978-3-0343-0074-2

Vol. 109 Ángeles Linde López & Rosalía Crespo Jiménez (eds)
Professional English in the European context. The EHEA challenge.
374 pages. 2010. ISBN 978-3-0343-0088-9

Vol. 110 Rosalía Rodríguez-Vázquez
The Rhythm of Speech, Verse and Vocal Music. A New Theory.
394 pages. 2010. ISBN 978-3-0343-0309-5

Vol. 111 Anastasios Tsangalidis & Roberta Facchinetti (eds)
Studies on English Modality. In Honour of Frank Palmer.
392 pages. 2009. ISBN 978-3-0343-0310-1

Vol. 112 Jing Huang
Autonomy, Agency and Identity in Foreign Language Learning and Teaching.
400 pages. 2013. ISBN 978-3-0343-0370-5

Vol. 113 Mihhail Lotman & Maria-Kristiina Lotman (eds)
Frontiers in Comparative Prosody. In memoriam: Mikhail Gasparov.
426 pages. 2011. ISBN 978-3-0343-0373-6

Vol. 114 Merja Kytö, John Scahill & Harumi Tanabe (eds)
Language Change and Variation from Old English to Late Modern English. A Festschrift for Minoji Akimoto
422 pages. 2010. ISBN 978-3-0343-0372-9

Vol. 115 Giuliana Garzone & Paola Catenaccio (eds)
Identities across Media and Modes. Discursive Perspectives.
379 pages. 2009. ISBN 978-3-0343-0386-6

Vol. 116 Elena Landone
Los marcadores del discurso y cortesía verbal en español.
390 pages. 2010. ISBN 978-3-0343-0413-9

Vol. 117 Maurizio Gotti & Christopher Williams (eds)
Legal Discourse across Languages and Cultures.
339 pages. 2010. ISBN 978-3-0343-0425-2

Vol. 118 David Hirsh
Academic Vocabulary in Context.
217 pages. 2010. ISBN 978-3-0343-0426-9

Vol. 119 Yvonne Dröschel
Lingua Franca English. The Role of Simplification and Transfer.
358 pages. 2011. ISBN 978-3-0343-0432-0

Vol. 120 Tengku Sepora Tengku Mahadi, Helia Vaezian & Mahmoud Akbari Corpora in Translation. A Practical Guide.
135 pages. 2010. ISBN 978-3-0343-0434-4

Vol. 121 Davide Simone Giannoni & Celina Frade (eds)
Researching Language and the Law. Textual Features and Translation Issues.
278 pages. 2010. ISBN 978-3-0343-0443-6

Vol. 122 Daniel Madrid & Stephen Hughes (eds)
Studies in Bilingual Education.
472 pages. 2011. ISBN 978-3-0343-0474-0

Vol. 123 Vijay K. Bhatia, Christopher N. Candlin & Maurizio Gotti (eds)
The Discourses of Dispute Resolution.
290 pages. 2010. ISBN 978-3-0343-0476-4

Vol. 124 Davide Simone Giannoni
Mapping Academic Values in the Disciplines. A Corpus-Based Approach.
288 pages. 2010. ISBN 978-3-0343-0488-7

Vol. 125 Giuliana Garzone & James Archibald (eds)
Discourse, Identities and Roles in Specialized Communication.
419 pages. 2010. ISBN 978-3-0343-0494-8

Vol. 126 Iria Pastor-Gómez
The Status and Development of N+N Sequences in Contemporary English Noun Phrases.
216 pages. 2011. ISBN 978-3-0343-0534-1

Vol. 127 Carlos Prado-Alonso
Full-verb Inversion in Written and Spoken English.
261 pages. 2011. ISBN 978-3-0343-0535-8

Vol. 128 Tony Harris & María Moreno Jaén (eds)
Corpus Linguistics in Language Teaching.
214 pages. 2010. ISBN 978-3-0343-0524-2

Vol. 129 Tetsuji Oda & Hiroyuki Eto (eds)
Multiple Perspectives on English Philology and History of Linguistics. A Festschrift for Shoichi Watanabe on his 80th Birthday.
378 pages. 2010. ISBN 978-3-0343-0480-1

Vol. 130 Luisa Chierichetti & Giovanni Garofalo (eds)
Lengua y Derecho. líneas de investigación interdisciplinaria.
283 pages. 2010. 978-3-0343-0463-4

Vol. 131 Paola Evangelisti Allori & Giuliana Garzone (eds)
Discourse, Identities and Genres in Corporate Communication. Sponsorship, Advertising and Organizational Communication.
324 pages. 2011. 978-3-0343-0591-4

Vol. 132 Leyre Ruiz de Zarobe & Yolanda Ruiz de Zarobe (eds)
Speech Acts and Politeness across Languages and Cultures.
402 pages. 2012. 978-3-0343-0611-9

Vol. 133 Thomas Christiansen
Cohesion. A Discourse Perspective.
387 pages. 2011. 978-3-0343-0619-5

Vol. 134 Giuliana Garzone & Maurizio Gotti
Discourse, Communication and the Enterprise. Genres and Trends.
451 pages. 2011. ISBN 978-3-0343-0620-1

Vol. 135 Zsuzsa Hoffmann
Ways of the World's Words.
Language Contact in the Age of Globalization.
334 pages 2011. ISBN 978-3-0343-0673-7

Vol. 136 Cecilia Varcasia (ed.) Becoming Multilingual.
Language Learning and Language Policy between Attitudes and Identities.
213 pages. 2011. ISBN 978-3-0343-0687-5

Vol. 137 Susy Macqueen
The Emergence of Patterns in Second Language Writing. A Sociocognitive Exploration of Lexical Trails.
325 pages. 2012. ISBN 978-3-0343-1010-9

Vol. 138 Maria Vittoria Calvi & Giovanna Mapelli (eds)
La lengua del turismo. Géneros discursivos y terminología.
365 pages. 2011.
ISBN 978-3-0343-1011-6

Vol. 139 Ken Lau
Learning to Become a Professional in a Textually-Mediated World. A Text-Oriented Study of Placement Practices.
261 pages. 2012. ISBN 978-3-0343-1016-1

Vol. 140 Sandra Campagna, Giuliana Garzone, Cornelia Ilie & Elizabeth Rowley-Jolivet (eds)
Evolving Genres in Web-mediated Communication.
337 pages. 2012. ISBN 978-3-0343-1013-0

Vol. 141 Edith Esch & Martin Solly (eds)
The Sociolinguistics of Language Education in International Contexts.
263 pages. 2012. ISBN 978-3-0343-1009-3

Vol. 142 Forthcoming.

Vol. 143 David Tizón-Couto
Left Dislocation in English. A Functional-Discoursal Approach.
416 pages. 2012. ISBN 978-3-0343-1037-6

Vol. 144 Margrethe Petersen & Jan Engberg (eds)
Current Trends in LSP Research. Aims and Methods.
323 pages. 2011. ISBN 978-3-0343-1054-3

Vol. 145 David Tizón-Couto, Beatriz Tizón-Couto, Iria Pastor-Gómez & Paula Rodríguez-Puente (eds) New Trends and Methodologies in Applied English Language Research II.
Studies in Language Variation, Meaning and Learning.
283 pages. 2012. ISBN 978-3-0343-1061-1

Vol. 146 Rita Salvi & Hiromasa Tanaka (eds)
Intercultural Interactions in Business and Management.
306 pages. 2011. ISBN 978-3-0343-1039-0

Vol. 147 Francesco Straniero Sergio & Caterina Falbo (eds)
Breaking Ground in Corpus-based Interpreting Studies.
254 pages. 2012. ISBN 978-3-0343-1071-0

Vol. 148 Forthcoming.

Vol. 149 Vijay K. Bhatia & Paola Evangelisti Allori (eds)
Discourse and Identity in the Professions. Legal, Corporate and Institutional Citizenship.
352 pages. 2011. ISBN 978-3-0343-1079-6

Vol. 150 Maurizio Gotti (ed.)
Academic Identity Traits. A Corpus-Based Investigation.
363 pages. 2012. ISBN 978-3-0343-1141-0

Vol. 151 Priscilla Heynderickx, Sylvain Dieltjens, Geert Jacobs, Paul Gillaerts & Elizabeth de Groot (eds)
The Language Factor in International Business.
New Perspectives on Research, Teaching and Practice.
320 pages. 2012. ISBN 978-3-0343-1090-1

Vol. 152 Paul Gillaerts, Elizabeth de Groot, Sylvain Dieltjens, Priscilla Heynderickx & Geert Jacobs (eds)
Researching Discourse in Business Genres. Cases and Corpora.
215 pages. 2012. ISBN 978-3-0343-1092-5

Vol. 153 Yongyan Zheng
Dynamic Vocabulary Development in a Foreign Language.
262 pages. 2012. ISBN 978-3-0343-1106-9

Vol. 154 Carmen Argondizzo (ed.)
Creativity and Innovation in Language Education.
357 pages. 2012. ISBN 978-3-0343-1080-2

Vol. 155 David Hirsh (ed.)
Current Perspectives in Second Language Vocabulary Research.
180 pages. 2012. ISBN 978-3-0343-1108-3

Vol. 156 Seiji Shinkawa
Unhistorical Gender Assignment in Lahamon's *Brut*. A Case Study of a Late Stage in the Development of Grammatical Gender toward its Ultimate Loss.
186 pages. 2012. ISBN 978-3-0343-1124-3

Vol. 157 Yeonkwon Jung
Basics of Organizational Writing: A Critical Reading Approach.
151 pages. 2014. ISBN 978-3-0343-1137-3.

Vol. 158 Bárbara Eizaga Rebollar (ed.) Studies in Linguistics and Cognition.
301 pages. 2012. ISBN 978-3-0343-1138-0

Vol. 159 Giuliana Garzone, Paola Catenaccio, Chiara Degano (eds)
Genre Change in the Contemporary World. Short-term Diachronic Perspectives.
329 pages. 2012. ISBN 978-3-0343-1214-1

Vol. 160 Carol Berkenkotter, Vijay K. Bhatia & Maurizio Gotti (eds) Insights into Academic Genres.
468 pages. 2012. ISBN 978-3-0343-1211-0

Vol. 161 Beatriz Tizón-Couto
Clausal Complements in Native and Learner Spoken English. A corpus-based study with Lindsei and Vicolse.
357 pages. 2013. ISBN 978-3-0343-1184-7

Vol. 162 Patrizia Anesa
Jury Trials and the Popularization of Legal Language. A Discourse Analytical Approach.
247 pages. 2012. ISBN 978-3-0343-1231-8

Vol. 163 David Hirsh
Endangered Languages, Knowledge Systems and Belief Systems.
153 pages. 2013. ISBN 978-3-0343-1232-5

Vol. 164 Eugenia Sainz (ed.)
De la estructura de la frase al tejido del discurso. Estudios contrastivos español/italiano.
305 pages. 2014. ISBN 978-3-0343-1253-0

Vol. 165 Julia Bamford, Franca Poppi & Davide Mazzi (eds)
Space, Place and the Discursive Construction of Identity.
367 pages. 2014. ISBN 978-3-0343-1249-3

Vol. 166 Rita Salvi & Janet Bowker (eds)
Space, Time and the Construction of Identity.
Discursive Indexicality in Cultural, Institutional and Professional Fields.
324 pages. 2013. ISBN 978-3-0343-1254-7

Vol. 167 Shunji Yamazaki & Robert Sigley (eds)
Approaching Language Variation through Corpora. A Festschrift in Honour of Toshio Saito. 421 pages. 2013. ISBN 978-3-0343-1264-6

Vol. 168 Franca Poppi
Global Interactions in English as a Lingua Franca. How written communication is changing under the influence of electronic media and new contexts of use.
249 pages. 2012. ISBN 978-3-0343-1276-9

Vol. 169 Miguel A. Aijón Oliva & María José Serrano
Style in syntax. Investigating variation in Spanish pronoun subjects.
239 pages. 2013. ISBN 978-3-0343-1244-8

Vol. 170 Inés Olza, Óscar Loureda & Manuel Casado-Velarde (eds)
Language Use in the Public Sphere. Methodological Perspectives and Empirical Applications
564 pages. 2014. ISBN 978-3-0343-1286-8

Vol. 171 Aleksandra Matulewska
Legilinguistic Translatology. A Parametric Approach to Legal Translation.
279 pages. 2013. ISBN 978-3-0343-1287-5

Vol. 172 Maurizio Gotti & Carmen Sancho Guinda (eds)
Narratives in Academic and Professional Genres.
513 pages. 2013. ISBN 978-3-0343-1371-1

Vol. 173 Madalina Chitez
Learner corpus profiles. The case of Romanian Learner English.
244 pages. 2014. ISBN 978-3-0343-1410-7

Vol. 174 Chihiro Inoue
Task Equivalence in Speaking Tests.
251 pages. 2013. ISBN 978-3-0343-1417-6

Vol. 175 Gabriel Quiroz & Pedro Patiño (eds.)
LSP in Colombia: advances and challenges.
339 pages. 2014. ISBN 978-3-0343-1434-3

Vol. 176 Catherine Resche
Economic Terms and Beyond: Capitalising on the Wealth of Notions.
How Researchers in Specialised Varieties of English Can Benefit from Focusing on Terms.
332 pages. 2013. ISBN 978-3-0343-1435-0

Vol. 177 Wei Wang
Media representation of migrant workers in China. Identities and stances
198 pages. 2018. 978-3-0343-1436-7

Vol. 178 Cécile Desoutter & Caroline Mellet (dir.)
Le discours rapporté: approches linguistiques et perspectives didactiques.
270 pages. 2013. ISBN 978-3-0343-1292-9

Vol. 179 Ana Díaz-Negrillo & Francisco Javier Díaz-Pérez (eds)
Specialisation and Variation in Language Corpora.
341 pages. 2014. ISBN 978-3-0343-1316-2

Vol. 180 Pilar Alonso
A Multi-dimensional Approach to Discourse Coherence. From Standardness to Creativity.
247 pages. 2014. ISBN 978-3-0343-1325-4

Vol. 181 Alejandro Alcaraz-Sintes & Salvador Valera-Hernández (eds)
Diachrony and Synchrony in English Corpus Linguistics.
393 pages. 2014. ISBN 978-3-0343-1326-1

Vol. 182 Runhan Zhang
Investigating Linguistic Knowledge of a Second Language.
207 pages. 2015. ISBN 978-3-0343-1330-8

Vol. 183 Hajar Abdul Rahim & Shakila Abdul Manan (eds.)
English in Malaysia. Postcolonial and Beyond.
267 pages. 2014. ISBN 978-3-0343-1341-4

Vol. 184 Virginie Fasel Lauzon
Comprendre et apprendre dans l'interaction. Les séquences d'explication en classe de français langue seconde.
292 pages. 2014. ISBN 978-3-0343-1451-0

Vol. 185 Forthcoming.

Vol. 186 Wei Ren
L2 Pragmatic Development in Study Abroad Contexts
256 pages. 2015. ISBN 978-3-0343-1358-2

Vol. 187 Marina Bondi & Rosa Lorés Sanz (eds)
Abstracts in Academic Discourse. Variation and Change.
361 pages. 2014. ISBN 978-3-0343-1483-1

Vol. 188 Giuditta Caliendo
Rethinking Community. Discourse, Identity and Citizenship in the European Union.
240 pages. 2017. ISBN 978-3-0343-1561-6

Vol. 189 Paola Evangelisti Allori (ed.) Identities in and across Cultures.
315 pages. 2014. ISBN 978-3-0343-1458-9

Vol. 190 Erik Castello, Katherine Ackerley & Francesca Coccetta (eds).
Studies in Learner Corpus Linguistics. Research and Applications for Foreign Language Teaching and Assessment.
358 pages. 2015. ISBN 978-3-0343-1506-7

Vol. 191 Ruth Breeze, Maurizio Gotti & Carmen Sancho Guinda (eds)
Interpersonality in Legal Genres.
389 pages. 2014. ISBN 978-3-0343-1524-1

Vol. 192 Paola Evangelisti Allori, John Bateman & Vijay K. Bhatia (eds)
Evolution in Genre. Emergence, Variation, Multimodality.
364 pages. 2014. ISBN 978-3-0343-1533-3

Vol. 193 Jiyeon Kook
Agency in Arzt-Patient-Gesprächen. Zur interaktionistischen Konzeptualisierung von Agency 271 pages. 2015. ISBN 978-3-0343-1666-8

Vol. 194 Susana Nicolás Román & Juan José Torres Núñez (eds)
Drama and CLIL. A new challenge for the teaching approaches in bilingual education.
170 pages. 2015. ISBN 978-3-0343-1629-3

Vol. 195 Alessandra Molino & Serenella Zanotti (eds)
Observing Norm, Observing Usage. Lexis in Dictionaries and in the Media.
430 pages. 2015. ISBN 978-3-0343-1584-5

Vol. 196 Begoña Soneira
A Lexical Description of English for Architecture. A Corpus-based Approach.
267 pages. 2015. ISBN 978-3-0343-1602-6

Vol. 197 M Luisa Roca-Varela
False Friends in Learner Corpora. A corpus-based study of English false friends in the written and spoken production of Spanish learners.
348 pages. 2015. ISBN 978-3-0343-1620-0

Vol. 198 Rahma Al-Mahrooqi & Christopher Denman
Bridging the Gap between Education and Employment. English Language Instruction in EFL Contexts.
416 pages. 2015. ISBN 978-3-0343-1681-1

Vol. 199 Rita Salvi & Janet Bowker (eds)
The Dissemination of Contemporary Knowledge in English. Genres, discourse strategies and professional practices.
171 pages. 2015. ISBN 978-3-0343-1679-8

Vol. 200 Maurizio Gotti & Davide S. Giannoni (eds)
Corpus Analysis for Descriptive and Pedagogical Purposes. ESP Perspectives.
432 pages. 2014. ISBN 978-3-0343-1516-6

Vol. 201 Ida Ruffolo
The Perception of Nature in Travel Promotion Texts. A Corpus-based Discourse Analysis.
148 pages. 2015. ISBN 978-3-0343-1521-0

Vol. 202 Ives Trevian
English suffixes. Stress-assignment properties, productivity, selection and combinatorial processes.
471 pages. 2015. ISBN 978-3-0343-1576-0

Vol. 203 Maurizio Gotti, Stefania Maci & Michele Sala (eds) Insights into Medical Communication.
422 pages. 2015. ISBN 978-3-0343-1694-1

Vol. 204 Carmen Argondizzo (ed.)
European Projects in University Language Centres. Creativity, Dynamics, Best Practice.
371 pages. 2015. ISBN 978-3-0343-1696-5

Vol. 205 Aura Luz Duffé Montalván (ed.)
Estudios sobre el léxico. Puntos y contrapuntos.
502 pages. 2016. ISBN 978-3-0343-2011-5

Vol. 206 Maria Pavesi, Maicol Formentelli & Elisa Ghia (eds)
The Languages of Dubbing. Mainstream Audiovisual Translation in Italy.
275 pages. 2014. ISBN 978-3-0343-1646-0

Vol. 207 Ruth Breeze & Inés Olza (eds)
Evaluation in media discourse. European perspectives.
268 pages. 2017. ISBN 978-3-0343-2014-6

Vol. 208 Vijay K. Bhatia & Maurizio Gotti (eds) Arbitration Discourse in Asia.
331 pages. 2015. ISBN 978-3-0343-2032-0

Vol. 209 Sofía Bemposta-Rivas, Carla Bouzada-Jabois, Yolanda Fernández-Pena, Tamara Bouso, Yolanda J. Calvo-Benzies, Iván Tamaredo (eds)
New trends and methodologies in applied English language research III. Synchronic and diachronic studies on discourse, lexis and grammar processing.
280 pages. 2017. ISBN 978-3-0343-2039-9

Vol. 210 Francisco Alonso Almeida, Laura Cruz García & Víctor González Ruiz (eds)
Corpus-based studies on language varieties.
285 pages. 2016. ISBN 978-3-0343-2044-3

Vol. 211 Juan Pedro Rica Peromingo
Aspectos lingüísticos y técnicos de la traducción audiovisual (TAV).
177 pages. 2016. ISBN 978-3-0343-2055-9

Vol. 212 Maria Vender
Disentangling Dyslexia. VenderPhonological and Processing Deficit in Developmental Dyslexia.
338 pages. 2017. ISBN 978-3-0343-2064-1

Vol. 213 Zhilong Xie
Bilingual Advantages. Contributions of Different Bilingual Experiences to Cognitive Control Differences Among Young-adult Bilinguals.
221 pages. 2016. ISBN 978-3-0343-2081-8

Vol. 214 Larissa D'Angelo
Academic posters. A textual and visual metadiscourse analysis.
367 pages. 2016. ISBN 978-3-0343-2083-2

Vol. 215 Evelyne Berger
Prendre la parole en L2. Regard sur la compétence d'interaction en classe de langue.
246 pages. 2016. ISBN 978-3-0343-2084-9

Vol. 216 David Lasagabaster and Aintzane Doiz (eds)
CLIL experiences in secondary and tertiary education: In search of good practices.
262 pages. 2016. ISBN 978-3-0343-2104-4

Vol. 217 Elena Kkese
Identifying Plosives in L2 English: The Case of L1 Cypriot Greek Speakers.
317 pages. 2016. ISBN 978-3-0343-2060-3

Vol. 218 Sandra Campagna, Elana Ochse, Virginia Pulcini & Martin Solly (eds)
Languaging in and across Communities: New Voices, New Identities. Studies in Honour of Giuseppina Cortese.
507 pages. 2016. ISBN 978-3-0343-2073-3

Vol. 219 Adriana Orlandi & Laura Giacomini (ed.)
Defining collocation for lexicographic purposes. From linguistic theory to lexicographic practice.
328 pages. 2016. ISBN 978-3-0343-2054-2

Vol. 220 Pietro Luigi Iaia
Analysing English as a Lingua Franca in Video Games. Linguistic Features, Experiential and Functional Dimensions of Online and Scripted Interactions.
139 pages. 2016. ISBN 978-3-0343-2138-9

Vol. 221 Dimitrinka G. Níkleva (ed.)
La formación de los docentes de español para inmigrantes en distintos contextos educativos.
390 pages. 2017. ISBN 978-3-0343-2135-8

Vol. 222 Katherine Ackerley, Marta Guarda & Francesca Helm (eds)
Sharing Perspectives on English-Medium Instruction.
308 pages. 2017. ISBN 978-3-0343-2537-0

Vol. 223 Juana I. Marín-Arrese, Julia Lavid-López, Marta Carretero, Elena Domínguez Romero, Ma Victoria Martín de la Rosa & María Pérez Blanco (eds)
Evidentiality and Modality in European Languages. Discourse-pragmatic perspectives.
427 pages. 2017. ISBN 978-3-0343-2437-3

Vol. 224 Gilles Col
Construction du sens : un modèle instructionnel pour la sémantique.
292 pages. 2017. ISBN 978-3-0343-2572-1

Vol. 225 Ana Chiquito & Gabriel Quiroz (eds)
Pobreza, Lenguaje y Medios en América Latina.
362 pages. 2017. ISBN 978-3-0343-2142-6

Vol. 226 Xu Zhang
English Quasi-Numeral Classifiers. A Corpus-Based Cognitive-Typological Study.
360 pages. 2017. ISBN 978-3-0343-2818-0

Vol. 227 María Ángeles Orts, Ruth Breeze & Maurizio Gotti (eds)
Power, Persuasion and Manipulation in Specialised Genres. Providing Keys to the Rhetoric of Professional Communities.
368 pages. 2017. ISBN 978-3-0343-3010-7

Vol. 228 Maurizio Gotti, Stefania Maci & Michele Sala (eds)
Ways of Seeing, Ways of Being: Representing the Voices of Tourism.
453 pages. 2017. ISBN 978-3-0343-3031-2

Vol. 229 Dino Selvaggi
Plurilingual Code-Switching between Standard and Local Varieties. A Socio-Psycholinguistic Approach
371 pages. 2018. ISBN 978-3-0343-2663-6

Vol. 230 Anca-Cristina Sterie
Interprofessional interactions at the hospital. Nurses' requests and reports of problems in calls with physicians.
371 pages. 2017. ISBN 978-3-0343-2734-3

Vol. 231 Xiaodong Zhang
Understanding Chinese EFL Teachers' Beliefs and Practices in the Textbook-Based Classroom.
189 pages. 2017. ISBN 978-3-0343-3053-4

Vol. 232 Manuela Caterina Moroni & Federica Ricci Garotti (Hrsg.)
Brücken schlagen zwischen Sprachwissenschaft und DaF-Didaktik.
345 pages. 2017. ISBN 978-3-0343-2667-4

Vol. 233 Dimitrinka Georgieva Níkleva
Necesidades y tendencias en la formación del profesorado de español como lengua extranjera
401 pages. 2017. ISBN 978-3-0343-2946-0

Vol. 234 Juan Santana-Lario & Salvador Valera (Hrsg.) Competing patterns in English affixation.
272 pages. 2017. ISBN 978-3-0343-2701-5

Vol. 235 Francisco Salgado-Robles
Desarrollo de la competencia sociolingüística por aprendices de español en un contexto de inmersión en el extranjero
241 pages. 2018. ISBN 978-3-0343-2323-9

Vol. 236 Maria Chiara Janner
Sguardi linguistici sulla marca. Analisi morfosintattica dei nomi commerciali in italiano
345 pages. 2017. ISBN 978-3-0343-2667-4

Vol. 237 Bárbara Herrero Muñoz-Cobo & Otman El Azami Zalachi La primavera del árabe marroquí.
192 pages. 2017. ISBN 978-3-0343-3104-3

Vol. 238 Consuelo Pascual Escagedo
El papel del oyente en la construcción de la conversación espontánea de estudiantes italianos en su interlengua y en su lengua materna
295 pages. 2017. ISBN 978-3-0343-3186-9

Vol. 239 Stefania M. Maci
The MS Digby 133 *Mary Magdalene*. Beyond scribal practices: language, discourse, values and attitudes.
336 pages. 2017. ISBN 978-3-0343-3256-9

Vol. 240 Eliecer Crespo-Fernández
Taboo in Discourse. Studies on Attenuation and Offence in Communication.
326 pages. 2018. ISBN 978-3-0343-3018-3

Vol. 241 Jana Altmanova, Maria Centrella, Katherine E. Russo (eds)
Terminology & Discourse / Terminologie et discours.
424 pages. 2018. ISBN 978-3-0343-2417-5

Vol. 242 Xavier Blanco et Inès Sfar (dir.)
Lexicologie(s) : approches croisées en sémantique lexicale.
442 pages. 2018. ISBN 978-3-0343-3056-5

Vol. 243 Yunfeng Ge
Resolution of Conflict of Interest in Chinese Civil Court Hearings. A Perspective of Discourse Information Theory.
302 pages. 2018. ISBN 978-3-0343-3313-9

Vol. 244 Carla Vergaro
Illocutionary Shell Nouns in English
322 pages. 2018. ISBN 978-3-0343-3069-5

Vol. 245 Paolo Frassi
L'adjectif en français et sa définition lexicographique.
270 pages. 2018. ISBN 978-3-0343-3394-8

Vol. 246 Suwilai Premsrirat and David Hirsh (eds)
Language Revitalization. Insights from Thailand
328 pages. 2018. ISBN 978-3-0343-3497-6

Vol. 247 Wei Wang
Researching Learning and Learners in Genre-based Academic Writing Instruction
282 pages. 2018. ISBN 978-3-0343-3297-2

Vol. 248 Isusi Alabarte, Alberto & Lahuerta Martínez, Ana Cristina (eds)
La comprensión lectora de lengua extranjera
Estudio de los factores de familiaridad, interés, género y métodos de evaluación
336 pages. 2018. ISBN 978-3-0343-3493-8

Vol. 249 Mercedes Eurrutia Cavero
Approche didactique du langage techno-scientifique Terminologie et discours
374 pages. 2018. ISBN 978-3-0343-3512-6

Vol. 250 Aurora Ruiz Mezcua (ed.)
Approaches to Telephone Interpretation Research, Innovation, Teaching and Transference
268 pages. 2018. ISBN 978-3-0343-3330-6

Vol. 251 Morini Massimiliano A Day in the News
A Stylistic Analysis of Newsspeak
188 pages. 2018. ISBN 978-3-0343-3507-2

Vol. 252 Ignacio Guillén-Galve & Ignacio Vázquez-Orta (eds.)
English as a Lingua Franca and Intercultural Communication Implications and Applications in the Field of English Language Teaching
414 pages. 2018. ISBN 978-3-0343-2763-3

Vol. 253 Bianca Del Villano
Using the Devil with Courtesy
Shakespeare and the Language of (Im)Politeness
216 pages. 2018. ISBN 978-3-0343-2315-4

Vol. 254 David Hirsh (ed.)
Explorations in Second Language Vocabulary Research
252 pages. 2018. ISBN 978-3-0343-2940-8

Vol. 255 Tania Baumann (ed.)
Reiseführer - Sprach- und Kulturmittlung im Tourismus / Le guide turistiche - mediazione linguistica e culturale in ambito turistico
270 pages. 2018. ISBN 978-3-0343-3402-0

Vol. 256 Ariadna Sánchez-Hernández & Ana Herraiz-Martínez (eds)
Learning second language pragmatics beyond traditional contexts
376 pages. 2018. ISBN 978-3-0343-3437-2

Vol. 257 Albert Bastardas-Boada, Emili Boix-Fuster, Rosa Maria Torrens (eds)
Family Multilingualism in Medium-Sized Linguistic Communities
336 pages. 2019. ISBN 978-3-0343-2536-3

Vol. 258 Yuyang Cai
Examining the Interaction among Components of English for Specific Purposes Ability in Reading. The Triple-Decker Model
296 pages. 2020. 978-3-0343-2913-2

Vol. 259 Catia Nannoni
Participe présent et gérondif dans la presse française contemporaine
176 pages. 2019. ISBN 978-3-0343-3631-4

Vol. 260 Nieves Rodríguez Pérez & Bárbara Heinsch (eds.)
Contextos multilingües. Mediadores interculturales, formación del profesorado de lenguas extranjeras
289 pages. 2019. ISBN 978-3-0343-3768-7

Vol. 261 Giuliana Elena Garzone, Mara Logaldo, Francesca Santulli (eds.)
Investigating Conflict Discourses in the Periodical Press
244 pages. 2020. ISBN 978-3-0343-3668-0

Vol. 262 Laura Nadal
Lingüística experimental y contraargumentación
233 pages. 2019. ISBN 978-3-0343-3791-5

Vol. 263 Claudia Claridge & Merja Kytö (eds.)
Punctuation in Context – Past and Present Perspectives
288 pages. 2019. ISBN 978-3-0343-3790-8

Vol. 264 Maurizio Gotti, Stefania Maci, Michele Sala (eds.)
Scholarly Pathways
530 pages. 2020. ISBN 978-3-0343-3860-8

Vol. 265 Ruth Breeze, Ana M. Fernández Vallejo (eds.)
Politics and populism across modes and media
350 pages. 2020. ISBN 978-3-0343-3707-6

Vol. 266 Jean Marguerite Jimenez
Understanding the Effects of Immediate Electronic Corrective Feedback on Second Language Development
252 pages. 2020. ISBN 978-3-0343-3815-8

Vol. 267 Sergio Rodríguez-Tapia, Adela González-Fernández (eds)
Lenguas y turismo: estudios en torno al discurso, la didáctica y la divulgación
380 pages. 2020. ISBN 978-3-0343-3881-3

Vol. 268 Ana Bocanegra-Valle (ed.)
Applied Linguistics and Knowledge Transfer. Employability, Internationalisation and Social Challenges
344 pages. 2020. ISBN 978-3-0343-3714-4

Vol. 269 Beatrice Garzelli
La traducción audiovisual español-italiano.Películas y cortos entre humor y habla soez
202 pages. 2020. ISBN 978-3-0343-4013-7

Vol. 270 Iván Tamaredo
Complexity, Efficiency, and Language Contact. Pronoun Omission in World Englishes
292 pages. 2020. ISBN 978-3-0343-3902-5

Vol. 271 Silvia Domenica Zollo,
Origine et histoire du vocabulaire des arts de la table. Analyse lexicale et exploitation de corpus textuels
239 pages. 2020. ISBN 978-3-0343-3890-5

Vol. 272 Paola Paissa, Michelangelo Conoscenti, Ruggero Druetta, Martin Solly (eds.)
Metaphor and Conflict / Métaphore et conflit
385 pages. 2021. 978-3-0343-4068-7

Vol. 273 María Martínez-Atienza de Dios,
Entre el léxico y la sintaxis: las fases de los eventos
178 pages. 2021. 978-3-0343-4173-8

Vol. 274 Noelia Castro-Chao,
Argument Structure in Flux. The Development of Impersonal Constructions in Middle and Early Modern English, with Special Reference to Verbs of Desire.
300 pages. 2021. 978-3-0343-4189-9

Vol. 275 Gabriella Carobbio, Cécile Desoutter, Aurora Fragonara (eds.)
Macht, Ratio und Emotion: Diskurse im digitalen Zeitalter / Pouvoir, raison et émotion: les discours à l'ère du numérique
246 pages. 2020. 978-3-0343-4184-4

Vol. 276 Miguel Fuster-Márquez, José Santaemilia, Carmen Gregori-Signes, Paula Rodríguez-Abruñeiras (eds.)
Exploring discourse and ideology through corpora
293 pages. 2021. 978-3-0343-3969-8

Vol. 277 Tamara Bouso
Changes in Argument Structure
The Transitivizing Reaction Object Construction
392. 2021. 978-3-0343-4095-3

Vol. 278 Maria Luisa Maggioni, Amanda Murphy (eds.)
Back to the Future. English from Past to Present
250 pages. 2021. 978-3-0343-4273-5

Vol. 279 Luisa Chierichetti
Diálogos de serie. Una aproximación a la construcción discursiva de personajes basada en corpus
246 pages. 2021. 978-3-0343-4274-2

Vol. 280 Cristina Lastres-López
From subordination to insubordination. A functional-pragmatic approach to if/si-constructions in English, French and Spanish spoken discourse
258 pages. 2021. 978-3-0343-4220-9

Vol. 281 Eleonora Federici, Stefania Maci (eds.)
Gender issues. Translating and mediating languages, cultures and societies
500 pages. 2021. 978-3-0343-4022-9

Vol. 282 José Mateo, Francisco Yus (eds.)
Metaphor in Economics and specialised Discourse
354 pages. 2021. 978-3-0343-4048-9

Vol. 283 Nicholas Brownlees (ed.)
The Role of Context in the Production and Reception of Historical News Discourse
376 pages. 2021. 978-3-0343-4181-3

Vol. 284 Catalina Fuentes Rodriguez, María Ester Brenes Peña, Víctor Pérez Béjar (eds.)
Sintaxis discursiva: construcciones y operadores en español
396 pages. 2021. 978-3-0343-4306-0

Vol. 285 Dominic Stewart
Frequency in the dictionary. A corpus-assisted contrastive analysis of English and Italian
176 pages. 2021. 978-3-0343-4368-8

Vol. 286 Carla Bouzada-Jabois
Nonfinite supplements in the recent history of English
320 pages. 2021. 978-3-0343-4226-1

Vol. 287 Sofía Bemposta Rivas
Verb-governed infinitival complementation in the recent history of English
320 pages. 2021. 978-3-0343-4227-8

Vol. 288 Mirella Agorni
Translating Italy for the Nineteenth Century. Translators and an Imagined Nation in the Early Romantic Period 1816–1830s
180 pages. 2021. 978-3-0343-3612-3

Vol. 289 David Hirsh (ed.)
Research Perspectives in Language and Education
276 pages. 2021. 978-3-0343-4219-3

Vol. 290 Federica Vezzani
Terminologie numérique : conception, représentation et gestion
238 pages. 2022. 978-3-0343-4394-7

Vol. 291 Stefania M. Maci
Evidential verbs in the genre of medical posters. A corpus-based analysis
498 pages. 2022. 978-3-0343-4521-7

Vol. 292 Francisco J. Álvarez-Gil
Stance devices in tourism-related research articles: A corpus-based study
170 pages. 2022. 978-3-0343-4555-2

Vol. 293 Annalisa Baicchi / Stefania Biscetti (eds.)
The Language of Fashion. Linguistic, Cognitive, and Cultural Insights
190 pages. 2022. 978-3-0343-4428-9

Vol. 294 Ana Maria Piquer-Píriz
E-learning in EMI. Academic language for university students
200 pages. 2022. 978-3-0343-4589-7

Vol. 295 Geneviève Henrot Sostero (ed.)
Alle radici della fraseologia europea
400 pages. 2023. 978-3-0343-4645-0

Vol. 296 Klara Dankova
Les fibres textiles entre synchronie et diachronie: études terminologiques
300 pages. 2023. 978-3-0343-4587-3

Vol. 297 Marta Carretero, Juana I. Marín-Arrese, Elena Domínguez Romero, Mª Victoria Martín de la Rosa (eds.) Evidentiality and Epistemic Modality. Conceptual and Descriptive issues
350 pages. 2023. 978-3-0343-3993-3

Vol. 298 Kim Grego, Alessandra Vicentini, Virpi Ylänne (eds.)
Age-Specific Issues. Language, Spaces, Technologies
300 pages. 2023. 978-3-0343-4411-1

Vol. 299 Giovanni Garofalo (ed.) Estudios de género asistidos por corpus. Enfoques multidisciplinarios
292 pages. 2022. 978-3-0343-4548-4

Vol. 300 Giuseppe Palumbo, Katia Peruzzo, Gianluca Pontrandolfo (eds.)
What's Special About Specialised Translation? Essays in Honour of Federica Scarpa
296 pages. 2023. 978-3-0343-4411-1

Vol. 301 Raquel P. Romasanta Probabilistic variability in clausal verb complementation in World Englishes.
390 pages. 2023. 978-3-0343-4703-7

Vol. 302 Giulia Adriana Pennisi A linguistic Insight into Legislative Drafting. Tradition and Change in the UK Legislation
330 pages. 2023. 978-3-0343-4700-6

Vol. 303 Javier Fernández-Cruz, Antonio Moreno-Ortiz
Economic terms in the news during the Great Recession. A diachronic sentiment and collocational analysis
193 pages. 2024. 978-3-0343-4778-5

Vol. 304 Stefania Maci, Mark McGlashan
(Critical) Discourse Studies and the (new?) normal. Analysing discourse in times of crisis.
400 pages. 2024. 978-3-0343-4767-9

Vol. 305 Ana Elvira, Ojanguren López
Predications in competition and the rise of serial verb constructions in English. The verbal and nominal complementation of Old English aspectual and manipulative verbs.
330 pages. 2024. 978-3-0343-4644-3

Vol. 306 Stefania Maci, Giovanni Garofalo (eds.)
Investigating Discourse and Texts. Corpus-Assisted Analytical Perspectives.
372 pages. 2023. 978-3-0343-4753-2

www.ingramcontent.com/pod-product-compliance
Ingram Content Group UK Ltd.
Pitfield, Milton Keynes, MK11 3LW, UK
UKHW041830100926
8556IPUK00002B/103

9 783034 347532